Creating Value with Big Data Analytics

Our newly digital world is generating an almost unimaginable amount of data about all of us. Such a vast amount of data is useless without plans and strategies that are designed to cope with its size and complexity, and which enable organisations to leverage the information to create value. This book is a refreshingly practical yet theoretically sound roadmap to leveraging big data and analytics.

Creating Value with Big Data Analytics provides a nuanced view of big data development, arguing that big data in itself is not a revolution but an evolution of the increasing availability of data that has been observed in recent times. Building on the authors' extensive academic and practical knowledge, this book aims to provide managers and analysts with strategic directions and practical analytical solutions on how to create value from existing and new big data.

By tying data and analytics to specific goals and processes for implementation, this is a much-needed book that will be essential reading for students and specialists of data analytics, marketing research, and customer relationship management.

Peter C. Verhoef is Professor of Marketing at the Department of Marketing, Faculty of Economics and Business, University of Groningen, The Netherlands. He also holds a visiting professorship in Marketing at BI Norwegian Business School in Oslo.

Edwin Kooge is co-founder of Metrixlab Big Data Analytics, The Netherlands. He is a pragmatic data analyst, a result-focused consultant, and entrepreneur with more than 25 years' experience in analytics.

Natasha Walk is co-founder of Metrixlab Big Data Analytics, The Netherlands. She is a data hacker, analyst, and talent coach with more than 20 years' experience in applied analytics.

This is a timely and thought-provoking book that should be on a must-read list of anyone interested in big data.

Sunil Gupta,
Edward W. Carter Professor of Business,
Harvard Business School, USA

This is one of the most compelling publications on the challenges and opportunities of data analytics. It paints not only a theoretical framework, but also navigates marketing professionals on organizational change and development of skills and capabilities for success. A must-read to unlock the full potential of data-driven and fact-based marketing!

Harry Dekker,
Media Director, Unilever Benelux, The Netherlands

Creating Value with Big Data Analytics offers a uniquely comprehensive and well-grounded examination of one of the most critically important topics in marketing today. With a strong customer focus, it provides rich, practical guidelines, frameworks and insights on how big data can truly create value for a firm.

Kevin Lane Keller,
Tuck School of Business, Dartmouth College, USA

No longer can marketing decisions be made on intuition alone. This book represents an excellent formula combining leading edge insight and experience in marketing with digital analytics methods and tools to support better, faster and more fact-based decision-making. It is highly recommended for business leaders who want to ensure they meet customer demands with precision in the 21st century.

Morten Thorkildsen,
CEO Rejlers, Norway; chairman of IT and communications company, Itera;
former CEO, IBM Norway (2003–13);
ex-chairman the Norwegian Computer Society (2009–13),
and visiting lecturer Norwegian Business School, Norway

Big Data is the next frontier in marketing. This comprehensive, yet eminently readable book by Verhoef, Kooge and Walk is an invaluable guide and a must-read for any marketer seriously interested in using big data to create firm value.

Jan-Benedict E.M. Steenkamp,
Massey Distinguished Professor of Marketing, Marketing Area Chair &
Executive Director AiMark, Kenan-Flagler Business School,
University of North Carolina at Chapel Hill, USA

This book goes beyond the hype, to provide a more thorough and realistic analysis of how big data can be deployed successfully in companies; successful in the sense of creating value both for the customer as well as the company, as well as what the pre-requisites are to do so. This book is not about the hype, nor about the analytics, it is about what really matters: how to create value. It is also illustrated with a broad range of inspiring company cases.

Hans Zijlstra,
Customer Insight Director, AIR FRANCE KLM, The Netherlands

Creating Value with Big Data Analytics

Making smarter marketing decisions

Peter C. Verhoef, Edwin Kooge and Natasha Walk

LONDON AND NEW YORK

First published 2016
by Routledge
2 Park Square, Milton Park, Abingdon, Oxon OX14 4RN

and by Routledge
711 Third Avenue, New York, NY 10017

Routledge is an imprint of the Taylor & Francis Group, an informa business

© 2015 Peter C. Verhoef, Edwin Kooge and Natasha Walk

The right of Peter C. Verhoef, Edwin Kooge and Natasha Walk to be identified as authors of this work has been asserted by them in accordance with sections 77 and 78 of the Copyright, Designs and Patents Act 1988.

All rights reserved. No part of this book may be reprinted or reproduced or utilised in any form or by any electronic, mechanical, or other means, now known or hereafter invented, including photocopying and recording, or in any information storage or retrieval system, without permission in writing from the publishers.

Every effort has been made to contact copyright holders for their permission to reprint material in this book. The publishers would be grateful to hear from any copyright holder who is not here acknowledged and will undertake to rectify any errors or omissions in future editions of this book.

Trademark notice: Product or corporate names may be trademarks or registered trademarks, and are used only for identification and explanation without intent to infringe.

British Library Cataloguing in Publication Data
A catalogue record for this book is available from the British Library

Library of Congress Cataloging in Publication Data
Verhoef, Peter C., author.
Creating value with big data analytics: making smarter marketing decisions / Peter Verhoef, Edwin Kooge and Natasha Walk.
  pages cm
  Includes bibliographical references and index.
  1. Consumer profiling. 2. Big data. 3. Marketing–Data processing. I. Kooge, Edwin. II. Walk, Natasha. III. Title.
  HF5415.32.V475 2016
  658.8'3–dc23
  2015027898

ISBN: 978-1-138-83795-9 (hbk)
ISBN: 978-1-138-83797-3 (pbk)
ISBN: 978-1-315-73475-0 (ebk)

Typeset in Bembo
by Sunrise Setting Ltd, Paignton, UK

Printed and bound in Great Britain by
TJ International Ltd, Padstow, Cornwall

To: Petra, Anne Mieke and Maurice

Contents

List of figures	xi
List of tables	xvi
Foreword	xvii
Preface	xix
Acknowledgements	xx
List of abbreviations	xxi

1 Big data challenges — 1
  Introduction 1
  Explosion of data 1
  Big data become the norm, but... 3
  Our objectives 4
  Our approach 4
  Reading guide 5

2 Creating value using big data analytics — 8
  Introduction 8
  Big data value creation model 9
  The role of culture 12
  Big data analytics 13
  From big data analytics to value creation 16
  Value creation model as guidance for book 21
  Conclusions 21

2.1 Value-to-customer metrics — 25
  Introduction 25
  Market metrics 26
  New big data market metrics 27
  Brand metrics 27
  New big data brand metrics 33
  Customer metrics 35
  New big data customer metrics 41

viii   Contents

    V2S metrics 42
    Should firms collect all V2C metrics? 44
    Conclusions 44

2.2 Value-to-firm metrics   49
    Introduction 49
    Market metrics 50
    Brand metrics 51
    Customer metrics 55
    Customer lifetime value 58
    New big data metrics 67
    Marketing ROI 70
    Conclusions 72

3   Data, data everywhere   75
    Introduction 75
    Data sources and data types 76
    Using the different data sources in the era of big data 85
    Data warehouse 87
    Database structures 88
    Data quality 89
    Missing values and data fusion 91
    Conclusions 91

3.1 Data integration   93
    Introduction 93
    Integrating data sources 93
    Dealing with different data types 95
    Data integration in the era of big data 100
    Conclusions 104

3.2 Customer privacy and data security   105
    Introduction 105
    Why is privacy a big issue? 106
    What is privacy? 107
    Customers and privacy 108
    Governments and privacy legislation 108
    Privacy and ethics 110
    Privacy policies 111
    Privacy and internal data analytics 112
    Data security 114
    Conclusions 116

4   How big data are changing analytics   118
    Introduction 118
    The power of analytics 119

Different sophistication levels 120
General types of marketing analysis 121
Strategies for analyzing big data 122
How big data changes analytics 127
Generic big data changes in analytics 132
Conclusions 137

4.1 Classic data analytics 140
Introduction 140
Overview of analytics 141
Classic 1: Reporting 141
Classic 2: Profiling 145
Classic 3: Migration analysis 150
Classic 4: Customer segmentation 155
Classic 5: Trend analysis market and sales forecasting 163
Classic 6: Attribute importance analysis 172
Classic 7: Individual prediction models 180
Conclusions 189

4.2 Big data analytics 193
Introduction 193
Big data area 1: Web analytics 194
Big data area 2: Customer journey analysis 199
Big data area 3: Attribution modeling 203
Big data area 4: Dynamic targeting 206
Big data area 5: Integrated big data models 212
Big data area 6: Social listening 216
Big data area 7: Social network analysis 221
Emerging techniques 226
Conclusions 226

4.3 Creating impact with storytelling and visualization 231
Introduction 231
Failure factors for creating impact 233
Storytelling 234
Visualization 238
Choosing the chart type 241
Conclusions 251

5 Building successful big data capabilities 253
Introduction 253
Transformation to create successful analytical competence 255
Building Block 1: Process 259
Building Block 2: People 263
Building Block 3: Systems 268

x   Contents

       Building Block 4: Organization 276
       Conclusions 282

6 **Every business has (big) data; let's use them**   285
       Introduction 285
       Case 1: CLV calculation for energy company 286
       Case 2: Holistic marketing approach by big data integration at an insurance company 289
       Case 3: Implementation of big data analytics for relevant personalization at an online retailer 293
       Case 4: Attribution modeling at an online retailer 298
       Case 5: Initial social network analytics at a telecom provider 301
       Conclusions 303

7 **Concluding thoughts and key learning points**   305
       Concluding thoughts 305
       Key learning points 306

Index   309

Figures

1.1	Effects of new developments including big data on GDP	2
1.2	Reading guide for book	6
2.1	Big data value creation model	9
2.2	Value-to-customer vs. value-to-firm	18
2.3	Classification of V2C and V2F metrics	20
2.4	Big data value creation model linked to chapters	22
2.1.1	Search results on "tablet" worldwide	27
2.1.2	Search interest in "big data" and "market research"	28
2.1.3	Example of tracking aided and spontaneous awareness through time	29
2.1.4	Example of brand preference of smartphone users, de-averaged to gender and age	30
2.1.5	Brand-Asset Valuator® model	30
2.1.6	Association network of McDonald's based on online data	34
2.1.7	Average number of likes and comments per product category	36
2.1.8	Development of intimacy and commitment over time	40
2.2.1	UK smartphone sales	50
2.2.2	Example of brand switching matrix	52
2.2.3	Brand revenue premium	54
2.2.4	Relationship lifecycle concept	55
2.2.5	The CLV model: the elements of customer lifetime value	60
2.2.6	Example of gross CLV distribution per decile	65
2.2.7	Customer equity ROI model	68
2.2.8	Customer engagement value: Extending CLV	69
2.2.9	Example of ROI calculation	71
3.1	Two dimensions of data: Data source versus data type	76
3.2	Example of Nielsen-Claritas information for a New York ZIP-code	78
3.3	Illustration of structured and unstructured data	79
3.4	Example of market data on the supply side for UK supermarkets	81
3.5	Example of market data on the demand side	81
3.6	Illustration of brand supply data extracted from internal systems	83
3.7	Illustration of brand demand based on market research	83

xii Figures

3.8	Illustration of a data model of customer supply data	85
3.9	Illustration of customer demand data (NPS)	86
3.10	The 5 "W"s model for assessment of data sources	87
3.11	Example of simple data table with customer as central element	89
3.12	Example of product data table derived from customer database	89
3.13	Net benefits of investing in data quality	90
3.1.1	The ETL process	94
3.1.2	The different data types	96
3.1.3	Overview of segmentation scheme used by Experian UK	97
3.1.4	External profiling using ZIP-code segmentation for clothing retailer	98
3.1.5	Presence of data types for Dutch firms	99
3.1.6	The challenges of data integration	101
3.2.1	Data protection laws around the globe	109
3.2.2	Effectiveness increase of Facebook advertising campaigns after addition of privacy button	113
3.2.3	Different ways of handling privacy sensitive data	114
4.1	Associations between customer analytics deployment and performance per industry	119
4.2	Different levels of statistical sophistication	120
4.3	Optimization of market share vs. revenue per price level	121
4.4	Classification of analysis types	121
4.5	Big data analysis strategies	123
4.6	Problem-solving process	124
4.7	Churn model results for telecom firm	125
4.8	Tesco's beer and diaper data	126
4.9	Different conversion rates after device switching	127
4.10	How big data are changing analytics	128
4.11	Impact of WhatsApp usage on the smartphone usage of a Dutch telecom company	129
4.12	Case example of multi-source data analysis of relation between brand performance and sales share	131
4.13	Different types of data approaches	134
4.14	Average top-decile lifts of model estimated at time	137
4.1.1	Different distributions causing similar averages	144
4.1.2	Example of time series for sales	145
4.1.3	Profiling new customers on age classification	146
4.1.4	Decile analysis for monetary value and retention rates	147
4.1.5	Gain chart analysis for book club	148
4.1.6	External profiling for a clothing retailer using Zip code segmentation	149
4.1.7	Sales share per customer segment for total coffee and fair trade coffee	150
4.1.8	Falling subscription base for a telecom provider	151
4.1.9	Decomposing subscription base in acquisition and churn	151

4.1.10	Migration matrix of customers of a telecom firm	152
4.1.11	Like-4-like analysis for value development of the customer base of a phone operator	153
4.1.12	Steps for execution of an L4L analysis	154
4.1.13	Example of a cohort analysis	155
4.1.14	Example of a survival analysis	156
4.1.15	Example of a dendrogram	160
4.1.16	Visualization clusters	161
4.1.17	Example of a cluster analysis of shoppers	162
4.1.18	Trend analysis	166
4.1.19	Effects of different marketing instruments on sales for a chocolate brand	169
4.1.20	Predictions for service quality time series of a European public transport firm	171
4.1.21	Effects of store attributes on store satisfaction	173
4.1.22	Attributes chosen for study on cab services	175
4.1.23	Example of a choice-based conjoint design for a cab study	177
4.1.24	Segmentation analysis for conjoint study on cab services	179
4.1.25	Response rate for different RFM-segments	182
4.1.26	Example of a decision tree using CHAID	183
4.1.27	Output of logistic regression mailing example in SPSS	185
4.1.28	Gains chart	187
4.2.1	Online purchase funnel	198
4.2.2	A/B testing	199
4.2.3	Effect of different touchpoints on advertising recall and brand consideration	201
4.2.4	Use of different channel for search and purchase: Webrooming vs. showrooming	201
4.2.5	Latent class segmentation based on customer channel usage	202
4.2.6	Revenues, costs, and profit per group with and without search channel catalog	203
4.2.7	Purchase funnel: Path to purchase on mobile handset	204
4.2.8	Comparison of effects estimated by attribution model and last click method	205
4.2.9	Closed-loop marketing process	207
4.2.10	Schematic overview of recommendation agent in hotel industry	209
4.2.11	Flu activity USA predicted by Google	212
4.2.12	Estimation results of multi-level model to assess performance of CFMs	215
4.2.13	Effects of marketing mix variables on brand performance using time-varying parameter models	216
4.2.14	Text analytics approach	218
4.2.15	Illustration of POS tagging	218
4.2.16	Illustration of a word cloud	219
4.2.17	Number of tweets by time and sentiment	221

4.2.18	Degree centrality	224
4.2.19	Betweenness centrality and closeness centrality	224
4.3.1	Information overload	232
4.3.2	Sweet spot of data, story and visual	233
4.3.3	Building blocks for a clear storyline	235
4.3.4	Analysis process vs. effective communication	236
4.3.5	Examples of different storylines for different purposes	238
4.3.6	Graph of Anscombe's Quartet data table	239
4.3.7	The picture superiority effect	240
4.3.8	Relationship charts	241
4.3.9	Comparison charts	242
4.3.10	Example of a bullet chart	243
4.3.11	Composition charts	244
4.3.12	Distribution charts	245
4.3.13	Chart suggestions—a thought starter	246
4.3.14	Pre-attentive attributes	247
4.3.15	Basic analytical patterns	248
4.3.16	From storyline to visuals to presentation	250
5.1	Shortage of supply in analytical talent	254
5.2	Changing role of the marketing intelligence department	256
5.3	Phases of the standard analytical process	259
5.4	Multi-disciplinary skills of an analyst	264
5.5	Possible big data staff profiles	265
5.6	Stepwise development of analytical competence within the firm	266
5.7	Number of vendors in marketing technology landscape represented in supergraphics of chiefmaric.com	269
5.8	Different layers of a big data analytical system	270
5.9	Linking data, analyses, actions and campaigns	274
5.10	Flow diagram of the adaptive personalization system developed by Chung, Rust and Wedel (2009)	276
5.11	Organization models for the analytical function	278
5.12	Different personality profiles of analysts and marketeers	279
6.1	Value drivers for an energy company	287
6.2	Contribution of each of the value drivers to CLV	287
6.3	Impact of different value driver improvements on CLV	288
6.4	The big data dashboard	290
6.5	The conceptual model for the holistic approach	292
6.6	From search/purchase behavior to product combinations	295
6.7	Algorithm for calculating product recommendations based on the product relation score	295
6.8	MapReduce programming model	296
6.9	Results of new way of working	297
6.10	Visualization of model being used	299
6.11	Comparison of effects for attribution model and last-click method	300

6.12	Comparison of complex model with simpler model	300
6.13	Results of cluster analysis on social network variables of telecom brand	302
7.1	Key learning points by chapter	306
7.2	Word cloud of our book	308

Tables

2.1.1	Example of items used to measure Rogers' adoption drivers	26
2.1.2	Definitions of BAV® components	31
2.1.3	Overview of different customer feedback metrics	37
2.1.4	Conceptualization of customer feedback metrics	38
2.1.5	Criteria for good metrics	44
4.1.1	Seven classic data analytics	142
4.1.2	Gains and lift scale	187
4.2.1	Seven big data analytics	195
4.2.2	How Internet choice differs from supermarket choice	198
5.1	Shifting focus of the marketing intelligence function	257

Foreword

Companies around the world are struggling with a vast amount of data, and can't make sense of it all. "Big data" has the promise of providing firms with significant new information about their markets, their products, their brands, and their customers—but currently, there's often a great divide between big data and truly usable insights that create value for the firm and the customer.

This book addresses this huge need. When I had the opportunity to read *Creating Value with Big Data Analytics: Making smart marketing decisions*, my first reaction was: Thank goodness! Where has this book been all my life? Finally, here's a book that provides a clear, detailed, and usable roadmap for big data analytics. I know that's hard to believe, but read on.

As I write this, Facebook has reached a new milestone of 1 billion users in a single day. Just think of the big data analytics opportunities from just that one day. Verhoef, Kooge and Walk have developed a theoretically sound and highly practical framework. Their value creation model just makes sense; it makes the complex simple. First, they clearly identify the goal of any analytic "job to be done", focusing on either (a) creating and measuring *value to the customer*, or (b) creating and measuring *value to the firm*. They further break these two goals down into three levels: *market* level, *brand* level and *customer* level. This clear delineation of six key analytic areas of focus, followed by practical, "how-to" guides for using and analyzing big data to answer questions in each of these key areas, is a highly executable approach, well grounded in rigorous scientific research.

They do a great job of achieving three key objectives:

1. Teaching us all how "big data" provide new opportunities to create value for the customer (so customers like our products and services better), and for the firm (so we make more profit), while also helping us to be mindful of key security and privacy issues. This framework makes the book work.
2. Teaching us specific analytic approaches that truly fit identifiable marketing questions and situations, and, most importantly, how to gain insights that lead to value creation opportunities—new growth opportunities, new customers, or growth from existing customers. This is the missing piece that this book does so well. One key advantage of this book is that it offers in-depth key analytic approaches for all areas of marketing, including analytic classics, new big data techniques, story-telling and visualization.

3   Teaching us how to develop a big data analytics capability focused on value creation—that delivers growth and positive ROI. By taking us through the entire process from getting the data, to integrating the data, to analysis, to insight, to value, to the role of the organization—the roadmap is complete, and ready for anyone to begin.

Who should read this book? Anyone who needs to understand customers, products, brands, markets or firms. CMOs and marketing executives should read this book—it provides great insights into how you can develop a successful big data analytics capability, and how to interpret insights from big data to fuel growth. Those individuals charged with insights within the organization should read this book: one of the key learnings from Verhoef, Kooge and Walk's approach is that you'll know what analysis to do, when, for what purpose, and with what data. That's huge! Data scientists should read this book—not because you need to learn the analysis techniques described here (you may be aware of many of them), but because it will strengthen your ability to gain insights on marketing problems and help you to communicate your ideas and insights to the rest of the organization. Even professors and students of analytics should read this book. It provides a rigorous approach to frame your thinking and build your analytic skills. And finally, if your head is swimming and you're overwhelmed with the opportunities and complexities of the "firehose" of big data, this book is for you.

I believe it's the Rosetta Stone we've all been looking for, finally answering critical questions: How do we create insights from big data for marketing? How do we create value from big data? How do we solve problems with big data? And how do we get a positive ROI on our investment in big data analytics? Whether you are just starting on your journey in big data analytics, or well on your way, you will learn a ton from this book.

The authors don't shy away from all the complexities and the messiness of big data and analytics. Rather, they make the complex manageable and understandable. They explain difficult analytic approaches clearly and show you when—and why—to use what technique. They provide a rare combination of science and practicality. Examples, cases and practical guidelines are clear, detailed and readable, taking you to that next step of getting to the business of analyzing your own big data to create value for your customers and your firm.

What more can I say? *Creating Value from Big Data Analytics: Making smart marketing decisions* offers in-depth, rigorous and practical knowledge on how to execute a successful big data analytics strategy that actually creates value. This is the first book that puts it all together. Thanks so much to Peter, Edwin and Natasha for writing the book that we all really needed.

Katherine N. Lemon, PhD
Accenture Professor and Professor of Marketing,
Carroll School of Management, Boston College
Executive Director, Marketing Science Institute (2015–2017)

Preface

When we started our careers in marketing analytics, it was a small discipline which attracted only minor attention from the boards of companies. Analytics was mainly developed in firms having a strong direct marketing focus, such as Readers Digest. Beyond that, research agencies were trying to develop analytical solutions for more brand-oriented companies. During our careers this situation has dramatically changed. Analytics have become a major discipline in many firms and scientific evidence strongly supports the performance impact of a strong analytics department. Successful examples in leading firms provide only more support for having a strong analytical function. Marketing has become more data-driven in the past decade!

This development has only become more prominent with the arrival of "big data". CEOs of banks, retailers, telecom providers, etc. now consider big data as an important growth opportunity in several aspects of their businesses. Despite this, we observe that many firms face strong challenges when developing big data initiatives. Many firms embrace big data without having a decent developed analytical function and without having sufficient knowledge in the organization on data analytics, let alone on big data analytics. We therefore believe there was an urgent need to write a book on creating value with big data analytics. In so doing, we strongly sympathized with the view that the existence of big data should not be considered a revolution; it rather builds on the strong developments in data and analytics in the past.

It was not just external big data developments that led us to write this book: some internal motivations induced us as well. All of us, at some point in our careers when we had built up extensive knowledge on marketing analytics, felt the need to share this knowledge with a broader audience, rather than only clients, fellow academics, and/or students. We had already developed material for master students and executives in specific specialized programs, such as masterclasses on customer value management and executive programs on customer centric strategies. However, when writing this book, we realized that this knowledge was not sufficient. The world of big data has created new analytical approaches that we had to dive into. Moreover, these developments inspired us to rethink our concepts and develop new frameworks. Overall, writing this book was a great learning experience for all of us. We hope that you will have a similar learning experience when you read this book.

Acknowledgements

Writing this book would not have been possible without the support of many people. Foremost we want to thank Kim Lijding who gave us considerable help in the final stages of the book, especially in getting the chapters organized. We also thank Hans Risselada PhD for some collegial feedback and the many marketing managers and marketing intelligence managers who provided valuable input for our book in the development process. We also acknowledge the support from Nicola Cupit from Routledge during the writing process. Finally, we want to emphasize that writing this book was a great and stimulating joint experience. So enjoy!

Peter C. Verhoef, Edwin Kooge and Natasha Walk

Abbreviations

ANCOVA	Analysis of covariance
ANOVA	Analysis of variance
APE	Average prediction error
APS	Adaptive personalization systems
ARMAX	Autoregressive moving average with x variables
ARPU	Average revenue per user
ATL	Above the line
B2B	Business-to-business
B2C	Business-to-customer
BAV	Brand asset valuator
BE	Brand equity
BRIC	Brazil Russia India China
BTL	Below the line
C2C	Customer-to-customer
CBC	Choice based conjoint
CDR	Call detail record
CES	Customer effort score
CFM	Customer feedback metrics
CHAID	Chi-square automatic interaction detection
CIV	Customer influence value
CKV	Customer knowledge value
CLM	Closed loop marketing
CLV	Customer lifetime value
CMO	Chief marketing officer
COGS	Costs of goods sold
CPC	Cost per click
CPO	Cost per order
CRM	Customer relationship management
CRV	Customer referral value
CSR	Corporate social responsibility
CTR	Click through rate
CVM	Customer value management
DASVAR	Double asymmetric vector autoregressive
DSI	Digital sentiment index

EBITDA	Earnings before interest, taxes, depreciation and amortization
ETL	Extract transform load
eWOM	Electronic word-of-mouth
FMCG	Fast-moving consumer goods
FTC	Federal Trade Commission
GDP	Gross domestic product
GMOK	Generalized mixture of Kalman filters model
GRPs	Gross rating points
IT	Information technology
KPI	Key performance indicator
LP	Loyalty program
MAPE	Mean absolute percentage error
MI	Marketing intelligence
MSE	Mean squared error
NBD	Negative binomial distribution
NLP	Natural language processing
NPS	Net promoter score
NSA	National Security Agency
OLAP	Online analytical processing
PCA	Principal component analysis
POS	Point-of-sale
POST	Part-of-speech-tagging
PSQ	Perceived service quality
RE	Relationship equity
RFM	Recency frequency monetary value
ROI	Return on investment
SBU	Strategic business unit
SEO	Search engine optimization
SKU	Stock-keeping unit
TAM	Technology acceptance model
UGC	User generated content
USP	Unique selling point
V2S	Value-to-society
VAR	Vector autoregressive
VARX	Vector autoregressive with x variables
VE	Value equity
V2C	Value-to-customer
V2F	Value-to-firm

1 Big data challenges

Introduction

One of the biggest challenges for today's management lies in the increasing prevalence of data. This is frequently referred to as "big data". A recent study by IBM among chief marketing officers (CMOs) indeed reports that big data or the explosion of data is considered a major business challenge (IBM, 2012). One of the main underlying drivers of this explosion is the increasing digitalization of our society, business and marketing. One can hardly imagine that consumers around the globe nowadays could live without smartphones, tablets, Facebook and Twitter. Marketing is probably one of the business disciplines most affected by new developments in technology. In the last decades, technological developments such as increasing data-storage capacity, increasing analytical capacity, increasing online usage, etc. have dramatically changed aspects of marketing. More specifically, we have seen the development of customer relationship management, or CRM (Kumar & Reinartz, 2005). This arrival of CRM posed challenges for marketing and raised issues on how to analyze and use all the available customer data to create loyal and valuable customers (Verhoef & Lemon, 2013). With the generation of even more data and other types of data, such as text and unstructured data, firms consider how to use such data as an even more important problem. A recent study by Leeflang and Verhoef in joint cooperation with McKinsey confirms this (Leeflang, Verhoef, Dahlström, & Freundt, 2014). They find that marketing is struggling with gaining customer insights from the increasing amount of available data. According to McKinsey, one of the main explanations is a lack of knowledge and skills on how to analyze data and how to create value from these data.

Explosion of data[1]

Data have been around for decades. However, thirty to forty years ago, these data were usually available at an aggregate level, such as a yearly or monthly level. With developments such as scanning technologies, weekly data became the norm. In the 1990s, firms started to invest in large customer databases, resulting in the creation of records of millions of customers in which information on purchase behavior, marketing contacts, and other customer characteristics were stored (Rigby, Reichheld, & Schefter, 2002). The arrival of the Internet and more recently of social media have led to a further explosion of data, and daily or even real-time data have become available to many firms. It is believed that getting value from these data is an important growth engine and will be of value to economies in the coming years (see Figure 1.1).

The Internet has become one of the most important marketplaces for transactions of goods and services. For example, online consumer spending in the United States already surpassed $100 billion in 2007, and the growth rates of online demand for information goods, such as books, magazines, and software, are between 25 and 50 percent (Albuquerque, Pavlidis, Chatow, Chen, & Jamal, 2012). In the United States digital music sales in 2011 exceeded physical sales for the first time in history (Fisch, 2013). Besides B2C and B2B markets, online C2C markets have grown in importance, with examples such as LuLu, eBay and YouTube. The number of Internet users by the end of 2014 was over 279 million in the United States and more than 640 million in China (Internet Live Stats, 2014). Worldwide, there are about 1.4 billion active users of Facebook at the end of the first quarter of 2015. On average Twitter users follow five brands (Ali, 2015). Companies are also increasingly investing in social media, indicated by worldwide marketing spending on social networking sites of about $4.3 billion (Williamson, 2011). Managers invest in social media to create brand fans,

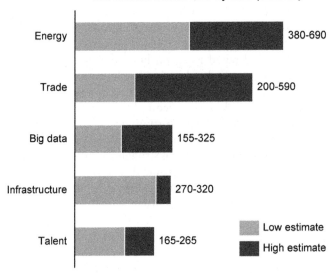

Figure 1.1 Effects of new developments including big data on GDP

Source: Figure adapted from McKinsey Global Institute (2013)

as this tends to have positive effects on firm word of mouth and loyalty (Uptal & Durham, 2010; De Vries, Gensler, & Leeflang, 2012). There are 32 billion searches on Google every month and 50 million Tweets per day. The use of social media also creates a tremendous increase in customer insights, including how consumers are interacting with each other and the products and services they consume. Blogs, product reviews, discussion groups, product ratings, etc. are all new important sources of information (Onishi & Manchanda, 2012; Mayzlin & Yoganarasimhan, 2012). The increasing use of online media, including mobile phones, also allows firms to follow customers in their customer journeys (Lemke, Clark, & Wilson, 2011).

Big data become the norm, but...

If one considers the popular press, big data have now become the norm and firms have started to understand that they might be able to compete more effectively by analyzing these data (e.g. Davenport & Harris, 2007). There are several popular examples of firms analyzing these data, such as IBM, Tesco, Capital One, Amazon, Google, and Netflix. But many companies struggle with getting value from these data. Besides, firms can easily become disappointed about their efforts regarding big data analytics, as we have seen in earlier data revolutions, such as CRM (e.g. Verhoef & Langerak, 2002). One problem was the dominant role of IT in CRM implementation. The same may happen with big data. Moreover, big data developments have stirred up vigorous discussion and public concern on privacy issues. These discussions and concerns have become even more prevalent as a consequence of the actions of Edward Snowden, who leaked documents that uncovered the existence of numerous global surveillance programs, many of them run by the NSA and the Five Eyes with the cooperation of telecommunication companies and European governments.[2] But still firms underestimate the privacy reactions of customers and societal organizations. For example, when the Dutch-based bank ING announced that they were going to use payment information to provide customers with personalized offers and advice, strong reactions on (social) media arose and even the CEO of the Dutch Central Bank said that banks should be very hesitant with this kind of big data initiative.

The problems with creating value from big data mainly arise due to a lack of knowledge and skills on how to analyze and use these big customer data. In addition, firms might overestimate the benefits of big data (Meer, 2013). One important danger is that firms start too optimistically and start thinking "too big", while actually lacking decent knowledge on the basics and challenges of good data analysis of already existing data, such as CRM and survey data, and how this can contribute to business performance. Firms start up large-scale big data projects with rather difficult data mining and computer science techniques and software programs, without a proper definition of the objectives of these projects and the underlying statistical techniques. As a consequence, firms invest heavily in big data but are likely to face a negative return of their big data investments.

Our objectives

Given the growing importance of big data, their economic potential, and the problems firms face on capitalizing on these opportunities, we believe there is an urgent need to provide managers with guidance on how to set up big data initiatives. By writing this book we aim to provide managers with this guidance. Specifically the main objectives of this book are threefold:

- Our first objective is to teach managers how the increasing presence of new and large data provides new opportunities to create value. For that reason, we discuss not only the increasing presence of these data, but also important value concepts. However, we also consider the possible dark sides of big data and specifically privacy and data security issues.
- As a second objective, we aim to show how specific analytical approaches are required, how value can be extracted from these data and new growth opportunities among new and existing customers developed.
- Thirdly, we discuss organizational solutions on how to develop and organize the marketing analytical function within firms to create value from big data.

Our approach

Although we believe in the potential power of analytics and big data, we aim to provide a more nuanced view on big data developments. In essence, we believe that the existence of big data in itself is not a revolution, it is rather an evolution of the increasing availability of data observed in recent decades as a result of scanner data developments, CRM data developments and online data developments. Big data are making data development more massive and this also leads to new data sources. Despite this, many analytical approaches remain similar and knowledge on, for example, how customer and marketing intelligence units have developed, remains valuable. Building on extensive academic and practical knowledge on multiple issues surrounding analytics, we have written a book that aims to provide managers and analysts with strategic directions, practical data and analytical solutions on how to create value from existing and new big data. To do so, this book has two specific approaches. First, we aimed to write a book that is useful for marketing decisions on multiple levels. Typically there has been a kind of disconnect between, for example, brand management and customer management (Leone et al., 2006). In this book we discuss the use of big data at three levels:

1. market level;
2. brand/product level; and
3. customer level.

We take this approach because we observe that big data have an impact on all these levels. Typical brand-oriented firms, such as Unilever and Phillips, are as interested in big data as firms with individual customer level data, such as ING and Amazon. Moreover, big data provide opportunities for data integration and insights using data from multiple levels.

Second, we have a unique combination of a scientific and practical approach to big data and customer analytics. Within marketing science we have observed increasing attention to customer and marketing analytics (Verhoef, Reinartz, & Krafft, 2010; Verhoef & Lemon, 2013), which has provided extensive knowledge on theoretical CRM concepts such as customer lifetime value (CLV). Furthermore, specific models have been developed, for example to predict customer loyalty and value (e.g, Neslin, Gupta, Kamakura, Lu, & Mason, 2006; Venkatesan & Kumar, 2004). However, despite this increasing presence, marketing science and analytical practice are frequently separated. Using our knowledge from science and practice, we aim to provide a scientifically solid, pragmatic and usable approach towards creating value from data within firms. We will provide a number of cases within each chapter to show how our discussed concepts and techniques can be used within marketing practice. We use a novel approach in the way this book is divided into chapters. The main chapters present an overarching discussion on the main theoretical and conceptual ideas on, for example, big data, value creation and analytics. Beyond that we have secondary in-depth chapters that aim to provide the interested readers (e.g. the data scientist) with much more in-depth knowledge on these specific concepts and analytics. As such, this book can be very valuable for (marketing) managers aiming to understand the core concepts of big data analytics in marketing, and also for marketing and customer intelligence specialists and data-scientists.

Reading guide

The structure of our book is displayed in Figure 1.2. We start with two general chapters (of which this introduction is the first). In these chapters we discuss our main underlying vision on big data and customer analytics and the relevance of analytics for firms. In Chapter 2 we discuss our main big data value creation model that will be used as a guidance for the following chapters. Next we have key chapters which focus on the business management level: we focus on the omnipresence of data (Chapter 3), analytics (Chapter 4) and the development of an analytical organization (Chapter 5). For Chapters 2, 3 and 4 we have written underlying in-depth chapters. For example, for value creation we focus on specific metrics of our value concepts: value-to-firm (V2F) and value-to-customer (V2C). Similarly, in-depth chapters on analytics discuss analytical classics, big data analytics and story-telling and visualization. As previously mentioned, the function of these in-depth chapters is to provide readers with more detailed knowledge and/or tools for each of the more high-level topics discussed in the higher-level chapters. In Chapter 6 we describe specific cases in (big data) analytics. We end by setting out the most important learning points.

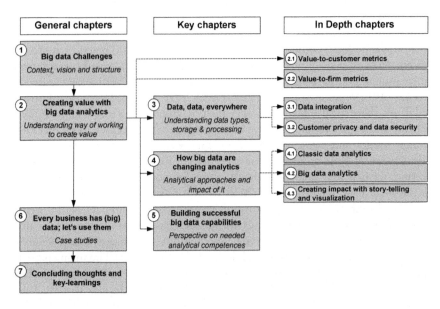

Figure 1.2 Reading guide for book

We urge the reader to start first with the general and key chapters. The in-depth chapters cannot be read independently from the general and key chapters! If one likes to have more detailed knowledge on specific topics one can later pick and choose from these in-depth chapters.

Notes

1 This section is based on Leeflang, Verhoef, Dahlström, & Freundt (2014).
2 See https://en.wikipedia.org/wiki/Global_surveillance_disclosures_(2013%E2%80%93present) (accessed September 14, 2015).

References

Albuquerque, P., Pavlidis, P., Chatow, U., Chen, K., & Jamal, Z. (2012). Evaluating promotional activities in an online two-sided market of user-generated content. *Marketing Science*, 31(3), 406–32.

Ali, A. (2015). *Why do we follow brands on social media?* Retrieved from Social Media Today. Retrieved June 10, 2015 from: www.socialmediatoday.com/social-business/asadali/2015-05-24/business-social-media-infographic.

Davenport, T., & Harris, J. (2007). *Competing on analytics – The new science of winning*. Harvard Business School Press.

De Vries, L., Gensler, S., & Leeflang, P. S. H. (2012). Popularity of brand posts on brand fan pages: An investigation of the effects of social media marketing. *Journal of Interactive Marketing*, 26(2), 83–91.

Fisch, K. (2013). *Did you know 3.0*. Retrieved January 19, 2013 from: www.youtube.com/watch?v=jp_oyHY5bug.

IBM. (2012). *Analytics: The real-world use of big data – How innovative enterprises extract value from uncertain data*. IBM Institute for Business Value. Retrieved September 11, 2015 from www.ibm.com/smarterplanet/global/files/se__sv_se__intelligence__Analytics_-_The_real-world_use_of_big_data.pdf

Internet Live Stats. (2014) *Internet Users by Country*. Retrieved from Internet Live Stats. Retrieved June 10, 2015 from www.internetlivestats.com/internet-users-by-country/.

Kumar, V., & Reinartz, W. (2005). *Customer Relationship Management: A Databased Approach*. USA: John Wiley and Sons.

Leeflang, P. S. H., Verhoef, P. C., Dahlström, P., & Freundt, T. (2014). Challenges and solutions for marketing in a digital era. *European Management Journal*, 32(1), 1–12.

Lemke, F., Clark, M., & Wilson, H. (2011). Customer experience quality: An exploration in business and consumer contexts using repertory grid technique. *Journal of the Academy of Marketing Science*, 3(6), 846–69.

Leone, R. P., Rao, V. R., Keller, K. L., Luo, A. M., McAlister, L., & Srivastava, R. (2006). Linking brand equity to customer equity. *Journal of Service Research*, 9(2), 125–38.

Mayzlin, D., & Yoganarasimhan, H. (2012). Link to success: How blogs build an audience by promoting rivals. *Management Science*, 58(9), 1651–1668.

McKinsey Global Institute. (2013). *Game changers: Five opportunities for US growth and renewal*. Retrieved from McKinsey.com. Retrieved September 11, 2015 from www.mckinsey.com/insights/americas/us_game_changers.

Meer, D. (2013). The ABCs of analytics. *Strategy Business*, 70, 6–8.

Neslin, S. A., Gupta S., Kamakura, W. A., Lu, J. X., & Mason, C. H. (2006). Defection detection: Measuring and understanding the predictive accuracy of customer churn models. *Journal of Marketing Research*, 43(2), 204–11.

Onishi, H., & Manchanda, P. (2012). Marketing activity, blogging and sales. *International Journal of Research in Marketing*, 2(3), 221–34.

Rigby, D. K., Reichheld, F. F., & Schefter, P. (2002). Avoid the four perils of CRM. *Harvard Business Review*, 82(11), 101–9.

Uptal, M. D., & Durham, E. (2010). One cafe chain's Facebook experiment. *Harvard Business Review*, 88(3), 26–26.

Venkatesan, R., & Kumar, V. (2004). A customer lifetime value framework for customer selection and resource allocation strategy. *Journal of Marketing*, 68(4), 106–215.

Verhoef, P. C., & Langerak, F. (2002). Eleven misconceptions about customer relationship management. *Business Strategy Review*, 13(4), 70–6.

Verhoef, P. C., & Lemon, K. N. (2013). Successful customer value management: Key lessons and emerging trends. *European Management Journal*, 31(1), 1–15.

Verhoef, P. C., Reinartz, W. J., & Krafft, M. (2010). Customer engagement as a new perspective in customer management. *Journal of Service Research*, 13(3), 247–52.

Williamson, D. A. (2011). *Worldwide social network ad spending: A rising tide*. Retrieved from eMarketer.com. Retrieved September, 2015 from www.emarketer.com/Report.aspx?code=emarketer_2000692.

2 Creating value using big data analytics

Introduction

Nowadays, the existence of big data is such a hype that firms are investing in big data solutions and organizational units to analyze these data and learn from them. We observe that firms are now, for instance, hiring big data scientists. This occurs in all sectors of the economy including telecom, (online) retailing, and financial services. Firms have a strong belief that analyzing big data can lead to a competitive advantage and can create new business opportunities.

However, at the same time experts are warning of too high expectations. Some commentators even consider big data as being only a hype that will mainly provide disappointing results.[1] David Meer (2013) suggests that taking a historical perspective on earlier data explosions shows specific patterns in the beliefs about the potential benefits. He specifically refers to the scanning revolution in the 1980s and the CRM revolution in the late 1990s (Verhoef & Langerak, 2002). Firms typically go through three stages:

1 Data enthusiasm—Investment phase
2 Data disappointment—Frustration disinvestment phase
3 Data realism—Reinvestment phase

In the first phase there are strong beliefs within a firm about the potential benefits that can be achieved. Frequently, top management is seduced by enthusiastic examples in the business press and effective sales strategies of IT, management consultants, and software providers. However, after some years the data explosion investments and initiatives provide mainly disappointing results and failed projects occur frequently. This induces firms to rethink their data strategies and sometimes disinvest in data initiatives and IT. This rethinking of strategies is usually the stepping stone towards a next phase with refined expectations, more realistic ambitions and a stronger focus on the value creating power of data-based initiatives and its return on investment (Verhoef & Lemon, 2013; Rigby & Ledingham, 2004).

Of course firms can go through these phases when implementing big data initiatives. However, this would certainly lead to value destruction, negative

ROIs, waste of resources, and enormous frustration. Instead of going through these phases, we propose that firms should have sound initial expectations on the value of potential big data. For this, it is essential to understand how big data can create value. Furthermore, it is our strong belief that firms should understand their analytical strategies and the approach they choose in analyzing available data.

In this chapter we lay out the foundations for a sound value-creating big data strategy. We discuss how big data can create value and what elements are required to create value.

Big data value creation model

One of the biggest challenges of big data is how firms can create value with big data. We have developed the big data value creation model to show how this value creation occurs (see Figure 2.1). This model has four elements:

1 Big data assets
2 Big data capabilities
3 Big data analytics
4 Big data value.

Big data assets

Assets are usually considered as resource endowments that a firm has accumulated over time. These assets can be tangible (e.g. plant) or intangible (e.g. brands, customer relationships). In the past, customer databases were considered important assets for firms (Srivastava, Tasadduq, & Fahey, 1998). For example, these

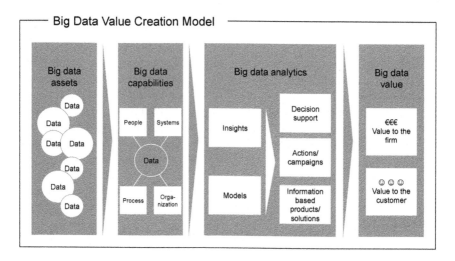

Figure 2.1 Big data value creation model

databases could be used to create stronger relationships with customers, achieve higher loyalty, and create more efficient and effective (cross)-selling techniques. In an era of big data, the data are no longer rare. One could actually argue that the data are no longer that valuable, as data are omnipresent, can be collected in multiple ways and are frequently publicly available to many firms (e.g. data on online reviews). In principle, we strongly sympathize with this view. However, we also observe that within firms there is actually a lack of knowledge on the mere presence of data within the firm itself and outside the firm. For example, one of the largest cable manufacturing companies in Europe only recently discovered that by diving into some internal billing data, they could gain valuable insights on loyalty and customer lifetime value (CLV) developments. We will discuss the different sources and types of data in Chapter 3.

Big data capabilities

We can see that the value of data is not in the mere presence of the data, but in the underlying capabilities able to exploit these data. We consider capabilities as the "glue" that enables big data—simultaneously with other assets—to be exploited to create value (Day, 1994). For example, using different data sources on customer experiences, one could learn how to improve these experiences, thereby also building on the qualitative input of key customers (relational asset) that may further improve the customer experience.

These underlying capabilities that can be used on big data concern:

1. People
2. Systems
3. Processes
4. Organization.

People

To exploit big data, people are very important. Without the right set of skilled big data experts it is not sensible to develop a big data strategy. Having intelligence departments with the right capabilities is of essential importance (Verhoef & Lemon, 2013). This is actually one of the biggest challenges for firms (Leeflang, Verhoef, Dahlström, & Freundt, 2014). Firms are now hiring big data scientists, but these people are difficult to find. As a consequence, firms have also chosen to educate big data scientists in-house through, for example, specific internal programs and academies (Verhoef & Lemon, 2013). Given that people are of essential importance for a successful big data strategy, we will devote a special chapter to how firms can develop a strong marketing intelligence capability (see Chapter 5).

Systems

With regard to systems, we strongly emphasize the importance of data integration and providing an integrated data ecosystem allowing the firm to analyze data from multiple sources. We still observe that within firms data are collected in different systems or databases, which are not sufficiently linked. This data integration requires specific data management skills and software. Data integration becomes even more difficult when firms are operating in multiple channels or in multiple countries where different systems are being used (Neslin et al., 2006). A key question for firms is to what extent data should be integrated, as the marginal returns on data integration might decline (Neslin et al., 2006). An important trend with systems is that, due to the size of big data, (cloud) solutions such as Hadoop have been developed. Similarly, we observe several new trends in available analytical software. One of the major trends is the development of open source "packages," such as R, which can be used for free. Although this involves a lot of programming, the programs are widely shared between communities of users, so that these packages become more easily accessible. We will have a more in-depth discussion on systems and specifically data-based solutions and software solutions in Chapter 5.

Process

Processes with regard to smart big data analytics mainly concern how firms organize the data input and storage, the accessibility of data to analytical teams and the communication between analytic teams and (marketing) management. The first two processes are relevant for smooth and real-time data accessibility. Importantly, these processes also involve how firms deal with privacy, data security issues, and legal issues with regard to data usage. Privacy and security have become a top priority for firms and both receive considerable attention among policy makers as a response to the increasing availability of big data and scandals involving big data. The trend seems to be that legislators are reducing the freedom of firms to use individual customer-level data. As a consequence, firms are becoming stricter with data usage and storage. For example, we know of firms that stored customer data covering several years, but now only store transaction data of customers for a maximum period of a year. Data security is becoming an issue: there have been many examples of hackers and criminal organizations being able to illegally get data on, for example, passwords, payment data (e.g. credit card numbers) and other personal data. Hackers are not the only problem—employees who are less careful with data (e.g. lose laptops or throw away data storage devices with sensitive data on them) can also cause security problems. Data compliance is thus an important element of big data processes. The usage of these data can hurt millions of customers around the globe. The other part of the processes concerns how marketing and analytical teams communicate. This involves a two-way communication. On the one hand marketing should clearly communicate to management the problems and challenges they face and how analytics could be helpful in solving them. On the other hand analytical teams should be able to effectively communicate their findings through insightful reports and marketing dashboards. Moreover, in an era where big data analytics can create value, analytical teams should be able to effectively communicate big data-based value-creating solutions to the management. These processes will probably develop in a natural way, but it might also be important to define processes up front in which, for example, marketing is required to get in touch with their analytical teams when a marketing problem (e.g. a decrease in loyalty) is observed. Processes on how marketing dashboards should be fuelled with relevant information over time should also be defined.

Organization

Beyond having good people, firms also need to devote attention to how big data and specifically big data analytics can be organized internally. One crucial question in this respect is whether analytics or intelligence departments can really have an impact on daily business. We observed several models on how the analytical function is embedded within firms. Typically, intelligence functions are separate staff departments that serve the marketing and sales functions with outcomes of their analyses, either on request or self-initiated. However, in order to have a stronger impact, some firms choose to integrate the intelligence department with the marketing/sales department. The underlying idea is that this will induce a stronger use of analytics within marketing decision making (Hagen et al., 2013). More likely, however, the result is a reduction in the independence of the analytics department, with negative consequences, such as a lack of innovation and not sufficiently thought-through analyses. A disadvantage of such an organization might also be that analytical knowledge is not used optimally within the organization as it is fragmented over multiple departments and/or functions.

The role of culture

One of the most prevalent issues in exploiting big data as an asset is the nature of the internal culture and the related processes. Traditionally, marketing has been a function that tended to rely on intuition and gut feeling. Fortunately, only having a good idea is no longer good enough in many firms (De Swaan Arons, Van den Driest, & Weed, 2014). In fact there is an increasing trend towards more data-driven or fact-based decision making, partially explained by a stronger emphasis on marketing accountability (Verhoef & Leeflang, 2009). Big data analytics can only survive within firms that embrace this trend and indeed are open to rely more on analytics and their resulting insights and models that provide ideas for innovation, or show the effectiveness of specific marketing actions, etc. This requires a strong move within firms and specifically marketing departments. This change in culture can be rather dramatic. Old-school marketers have to change their decision-making style and have to gain more knowledge on analytics and how they can be used to make smarter marketing decisions. This requires intensive education programs for—or in extreme cases replacement of—these marketers. One specific challenge, though, is how the analytical left-brain culture can be combined with a more creative/intuitive right-brain culture (Leeflang et al., 2014; De Swaan Arons et al., 2014). In Chapter 5 we will discuss the issues surrounding big data capabilities.

Big data analytics

Reading a book about big data and analytics, one would probably expect that analytics would deserve immediate attention. However, analytics not embedded in the organization without the relevant data, culture, and systems will have limited impact and value-creating potential. When discussing big data analytics, we make a distinction between two different forms of analytics:

- Analytics focusing on gaining insights
- Analytics aiming to develop models to improve decision making.

We define big data insights usually as descriptive findings resulting from data analyses that provide input into marketing decisions. Models are purposely developed to direct and support marketing decisions. Model development is almost like an R&D task in which analysts work to an end goal on a model, which is accepted by the management of the department and users of the models (e.g. Van Bruggen & Wierenga, 2010).

The developed insights and models can create value for firms in three ways:

- Decision support for marketing
- Improved actions and campaigns
- Information-based products and solutions

Using the developed insights and models firms can potentially make more informed decisions on where to allocate their marketing budgets. Results of a model can show the specific effectiveness of an advertising channel. For example, when De Vries (2015) showed the limited influence of social media on acquisition, one could question whether a firm should heavily focus on social media to attract new customers. Leeflang et al. (2014) distinguish between two different models that can be developed to drive marketing decision making:

- Idiosyncratic, usually more sophisticated models developed to tackle specific marketing problems
- Standardized models that have become important tools to improve the quality of tactical marketing decisions.

The marketing literature has identified many standardized models (e.g. ScanPro), which are mainly delivered by marketing research agencies such as AC Nielsen, IRI and Research International (Hanssens, Leeflang, & Wittink, 2005). These standardized models can be filled with available data within firms and research agencies. We expect that research agencies will provide more standardized solutions on how big data can be integrated to gain customer insights and estimate the relationships between marketing instruments and marketing outcomes.

The improvement of actions and campaigns is mainly relevant in a CRM environment. It mainly has to do with whom to target, when to target and with what message. It has been shown that through effective selection of customers, the ROI of campaigns can be improved (e.g. Bult & Wansbeek, 1995). It has been observed that customization of messages and offers, specifically in an online environment, can be very valuable (Ansari & Mela, 2003). In a big data environment this now occurs in real-time, and is also known as behavioral targeting. This can, however, have negative side effects as it may be considered intrusive (Van Doorn & Hoekstra, 2013).

A relatively new development in the era of big data is the use of results of analyses and models to develop information-based products and solutions that specifically focus on customers to create value for these customers. For example, a novel player in the Dutch banking sector, KNAB bank, is explicitly providing data-based solutions to their customers to advise them how to use their available money (e.g. put it in a savings account). The Dutch railways provide a service to their customers in which, based on actual information on traffic and trains, the fastest transport mode is recommended (Leeflang et al., 2014). Nobel prize winner Rich Thaler believes that these solutions, either developed by suppliers themselves or by other, frequently independent, infomediaries, will become important in helping customers to make more informed decisions (Thaler & Tucker, 2013).

Strategies for analyzing big data

The presence of big data provides huge opportunities for analytical teams. One of the easiest ways of using it is probably just to start up analyses and start digging into the available data. By digging in the data, one might gain very interesting insights, which can guide marketing decisions. The most famous example in this respect is the UK-based retailer Tesco: when analyzing data of their loyalty card, they discovered that consumers buying diapers also frequently buy beer and chips (Humby, Hunt & Phillips, 2008). Although such an example can be inspiring, we posit that before starting up an analytical exercise, one should clearly understand the benefits and disadvantages of this specific analysis strategy as well as that of other strategies. Therefore we strongly advise a more problem-driven approach instead of a rather exploratory findings approach. We discuss these strategies in more depth in Chapter 4.

Big data is changing analytics

Big data is believed to change analytics as big data has specific characteristics known as the 3Vs of big data, posing specific challenges for researchers and managers (Taylor, Cowls, Schroeder, & Mayer, 2014; Leeflang et al., 2014):

- Increasing data **V**olume
- Increasing data **V**elocity
- Increasing data **V**ariety

The increasing volume of data implies that databases become very large, and the analysis of data of millions of customers with hundreds of characteristics is no longer an exception (e.g. Reimer, Rutz, & Pauwels, 2014). Data are also arriving more quickly, which induces faster analysis and faster action (Leeflang et al., 2014). We have been moving from yearly data to monthly data, to weekly data, to daily data and now even to data per hour/minute. Finally, the data are becoming more complex as they arrive in different formats. In the past numerical data was the standard. Nowadays, more unstructured data such as text and audio data are also available, and also video data through, for example, YouTube. Other examples include data on Facebook postings, and GPS data from mobile devices. The three Vs have been extended to five Vs, where **V**eracity and **V**alue have been added. Veracity refers to the messiness and trustworthiness of data. With the increasing availability of data, not all data are as reliable as one would like. Hence, data quality can be low. For example, it is known that customer reviews are being manipulated. Value is considered as the value that is captured from analyzing and using the data. Although we clearly do acknowledge that value should be captured (see our big data value creation model) it is not a specific characteristic of big data, which is changing analytics.

How these big data are changing marketing analytics is not as clear. Marketing scientists have argued the following: high volume of data implies the need for models that are scalable; high velocity opens opportunities for real-time, or virtually real-time marketing decision making that may or may not be automated; and high variety may require integration across disciplines with the corresponding sensitivity to various methods and philosophies of research.[2] In sum, this suggests that models should easily be estimated on large sample sizes, whereas analytics should be done in such a way that it can provide immediate results, and finally new methodologies from other disciplines, such as computer science and linguistics, should be integrated.

However, we also warn analysts and managers that despite the different characteristics of big data compared to traditional data, one should also be careful of immediately moving into a totally different analysis mode. For example, despite the huge volume of data available, analysis can still be done on smaller samples of the available data. The information present in unstructured data may also be more limited than expected. DeVries (2015) recently showed that the additional explanatory power of Facebook "likes" in explaining sales is rather limited. It is our contention that in order to be a good big data analyst and to use big data in a good fashion, one should master the basics of analytics rather than moving immediately into grand big data analytical exercises without actually knowing what one is doing.

The power of visualization

Analysts with a left-brain who are trained in statistics will find it easy to understand numerical outcomes of analyses. However, for many other people understanding the meaning of numbers is quite difficult. Presentation of analyses (and their results) is therefore a crucial task when analyzing the data. One way to have more impact is to visualize the data (that is, using visual aids in data presentation), because humans in general look for structures, anomalies, trends, and relationships. Visualization supports this by presenting the data in various forms with different interactions. It can provide a powerful qualitative overview of data and analytical results. It can also show the important relationships in the data (Grinstein & Ward, 2002). We believe that visualization is a very important analytical capability whose importance is frequently neglected. It does, however, allow researchers to have more impact on daily marketing decisions, as it enhances the accessibility of analytical results for especially right-brain trained marketing executives. Despite this, one should also be very careful. Visualization can lead to an oversimplification of results (e.g. by providing a scatter plot of a spurious correlation) or can easily overestimate the found effects with some scaling tricks on graphical axes. Hence, one should also be careful not to communicate a statistical illusion when visualizing the data.

From big data analytics to value creation

We consider three methods by which big data analytics can create value for customers and firms. First, big data analytics can create important new insights that improve marketing decision making. For example, big data analytics can show how firms can improve customer satisfaction through improving, for example, the specific features of the service experience. By having these insights marketing budgets can be allocated more effectively. Instead of relying on intuition, brand managers can, for example, invest in a positioning strategy that effectively differentiates brands from competitors.

A second value-creation benefit of big data analytics is the development of more effective marketing campaigns, and more specifically more effective targeting of campaigns by selecting the right customers. Where early analytics were mainly focused on immediate response to campaigns (e.g. Feld, Frenzen, Krafft, Peters, & Verhoef, 2013; Bult & Wansbeek, 1995), a longer-term focus is now strongly advocated, achieved by considering the impact of marketing campaigns on CLV and customer equity (e.g., Venkatesan & Kumar, 2004; Rust, Lemon, & Zeithaml, 2004). The effectiveness of both approaches has been shown extensively in the scientific literature. Importantly, these approaches have also been applied in business and have been shown to increase firm value (Kumar & Shah, 2009). Another development is that, especially in an online environment, real-time behavioral targeting is being used to adapt online environments and advertising to specific considered needs of the customer.

A third value-creation benefit is the development of big-data-based solutions for customers. These solutions directly have an impact on customers and should create more value for them. Frequently, this involves an improvement of the service experience in several stages of the purchase process. For example, specific tools can be developed to help customers make better purchase decisions using smart algorithms (e.g. Thaler & Tucker, 2013).

Value creation concepts

Value creation should be the ultimate objective of every big data strategy. However, value creation is one of those terms that is easily written down without a full and complete understanding of the topic. Importantly, we consider value from two perspectives:

1. Value to the customer (V2C)
2. Value to the firm (V2F)

These two perspectives are not novel. In fact the classical definitions of marketing put forward in basic marketing text books (e.g., Kotler & Armstrong, 2014) emphasize that marketing should focus on creating superior value for customers (through high quality, attractive brand propositions and striving for an appropriate relationship), and that firms can capture value from customers in return for this value creation. This is sometimes also referred to as "value delivery" and "value extraction." Value extraction from customers is considered to be a direct consequence of value delivery. Value extraction occurs by paid price premiums, higher loyalty rates (lower churn), higher revenues per customers and stronger customer advocacy (Reichheld, 1996; Srivastasva et al., 1998). Scientific research indeed suggests that firms which provide more value to customers they tend to have a stronger financial performance (Anderson, Fornell, & Mazvancheryl, 2004).

Balance between V2F and V2C

Firms can be classified on two value dimensions (see Figure 2.2). A high value delivery and high value extraction strategy is considered as a win-win strategy. It is usually seen as the best strategy for firms. Despite this, we frequently observe that firms tend to outperform on a single value dimension (upper left and bottom right cells). This can have dramatic consequences. Frequently, firms tend to focus on value extraction solely: examples can be found in many sectors. A dramatic example is the banking industry. There has been a strong focus on shareholders' value within banks, inducing them to focus less on customers and the delivery of value to customers. The crisis in 2008, with many banks facing difficult problems, showed that this sole focus on value extraction can have severe consequences for firms and society (Verhoef, 2012). Firms in other industries sometimes focus solely on V2F, to their detriment. For example, the main focus of the CEO of the Dutch Telco-incumbent KPN was on creating value for shareholders. As a consequence, marketing management had a strong focus on CLV creation through communication tactics and contractual offers (i.e. moving from one-year to two-year contracts, minute rounding or other short-term pricing tactics). Data analysis of their CRM database, looking for potential churn candidates, was an important element of that strategy. In terms of value delivery to shareholders this strategy was rewarding: this is reflected in the top 100 position for the former Dutch Telco CEO in a recent Harvard Business Review list of CEOs that were successful in creating shareholder value (Hansen, Ibarra, Peyer & Von Bernuth, 2013). Despite this, after he stepped down his strategy was criticised for putting too little emphasis on the customer, resulting in the delivery of insufficient value to customers.[3] Specifically, the presumed lack of investments in service quality and innovation was considered as a weakness of that strategy. In fact, one of the first strategies of the new CEO was to announce that Dutch Telco would invest more in service and that excellent service delivery to customers would be a key strategic focus. The practice of Dutch Telco was rather typical of many Telco companies around the globe. Actually, many firms were criticised for poor service and taking advantage of customers through, for example, using complex pricing plans. In the US, Virgin Mobile was one of the firms to address this criticism, by developing customer friendly pricing plans and focusing on a superior service (McGovern, 2007).

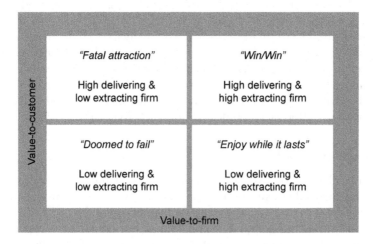

Figure 2.2 Value-to-customer vs. value-to-firm

Source: Adapted from Reinartz (2011), and Wiesel et al. (2011)

A mismatch between delivered customer value and extracted firm value can also occur (upper left cell). These firms are rather attractive for customers, but the firms fail to extract more value through, for example, achieved higher loyalty and higher price premiums. Many starting online firms struggle here; they provide much value in terms of free services, and lower prices, etc. but find it difficult to keep customers and/or ask for fees for the services they provide. Empirical research, however, shows that while firms are frequently in the downward "Enjoy while it lasts cell," the number of firms in the upper-left "Fatal attraction" cell is rather limited (Bouma et al., 2010). We do, however, find a number of examples of firms in the "Doomed-to-fail" cell, where firms provide low customer value and are unable to extract sufficient value. Firms in this cell are in a dangerous position, as their value proposition and delivery requires strong investment, while due to their inability to extract value they might lack long-term resources for these investments. Consider Nokia: with a decreasing attractiveness for customers and a low repeat purchase rate it now no longer exists as an independent firm, but has been acquired in 2013 by a firm that had sufficient financial resources to invest in the Nokia brand and its underlying products—Microsoft.

V2S: Extending value creation

The above value concepts are sometimes extended. Especially in an era where firms are considered to also have a societal function and an increased focus on, for example, corporate social responsibility, a focus on only V2C and V2F is not sufficient (Korschun, Bhattacharya, & Swain, 2014; Porter & Kramer, 2011). In fact banks have not only been criticised for insufficient focus on customers, but also for insufficient consideration of society as a whole (Verhoef, 2012). One could therefore suggest extending the value concept by also taking into account value delivery to society (V2S). This could be done in many ways. Some firms, such as Unilever, consider sustainability as one of their core elements in their corporate strategy and aim to show that in their business operation, including brand propositions. However, Procter & Gamble is using a more tactical approach and uses specific activities at the brand level, such as dental education programs in Hispanic neighbourhoods in the US, to show their involvement with local societies.

V2S can partly be reflected in the delivered value to customers. Indeed Rust, Zeithaml and Lemon (2000), for example, consider brand ethics as an integral part of the delivered value by brands. Similarly, corporate social responsibility is considered as a driver of customer satisfaction (Korschun et al., 2014) and customer satisfaction functions as an important mediator in the effect of corporate social responsibility on customer and firm performance (Luo & Bhattacharya, 2009; Onrust, Verhoef, Van Doorn, & Bügel, 2014). In this book we will mainly take this perspective and consider V2S as a driver of V2C. We also observed that corporate reputation measures can be heavily correlated with customer satisfaction metrics over time. In this book we will therefore not specifically differentiate between V2S and V2C. Instead we consider V2S to be a driver of V2C.

Metrics for V2F and V2C

Metrics have become very important due to the increasing attention for accountability within firms and the resulting consequences for marketing departments (Verhoef & Leeflang, 2009). Metrics are measuring systems that quantify trends, dynamics, or characteristics (Farris, Bendle, Pfeifer, & Reibstein, 2010). There are numerous metrics in marketing that can be measured. Farris et al. (2010) discuss more than fifty metrics that every executive should master. We classify metrics into V2C and V2F metrics. V2F metrics are usually much more transaction-oriented and focus on concrete market outcomes that can be related to monetary consequences for the firm. V2C metrics typically focus on the evaluation of value by customers.

Beyond the distinction between V2C and V2F metrics, we distinguish between metrics at the market, brand, and customer level (see Figure 2.3). V2C metrics typically focus on the evaluation of value by customers. V2C metrics at the market level include issues such as product awareness and penetration of new products and services. Brand level V2C metrics focus on brand evaluations and brand knowledge of customers. For example, brand awareness would be a typical V2C metric but so also are brand consideration and brand attitudes. Some of these brand attitudes, such as brand uniqueness and brand innovativeness, are considered as input for mere attitudinal based brand equity measures. At the customer level, typical metrics are customer satisfaction and relationship

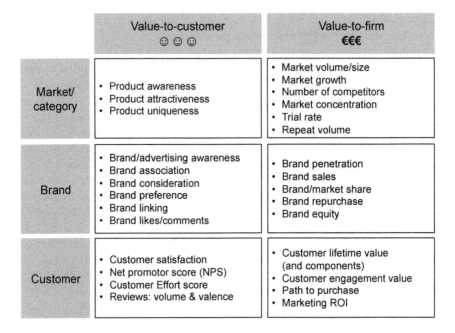

Figure 2.3 Classification of V2C and V2F metrics

quality measures. Sometimes these metrics are referred to as customer feedback metrics (e.g. De Haan, Verhoef, & Wiesel, 2015). A very popular V2C metric is the net promotor score. One might argue that operational measures, such as the number of complaints, or the number of reported problems with the product or service, can also be considered as V2C metrics. Although these metrics are typically not evaluations of customers and could be mainly be considered as input for customers' perceived value, they could be very valuable measures reflecting the delivered value to customers (e.g., Gijsenberg, Van Heerde, & Verhoef, 2015). In this era of big data, these metrics have become more available and they should definitely be considered in an extended V2C value creation analysis.

Typical V2F metrics at the market level are market volume, category sales, market size, and number of customers. These V2F metrics are generally not so firm specific. At the brand level, one would measure brand or market share and brand sales, and also brand equity, which is a more monetary evaluation of a brand's value. A measure that can be used here is revenue or price premium (Ailawadi, Lehmann, & Neslin, 2003). At the customer level, CLV is a customer metric that has received enormous attention in the last decade. It can be considered as a key V2F customer metric that really tries to capture the monetary value generated by an average customer over his or her relationship with firms. This measure can be extended by also considering Customer Engagement Value (Kumar et al., 2010), that may include outcomes, such as referrals and actual word of mouth (e.g. Bijmolt et al., 2010). An in-depth discussion of V2C and V2F metrics can be found in Chapters 2.1 and 2.2.

Value creation model as guidance for book

As noted above, the different elements of the big data value creation model are discussed in different chapters that are yet to come. We extend the diagram of the model (Figure 2.1) with references to the relevant chapters (see Figure 2.4), as we also referred to in the above text. This figure nicely summarizes how the chapters relate to each element in our big data value creation model. Furthermore, in each chapter we start with this model to show where this chapter fits within this model—that is, guiding our discussion on how big data can be used for smart marketing decisions. In Chapter 6 we discuss how firms can create value through an integrated approach of big data as depicted in our model. This will provide some useful applications on how the building blocks of big data analytics jointly can be used within firms.

Conclusions

In this chapter we have discussed the big data value creation model in marketing. Understanding this model is essential to understanding the value-creation potential of big data analytics. Big data assets and capabilities are the important building blocks underlying big data value creation. The capabilities involve systems, people, processes, and the organization. If capabilities are present, big

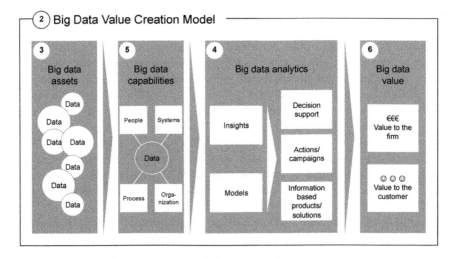

Figure 2.4 Big data value creation model linked to chapters

data analytics can be deployed. These big data analytics can create marketing insights and models that subsequently can improve marketing decision making, and improve the success of actions and campaigns. Moreover, it can be used to develop information-based products and solutions. We consider value as a multi-dimensional construct consisting of value creation to customers (V2C) and value creation to firms (V2F). The use of big data analytics can result in both more V2C and V2F.

Notes

1 See comment by by Nassim Nicolas Taleb that big data is "bullshit" at www.automatiseringgids.nl/nieuws/2013/41/big-data-is-bullshit (accessed September 13, 2015).
2 http//pubsonline.informats.org/page/mksc/calls-for-papers
3 The former CEO disagrees and claims that he was not investing insufficiently in service and innovation: see www.mt.nl/332/76174/business/ad-scheepbouwer-had-ik-dan-minder-winst-moeten-maken.html (accessed September 13, 2015).

References

Ailawadi, K. L., Lehmann, D. R,, & Neslin, S. A. (2003). Revenue premium as an outcome measure of brand equity. *Journal of Marketing*, 67(4), 1–17.
Anderson, E. W., Fornell, C., & Mazvancheryl, S. K. (2004). Customer satisfaction and shareholder value. *Journal of Marketing*, 68(4), 172–85.
Ansari, A., & Mela, C. F. (2003). E-Customization. *Journal of Marketing Research*, 40(2), 131–45.
Bijmolt, T. H. A., Leeflang, P. S. H., Block, F., Eisenbeiss, M., Hardie, B. G. S., Lemmens, A., & Saffert, P. (2010). Analytics for customer engagement. *Journal of Service Research*, 13(3), 341–56.

Bouma, J. T., Bügel, M. S., Verhoef, P. C., Alleman, T., Wiesel, T., & Wesselius, T. (2010). Dutch customer performance index: Het nieuwe meten van klantprestaties. *Tijdschrift voor Marketing*, 4, 58–63.
Bult, J. R., & Wansbeek, T. J. (1995). Optimal selection for direct mail. *Marketing Science*, 14(4), 378–94.
Day, G. S. (1994). The capabilities of market-driven organizations. *Journal of Marketing*, 58(4), 37–52.
De Haan, E., Verhoef, P. C., & Wiesel, T. (2015). The predictive ability of different customer feedback metrics for retention. *International Journal of Research in Marketing*, 32(2), 195–206.
De Swaan Arons, M., Van den Driest, F., & Weed, K. (2014). The ultimate marketing machine. *Harvard Business Review*, 92(7/8), 54–63.
De Vries, L. (2015). *Impact of Social Media on Consumers and Firms*. Doctoral Dissertation, University of Groningen.
Farris, P. W., Bendle, N. T., Pfeifer, P. E., & Reibstein, D. J. (2010). *Marketing metrics: The definitive guide to measuring marketing performance*. USA: Pearson Education.
Feld, S., Frenzen, H., Krafft, M., Peters, K., & Verhoef, P. C. (2013). The effects of mailing design characteristics on direct mail campaign performance. *International Journal of Research in Marketing*, 30(2), 143–59.
Gijsenberg, M. J., Van Heerde, H. J., & Verhoef, P. C. (2015). Losses loom longer than gains: Modeling the impact of service crises on customer satisfaction over time. *Journal of Marketing Research*, 52(5), 642–56.
Grinstein, G. G., & Ward, M. O. (2002). Introduction to data visualization. In U. Fayyad, G. Grinstein & A. Wierse, (Eds), *Information Visualization in Data Mining and Knowlegde Discovery* (pp. 21–46). USA: Morgan Kaufmann Publishers.
Hagen, C., Khan, K., Ciobo, M., Miller, J., Wall, D., Evans, H., & Yaday, Y. (2013). Big data and the creative destruction of today's business models. *Holland Management Review*, 148(4), 25–37.
Hansen, M. T., Ibarra, H., Peyer, U., & Von Bernuth, N. (2013). The best-performing CEOs in the world. *Harvard Business Review*, 91(1/2), 81–95
Hanssens, D. M., Leeflang, P. S. H., & Wittink, D. R. (2005) Market response models and marketing practice. *Applied Stochastic Models in Business & Industry*, 21(4/5), 423–34.
Humby, C., Hunt, T., & Phillips, T. (2008). *Scoring points: How Tesco is winning customer loyalty*. Philadelphia: Kogan Page Publishers.
Korschun, D., Bhattacharya, C. B., & Swain, S. D. (2014). Corporate social responsibility, customer orientation, and the job performance of frontline employees. *Journal of Marketing*, 7(3), 20–37.
Kotler, P., & Armstrong, G. (2014). *Principles of Marketing*. USA: Pearson Education.
Kumar, V., & Shah, D. (2009). Expanding the role of marketing: From customer equity to market capitalization. *Journal of Marketing*, 73(6), 119–36.
Kumar, V., Aksoy, L., Donkers, B., Venkatesan, R., Wiesel, T., & Tillmanns, S. (2010). Undervalued or overvalued customers: Capturing total customer engagement value. *Journal of Service Research*, 13(3), 297–310.
Leeflang, P. S. H., Verhoef, P. C., Dahlström, P., & Freundt, T. (2014). Challenges and solutions for marketing in a digital era. *European Management Journal*, 32(1), 1–12.
Luo, X., & Bhattacharya, C. B. (2009). The debate over doing good: Corporate social performance, strategic marketing levers, and firm-idiosyncratic risk. *Journal of Marketing*, 73(6), 198–213.

McGovern, G. (2007). *Virgin mobile USA: Pricing for the very first time (case 9-504-208)*. Boston: Harvard Business School Press.

Meer, D. (2013). The ABCs of analytics. *Strategy Business*, 70, 6–8.

Neslin, S. A., Grewal, D., Leghorn, R., Shankar, V., Teeling, M. L., Thomas, J. S., & Verhoef, P. C. (2006). Challenges and opportunities in multichannel customer management. *Journal of Service Research*, 9(2), 95–112.

Onrust, M., Verhoef, P. C., Van Doorn, J., & Bügel, M. S. (2014). *When doing good leads to increased customer loyalty: Why weak firms can benefit from CSR*. Working Paper, University of Groningen.

Porter, M. E., & Kramer, M. R. (2011). Creating shared value. *Harvard Business Review*, 89(1/2), 62–77.

Reichheld, F. F. (1996). *The loyalty effect: The hidden force behind growth, profits, and lasting value*. USA: Harvard Business School Press.

Reimer, K., Rutz, O. J., & Pauwels, K. (2014). How online consumer segments differ in long-term marketing effectiveness. *Journal of Interactive Marketing*, 28(4), 271–84.

Reinartz, W. (2011). Presentation on customer management on Dutch customer performance awards.

Rigby, D. K., & Ledingham, D. (2004). CRM done right. *Harvard Business Review*, 82(11), 118–29.

Rust, R. T., Lemon, K. N., & Zeithaml, V. A. (2004). Return on marketing: Using customer equity to focus marketing strategy. *Journal of Marketing*, 68(1), 109–27.

Rust, R. T., Zeithaml, V. A., & Lemon, K. N. (2000). *Driving customer equity: How customer lifetime value is reshaping corporate strategy*. New York: The Free Press.

Srivastava, R. K., Tasadduq, A. S., & Fahey, L. (1998). Market-based assets and shareholder value: A framework for analysis. *Journal of Marketing*, 62(1), 2–18.

Taylor, L., Cowls, J., Schroeder, R., & Meyer, E. T. (2014). Big data and positive change in the developing world. *Policy & Internet*, 6(4), 418–44.

Thaler, R. H., & Tucker, W. (2013). Smarter information, smarter consumers. *Harvard Business Review*, 91(1), 45–54.

Van Bruggen, G. H., & Wierenga, B. (2010). Marketing decision making and decision support: Challenges and perspectives for successful marketing management support systems. *Foundations and Trends® in Marketing*, 4(4), 209–332.

Van Doorn, J., & Hoekstra, J. C. (2013). Customization of online advertising: the role of intrusiveness. *Marketing Letters*, 24, 339–51.

Venkatesan, R., & Kumar, V. (2004). A customer lifetime value framework for customer selection and resource allocation strategy. *Journal of Marketing*, 68(4), 106–215.

Verhoef, P. C. (2012). *Klanten centraal in de bankensector*. White paper, Monitoring Commissie Code Banken, the Netherlands.

Verhoef, P. C., & Langerak, F. (2002). Eleven misconceptions about customer relationship management. *Business Strategy Review*, 13(4), 70–6.

Verhoef, P. C., & Leeflang, P.S.H. (2009). Understanding the marketing department's influence within the firm. *Journal of Marketing*, 73(2), 14–37.

Verhoef, P. C., & Lemon, K. N. (2013). Successful customer value management: Key lessons and emerging trends. *European Management Journal*, 13(1), 1–15.

Wiesel, T., Alleman, T., Bouma, J. T., Bügel, M. S., de Haan, E., Hoving-Wesselius, T., & Teunter, L. (2011). Customer performance impact: interessante relaties tussen DCPI, NPS en omzet. Customer Insights Center Rapport CIC-2011-02, University of Groningen.

2.1 Value-to-customer metrics

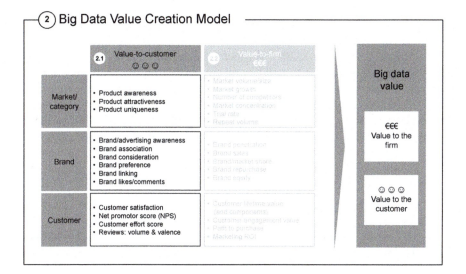

Introduction

Value-to-customer (V2C) metrics focus on the delivered value to customers. Sometimes these metrics also refer to "share of heart" metrics or "share of mind" metrics. In essence, these metrics indeed focus on what a firm achieves in a customer's mind and whether it results in positive cognitive and affective responses. These metrics in themselves do not reflect any value beyond what customers know and feel. However, they can indeed be linked to value-to-firm (V2F) metrics and extensive research has shown substantial effects of different V2C metrics on V2F metrics.

In this chapter we will discuss the main V2C metrics, distinguishing between market, brand, and customer metrics. Within each of these metrics, we will discuss standard metrics and new big data metrics. Next to V2C metrics, we will also pay some attention to value-to-society (V2S) metrics, such as corporate social responsibility.

Market metrics

V2C market metrics are mainly relevant in the early phases of a product's life-cycle, as different firms aim to communicate the value and relevance of newly introduced products and services. The important framework is the adoption model as proposed by Rogers (1995): he suggests that new products can be evaluated based on several dimensions: relative advantage, complexity, compatibility, observability, and trialability. In a broader sense, metrics could focus on the knowledge of products (product awareness) and beliefs, and on the value offered by products (product attractiveness and product uniqueness). These metrics are typically measured with surveys among potential customers using extensive scales. In Table 2.1.1 we show an example of how these constructs are being measured for the adoption of an online grocery channel. The validity of these dimensions has been shown frequently, and indeed customer perceptions of these advantages predict usage intentions of new product innovations (e.g., Arts, Frambach, & Bijmolt, 2011; Verhoef & Langerak, 2001).

Another frequently used model in this respect is the so-called "technology acceptance model" (TAM). This model builds on the theory of reasoned action and suggests that there are two main attitudes to be considered for new technologies: ease of use and usefulness (e.g. Davis 1989; Davis, Bagozzi, & Warshaw, 1989). This model has also been tested frequently for mainly IT-based innovations and its validity has been shown (King & He, 2006). In an online context the TAM model has been extended by including the effects of trust and perceived risk (Venkatesh & Bala, 2008).

Table 2.1.1 Example of items used to measure Rogers' adoption drivers

Perceived relative advantage
Electronic shopping is less exciting
Using electronic shopping saves much time
Using electronic shopping makes me less dependent of opening hours
Perceived compatibility
Electronic shopping suits my person
Electronic shopping requires few adaptations in my personal life
Electronic shopping yields few problems for me
Perceived complexity
Electronic shopping is complex, because I cannot feel and see the products
With electronic shopping it is hard to find the needed products
With electronic shopping it is difficult to order products
With electronic shopping it is problematic to compare products
Electronic shopping is complex
Intention to adopt electronic grocery shopping
Please indicate on the response scale from 0 to 10 to which extent you intend to use electronic shopping to obtain your groceries in the near future

Source: Adapted from Verhoef & Langerak (2001)

New big data market metrics

Big data developments, and specifically online conversation on products and products usage, may provide firms with a deeper understanding of how customers view and use products. Of specific use here could be statistics on the use of different search terms on search engines such as Google and Yahoo. These search terms may show initial interest in products and brands.

A tool used for this is Google trends. In Figure 2.1.1 we show the search results for "tablet" as a product over time. As one can observe, the number of search requests for tablets has increased over time, and one can also observe some peaks. New product introductions of, for example, the iPad could cause these peaks.

Similar figures can be derived from multiple, also more generic, search terms. In Figure 2.1.2 we show search results for big data and market research. Here you clearly see that interest in market research is declining, whereas there is a strong and increasing interest in big data. Importantly, Google trends can also show the interest across, for example, different geographical markets and specific cities across the globe.

Brand metrics

V2C brand metrics are frequently collected on a continuous basis. For many firms it is very important to continuously measure indicators of their brand performance and, related to that, to track the outcomes of advertising campaigns. Many research and advertising agencies around the globe, such as Young & Rubicam, have developed standard brand performance measurements. Importantly, brand metrics are collected among all customers in the market place, as firms aim to measure the position of brands relative to competing brands. This contrasts with

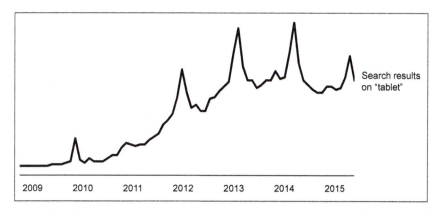

Figure 2.1.1 Search results on "tablet" worldwide

Source: Adapted from Google trends (2015)

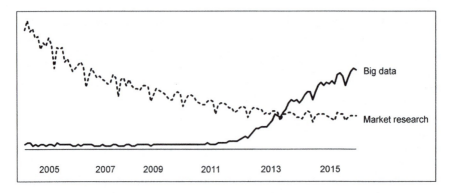

Figure 2.1.2 Search interest in "big data" and "market research"

Source: Adapted from Google trends (2015)

customer metrics, which typically are measured among existing customers of a firm or brand.

Traditional brand performance measures can be structured around the sales funnel from being aware to final purchase of the brand and subsequent resulting loyalty. Brand metrics can also be classified based on their focus. Broadly, one could distinguish between cognitive brand metrics focusing on customers' knowledge of a brand and affective measures focusing on customers' feelings and emotions towards a brand (Hanssens, Pauwels, Srinivasan, Vanhuele, & Yildirim, 2014).

A typical cognitive brand metric is brand awareness, which measures whether customers know the brand. Brand awareness can be unaided or spontaneous, reflecting top-of-mind awareness and aided brand awareness (see Figure 2.1.3 for a trend-line on these two brand metrics). Especially for strong brands, such as Coca Cola and Apple, brand awareness metrics are close to 100% and do not vary much over time. The added value of this brand awareness metric for these brands could be relatively small. For unknown brands, tracking brand awareness can provide very useful information. Beyond brand awareness firms also frequently measure "advertising awareness," which focuses on whether consumers are aware of (usually) a recent brand's advertising campaign.

At a deeper level, customers gain more knowledge about the brand. This may be reflected in specific brand associations, such as whether it is an innovative brand or a high-quality brand. These associations are likely to vary more between brands and over time, as brands have developed specific positioning strategies. In contrast with brand awareness metrics, these metrics are likely to change more over time (e.g. Mizik & Jacobson, 2009; Hunneman, Verhoef, & Sloot, 2015).

Brand metrics that are closer to the final purchase concern brand consideration, and brand preference or brand liking. Brand consideration metrics focus on whether brands are in the set of brands that customers consider buying.

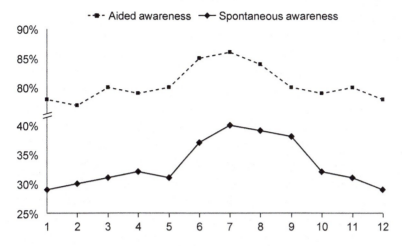

Figure 2.1.3 Example of tracking aided and spontaneous awareness through time

Brand consideration is traditionally considered as a necessary condition for brands to be purchased. However, brands can easily enter a consideration set, when they are, for example, in promotion or there is effective in-store communication (e.g. Baxendale, Macdonald, & Wilson, 2015; Van Nierop et al. 2010).

Brand preference measures whether customers prefer a specific brand over competing brands. High brand preference levels for brands should typically lead to higher market shares for brands. One could argue that a brand preference measure is so close to behavior that it might actually be a V2F metric. In Figure 2.1.4, we provide an example of the brand preference for multiple smartphone brands and how these preference measures vary between different market segments. As one can observe, the Apple iPhone is the most preferred brand in 2011, but that this preference varies between segments.

An alternative measure being used is brand liking, which is also a metric focusing on the affective attraction of a brand. It is typically measured with a question, where customers have to state their liking of a brand, for example by using a scale such as 1 = "not like the brand," to 7 = "like enormously." (Hanssens et al., 2014).

Brand-asset valuator®

One of the most influential V2C brand measurement systems is the one developed and used by Young & Rubicam. They developed the Brand-Asset Valuator® (BAV). This brand-asset valuator focuses on multiple dimensions of the brand (see Figure 2.1.5).

30 *Value-to-customer metrics*

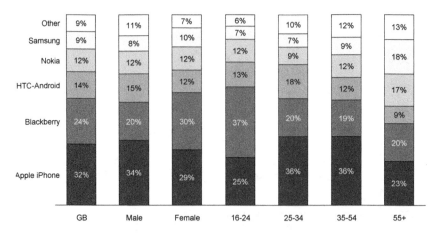

Figure 2.1.4 Example of brand preference of smartphone users, de-averaged to gender and age

Source: Adapted from Ofcom omnibus research, March 2011

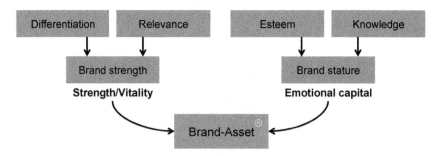

Figure 2.1.5 Brand-Asset Valuator® model

Source: adapted from Young & Rubicam[1]

The BAV distinguishes between brand strength and brand stature. Each of these measures can then be subdivided into underlying metrics: differentiation and relevance for brand strength and esteem and knowledge for brand stature. In some updated models of BAV, brand energy is also measured (Mizik & Jacobson, 2009). The measures and definitions for each of these dimensions, including brand energy, are provided in Table 2.1.2.

Do brand metrics matter?

Collecting the brand metrics discussed above provides firms with early information on the future health of their brands. For example, changes in brand consideration may signal that somewhere in the near future brand market share

Table 2.1.2 Definitions of BAV® components

BAV pillar	Underlying perceptual metrics	Survey scale	BAV data	Meaning and role of the pillar
Differentiation	1 Unique 2 Distinctive	Yes/no Yes/no	% responding "yes" % responding "yes"	Perceived distinctiveness of the brand. Defines the brand and reflects its ability to stand out from competition. Is the "engine of the brand train;… if the engine stops, so will the train."
Relevance	1 Relevant to me	1-7 scale	Average score	Personal relevance and appropriateness and perceived importance of the brand. Drives market penetration and is a source of brand's staying power.
Esteem	1 Personal regard 2 Leader 3 High quality 4 Reliable	1-7 scale Yes/no Yes/no Yes/no	Average score % % responding "yes" % responding "yes" % responding "yes"	Level of regard consumers hold for the brand and valence of consumer attitude. Reflects how well the brand lives up to its promises.
Knowledge	1 Familiarity with the brand	1-7 scale	Average score	Awareness and understanding of the brand identity. Captures consumer intimacy with the brand. Results from brand-related (marketing) communications and personal experiences with the brand.
Energy (new pillar)	1 Innovative 2 Dynamic	Yes/no Yes/no	% responding "yes" % responding "yes"	Brand's ability to meet consumers' needs in the future and to adapt and respond to changing tastes and needs. Indicated future orientation and capabilities of the brand.

Source: Adapted from Mizik & Jacobson (2009: 16)

might decline. As noted, it also provides information on the competitive positioning of the brand compared with other brands. This information may help firms to redefine positioning strategies and the communicated USP. For example, if the price image of supermarkets is changing, supermarkets may want to change their retail mix in such a way that, for example, this price image is improved (e.g. Hunneman et al., 2015; Van Heerde, Gijsbrechts, & Pauwels, 2008).

Research has also considered the impact of brand metrics on V2F metrics. Mizik and Jacobson (2009) studied the impact of the BAV® measure on shareholder value metrics. They essentially show that positive changes in energy and relevance perceptions increase shareholder value metrics. No effects on the other three dimensions are found. These results suggest that only specific brand metrics can be considered as indicators for future business success.

Brand metrics have not only been linked to shareholder value metrics, but also to V2F metrics, such as brand sales. Srinivasan, Vanhuele and Pauwels (2010) label these metrics as "mind-set metrics" and assess the joint impact of past sales, marketing mix variables, and mind-set metrics on brands' sales performance. Their studies consistently show that marketing mix variables impact these metrics and that the studied brand metrics also impact sales performance. However, there are substantial differences between brands (Hanssens et al., 2014).

Hanssens et al. (2014) suggest good V2C brand metrics should do well on three criteria. They should:

1 have potential for growth;
2 have some stickiness; and
3 be responsive to marketing efforts.

The first criterion refers to whether the metric can indeed change and grow over time. This frequently does not hold for brand awareness metrics, as a natural ceiling is often reached. The stickiness of the metric focuses on the fact that the metric does not change too much over time. There should be some staying power, which may result from inertia or lock-in. The responsiveness to marketing efforts refers to marketing's ability to "move the needle" on the V2C metric. If a V2C metric does not respond to changes in the marketing mix, it is probably not a very effective metric.

What about brand equity?

A common term used in the branding world is "brand equity." Brand equity (BE) can have different meanings. Depending on the measurement, it is sometimes considered as just another V2C metric whereas others consider it more a V2F metric. Branding expert Kevin Lane Keller considers customer-based BE as that part of customers' behavioral response that can be attributed to the brand. For example, if customers are paying a price premium for a brand, this could be an indicator of BE (Ailawadi, Neslin, & Lehmann, 2003). The definition of BE indicates that it is mainly a V2F metric reflecting the (financial) value of the brand. In fact firms like Interbrand focus on this value of the brand, when making a list of the top 100 global brands.

Some researchers measure BE using attitudinal customer metrics that focus on measures such as brand strength and brand uniqueness (Verhoef, Langerak, & Donkers, 2007). In fact, in his BE model, early brand guru David Aaker includes brand associations and brand quality as indicators of BE (Aaker, 2009). Brand associations could be quality, innovativeness, but also associations, such as hip, young, etc. Examples of brands with strong brand associations include BMW and Nike.

New big data brand metrics

The metrics discussed so far are rather traditional and have been around for years. Only recently we have started to understand the actual impact of these metrics on brand performance outcomes. Being able to combine different data sources, together with continuous collection of brand metrics data, allowed researchers to do so.

Particularly as a result of online and social media developments, where customers share their opinions about brands and may also indicate their liking of brands, new sources for data on brands have been developed. This is sometimes referred to as "user generated content" (UGC). Importantly, this UGC can be collected and analyzed to create brand metrics. We consider the following specific new big data metrics:

- Digital brand association networks
- Summarized digital brand metrics
- Social media brand metrics.

Digital brand association networks

When writing their opinion about brands, customers may share different opinions in words about brands. For example, they may share somewhere on a blog that Apple is considered innovative, whereas Samsung is considered as a real Asian brand. Similarly, ideas on brands such as Nike and Adidas can be shared. Researchers have developed methods to collect these data and to analyze them, thereby considering the valence of these words. In Figure 2.1.6 an association network for McDonalds is shown, based on digital data. As one can observe from this network, the main association for McDonalds is "yummy"; however, negative associations are service, taste and the offered volume (not enough). We will discuss methods to analyze text data in greater detail in Chapter 3.1.

Digital summary indices

With digital brand associations we are mainly interested in actual associations, providing managers with more knowledge on what customers actually think about a brand. Research agencies have now developed methods to assess how positive or negative customers' views are when they discuss brands online.

34 *Value-to-customer metrics*

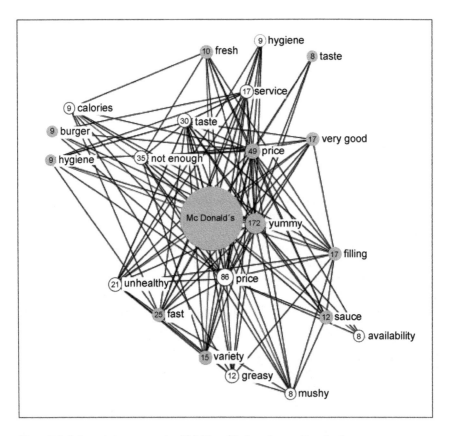

Figure 2.1.6 Association network of McDonald's based on online data[a]

Source: Adapted from Gensler, Völckner, Egger, Fischbach, & Schoder (2015)

Note
a Grey (white) circles represent favorable (unfavorable) brand associations. Numbers in circles represent normalized, weighted degree centrality (per mill)

Using text analytics, the valence of words is then assessed. Based on dictionaries, such as the dictionary of affect, the negativity and positivity of these words can be assessed. Whereas in the past this was done manually (e.g. Verhoef, Antonides, & De Hoog 2004), this is now done automatically using text analysis programs. Based on this positive and negative valence for brands, a valence score can be calculated. These valence scores are related to the sales of brands; correlations with shareholder value metrics have also been reported (e.g. Tellis & Johnson, 2007; Onishi & Manchanda, 2012). These digital summary indices are also referred to as electronic word-of-mouth, or eWOM (Trusov, Bucklin, & Pauwels, 2009).

Especially in the last decade, specialized companies have developed specific brand metrics that can summarize customer online discussions. One example is the digital sentiment index (DSI) as developed by Oxyme/Metrixlab in cooperation with researchers from the University of Münster. The DSI incorporates the sentiment concerning products, services, or brands throughout the most important platforms in a single measure. Furthermore, DSI also tracks competitors and one can simply derive direct comparisons with them. DSI is used for more than a hundred brands in Germany, USA, UK, France, the Netherlands, Finland, and Sweden.

Social media brand metrics

Not only do customers discuss brands online in social media, but also the brands themselves actively use social media for promotion purposes. Customers can visit these brand pages on, for example, Facebook. Customers can react to these brand pages by pushing on the "like" button and by providing comments. The numbers of brand likes and brand comments are considered two relevant social media brand metrics. The number of brand likes may be an indicator of brand preference among customers. The number of comments may indicate some brand involvement. Importantly, the content of social media marketing campaigns affects both metrics. For example, brands get more likes when they include a contest in the campaign and include a video (De Vries, Gensler, & Leeflang, 2012). Not surprisingly, more comments are received when a question is being asked in the campaign. Overall, one could doubt the value of these metrics as real V2C brand metrics. Still, the number of likes and comments can be substantial, although it varies considerably between brands and industries (see Figure 2.1.7). To some extent, they mainly reflect reactions to the social media presence of a specific brand, while brand knowledge and attitudes are based on multiple interactions in multiple channels and touch points. Finally, we note that social media brand metrics and the content of discussions on social media of brands may contribute to the summary digital brand metrics, such as DSI.

Customer metrics

V2C customer metrics are frequently labeled as customer feedback metrics by marketing researchers. Customer feedback metrics (CFMs) have become very popular. Firms are aiming to improve the customer experience across multiple touch points and are seeking ways of measuring this experience. Targets are set on these metrics and continuous measurement occurs. In some cases specific feedback mechanisms are built in. Such a mechanism is the so-called customer feedback loop. In this loop customers give feedback to a firm on a specific service event and subsequently they are called back when they score low on this metric, and are asked about what is behind this low score. Firms then try to solve these issues, which hopefully results in a higher performance. All these

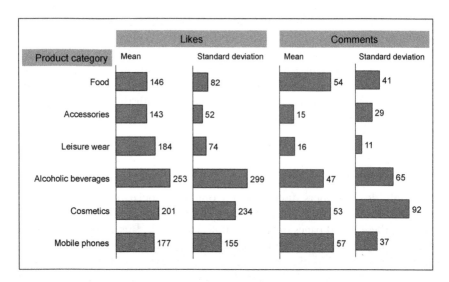

Figure 2.1.7 Average number of likes and comments per product category

Source: Adapted from De Vries, Gensler, & Leeflang (2012: 87)

kinds of systems result in series of customer feedback metrics of thousands of different customers over time. The most popular metrics are the net promoter score (NPS), customer satisfaction, and the more recent customer effort score (CES). These metrics can be measured in different ways. In Table 2.1.3 the exact questions and operationalizations are discussed:

We distinguish between these metrics on two dimensions. The first dimension was introduced by Bolton, Lemon and Verhoef (2004) and more recently by Zeithaml, et al. (2006), who focus on the time span of measures and distinguish between more backward-looking and more forward-looking metrics. Forward-looking CFMs focus on what customers plan to do in the future and may signal something about the future performance of the relationship. The NPS introduced by Reichheld (2003) is an example of a forward-looking CFM, since it considers the willingness to recommend a firm in the future, which may also signal a customer's future relationship with the firm (e.g. Zeithaml et al., 2006). Backward-looking metrics focus on the past and current customer performance of a company towards customers.

The CES is a typical backward-looking CFM, as it measures the perceived service performance from a past specific experience (Dixon, Freeman, & Toman, 2010). It is based on a single question ("How much effort did you personally have to put forth to handle your request?"), and measured on a five-point scale. Dixon et al. (2010) suggest that the CES is a better predictor of repurchase (intentions) and increased spending than the NPS or customer satisfaction.

Table 2.1.3 Overview of different customer feedback metrics

CFM	Measurement
1 Customer satisfaction	"All in all, how satisfied or unsatisfied are you with [company X]?" (1 = very unsatisfied, 7 = very satisfied).
2 Top-2-box customer satisfaction	A dummy at the customer level indicating if the customer has given a score of six or seven on the customer satisfaction question. At the firm (industry) level this is the proportion of customers of that firm (industry) that gave a score of 6 or 7.
3 Net promoter score (NPS)	"How likely is it that you would recommend [company X] to a friend or colleague?" (0 = very unlikely, 10 = very likely). Respondents who gave a score of 0-6 are "detractors," those who gave a 7 or 8 are "passives," and those who gave a 9 or 10 are "promoters." Subtracting the proportion of promoters from the proportion of detractors provides the NPS at the firm level (Reichheld, 2003).
4 NPS-value	The untransformed NPS score (on the 0-10 range) provided by the customer.
5 Customer effort score (CES)	"Did you try to contact [company X] with any kind of request?" (yes/no) If yes, the following question is asked: "How much effort did you personally have to put forth to handle your request?" (1 = very low effort, 5 = very high effort).

Source: Adapted from De Haan, Verhoef, & Wiesel (2015)

Finally, customer satisfaction focuses more on an overall evaluation of the interactions between the customer and the firm over time, and tends to have a more present focus (Verhoef, 2003), although it may also be based on past experiences.

The second dimension we use is about how the measurement scale of the CFM is used. There are advocates of not looking at the mean value of the scale, but at the proportion of people responding very positively and/or very negatively. An example of this is "top-2-box customer satisfaction," which measures the proportion of customers filling in the two highest-scoring points for their overall[2] customer satisfaction (Morgan & Rego, 2006). The calculation underlying the official NPS also distinguishes between very positive, moderate, and negative responses (Reichheld, 2003). Transformations can theoretically be defended, as it has been shown that customers mainly focus on extreme experiences and therefore the effects of CFMs can be rather non-linear (e.g. Van Doorn & Verhoef, 2008; Streukens & De Ruyter, 2004). Moreover, service marketing experts promise to delight customers, implying that customers should evaluate firms with extreme scores on the CFM scales (Oliver, Rust, & Varki, 1997). Firms can, however, also choose not to use a transformation, and instead make use of the full scale, for example the 0–10 scale of the NPS. If we combine the two dimensions, we end up with the three-by-two classification matrix as provided in Table 2.1.4.

Table 2.1.4 Conceptualization of customer feedback metrics

		Pre-defined data		
		Past focus	*Present focus*	*Future focus*
Part of the scale used	Full scale	Customer effort score (CES)	Customer satisfaction	NPS Value
	Focus on extremes		Top-2-box customer satisfaction	Official NPS

Source: Adapted from De Haan, Verhoef, & Wiesel (2015)

Is there a silver metric?

Proponents of different metrics propose that their metrics have the best performance for predicting future growth and customer retention. For example Reichheld (2003) strongly advocates the NPS, while Dixon et al.(2010) believe and show that CES has a very strong performance in predicting customer loyalty, going beyond the performance of other competing metrics. Not surprisingly, academics questioned these claims and have investigated the actual quality of these metrics. Typically they compared the performance of different metrics in predicting future business growth and customer loyalty. Initial studies were not so positive about the performance of the NPS and tended to prefer customer satisfaction (e.g. Keiningham, Cooil, Aksoy, Andreassen, & Weiner, 2007). However, more recent studies actually show smaller differences between customer satisfaction and NPS (e.g. Van Doorn, Leeflang, & Tijs, 2013). In a recent study we analyzed the performance of the metrics for customer retention (De Haan et al., 2015). Here we again find no clear winner. NPS and customer satisfaction score equally well. The CES is, however, doing very poorly. We also observe that there might be some benefits in combining metrics, suggesting that at least firms should monitor multiple metrics (e.g. NPS and satisfaction). This would imply making use of dashboards involving multiple metrics. Based on existing knowledge and practical insights we have the following recommendations for firms:

- Rely on overall metrics with a present or future focus.
- It is very valuable to analyze the development of the top scores of metrics (e.g. top-2 boxes).
- Do not immediately adopt new metrics promising superior performance, but carefully consider the actual performance.
- Measure multiple metrics and report in a dashboard.

Other theoretical relationship metrics

Especially within the CRM literature, other metrics or customer attitudes have been discussed and have gained attention. These metrics mainly focus on the quality of the customer relationship. Customer satisfaction can be an indicator of this quality, although this attitude usually focuses more on the cognitive side of the relationship, being the mere evaluation of the delivered products and services (Bolton et al., 2004). The most specific metric that has been proposed is commitment, defined as the enduring desire to continue a valued relationship (Moorman, Zaltman, & Desphande, 1992). In general this attitude reflects a more emotional evaluation and also considers the future development of the relationship. Researchers have also considered several forms of commitment (e.g. Verhoef, Franses, & Hoekstra, 2002):

- *Affective commitment*: psychological attachment of a customer to the firm, based on feelings of identification, loyalty, and affiliation (Gundlach, Ravi, & Mentzer, 1995).
- *Calculative commitment*: the extent to which customers perceive the need to maintain a relationship given anticipated termination or switching costs (Geyskens, Steenkamp, Scheer, & Kumar, 1996).
- *Normative commitment:* a customer's obligation-based attachment to an organization, marked by feelings of guilt or unease in leaving the organization (e.g., Melancon, Noble, & Noble, 2011).

Affective commitment has been shown to be a predictor of retention, share of wallet and word-of-mouth (Verhoef, 2003). The two other forms of commitment arise from merely negative motivations to stay in a relationship and can even be detrimental for relationship development (Verhoef et al., 2002).

Interestingly, based on the theory of love developed by the psychologist R. J. Sternberg (1986), Bügel, Verhoef and Buunk (2011) propose "customer intimacy" as a novel customer attitude. In their analysis this measure involves both passion about the relationship and the perceived intimacy between the customer and the firm. Their results suggest a strong correlation between commitment and customer intimacy. However, customers feel stronger commitment than intimacy. Remarkably, they also show that the level of intimacy develops during the customer lifecycle from relatively high in the very early phases of the relationship, while it drops in later phases before rising again (see Figure 2.1.8). Overall, we observe no strong use of these metrics within practice, despite the fact that they have been very well received within academic research. It seems that these measures are considered highly theoretical, without a strong adoption within marketing practice (e.g., Roberts, Kayandé, & Stremersch, 2014).

Another customer metric that gained attention is customer trust. Trust is defined as customers' confidence in the quality and reliability of the services provided (Garbarino & Johnson, 1999). Researchers have also proposed that one should distinguish between reliability and benevolence. Reliability focuses on the fact that a firm acts on its promises, while benevolence considers the fact that a firm not only cares about a firm's interests, but also the customer's interest, and acts on that (Geyskens et al., 1996). Trust has gained renewed attention as a result of the multiple crises firms and customers have been (and still are)

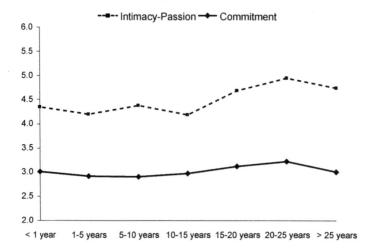

Figure 2.1.8 Development of intimacy and commitment over time

Source: Adapted from Bügel, Verhoef, & Buunk (2011: 253)

confronted with. In particular the financial crisis has stirred up distrust in banks and the banking sector (Verhoef, 2012).

A final theoretical metric is "payment equity" or "price fairness," defined as customers' perceived fairness of the price paid for their consumed services of products (Bolton & Lemon, 1999). In contrast with other metrics, this metric strongly focuses on a single instrument: price. It has been shown that it can predict service usage. However, other studies have shown its predictive power for retention and the purchase of additional services to be absent (Verhoef, 2003; Verhoef et al., 2002).

Customer equity drivers[3]

Within customer management the customer equity model as developed by Rust, Zeithaml, and Lemon (2000) has been influential. They consider customer equity—the net present value of all future and current customers—as a very important outcome variable in customer-centric firms. Conceptually they consider three drivers:

- value equity (VE), defined as customers' objective assessment of the utility of services based on perceptions of "what is given up" for "what is received." VE reflects the outcome of customers' comparisons between their own expectations and firms' performance;
- brand equity (BE), which reflects customers' subjective and intangible assessment of the brand image; and

- relationship equity (RE), defined as customers' assessments of their interactions with the firm. This factor depends on customers' relationships with sales and service persons, loyalty programs, customer communities/networks, and so forth. Positive RE provides relatively more financial and social benefits to customers (Rust, Zeithaml & Lemon, 2000). This enhances feelings of reciprocity and benevolence, which should positively influence loyalty (Selnes & Gønhaug, 2000).

These drivers can be measured with attitude-like questions in which customers evaluate the performance of firms and brands on these dimensions. There is sufficient evidence to indicate that these drivers contribute to customer loyalty. However, the importance of each of these drivers may differ between industries, firms, and customers (e.g. Ou, DeVries, Wiesel, & Verhoef, 2014). For example, BE and VE are more relevant for firms offering innovative services.

New big data customer metrics

Big data customer V2C metrics mainly arise from online interactions, but also from internal data sources, which are frequently neglected.

Internal data sources

Within CRM databases the focus has been strongly on collecting transaction data. However, firms have many interactions with customers that can be used as indicators for V2C. In general we advocate paying more attention to this information. For example, firms can collect complaints of customers. A complaint is certainly a V2C indicator and can probably predict switching behavior. We note that, according to the service recovery paradox, firms acting on complaints can increase customer loyalty (Van Doorn & Verhoef, 2008). Also personal contacts with customers can be indicators of V2C. More deeply personal contacts (e.g. email-conversations, call center contacts) can be analyzed and the positivity or negativity of these contacts can be assessed (Verhoef, Antonides, & De Hoog, 2004).

Other internal data sources can provide information on the actual delivered value to customers and specifically use internal operations data. These data can be customer-specific or measured at a more aggregate level. An example of customer specific data might involve the resolution time of a service problem for a specific customer. Bolton et al. (2008) show that operational data can indeed predict the probability of contract renewal and the level of service upgrading. The delivered service performance can also be measured at a more aggregate level. For example, for railway firms the percentage of trains with a specific delay or the percentage of unsuccessful connections between trains can be an internal measure for the actual delivered value (Gijsenberg et al., 2015). One important issue is that these internal measures do not reflect the actual perception of the delivered value. Perceptions frequently arise from a comparison of the expected service level and the delivered service level. Expectations are, however, frequently based on the past and thus having time series data on the delivered performance may create a more accurate understanding (Gijsenberg et al., 2015).

Online sources

The most important online customer metric is customer reviews. Reviews of firms and specific products are placed online and frequently involve relatively independent websites, such as Tripadvisor or Zoover. Also, online retailers allow consumers to provide reviews of sold products. An online survey of 2,005 American shoppers showed that 65% of potential shoppers selected a brand that was only in their consideration set as a result of online reviews (Weber Shandwick, 2012). This suggests that reviews can be very powerful and influential in steering customer choices online. Indeed, the effect of reviews on sales is significant and substantial with a mean elasticity of 0.35 increase for review volume and 0.65 for review valence (Floyd, Freling, Alhoqail, Cho, & Freling, 2014). Here "review volume" is a measure for the number of reviews and "reviews valence" is a measure of the positivity of the review. However, there is considerable variation in the effectiveness of reviews. Reviews have stronger predictive effects for products with a high customer involvement, while third party and critic reviews have a stronger effect than normal customer reviews.

Note that in an online context the differences between brand metrics and customer metrics become blurred. Customer reviews can be used as input for the creation of summary brand metrics. Furthermore, customer reviews also are considered as eWOM. Despite this it is rather clear that reviews are becoming very important. They clearly affect sales as customers include reading these reviews in their purchase decision. If, for example, a hotel has poor reviews, fewer customers will be likely to book that hotel.

V2S metrics[4]

The V2C concept can also be extended to focus on the societal value of firms. Many firms are developing strategies and initiatives to, for example, improve their sustainability. Such initiatives are significant elements of the corporate strategy of many (multi) national corporations (Beard et al., 2011; Porter & Kramer, 2011), whose CEOs, such as Paul Polman of Unilever, assert that businesses can be a positive force for good in the world and that this approach is in the interests of all firms' stakeholders.

Firms also collect metrics to measure their performance on these societal strategies. These metrics are typically not the responsibility of marketing, but mainly are administered by staff departments responsible for sustainability and/or corporate reputation. Within the management and marketing literature, there is one metric receiving considerable attention: corporate social responsibility (CSR).

Corporate social responsibility

CSR is a firm's commitment to ensure societal and stakeholder well-being through discretionary business practices and contributions of corporate resources (Du, Bhattacharya & Sen, 2010; Kotler & Lee, 2005; Luo & Bhattacharya, 2006). As a broad concept, CSR can include business practices as diverse as cash donations to charity, equitable treatment of workers, and an environmentally friendly production policy. Yet, although CSR goes beyond the interests of the firm to benefit society (McWilliams & Siegel, 2001), many firms additionally strive to "do better by doing good" and gain competitive advantages through CSR (Prout, 2006). Frequently CSR is seen as a kind of perception measure similar to satisfaction, and involves seeking opinions on statements such as "this company emphasizes the importance of its social responsibilities" and "this company provides an evident social contribution" (Du, Bhattacharya & Sen, 2007). There is evidence that companies performing well on CSR have a higher performance. However, the effects on customer behavior (i.e. retention) are less straightforward. In fact CSR is believed to have an indirect effect on loyalty through improving customer attitudes (e.g. Onrust, Verhoef, Van Doorn, & Bügel, 2014). From a big data perspective marketing analytics should be aware that these data are frequently collected within firms. However, as noted earlier, these data are typically not owned by marketing but by corporate level departments.

Corporate reputation

Corporate reputation is a rather general metric that measures the reputation of firms at the corporate level. It is a high-level metric that involves multiple stakeholders. Fombrun and Van Riel (1997) define corporate reputation as a collective representation of a firm's past actions and results that describes the firm's ability to deliver valued outcomes to multiple stakeholders. It gauges a firm's relative reputation both internally with employees and externally with its stakeholders, in both its competitive and institutional environments. Several measurement systems have been developed to measure corporate reputation. The Reputation Institute has developed RepTrack®, which measures corporate reputations of firms across the globe. These measures are being used by leading firms. RepTrack® involves examining the relationship between the emotional connection, or "Pulse," with any given stakeholder, alongside perceptions of seven underlying rational connections or "dimensions" identified as: (1) products/services; (2) innovation; (3) workplace; (4) citizenship; (5) governance; (6) leadership; and (7) performance. Inside each dimension lie specific attributes that can be customized for clients to allow for program and message-ready analysis.[5] The main difference between reputation metrics and brand metrics is that reputation metrics are measured at the firm level and not at the brand level. In addition, brand metrics usually focus only on customers as a stakeholder, whereas reputation metrics involves multiple stakeholders.

Should firms collect all V2C metrics?

A reader of this in-depth chapter might wonder whether firms should collect all the mentioned metrics. Our answer to this is a definite No! Firms should focus on a limited number of metrics and include them in a marketing dashboard. Managers should then strive to influence these metrics with marketing strategies. We specifically observe that many firms are not following this path. They collect a plethora of V2C metrics in different layers in the organization. For example, many firms collect satisfaction data, data on NPS, brand-metrics, digital sentiment metrics, and corporate reputation metrics. Satisfaction and NPS data are mainly under the ownership of the marketing research department. Marketing management and communication are mainly interested in brand metrics, whereas corporate strategy owns the corporate reputation metrics. The use of multiple measures results in strong discussions on which metrics to use, instead of how they could be influenced and how their use could give value to the firm. When these metrics are being analyzed it frequently becomes clear that there are actually strong correlations between many of them. An in-depth comparison of each of these metrics using specific criteria developed by Ailawadi et al. (2003) on what good metrics are (see Table 2.1.5) can be useful to select a reduced set of V2C metrics.

Conclusions

In this chapter we have provided an overview of the main V2C metrics. Most attention has been given to the metrics at the brand and customer level. These metrics have been developed strongly in science and practice. Importantly, big data developments have enriched the set of metrics. The main development here is the fact that customers share their thoughts and feelings of brand and services online. This results in many new metrics, which can be useful for managers. However, some of these metrics are also rather specific. Further, firms should consider internal data sources that can give information on the provision

Table 2.1.5 Criteria for good metrics

1. Theory-based
2. Complete
3. Diagnostic
4. Future potential
5. Objective
6. Based on existing data
7. A single number
8. Intuitive and trustworthy for top management
9. Robust and reliable
10. Validated with other outcome measures

Source: Adapted from Ailawadi, Neslin, & Lehmann (2003)

of V2C. These metrics can be powerful indicators of V2C. Finally, we discussed V2S metrics, which are frequently collected at the corporate level.

Notes

1 See http://young-rubicam.de/tools-wissen/tools/brandasset-valuator/?lang=en (accessed September 15, 2015).
2 This part of the text is derived from De Haan et al. (2015).
3 This section is based on Ou, De Vries, Wiesel and Verhoef (2014).
4 This section is partially based on Onrust et al. (2014).
5 www.reputationinstitute.com/about-reputation-institute/the-reptrak-framework.

References

Aaker, D. A. (2009). *Managing brand equity*. Simon and Schuster. New York: The Free Press.
Ailawadi, K. L., Neslin, S. A., & Lehmann, D. R. (2003). Revenue premium as an outcome measure of brand equity. *Journal of Marketing*, 67(4), 1–17.
Arts, J., Frambach, R. T., & Bijmolt, T. H. A. (2011). Generalizations on consumer innovation adoption: A meta-analysis on drivers of intention and behavior. *International Journal of Research in Marketing*, 28(2), 134–44.
Baxendale, S., Macdonald, E., Wilson, H. N. (2015). Impact of different touchpoints on brand consideration. *Journal of Retailing*, 91(2), 235–53.
Beard, A., Hornik, R., Wang, H., Ennes, M., Rush, E., & Presnal, S. (2011). It's hard to be good. *Harvard Business Review*, 89(11), 88–96.
Bolton, R. N., & Lemon, K. N. (1999). A dynamic model of customers' usage of services: Usage as an antecedent and consequence of satisfaction. *Journal of Marketing Research*, 36(2), 171–86.
Bolton, R. N., Lemon, K. N., & Verhoef, P. C. (2004). The theoretical underpinnings of customer asset management: A framework and propositions for future research. *Journal of the Academy of Marketing Science*, 32(3), 271–92.
Bolton, R. N., Lemon, K. N., & Verhoef, P. C. (2008). Expanding business-to-business customer relationships: Modeling the customer's upgrade decision. *Journal of Marketing*, 72(1), 46–64.
Bügel, M. S., Verhoef, P. C., & Buunk, A. P. (2011). Customer intimacy and commitment to relationships with firms in five different sectors: Preliminary evidence. *Journal of Retailing & Consumer Services*, 18(4), 247–58.
Davis, F. D. (1989). Perceived usefulness, perceived ease of use, and user acceptance of information technology. *MIS Quarterly*, 13(3), 319–40.
Davis, F. D., Bagozzi, R. P., & Warshaw, P. R. (1989). User acceptance of computer technology: A comparison of two theoretical models. *Management Science*, 35(8), 982–1003.
De Haan, E., Verhoef, P. C., & Wiesel, T. (2015). The predictive ability of different customer feedback metrics for retention. *International Journal of Research in Marketing*, 32(2), 195–206.
De Vries, L., Gensler, S., & Leeflang, P. S. H. (2012). Popularity of brand posts on brand fan pages: An investigation of the effects of social media marketing. *Journal of Interactive Marketing*, 26(2), 83–91.
Dixon, M., Freeman, K., & Toman, N. (2010). Stop trying to delight your customers. *Harvard Business Review*, 88(7/8), 116–22.

Du, S., Bhattacharya, C. B., & Sen, S. (2007). Reaping relational rewards from corporate social responsibility: The role of competitive positioning. *International Journal of Research in Marketing*, 24(3), 224–41.

Du, S., Bhattacharya, C. B., & Sen, S. (2010). Maximizing business returns to corporate social responsibility (CSR): The role of CSR communication. *International Journal of Management Reviews*, 12(1), 8–19.

Dwyer, F. R., Schurr, P. H., & Oh, S. (1987). Developing buyer-seller relationships. *Journal of Marketing*, 51(2), 11–27.

Floyd, K., Freling, R., Alhoqail, S., Cho, H. Y., & Freling, T. (2014). How online product reviews affect retail sales: A meta-analysis. *Journal of Retailing*, 9(2), 217–32.

Fombrun, C. J., & Van Riel, C.B.M. (1997). The reputational landscape. *Corporate Reputation Review*, 1(1/2), 5–13.

Garbarino, E., & Johnson, M. (1999). The different roles of satisfaction, trust, and commitment in customer relationships. *Journal of Marketing*, 63(2), 70–87.

Gensler, S., Völckner, F., Egger, M., Fischbach, K., & Schoder, D. (2015). Listen to your customers: Insights into brand image using online consumer-generated product reviews. *International Journal of Electronic Commerce*, 20(1), 112–41.

Geyskens, I., Steenkamp, J.-B. E. M., Scheer, L. K., & Kumar, N. (1996). The effects of trust and interdependence on relationship commitment: A transatlantic study. *International Journal of Research in Marketing*, 13(4), 303–17.

Gijsenberg, M. J., Van Heerde, H. J., & Verhoef, P. C. (2015). Losses loom longer than gains: Modeling the impact of service crises on customer satisfaction over time. *Journal of Marketing Research*, 52(5), 642–56.

Gundlach, G. T., Ravi, S. A., & Mentzer, J. T. (1995). The structure of commitment in exchange. *Journal of Marketing*, 64(3), 34–49.

Hanssens, D. M., Pauwels, K. H., Srinivasan, S., Vanhuele, M., & Yildirim, G. (2014). Consumer attitude metrics for guiding marketing mix decisions. *Marketing Science*, 33(4), 534–50.

Hunneman, A., Verhoef, P. C., & Sloot, L. M. (2015). The impact of consumer confidence on store satisfaction and share of wallet formation. *Journal of Retailing*, 91(3), 516–32.

Keiningham, T. L., Cooil, B., Aksoy, L., Andreassen, T. W., & Weiner, J. (2007). The value of different customer satisfaction and loyalty metrics in predicting customer retention, recommendation, and share-of-wallet. *Managing Service Quality*, 17(4), 361–84.

King, W. R., & He, J. (2006). A meta-analysis of the technology acceptance model. *Information & Management*, 43(6), 740–55.

Kotler, P., & Lee, N. (2005). *Corporate Social Responsibility—Doing the most good for your company and your cause.* New Jersey: John Wiley and Sons.

Luo, X., & Bhattacharya, C. B. (2006). Corporate social responsibility, customer satisfaction, and market value. *Journal of Marketing*, 70(4), 1–18.

McWilliams, A., & Siegel, D. (2001). Corporate Social Responsibility: A theory of the firm perspective. *Academy of Management Review*, 26(1), 117–27.

Melancon, J. P., Noble, S. M, & Noble, C. H. (2011). Managing rewards to enhance relational worth. *Journal of the Academy of Marketing Science*, 39(3), 341–62.

Mizik, N., & Jacobson, R. (2009). Valuing branded businesses. *Journal of Marketing*, 73(6), 137–53.

Moorman, C., Zaltman, G., & Deshpande, R. (1992). Relationship between providers and users of market research: The dynamics of trust within and between organizations. *Journal of Marketing Research*, 29(3), 314–28.

Morgan, N. A., & Rego, L. L. (2006). The value of different customer satisfaction and loyalty metrics in predicting business performance. *Marketing Science*, 25(5), 426–39.

Oliver, R. L., Rust, R. T., & Varki, S. (1997). Customer delight: Foundations, findings, and managerial insight. *Journal of Retailing*, 73(3), 311–36.

Onishi, H., & Manchanda, P. (2012). Marketing activity, blogging and sales. *International Journal of Research in Marketing*, 2(3), 221–34.

Onrust, M., Verhoef, P. C., Van Doorn, J., & Bügel, M. S. (2014). *When doing good leads to increased customer loyalty: Why weak firms can benefit from CSR*. Working paper, University of Groningen.

Ou, Y.-C., De Vries, L., Wiesel, T., & Verhoef, P. C. (2014). The role of consumer confidence in creating customer loyalty. *Journal of Service Research*, 17(3), 229–354.

Porter, M. E., & Kramer, M. R. (2011). Creating shared value. *Harvard Business Review*, 89(1/2), 62–77.

Prout, J. (2006). Corporate responsibility in the global economy: A business case. *Society and Business Review*, (2), 184–91.

Reichheld, F. F. (2003). The one number you need to grow. *Harvard Business Review*, 81(12), 46–54.

Roberts, J. H., Kayande, U., & Stremersch, S. (2014). From academic research to marketing practice: Exploring the marketing science value chain. *International Journal of Research in Marketing*, 3(2), 127–40.

Rogers, E. M. (1995). *The diffusion of innovations*. New York: The Free Press.

Rust, R. T., Zeithaml, V. A., & Lemon, K. N. (2000). *Driving customer equity: How customer lifetime value is reshaping corporate strategy*. New York: The Free Press.

Selnes, F., & Gønhaug, K. (2000). Effects of supplier reliability and benevolence in business marketing. *Journal of Business Research*, 49(3), 259–71.

Srinivasan, S., Vanhuele, M., & Pauwels, K. (2010). Mindset metrics in market response models: An integrative approach. *Journal of Marketing Research*, 47(4), 672–84.

Sternberg, R. J. (1986). A triangular theory of love. *Psychological Review*, 93, 119–35.

Streukens, S., & De Ruyter, K. (2004). Reconsidering nonlinearity and asymmetry in customer satisfaction and customer loyalty models: An empirical study in three retail service settings. *Marketing Letters*, 15(2/3), 99–111.

Tellis, G. J., & Johnson, J. (2007). The value of quality. *Marketing Science*, 26(6), 758–73.

Trusov, M., Bucklin, R. E., & Pauwels, K. (2009). Effects of word-of-mouth versus traditional marketing: Findings from an Internet social networking site. *Journal of Marketing*, 73(5), 90–102.

Van Doorn, J., & Verhoef, P. C. (2008). Critical incidents and the impact of satisfaction on customer share. *Journal of Marketing*, 72(4), 123–42.

Van Doorn, J., Leeflang, P.S.H., & Tijs, M. (2013). Satisfaction as a predictor of future performance: A replication. *International Journal of Research in Marketing*, 30(3), 314–8.

Van Heerde, H. J., Gijsbrechts, E., & Pauwels, K. (2008). Winners and losers of a major price war. *Journal of Marketing Research*, 45(5), 499–518.

Van Nierop, E., Bronnenberg, B., Paap, R., Wedel, M., & Franses, P. H. (2010). Retrieving unobserved consideration sets from household panel data. *Journal of Marketing Research*, 47(1), 63–74.

Venkatesh, V., & Bala, H. (2008). Technology acceptance model 3 and a research agenda on interventions. *Decision Sciences*, 39(2), 273–315.

Verhoef, P. C. (2003). Understanding the effect of customer relationship management efforts on customer retention and customer share development. *Journal of Marketing*, 67(4), 30–45.

Verhoef, P. C. (2012). *Klanten centraal in de bankensector*. White paper, Monitoring Commissie Code Banken, the Netherlands.

Verhoef, P. C., & Langerak, F. (2001). Possible determinants of consumers' adoption of electronic grocery shopping in the Netherlands. *Journal of Retailing and Consumer Services*, 8(5), 275–85.

Verhoef, P. C., Antonides, G., & De Hoog, A. N. (2004). Service encounters as a sequence of events the importance of peak experiences. *Journal of Service Research*, 7(1), 53–64.

Verhoef, P. C., Franses, P. H., & Hoekstra, J. C. (2002). The effect of relational constructs on customer referrals and number of services purchased from a multiservice provider: Does age of relationship matter? *Journal of the Academy of Marketing Science*, 30(3), 202–16.

Verhoef, P. C., Langerak, F., & Donkers, B. (2007). Understanding brand and dealer retention in the new car market: The moderating role of brand tier. *Journal of Retailing*, 83(1), 97–113.

Weber Shandwick/KRC Research (2012). *Buy It, Try It, Rate It*. Retrieved September 9, 2015 from www.webershandwick.com/uploads/news/files/ReviewsSurveyReportFINAL.pdf

Zeithaml, V. A., Bolton, R. N., Deighton, J., Keiningham, T. L., Lemon, K. N., & Petersen, J. A. (2006). Forward-looking focus can firms have adaptive foresight? *Journal of Service Research*, 9(2), 168–83.

2.2 Value-to-firm metrics

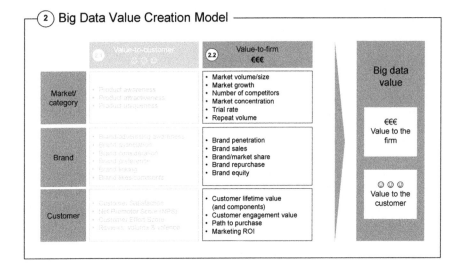

Introduction

Value-to-firm metrics focus on the value delivered by customers to firms. These metrics are typically behavioral and are frequently financial in nature. As with the V2C metrics, firms can choose from a plethora of V2F metrics. Some of them, such as brand sales and market share, have been around for a long time, while others, such as customer lifetime value (CLV) are relatively new. Big data developments have created new V2F metrics. Especially in digital environments, many new metrics have been developed and are now being used in digital marketing. The challenge for firms is how to interpret and use these new metrics and link them to existing metrics (Leeflang, Verhoef, Dahlström, & Freundt, 2014).

In this in-depth chapter we discuss several V2F metrics and their meaning. We again divide metrics into market metrics, brand metrics and customer metrics. We will also discuss new big data metrics, thereby specifically focusing on customer engagement metrics and customer journey metrics.

50 Value-to-firm metrics

Market metrics

At the market level, firms will mainly be interested in metrics that show the attractiveness of the market. These market size metrics are relevant for firms when they make strategic market entry decisions and strategic portfolio decisions. Based on these types of analyses a company such as Royal Dutch Phillips can make strategic decisions: it decided to retract from the electronics- and lightning market to focus on health. Market metrics are also very important when considering new product sales. We therefore distinguish between two types of market metrics:

1   Market attractiveness metrics
2   New product sales metrics.

Market attractiveness metrics

Typical market metrics being used are:

- Market size: The total market demand in terms of number of (potential) customers (i.e. target population), units or $ sales (see Figure 2.2.1 on UK smartphone sales)
- Market growth: The annual growth of the market
- Number of competitors
- Market concentration: This metric measures whether the market is dominated by a few players or whether many players have relative equal positions in the market. The so-called Herfindahl Index is used to measure this. It is defined for a specific market with J firms as:

$$Herfindahl\ Index = \sum_{j=1}^{J} Market\ Share_j^2 \qquad (2.2.1)$$

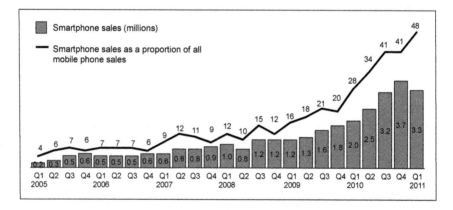

Figure 2.2.1 UK smartphone sales

Source: Adapted from GfK Retail & Technology[1]

and can vary between 0 and 1, with 1 representing a very concentrated market with a monopolist having 100% of the market.

One problem that firms face is how to define the market and competition. This is becoming rather difficult, because of market fragmentation. For example, strong retailers such as Tesco not only sell fast-moving consumer goods, but also telecom subscriptions and financial services. Similarly, new players are entering the market in this digital era. Google, for example, can become a competitor of online retailers when they are actively starting Google Shop; banks are confronted with the growth of new payment forms such as Paypal and Bitcoins and are also worried about Google getting into banking.

New product sales metrics

For forecasting new product sales it is considered important to use several metrics (e.g., Farris, Bendle, Pfeifer, & Reibstein, 2006):

- Trial rate: The number of first-time new product users as a percentage of the target population
- Repeat volume: Number of repeat buyers multiplied by the number of products they buy in each purchase, multiplied by the number of times they purchase per period
- Penetration rate: Number of repeat users plus number of new trials, divided by the market population.

Based on these figures, volume projections of the market can be made. A very simple equation for sales volume is for example:

Sales volume = Penetration rate × Purchase frequency × Units purchased

Note that so far we describe the above metrics at the product level. However, similar metrics can be calculated for (new) brands.[2]

Brand metrics

We consider two types of V2F brand metrics:

1 Brand market performance metrics
2 Brand valuation metrics.

Brand market performance metrics

Brand market performance metrics focus on the actual performance of brands in the market. Traditional brand metrics are well known and are very frequently measured: brand penetration, brand sales, and market share. Brand sales can be measured internally. Brand penetration and market share data are more difficult to measure as information on the whole market is required. In some markets, such as the FMCG (fast-moving consumer goods) market, these metrics are measured daily or weekly using scanning technologies by market research firms such as GfK, AC Nielsen, and IRI. In many other markets, for example financial services and telecom, data on market shares are less frequently measured. One specific issue is that in these markets, data collection on actual purchases is not well organized, or is fairly difficult to execute. For example, when measuring market shares in the insurance industry, customers have to report accurately on their ownership of insurance and the firms they purchased from. It is questionable whether this can be done in an accurate way.

Next to these more aggregate brand market performance metrics, firms also frequently measure brand loyalty metrics. These metrics could be based on stated intentions, such as brand repurchase intentions. This can be measured using scales, such as for example a Juster scale where 0 = will absolutely not repurchase, and 10 = will absolutely repurchase (Juster, 1969). However, one could also use scales in which customers have to divide 100 points across brands in the market place—called a constant sum scale (Rust, Lemon, & Zeithaml, 2004). This will more accurately reflect the fact that customers frequently buy multiple brands and are frequently not loyal to one specific brand. This purchase behavior of multiple brands has been referred to as "polygamous loyalty" (e.g. Dowling & Uncles, 1997). Actual brand loyalty metrics concern the brand repurchase rate, which is the percentage of customers purchasing a specific brand that will repurchase the brand on the next purchase occasion as well. It is important to note that a no-purchase on this next purchase occasion can be followed by a repurchase of the brand in a subsequent period. Using this information, a so-called "switching matrix" can be formed (see Figure 2.2.2). In this matrix, one observes the repurchase rates of a brand and the switching probabilities to other brands in the market. In this specific example, the switching probability from brand A to B is 20%, whereas the probability of customers switching back to brand A in the subsequent purchase occasion is 10%. Notably, this switching matrix not only can be based on actual repurchase rates, but can also use the constant sum scale of the division of 100 points across brands (Rust et al., 2004).

Brand	A (%)	B (%)	C (%)
A	**70%**	20%	10%
B	10%	**80%**	10%
C	0%	20%	**80%**

Figure 2.2.2 Example of brand switching matrix

Within marketing science the relationship between market share and brand repurchase rates has been studied, and the general finding is that there is a strong relationship between them. In particular, the school around former London-based marketing professor Andrew Ehrenberg, with followers such as Byron Sharp, has aimed to demonstrate that this empirical relationship can be shown in many markets. One of the most important implications of this is that brands with a high market share have a high repurchase rate and that brands with low market shares have a low repurchase rate. There are some exceptions, such as a niche brand targeting a specific market segment, with loyal customers. One of the conclusions Ehrenberg and colleagues draw is that firms should not believe too strongly in the need to create loyal customers. They are therefore very critical on loyalty strategies, such as loyalty programs (Dowling & Uncles, 1997; Sharp, 2010). However, although one could draw this conclusion, these analyses only provide a current status quo. There is sufficient evidence that loyalty strategies can create a higher repurchase rate for brands (e.g. Leenheer, Bijmolt, Van Heerde, & Smidts, 2007).

As well as looking at the revenue side of brands, brand investment can also be measured. These brand investments could involve, for example, advertising costs. The results of these advertising costs are measured with so-called "gross rating points" (GRPs). This is calculated as the percentage of the reached target market multiplied by the exposure frequency of the advertisement.

Brand evaluation metrics

As brands are very important assets for firms, there has been strong attention on how to financially evaluate these brands; in particular, financially oriented brand equity (BE) metrics have been developed. These metrics differ from the V2C BE metrics that typically focus on customer-based BE and focus only on awareness and attitudinal measures, such as brand preference. Probably the best known financially oriented BE metric is the one developed by Interbrand. Each year they develop this to calculate the BE of global brands such as Coca-Cola, Apple, and BMW and publish a top 100. For years Coca-Cola was the most valued brand, until Apple took over the first position in 2013, followed by Google. The Interbrand measure[3] is based on three pillars: financial performance of the brand, role of the brand in purchase decisions, and brand strength, which is the ability of the brand to create brand loyalty.[4] The exact methodology of this metric is not fully shared and therefore represents a black box for many researchers. Beyond these well-known metrics, academic researchers have also proposed some metrics to evaluate BE. We discuss some of these here: the list is by no means fully exhaustive:

- Brand equity share holder value approach: Using this approach BE is based on the market value of the firm (Simon & Sullivan, 1993). This market value is decomposed into tangible and intangible assets. The value of intangible assets consists of R&D (i.e. patents), value of industry factors (e.g. monopoly positions), and the value of the brand.

- Brand equity preference-based approach: With this approach, researchers aim to measure the ability of the brand to attract and keep customers. This can be done using conjoint analysis (see Chapter 4.1) in which the utility of a number of product variants consisting of several attributes including the brand attribute is assessed using several methodologies (e.g. choices between alternative products, product evaluations). A stronger impact of the brand attribute on the product utility reflects higher BE. Although using a different methodological approach, researchers have also developed BE metrics using demand models. In this approach the choice for a specific brand over time is modeled using product attributes and marketing mix variables as explanatory variables. The value of the brand constant in the model is a measure for BE as it reflects the power to attract and keep customers beyond the effects of product attributes and marketing (Sriram, Balachander, & Kalwani, 2007).
- Brand equity price premium approach: This BE metric focuses on the ability of brands to ask a higher price from customers. A measure used here is "willingness to pay." A higher willingness to pay signals a higher BE. One problem with this measure is that it is subjective, as it is based on customer surveys and it is difficult to quantify financially. Another metric involves measuring the price premium of a brand. Ailawadi, Lehmann and Neslin (2003) propose the revenue premium as a measure. This measure is a combination of brand unit sales and brand price premium and measures the price difference of the brand with a generic brand and the unit sales difference with that generic brand (see Figure 2.2.3). The challenge is to find a good generic brand. In their study, Ailawadi et al. (2004) use the private label (store brand) as the generic brand.

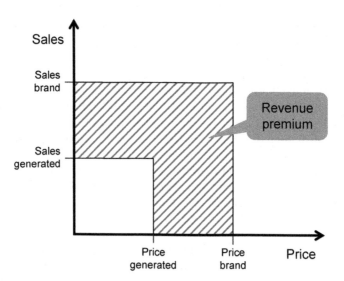

Figure 2.2.3 Brand revenue premium

Source: Adapted from Ailawadi et al., 2004

Interestingly, studies report strong correlations of BE metrics with product market metrics. For example, Ailawadi et al. (2003) show that their revenue premium measure is relatively strongly correlated with measures like market share. One could probably debate about the additional value of BE metrics over and above frequently used brand metrics, such as market share. One problem with these metrics is that they are frequently short-term oriented, while BE is more long-term oriented. Financial BE metrics should be diagnostically about a brand's long-term health; this goes beyond sales and could consider factors such as the attractive power of brands, price premiums and financial value.

Customer metrics

Customer metrics focus on the behavior of individual customers in their relationships with the firm. We adopt the so-called "relationship lifecycle" as an underlying model of many of these metrics (Dwyer, Shurr, & Oh, 1987). In this relationship lifecycle, the trajectory of an individual customer moving from a prospective customer, to a customer, and finally a defecting customer is considered (see Figure 2.2.4).

Based on the relationship lifecycle concept one can distinguish three types of metrics:

1 Customer acquisition metrics, which focus on the first phase of attracting customers
2 Customer development metrics, which focus on how the relationship develops after acquiring the customers
3 Customer value metrics, which consider the financial value of the customer during the relationship and can involve both the acquisition phase and relationship development phase.

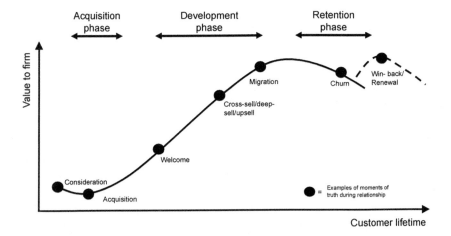

Figure 2.2.4 Relationship lifecycle concept

Customer acquisition metrics

Customer acquisition metrics consider how customers respond to acquisition actions. From a customer perspective we mainly consider individual customer acquisition techniques, such as direct marketing efforts, telemarketing, etc. On a more aggregate level, firms will be interested in the number of customers acquired through these different channels. From a cost perspective they would like to know the acquisition costs (per customer). Importantly, we also suggest considering the value of the acquired customers. Firms constantly fall into the trap of acquiring many customers with attractive price offers who are likely to be unprofitable and will switch frequently after one year (Lewis, 2006). When evaluating acquisition campaigns two specific metrics are frequently considered:

- Response rate: the number of customers responding to a campaign divided by the number of total customers approached with a campaign
- Conversion rate: the number of customers acquired divided by the number of customers responding to a campaign.

Feld, Frenzen, Krafft, Peters, & Verhoef (2013) discuss some intermediate metrics to evaluate campaigns in addition to the above-mentioned metrics. They report on the opening rate of a direct mailing and the keeping rate of the direct mailing.

Customer development metrics

Customer development metrics concern many dimensions of relationship development (e.g. Bolton, Lemon, & Verhoef, 2004). Specifically, we consider three types of metrics:

1. Relationship continuation or length metrics
2. Relationship expansion metrics
3. Relationship costs and risk metrics.

Relationship length metrics

These metrics focus on the continuation of the relationship. Specific metrics concern:

- Churn or customer defection: The percentage of customers quitting the relationship with the firm
- Customer retention: The percentage of customers continuing the relationship with the firm (1 − customer churn/defection)
- Customer lifetime/relationship length: The (expected) length of the relationship between the customer and the firm

- Purchase frequency: The number of times a customer purchases from a company in a specific time period
- Recency: Time since last purchase.

One specific metric you could consider here is the win-back percentage of defected customers. Win-back metrics become prevalent when firms actively approach churned customers to become customers again.

Relationship expansion metrics

Relationship expansion concerns metrics that focus on the growth of the relationship. This expansion can involve multiple metrics:

- Average number of products/services sold per customer
- Cross-buying rate: The percentage of customers purchasing additional products or services from a company
- Upgrading rate: The percentage of customers upgrading their products or services to a higher level (e.g. upgraded service contract)
- Adoption rate: The percentage of customers purchasing the newly introduced product or service
- Customer share: The number of products or services purchased by a customer from a firm divided by the number of products or services purchased by a customer in that specific product category
- Share of wallet: The money spent by a customer at a firm divided by the money spent by a customer in that specific product category.

The first four measures can be gained from the customer database. The share metrics provide information on the relative loyalty position of a firm for a specific customer. In order to calculate these metrics additional data on the purchase behavior of customers in a specific category is required (Verhoef, 2003). Higher cross-buying rates should usually also be reflected in higher values for the share metrics. Importantly, recent research suggests that cross-buying can indeed have positive profit consequences, but not all customers with large cross-buying percentages are profitable (Shah, Kumar, Qu, & Chen, 2012).

Relationship costs and risk metrics

During the relationship, firms also invest in the customer relationship. Investments focus on developing the relationship and can, for example, include the costs of a loyalty program. We discuss these costs in more depth in the next section on CLV. Costs may mainly involve the costs to serve an individual. Importantly, these costs may vary considerably between customers. One specific risk that firms frequently face is that customers might not pay. In this regard measuring the debt risk of the customer base and individual customers is of essential importance, especially for firms delivering products or services before the payment is received (e.g. utilities, telecom). Debt risk can be modeled and predicted (L'Hoest-Snoeck, Van Nierop, & Verhoef, 2015). For retailers the number of product returns has also become an important cost-related metric. Returns occur when customers order a product that does not deliver what they actually hoped for. Frequently, customers can return these products for free and firms are obliged to receive them back—and have to pay back the price paid. Reducing return rates has become one of the top priorities for online retailers, such as Zalando, in order to improve profitability. Overall, Shah et al. (2012) suggest that firms should consider metrics that reveal so-called "adverse behavior" of customers, which may involve debt risk, large service costs, and product returns. Interestingly, customers show a pattern in these adverse behaviors and thus in targeting policies firms can choose not to offer these customers attractive offers (Shah et al., 2012).

Customer value metrics

The metrics discussed so far focus on actual behavior during the relationship lifecycle. Customer value metrics consider the resulting financial value of customers. Value metrics can be divided based on the forward-looking nature of these metrics. Non-forward-looking value metrics focus on the current status of a customer and involve customer revenue or the monetary value of a customer, customer margin, and customer profitability. Forward-looking metrics consider the expected value of customers in the future. The most prominent metric in this regard is customer lifetime value. This metric has gained so much attention in the literature—and has been accepted in practice—that we devote an extensive discussion of this metric in this chapter.

Customer lifetime value

Customer lifetime value (CLV) is a metric that has taken off with the strong development of customer relationship management (CRM). This metric is typically used to evaluate the value of customers. CLV is frequently defined as "the present value of the future cash flows attributed to the customer during his/her entire relationship with the company" (Farris, Bendle, Pfeifer, & Reibstein, 2010). In this definition, CLV assesses the total value delivered by a customer. However, firms are frequently more interested in the future value of customers. CLV can then be considered as a forward-looking customer centric metric, based on assumptions and predictions, and can be defined as the net present expected value of a customer. In other words, value created in the past is not taken into account when calculating the value of a customer or customer base. However, past customer value can be a predictor of future value (e.g. Donkers, Verhoef, & De Jong, 2007). CLV is a very important metric, because (when calculated properly) it can be the link between the marketing and the financial department and create the common platform to bring these worlds together. Furthermore, there is sufficient evidence to show that, when calculated properly, CLV can be a good indicator for firm valuation (e.g. Gupta, Lehmann, & Stuart, 2004), especially in those industries/companies where customers are the biggest asset and markets are rather stable. A very simple definition of CLV for customer i at time t = 0 and where "d" is the discount rate is:

$$CLV_{i,t} = \sum_{t=0}^{T} \frac{Margin_{i,t}}{(1+d)^t} \qquad (2.2.2)$$

In this definition we assume that each year a specific margin is earned per customer. These margins are summed over time until a chosen end point T. Typically, periods of 3–5 years are used for CLV-calculations (Rust, Zeithaml, & Lemon, 2000). A discount rate is used to make the future earnings present. This discount rate is set in cooperation with the finance department. A high discount rate implies that future earnings contribute less to CLV and may signal that firms value these future earnings less. This implies a more short-term orientation.

CLV and its components

For a proper CLV calculation, it is crucial that in building the underlying CLV model, the assumptions, components, and outcomes are adopted and accepted by both the marketing and the finance department. By the CLV model we mean the different components of CLV, how they are calculated and how they are interrelated. The main components of CLV (see also Figure 2.2.5) are:

1 Margin or EBITDA
2 Expected lifetime
3 One time investments.

Margin

Margin or EBITDA is the result of the revenues generated per customer minus operational costs. For pure calculations, especially in capital intensive industries, depreciation should also be taken into account, but we will skip over this to prevent unnecessary complexity. Usually for the revenue part we only look at the billed revenue, meaning that discounts given have been deducted from the gross revenue. Especially when discounts are substantial and can differ between customers, there can be a considerable difference between gross revenue and net revenue. Using the charged amount also implies that we will use the frequency of billing (for example monthly) in a contractual setting as the time unit to be used in our CLV model.

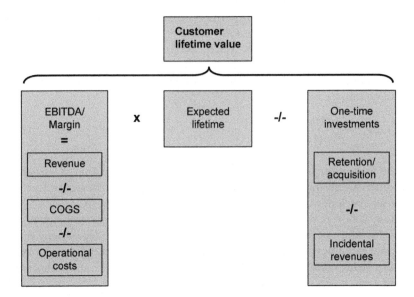

Figure 2.2.5 The CLV model: the elements of customer lifetime value

Since we are calculating the CLV, for a multi-product organization we should sum the revenue per product generated by the customer. Expecting the customer to stay with the organization for many billing cycles, ideally many years, it will be necessary to calculate the net present value of future revenues (see Equation 2.2.2). In other words, a euro or dollar collected next year is worth less than the euro/dollar of this year. We will discuss this further when explaining lifetime calculation. To obtain the margin from revenues, costs have to be deducted from revenues. We distinguish two types of costs:

- Costs of goods sold (COGS): the cost directly associated with the product usage (for example minutes called for a telco company) or manufacturing of the product;
- Overhead costs: the costs of the organization not directly related to product usage or manufacturing, for example the IT department, the call center, real estate etc.

It is important that the total costs of the organization are allocated to one of these two buckets, to prevent missing certain costs, but also to prevent double counting. Since the elements of COGS are directly linked to a single product they can be easily allocated to individual customers buying and/or using different products. Calculating the COGS is normally part of typical cost price calculations every organization should have. To build a good CLV model, the COGS ideally should be decomposed as much as possible, to cope with different cost prices per type of product/service. For example, for a telco company the cost price of a text message might be lower than the cost price of a minute called and a minute called can be further broken down into a minute called on the company's own network or on the network of another organization. Having the COGS per customer, based on total product usage (built up from the different components of product usage) can already result in large differentiation within the customer base: for example, customers paying the same fixed subscription fee, with differences in type and intensity of usage, can result in completely different margins.

For the operational cost centers, the first step is to identify the large cost buckets in the company's P&L account. For the largest cost buckets our challenge is to identify the drivers of customer behavior of these costs, in order to define the right allocation methodology of these costs. Let's take for example the yearly total costs of the call center (human resources, tooling, housing, infrastructure, etc.). Obviously the costs are driven by the number of customers calling, or more specifically by the number of calls and perhaps the duration per call. These numbers can be used to allocate the costs of the call center to individual customers. However, part of these total costs should be allocated to all customers, since even if not one customer calls (not realistic but let's assume), the organization still would have a call center with all its fixed costs in place. That's why non-calling customers should also be allocated part of the call center costs. Typically, this is done by analyzing which part of the total costs are fixed and divide these by the total number of customers, and use the customer behavior drivers for allocating all other costs. For the smaller cost buckets, the easiest way is to just spread these costs across all customers. In Box 2.2.1 we provide an example of allocation of costs to guide analysts further.

Box 2.2.1 Example of cost allocation options from simple to complex

- Total yearly cost of call center is 10 million euros.
- Total number of customers is 1 million.

Input on possible drivers of cost allocation to individual customers:

- Total number of calls is 2 million.
- Total number of customers with at least one call is 500k.
- Average number of calls per calling customer is thus 4 calls.
- The highest number of calls per customer is 25.
- 20% of the calls are about billing, 60% are technical questions, 20% are contract or transaction related.

- Billing calls take on average 2 minutes, technical calls 15 minutes and contract/transaction calls 10 minutes.
- 20% of costs are fixed, 80% are variable.

Different options for cost allocation, from simple to complex:

Option 1. Flat allocation
Divide the total costs of calls by the total number of customers: 10 million/1 million and allocate 10 euros per customer.

Option 2. Fixed and variable split
Divide the 80% variable part of the costs by the number of calling customers: 8 million/500k = 16 euros and add 20% of the fixed costs (2 million) divided by the total number of customers = 2 million/1 million = 2 euros. This means that a calling customer gets 18 euros of costs allocated and a non-calling customer 2 euros.

Option 3. Call ratio
As in option 2, a non-calling customer gets 2 euros of costs allocated, but now we allocate the other 80% of the costs by looking at the number of calls per customer. Per call this means 8 million variable costs/2 million calls = 4 euros per call. In other words, a customer with 25 calls will get (25 × 4) + 2 euros of costs allocated = 102 euros, while on average a calling customer will still get (4 × 4) + 2 = 18 euros of costs allocated.

Option 4. Type of call
The total minutes called are (400,000 × 2) + (1,200,000 × 15) + (400,000 × 10) = 22,800,000. This means that every minute called costs 8 million/22.8 million = 0.35 euro per minute. So a billing call costs 0.35 × 2 minutes = 0.70 euro, a technical call 0.35 × 15 = 5.27 and a transaction call 0.35 × 10 = 3.50 euros. This means that a calling customer with a technical call and a transaction call will get in total 5.27 + 3.50 + 2.00 = 10.77 euros allocated.

Other options can be built up, for example by a further specification of the typical costs per type of call, or by taking into account the actual minutes necessary for a call. So the above is not exhaustive, but shows how further cost differentiation based on the drivers and type of customer behavior and characteristics can help in cost allocation. In this the database and the database analyses by the data-analysts play an important role.

Lifetime

Lifetime is the metric that indicates the total (expected) remaining duration of the relationship. This is the metric with the highest impact (due to the multiplier on the margin it delivers); however, it is also the most complex to calculate. A first distinction that should be made is between the two different types of relationships (Fader & Hardie, 2010):

1 The contractual setting: the customer commits for a certain period to use a service or product and cannot leave without good reasons (death, moving abroad, etc.) within this period. This type of setting is often seen in utilities, telecoms, and insurance. In this setting the minimum lifetime is the remaining duration of the contract. When the contract ends there is probability that the customer continues and renews the contract. This continuation is observed. Usually the customer has to do something (e.g. send a letter, fill in a form, call) to end the contract.
2 The non-contractual setting: the customer has no contractual commitment to the organization and can decide at any moment to switch or stop using the product or service and has no obligation to communicate this to the organization. This kind of behavior is very typical in (online) retailing and with fast-moving consumer goods. In this setting lifetime is based on the probability of future usage or buying of the product or service. Typically switching is not observed in non-contractual settings, as customers do not have to end a contract. They just stop buying. As such one never knows when a relationship ends.

There are different drivers that influence customer lifetime, such as usage, past relationship duration, socio-demographics, and products used. These drivers can be included in models to predict lifetime. Typically, different models are used for contractual settings than for non-contractual settings. For contractual settings analysts tend to use discrete choice models, such as the logit-model (e.g., Donkers et al., 2007) (see Chapter 4.1). For non-contractual settings duration models or negative binomial distribution (NBD) models are used (Fader & Hardie, 2010).

Investments

We consider as investments all net organizational expenses that are spent from a multi-period perspective on the customer relationship and that are not covered by the COGS or operational cost centers and that result in "out-of-pocket" for the organization. One-time revenues are subtracted from the total of these expenses (for example, the fee collected for connecting a subscription for a mobile telco). Components of these investments can be, for example:

- A subsidy on delivered hardware
- Gadgets/premiums
- Marketing campaigns above the line (ATL) and below the line (BTL) (where the costs of the campaigns are allocated to the conversion)
- Channel costs, such as fees to be paid to intermediaries
- … and so on.

These investments are made in the beginning of the relationship (acquisition investments) to compose an appealing offer to the new potential client, or at the potential end of the relationship (for example, as the contract is expiring), in order to renew the contract (retention investments). These investments in the customer relationship differ largely per industry and are based on the expected revenue stream during the relationship, the costs of the relationship, and the expected length of the relationship. Since in the contractual setting the minimum revenues and length of the relationship are known, creating a lower level of uncertainty, this will often result in higher upfront investments. In certain industries such as insurance, telecoms, or utilities this might result in investment per new contract of several hundreds of euros/dollars. In the non-contractual setting these upfront investments are usually low, due the much higher uncertainty of future revenues and lifetime. Even small investments are difficult to earn back. For example, small investments to acquire new customers for the US online grocery start-up Retail Relay were higher than the expected CLV of a new customer (Venkatesan, Farris, & Wilcox, 2014).

As we have seen earlier in this chapter when discussing the calculation of margin and lifetime per individual customer and the outcome of the combined metrics (which we call gross CLV), one can expect big differences between individual customers (see Figure 2.2.6). This means that an organization that is trying to balance gross CLV and investments can use investments and especially the differentiation in the investments as a way to optimize its commercial efforts.

Calculating customer lifetime value

For calculating the actual CLV, based on our CLV model and its components, we will need a formula to incorporate all elements in order to calculate a CLV per individual customer that can be expressed as a euro/dollar amount. At a minimum level, firms need to have data on customer margins and expected lifetime. Beyond that, especially when calculating the value of a new customer, data on investments in acquisition or retention should be taken into account. Extensive literature on CLV has proposed several more extended CLV models (e.g., Berger & Nasr, 1999; Venkatesan & Kumar, 2004; L'Hoest-Snoeck et al., 2015). We specifically discuss a more extensive version of the simple equation in which we include the retention rate (r) to account for the expected lifetime of individual customers, thereby taking into account the possibility that

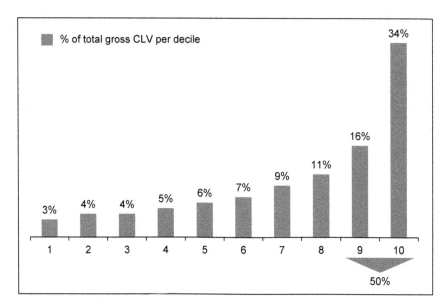

Figure 2.2.6 Example of gross CLV distribution per decile

earnings from customers may drop because customers churn and that firms invest in acquisition:

$$CLV_{i,t} = -\text{Acquistion/Retention Investment}_i + \sum_{t=0}^{T} \frac{(r_{i,t})^t \times \text{Margin}_{i,t}}{(1+d)^t} \quad (2.2.3)$$

An easy way to calculate CLV is to take T to infinity. After some mathematical computations the following simple formula is achieved for the calculation of the CLV for customer i:

$$CLV_i = -\text{Acquistion/Retention Investment}_i + \text{margin}_i \left(\frac{r_i}{1+d-r_i}\right) \quad (2.2.4)$$

Each of the above component models can be used to forecast the individual retention rates and margins. For example, retention rates can be predicted using a logistic regression model. More extensive versions of the above models can be developed; one way might be to consider margin growth through, for example, reduced costs or increased revenues from cross-buying or upgrading. We refer to Berger and Nasr (1999) for an extensive discussion of these basic models. Donkers et al. (2007) also discuss many models that differ in complexity. Interestingly, they show that in their setting, the simple forecast rule of today's customer profit is next years' profit has the strongest predictive performance.

Getting started with CLV: Be pragmatic

In building a CLV model, one should realize that it is quite impossible to build a full blown CLV model from scratch. In reality a phased approach is much more realistic and can help in processing new insights on the dynamics of the CLV model. Defining the different phases in a pragmatic way on a project basis can help the organization gain experience with CLV at an early stage and reduce the probability of failure. Starting with a too complex model in the beginning can result in disappointment, the loss of organizational acceptance, inaccurate results, and delays in delivery. It is good to know that there are many pragmatic approaches and rules of thumb available to realize a first CLV model for quick results.

Let's start with the CLV formula:

$$CLV_i = -\text{Acquistion/Retention Investment}_i + \text{margin}_i \left(\frac{r_i}{1+d-r_i}\right) \quad (2.2.5)$$

- The first component, the (monthly) margin (revenues minus costs), could be simplified by just taking a percentage of the revenue. This could be further refined by specifying this margin percentage per product, assuming that per product a cost allocation model delivers this percentage, differentiating this per product. A next step in margin calculation could be to take the largest cost buckets and try to allocate them based on consumer behavior.
- A good proxy of the lifetime of the customer, based on the retention rate (r) in the formula above for a contractual setting, can be obtained by assuming that the lifetime equals the duration of the first contract. In a non-contractual setting one could take the buying frequency per year (or other timeframe) as an indicator of lifetime. It might be clear that the above proxies are still a rather rough proxy of the real lifetime, with only a little differentiation per customer. So a next step could be to build a first basic churn prediction model to allocate customers into churn buckets and assigning a churn (in a contractual setting) or inactivity (in a non-contractual) setting probability per segment.
- The easiest way to estimate the investments in acquisition or retention is to take the total investments and divide this by the total number of transactions for new or renewing customers. This could be refined by splitting these total costs in acquisition and retention investment and dividing this by either the number of acquisitions or the number of retentions. The next step could be to specify the investments per channel and/or product.

In Chapter 6, one of the cases we will discuss will be a CLV case for a large energy company that tried to model CLV over the customer base, to assess the importance of every element of the CLV formula. We also suggest taking a look at the numerous calculators that can be used as a guide in building your own CLV model. Specifically we would like to mention the calculator developed by Harvard Business School.[5] Even the basic version is a very nice example of how to calculate CLV.

Customer equity

Customer equity is closely related to CLV. The metric, as successfully proposed by Rust et al. (2000), is the summation of all CLVs of current and future customers of a firm. As such it is broader than CLV because it considers all customers and also future customers. Hence, it considers both the value of existing relationships resulting from customer loyalty and the ability of the firm to attract new valuable customers. To achieve this, Rust et al. (2000) use a switching matrix approach, in which customers can switch between suppliers. In subsequent work Rust et al. (2004) show that firms can calculate the consequences of investments in drivers that increase the value delivered to customers (reflected in customer perceptions on customer equity), by considering acquisition and retention consequences and subsequent effects on CLV and customer equity. By comparing the investments in value creation (e.g. increasing leg space in airplanes) with the customer equity changes, a marketing ROI can be calculated (see Figure 2.2.7).

New big data metrics

As a result of the development of big data, we can consider two important new areas that require additional metrics:

- Customer engagement
- Digital customer journey.

Customer engagement

The increasing presence of social media has stirred up attention for the non-transactional behavior of customers. Customers not only add value with their purchase behavior, but may also add value by sharing their experiences online, influencing other customers and providing input through co-creation. This non-transactional behavior is frequently referred to as "customer engagement behavior" (van Doorn et al., 2010; Hoyer, Chandy, Dorotic, Krafft, & Singh, 2010). This behavior results in a possible need for additional metrics, such as:

- The number of referrals per customer
- The number of relationships of a customer with other customers

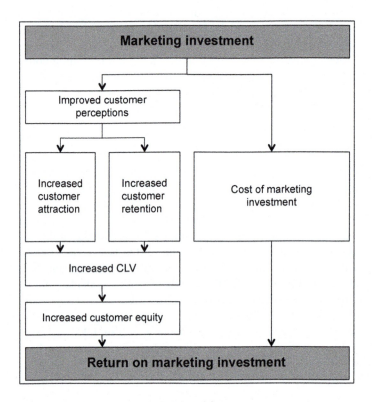

Figure 2.2.7 Customer equity ROI model

Source: Adapted from Rust, Lemon and Zeithaml (2004)

- The number of ideas (e.g. new products, service improvements) of customers provided to a firm
- The influential power of customers (i.e. measured by opinion leadership or social network variables; see for example Risselada, Verhoef, & Bijmolt, 2015).

One problem with these metrics is that they are frequently difficult to measure as it may involve social network information and/or self-reports on influence. We will reflect on this in more depth in the in-depth Chapter 4.2 on analytics, where we discuss social network analytics. Firms have, however, been able to collect data in their databases on referrals and potentially on numbers of ideas (e.g. through measuring complaints). The importance of customer engagement also implies an extension of the CLV concept. Specifically Kumar, Donkers, Venkatesan, Wiesel, and Tillmanns (2010) introduced the concept of "customer engagement value." Within this concept three new additional value components are introduced: customer referral value (CRV), customer influence value (CIV) and customer knowledge value (CKV), as shown in Figure 2.2.8.

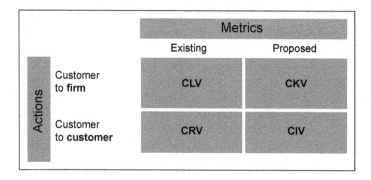

Figure 2.2.8 Customer engagement value: Extending CLV
Source: Kumar et al. (2010)

Kumar et al. (2010) distinguish between customer-to-customer (C2C) and customer-to-firm (C2F) values. CRV and CIV are C2C values, whereas CLV and CKV are C2F values. CRV has been operationalized and measured using actual referral behavior in work by Kumar and colleagues (Kumar et al., 2010; Kumar, Bhaskaran, Mirchandani, & Shah, 2013). Interestingly, they show that customers with a medium CLV have the highest CRV. CIV is more difficult to measure, because of the need for network data. Kumar et al. (2013) measured CIV for the social media campaign of an Indian ice-cream retailer, Hokey Pokey. They calculated both CLV and CIV and summing these metrics they calculated the ROI of the social media campaign.

Customer journey metrics: Path to purchase

The digital revolution has led to a new omni-channel environment (e.g. Verhoef, Kannan, & Inman, 2015). Customers are now developing their own path to purchase. They browse and search online, switch between offline and online channels, use multiple devices, etc. and are still being influenced by traditional advertising. In sum, different customers face brands at different touchpoints that may affect different customers in different ways (e.g. Baxendale, Macdonald, & Wilson, 2015). This new development also results in a mix of new brand and customer metrics. At the brand level we may, for example, observe the number of click throughs on a banner ad. For customers, firms may observe conversion rates. However, for prospective customers these metrics are less easy to measure. For firms it is still important to understand this path to purchases and to measure specific outcomes along this path to purchase, for both customers and prospective customers. (e.g., Verhoef et al., 2015; Li & Kannan, 2014). This results in a set of new, different digital metrics:

- Number of website visits: when paying other websites to show your advertisement and/or banner the associated cost is measured against the costs per 1000 views/eyeballs (CPM=Cost per mille)
- Click through rates: The percentage of customers viewing an online ad, search engine outcome, etc. clicking on the ad to visit the referred website; the financial metric to represent the associated costs when, for example, showing an online advertisement via Google—cost per click (CPC)
- Purchase conversion rate: The number of purchases after a website visit divided by the number of website visits. The financial metric to show the costs of advertisements or online activities is cost per order/transaction (CPO)
- Average order size: The average order size of each purchase
- Costs of each unique touchpoint
- Channel switching: The migration patterns of customer to other channels (especially relevant when firms aim to migrate customers to low-cost channels (e.g., Trampe, Konuş, & Verhoef, 2014; Gensler, Verhoef & Böhm, 2012)
- Research shopping percentage: Percentage of customers searching in one channel and purchasing in another channel (e.g. Verhoef, Neslin, & Vroomen, 2007). One specific form of this is the showrooming percentage, where the search channel is the store and the purchase channel is online (Rapp, Baker, Bachrach, Ogilvie, & Beitelspacher, 2015).

We will discuss customer journey analytics and paths to purchase models in more depth in Chapter 4.2. One specific concern managers face is to link investments in different (digital) acquisition channels to purchase outcomes. This is not so trivial, as customers may be influenced by multiple channels or touchpoints in their purchase decisions and specific channels (e.g. search engines) are by definition closer to the purchase decision than other channels (e.g. advertising). Firms require strong attribution models to quantify the contribution of every channel.

Marketing ROI

One final metric that firms are interested in is the ROI of marketing investments. We have already briefly mentioned this in our discussion of the customer equity metric, since ROI is directly related to current and future CLV. The ROI on marketing investments is calculated as the additional CLV divided by marketing investment.

Ideally marketing ROI should cover all possible marketing activities that can be deployed and not just the (direct) marketing activities addressing new and existing customers. Furthermore, the measure to calculate ROI should not be based on sales volume, but ideally on created CLV, and it should also take into account the extent to which marketing activities contribute to V2C metrics (see Figure 2.2.9).

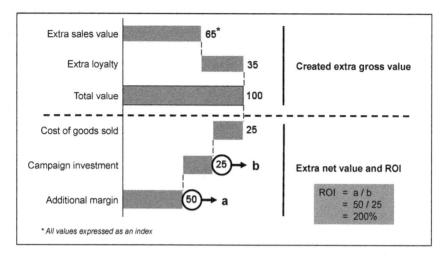

Figure 2.2.9 Example of ROI calculation

In fact, a marketing ROI calculation should also encompass, for example, investments made in ATL campaigns, specific brand activities, and other marketing mix elements. But there are few cases that successfully show marketing ROI as a holistic (i.e. analyzing CLV and V2C effects of the whole marketing mix) approach.

There are several reasons why this is not common practice:

- The relationship between, for example, an ATL campaign and the extra CLV created is very difficult to assess. This is because there are all kinds of possible interferences on the final effect (if any) on CLV. However, there is a whole world of studies and projects going on trying to make marketing mix models in order to quantify these relations.
- Integrating all data sources, in order to measure all the efforts being deployed and their effect on intermediate KPIs like brand awareness, market share etc. instead of measuring the effect on CLV, is very complex. This challenge of data integration and how to deal with it will be discussed in depth in Chapter 3.1.
- Furthermore, CLV might raise some discussions within the organization, because some of the elements of the CLV calculation are considered either a black box or are based on assumptions (like, for example, expected lifetime) that are not indisputable. In these cases organizations might choose to fall back on sales or sales revenues instead of CLV for marketing ROI calculations.
- There is a lack of an organization-wide accepted segmentation of customers and the market that can be identified in all sources in scope. Not only does this limit the possibilities of data integration, but it also limits the action ability of initiatives to improve the marketing ROI.

Conclusions

In this chapter we have discussed V2F metrics at both the market, brand, and customer level. It is clear that there is a plethora of metrics from which firms can choose. This actually holds for both V2C and V2F metrics. We have aimed to provide an overview of rather frequently used metrics, but acknowledge that one can easily come up with many other relevant (or irrelevant) metrics. For interested readers we refer to Farris et al. (2006), who provide a very extensive discussion of multiple metrics for multiple areas of marketing. Importantly, we also discussed some new big data metrics. Specifically, we focused on customer engagement metrics and customer journey metrics, as we believe that major developments are occurring here. A clear understanding of these metrics will be required to actually implement big data analytics to show the ROI of (additional) marketing investments.

Notes

1. See http://followthatapp.co.uk/2011/08/10/uk-smartphone-sales-statistics (accessed September 17, 2015).
2. We refer to Farris et al. (2006) for a detailed discussion on some of these metrics and how they can be used to calculate sales volumes. In our Chapter 4.1 we also discuss some market forecasting techniques.
3. Other agencies have also developed BE metrics. The Interbrand metric is, however, best known and the most influential, and we therefore have included this metric in this chapter and ignored some other metrics of commercial agencies.
4. See www.interbrand.com (accessed September 14, 2015).
5. See https://cb.hbsp.harvard.edu/cbmp/resources/marketing/multimedia/flashtools/cltv/index.html (accessed September 14, 2015).

References

Ailawadi, K. L., Lehmann, D. R., & Neslin, S. A. (2003). Revenue premium as an outcome measure of brand equity. *Journal of Marketing*, 67(4), 1–17.

Baxendale, S., Macdonald, E. K., & Wilson, H. N. (2015). The impact of different touchpoints on brand consideration. *Journal of Retailing*, 91(2), 235–53.

Berger, P. D., & Nasr, N. I. (1999). Customer lifetime value: Marketing models and applications. *Journal of Interactive Marketing*, 12(1), 17–30.

Bolton, R. N., Lemon, K. N., & Verhoef, P. C. (2004). The theoretical underpinnings of customer asset management: A framework and propositions for future research. *Journal of the Academy of Marketing Science*, 32(3), 271–92.

Donkers, B., Verhoef, P. C., & De Jong, M. G. (2007). Modeling CLV: A test of competing models in the insurance industry. *Quantitative Marketing and Economics*, 5, 163–90.

Dowling, G. R., & Uncles, M. (1997). Do customer loyalty programs really work? *Sloan Management Review*, 38(2), 71–82.

Fader, P. S., & Hardie, B. G. (2010). Customer-base valuation in a contractual setting: The perils of ignoring heterogeneity. *Marketing Science*, 29(1), 85–93.

Farris, P. W., Bendle, N. T., Pfeifer, P. E., & Reibstein, D. J. (2006). *Marketing metrics: Fifty+ metrics every marketer should know*. Philadelphia: Wharton School Publishing.

Farris, P. W., Bendle, N. T., Pfeifer, P. E., & Reibstein, D. J. (2010). *Marketing metrics: The Definitive guide to measuring marketing performance.* Upper Saddle River, NJ: Pearson Education.

Feld, S., Frenzen, H., Krafft, M., Peters, K., & Verhoef, P. C. (2013). The effects of mailing design characteristics on direct mail campaign performance. *International Journal of Research in Marketing*, 30(2), 143–59.

Gensler, S., Verhoef, P. C., & Böhm, M. (2012). Understanding consumers' multichannel choices across the different stages of the buying process. *Marketing Letters*, 23(4), 987–1003.

Gupta, S., Lehmann, D. R., & Stuart, J. A. (2004). Valuing Customers. *Journal of Marketing Research*, 4(1), 7.

Hoyer, W. D., Chandy, R., Dorotic, M., Krafft, M., & Singh, S. S. (2010). Consumer cocreation in new product development. *Journal of Service Research*, 13(3), 283–96.

Juster, F. T. (1969). Consumer anticipations and models of durable goods demand. In Mincer, J. (1969). *Economic Forecasts and Expectations.* New York: National Bureau of Economic Research.

Kumar, V., Bhaskaran, V., Mirchandani, R., Shah, M. (2013). Creating a measurable social media marketing strategy for Hokey Pokey: Increasing the value and ROI of intangibles & tangibles. *Marketing Science*, 32(2), 194–212.

Kumar, V., Donkers, A. C., Venkatesan, R., Wiesel, T., & Tillmanns, S. (2010). Undervalued or overvalued customers: Capturing total customer engagement value. *Journal of Service Research*, 1(3), 297–310.

L'Hoest-Snoeck, S., Van Nierop, E., & Verhoef, P. C. (2015). Customer value modelling in the energy market and a practical application for marketing decision making. *International Journal of Electronic Customer Relationship Management*, 9(1), 1–32.

Leeflang, P. S. H., Verhoef, P. C., Dahlström, P., & Freundt, T. (2014). Challenges and solutions for marketing in a digital era. *European Management Journal*, 32(1), 1–12.

Leenheer, J., Bijmolt, T. H. A., Van Heerde, H. J., & Smidts, A. (2007). Do loyalty programs really enhance behavioral loyalty? An empirical analysis accounting for self-selecting members. *International Journal of Research in Marketing*, 24(1), 31–47.

Lewis, M. (2006). Customer acquisition promotions and customer asset value. *Journal of Marketing Research*, 4(2), 195–203.

Li, H. A., & Kannan, P. K. (2014). Attributing conversions in a multichannel online marketing environment: An empirical model and a field experiment. *Journal of Marketing Research*, 5(1), 40–56.

Rapp, A., Baker, T. L., Bachrach, D. G., Ogilvie, J., & Beitelspacher, L. S. (2015). Perceived customer showrooming behavior and the effect on retail salesperson self-efficacy and performance. *Journal of Retailing*, 91(2), 358–69.

Risselada, H., Verhoef, P. C., & Bijmolt, T. H. A. (2015). Indicators of opinion leadership in customer networks: Self reports and degree centrality. *Marketing Letters*. Forthcoming.

Rust, R. T., Lemon, K. N., & Zeithaml, V. A. (2004). Return on marketing: Using customer equity to focus marketing strategy. *Journal of Marketing*, 68(1), 109–27.

Rust, R. T., Zeithaml, V. A., & Lemon, K. N. (2000). *Driving customer equity: How customer lifetime value is reshaping corporate strategy.* New York: The Free Press.

Shah, D., Kumar, V., Qu, Y., & Chen, S. (2012). Unprofitable cross-buying: Evidence from consumer and business markets. *Journal of Marketing*, 76(3), 78–95.

Sharp, B. (2010). *How brands grow.* Australia & New Zealand: Oxford University Press.

Simon, C. J., & Sullivan, M. W. (1993). The measurement and determinants of brand equity: A financial approach. *Marketing Science*, 12(1), 28–52.

Sriram, S., Balachander, S., & Kalwani, M. U. (2007). Monitoring the dynamics of brand equity using store-level data. *Journal of Marketing*, 71(2), 61–78.

Trampe, D., Konuş, U., & Verhoef, P. C. (2014). Customer responses to channel migration strategies toward the e-channel. *Journal of Interactive Marketing*, 28(4), 257–70.

Van Doorn, J., Lemon, K. E., Mittal, V., Naβ, S., Pick, D., Pirner, P., Verhoef, P. C. (2010). Customer engagement behavior: Theoretical foundations and research directions. *Journal of Service Research*, 13(3), 253–66.

Venkatesan, R., & Kumar, V. (2004). A customer lifetime value framework for customer selection and resource allocation strategy. *Journal of Marketing*, 68(4), 106–215.

Venkatesan, R., Farris P., & Wilcox R. T. (2014). *Cutting-edge marketing analytics, real world cases and data sets for hands on learning*. Upper Saddle River, New Jersey: Pearson Education.

Verhoef, P. C. (2003). Understanding the effect of customer relationship management efforts on customer retention and customer share development. *Journal of Marketing*, 67(4), 30–45.

Verhoef, P. C., Kannan, P. K., & Inman, J. (2015). From multi-channel retailing to omni-channel retailing: Introduction to the special issue on multi-channel retailing. *Journal of Retailing*, 9(2), 174–81.

Verhoef, P. C., Neslin, S. A., & Vroomen, B. (2007). Browsing versus buying: Determinants of customer search and buy decisions in a multi-channel environment. *International Journal of Research in Marketing*, 24(2), 129–48.

3 Data, data everywhere

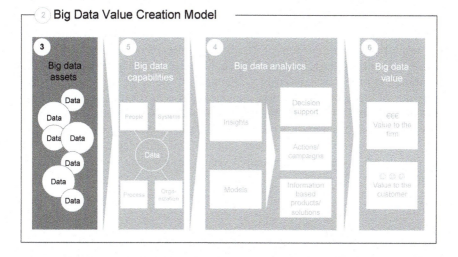

Introduction

In this world of big data everything starts with dealing with the overload and variety of data that are available, to help realize the ambitious objectives of value creation with big data analytics. And that's why data is at the core of this book. Earlier, we explained why we talk about "big" data (by using the three Vs model). One of the three 'V's was variety. This represents the fact that data nowadays are arising from more and more sources, and that in fact data can be found everywhere. In this chapter we will elaborate on this variety of data sources. We will discuss what kind of data sources can be distinguished and how all these data can be categorized, as well as how data should be processed and stored. Specific attention will be given to data quality and data security. We will follow the same structure as in other chapters, meaning that we will discuss market data sources, product and brand data sources, and data sources with customer data—all with a specific focus on new data sources that have become available.

76 *Data, data everywhere*

In Chapter 3.1 we will discuss data integration: how to extract, transform, and load data, how to create all types of variables in the commercial data environment and how to physically integrate data sources from different aggregation levels. In Chapter 3.2 the subject will be big data privacy issues and security. For companies, as well as for their customers, privacy and security are very real themes that are being discussed almost daily on TV and in newspapers—and definitely should be discussed within the context of this book.

Data sources and data types

Firms have many different data sources at their disposal for filling their commercial data environment. By a commercial data environment we mean the technical infrastructure where all data is stored, processed, and accessed, coming from all kinds of sources to be used for commercial steering. In this environment, we see nowadays a combination of "traditional" data warehousing technology combined with modern big data tooling, like Hadoop, MapReduce, etc. This combination of technology enables dealing with the challenges posed by the existence of different types of data sources, and specific challenges in data volume and variety. In Chapter 5 we will discuss this more in depth. Within these data sources, we distinguish between internal versus external data sources and structured versus unstructured data sources. The different combinations of internal versus external and structured versus unstructured data are shown in Figure 3.1.

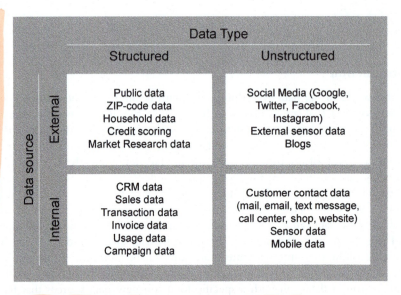

Figure 3.1 Two dimensions of data: Data source versus data type

Source: Adapted from Nair and Raman (2012)

A first important distinction in these data sources is between external and internal data sources.

External data sources versus internal data sources

External data sources are not present within the firm and are frequently purchased and added to the commercial data environment from (or collected by) external data vendors. Important examples of these data are ZIP-code or household datasets. In ZIP-code datasets, information is provided on the characteristics of households living in that ZIP-code, such as average income level, education level, average house-price, etc. This information can be linked to individual customers through the ZIP-code of the customer. More and more vendors are transforming their ZIP-code datasets into household datasets, by enriching ZIP-code datasets with information obtained from omnibus questionnaires and publicly available datasets for commercial use (such as information on the sale of houses, including house prices). This transformation helps to create more powerful profiles of households, instead of having to make use of extrapolations for all households in a ZIP-code.

Other external information may, for example, involve the financial creditworthiness of a customer. Credit card firms such as American Express, Mastercard, and Visa have good knowledge of whether a consumer is creditworthy, by analyzing the use of their credit card. More and more firms (e.g. Mastercard) are starting to exploit their datasets to be used as an external data source for checks of creditworthiness, for example with telecom providers.

Important suppliers of external consumer data are Experian, Axciom, and Nielsen-Claritas. External B2B data are provided by firms such as Graydon and Dun & Bradstreet. External consumer data are frequently used for target marketing purposes and for profiling current customers in terms of socio-demographics, lifestyle, and psychographic variables. Suppliers such as Nielsen-Claritas have developed detailed segmentation systems, in which each household belongs to a certain psychographic-lifestyle segment, such as young families, rural families, young urban professionals, etc. (see Figure 3.2).

Another kind of external data is marketing research data, mostly collected for firms by their market research agencies. These agencies often have large panel sets, with respondents in place to perform quantitative market research on topics such as brand performance, campaign evaluation, media effectiveness, and product innovation. Market research can also be realized by using data of the firm's own customers, such as customer satisfaction or NPS, usually collected by external marketing research suppliers. Depending on privacy regulations, customer permission, and/or the specific research professional code, market research data can be included in the commercial data environment as well.

Furthermore, firms may collect competitive intelligence data on competitive actions. These data are usually not internally present, and can be collected by marketing intelligence departments. Research has shown that competitive

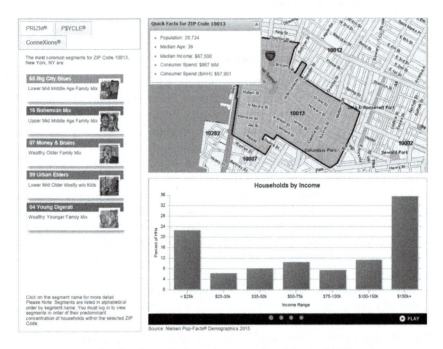

Figure 3.2 Example of Nielsen-Claritas information for a New York ZIP-code
Source: Claritas.com[1]

actions, such as competitive advertising, have an impact on customer behavior (Prins & Verhoef, 2007).

Another type of fast-growing external data are data from social media. These data come from parties like Facebook, Twitter, LinkedIn, and Instagram, all of which have huge user bases, so that often a substantial proportion of a firm's customers participate in these social media. Linking these data to the commercial data environment is quite a challenge and not yet a common practice. This is mainly due to the highly unstructured way these data are being created. Firms are collecting these data by using platforms like Radian6 for social media monitoring, but are still struggling to interpret the data and integrate these platforms with their commercial environment.

Internal data sources are already present within the firm and may include point-of-sales data, transaction data, invoice data, contact data, and usage data. These internal data sources are gathered and stored in the data warehouse. Internal data can be considered to be very powerful. The possession of information from internal data is important if customer behavior is to be described, understood, and predicted. However, these data sources need a lot of data preparation in order to create valuable information. Within customer value management (CVM) this is the most frequently stored data (Verhoef, Spring,

Hoekstra, & Leeflang, 2002). Also many models aiming to optimize the customer value only use internal data (e.g. Venkatesan & Kumar, 2004).

Structured versus unstructured data

An alternative way to structure data sources is to make a distinction between structured and unstructured data sources. Structured data are data that come in a fixed format, based on a detailed record and variable structure, good labeling of values in the database, and high data quality. The invoice data mentioned earlier (internal data) and ZIP-code data (external data) are good examples of highly structured data. On the other side of the coin we have unstructured data. These data are often very bulky in size, without a fixed format, containing a lot of free format text and often need a good deal of data interpretation and data reduction in order to create usable information. Examples of these data sources are data from customer contact (internal data), where customers and their questions or remarks are often registered in free format text, and social media data (external data) contained in Twitter messages, Facebook comments, etc. Figure 3.3 shows an example of how unstructured data can be transformed into structured data.

A special remark should be made about mobile data. Mobile data (in Figure 3.1 depicted as internal, unstructured data) is a rather new phenomenon that took off with the increase of smartphone and tablet penetration. This kind of data is quite unique since it offers organizations the possibility not only to monitor what customers are doing, but also where they are doing it—thereby giving big opportunities to all kinds of location-based services. Installed apps give the customer access to products and services that offer all kinds of service and transaction functionalities. Since the usage of data generated by these apps is often not yet integrated within the architecture of the commercial data environment,

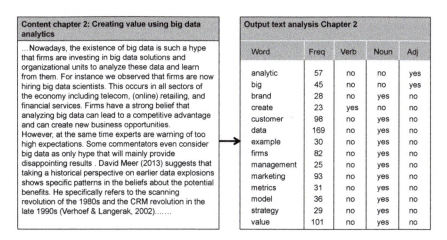

Figure 3.3 Illustration of structured and unstructured data

and because the data from these apps are often unstructured, there is still pioneering work to be done in this area.

Market data

Another lens for discussing data sources is our breakdown by market, brand/product, and customer. This is not only useful from the perspective of the big data challenge but also it creates awareness about the differences between the data sources for market, product/brand, and customers, differences that arise due to scope, detail, and power of the data source at hand. We define two types of market data:

1   Market data on the supply side: Data that describe and explain metrics like market size, market volume, market share, market development, media spend etc. for all players in the market. Ideally with the possibility to be shown per competitor in the market.
2   Market data on the demand side: Data that describe the consumers in the market, their buying and spending behavior, their socio-demographics (e.g. age, household size, income), and their needs.

Market data on the supply side is often collected by agencies that aggregate, for example, sales figures from different suppliers in order to create a market overview. Sometimes this can be an agency that operates for the whole industry. For example, employment agencies in the Netherlands all deliver their placements per 4-week period to ABU, an organization that collects this data for the whole industry and delivers this back at an aggregated level. Another example is Nielsen, which collects scanning data and creates detailed sales figures based on this (see Figure 3.4).

Market data on the demand side is mainly collected by research agencies. An example is GfK, which creates, for instance, an overview of the insurance market by asking consumers details of their insurance papers. The main difference with supply-side data is how the data are collected. Demand-side data are built up from the users or buyers of products or services, often at the household level, as far as it concerns consumers. We can consider the external data as provided by vendors like Experian (see above) also as an example of market data, since these are built up from the consumer/demand-side perspective at the household or ZIP-code level. Market data on the demand side are not only data on product usage or product-buying and socio-demographics, they can also consist of more "soft data," describing consumer needs and values as they exist in the market. These datasets categorize consumers in segments like "cosmopolitans" or "post-materialists" as used by, for example, Motivaction, a Dutch research agency. These groups display specific needs with respect to a certain industry or product category. In Figure 3.5 the mentality milieu segmentation of Motivation is displayed as an example of market data on the demand side.

	% share, 12 weeks to 16 August 2014	% share, 12 weeks to 17 August 2013	% sales change vs. Same 12 weeks year ago
TESCO	28.2%	29.7%	-5.9%
ASDA	16.3%	16.1%	0.3%
SAINSBURY	16.2%	16.2%	-0.7%
MORRISONS	11.0%	11.3%	-3.3%
CO-OPERATIVE	5.9%	6.0%	-1.0%
ALDI	5.4%	4.2%	26.2%
WAITROSE	4.9%	4.7%	4.6%
LIDL	4.1%	3.4%	20.9%
MARKS AND SPENCER	3.1%	3.0%	2.3%
ICELAND	2.1%	2.1%	-0.7%

Figure 3.4 Example of market data on the supply side for UK supermarkets

Source: adapted from Nielsen TotalTill, Nielsen Homescan (2014)[2]

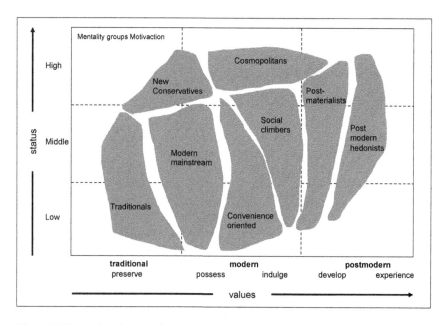

Figure 3.5 Example of market data on the demand side

Source: Motivaction[3]

By definition market data have the broadest scope, as their aim is to represent the total market for an industry or product/service. However, since collecting this kind of data can be very costly, the data may sometimes not be as detailed as desired and sometimes also be outdated, since regularly updating is costly as well. This of course limits the power of the use of these kinds of data sources.

Big data influence on market data

Alternatives for traditional market data are arising, especially due to developments like open data projects, where governments and organizations share their data using the enormous power of digitalization and online data. As an example, by analyzing the data from the app called "Slice" (an app that helps customers to keep track of purchases and store receipts) a very good estimate was made of recently sold units of the new Apple watch. Another example is data collected by all kind of comparison sites. They all have a good perspective on market volumes and transactions, especially since the online share of transactions in all industries is still rising very fast (mainly in the orientation phase of the buying process) and possible biases are reducing.

Brand data

For brand data we again make a distinction between:

1. Brand data on the supply side: Data that describe the volume and market share of specific brands/products
2. Brand data on the demand side: Data that describe and explain how (potential) customers judge a certain brand.

Brand data have a limited scope in that they focus only on brands and their performance. Collecting these kinds of data, especially for the demand side, is a costly effort. To collect these data, research is necessary, and this brings up discussions about the quality and validity of results.

For brand data on the supply side there are actually no specific data sources built up. Either these data are a subset or cross-section of the above-mentioned market data (for example, to calculate the market share of a specific brand) or they are extracted from the systems that store the sales per brand for the organization (see discussion of customer data later in this chapter). In Figure 3.6 we show an example of what this type of data might look like.

Brand data on the demand side (see the example in Figure 3.7) focuses on the different steps in the customer orientation process, as measured by brand funnels with steps such as brand awareness, brand consideration, and brand preference (see Chapter 2.1). These kinds of data are collected by conducting (online) market research that is performed in longitudinal studies.

	Product revenue	Unique purchasers	Quantity	Average price	Average QTY
Brand A	$2,072,610	57,700	100,123	$21	1.7
Brand B	$903,384	11,425	15,001	$79	1.3
Brand C	$675,810	10,800	23,400	$63	2.2
Brand D	$614,250	14,175	18,980	$43	1.3
Brand E	$547,020	14,600	25,576	$37	1.8

Figure 3.6 Illustration of brand supply data extracted from internal systems

	Total	US	UK	China	Italy
Base: All likely to purchase a smartwatch	**747**	**64**	**48**	**340**	**295**
Samsung Gear	37%	31%	25%	34%	43%
Apple Watch	25%	28%	17%	36%	13%
Sony SmartWatch	6%	6%	6%	5%	8%
Motorola Moto 360	2%	0%	6%	3%	1%
Garmin Forerunner	2%	2%	6%	2%	2%
Z1 Android Watch-Phone	2%	2%	4%	2%	1%
GEAK Watch	2%	0%	0%	2%	2%
LG G Watch	2%	0%	2%	0%	3%
Timex Datalink	2%	2%	0%	3%	0%
NikeFuel	1%	8%	4%	0%	1%
MetaWatch Strata	1%	2%	0%	0%	1%
Fashion S9110	1%	3%	0%	1%	0%
Hyundai MB 910	1%	2%	0%	1%	0%
Other	1%	3%	0%	1%	0%
Not Sure	14%	9%	23%	10%	17%

Figure 3.7 Illustration of brand demand based on market research
Source: adapted from UBS Evidence Lab[4]

Big data influence on brand data

In these days of big data, brand data can also be collected by listening into social media to measure brand sentiment, not to replace but to add to brand data collected by research. Reviews and ratings can also be an important big data source for measuring and collecting brand data. To prevent biases we suggest that these kinds of new data sources are analyzed in combination with traditional sources, instead of fully replacing them.

Customer data

Although the distinction between supply and demand data can also be made for customer data, there is as much customer data available on the supply side as there is on the demand side:

1. Customer data on the supply side: Data that describes the (historical) product and services used by the customer during the relationship with the organization
2. Customer data on the demand side: Data that describes the expectations, satisfaction, and interactions of the customer with the organization.

Customer data is different from market and brand data in several ways: customer data is often very detailed and accurate (especially since billing data is the life-blood of the organization) and by definition only covers customers (and sometimes prospects and ex-customers). So it has a narrower scope and has become (from the moment organizations were successful in extracting and storing this data) very powerful in the commercial steering process.

Customer data on the supply side are mainly stored in the CRM systems of the organization (see Figure 3.8 for an example of a relational marketing database environment). In a contractual setting the billing data are an important source for identifying the customer and assessing the financial value of the customer, as well as helping to analyze product holding and usage. In a non-contractual setting where customer identification is not always possible these data are often limited to data on the product level, stating usage and buying of products, including repeat purchase.

Customer data from the demand side (see Figure 3.9) come from market research on the customer base, doing research on metrics such as NPS or customer satisfaction, or from interactions between the customer and the organization, for example in a call center, shop, or on a website. Because these data are often (at least partly) unstructured, interpretation and analysis of them is necessary to transform them into information and knowledge.

Big data influence on customer data

The influence of big data on customer data can be found in the large internal, unstructured datasets that are being built up and that are more and more

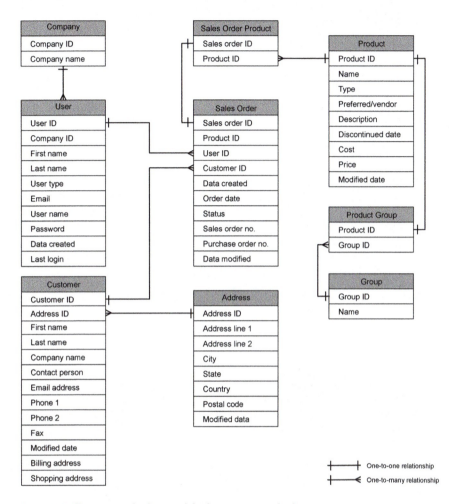

Figure 3.8 Illustration of a data model of customer supply data

within the scope of the data analyst. Also, the online presence of organizations designed to help them to serve their customers, is something that is creating big data—for example, in the "my [organization name]" environment that many organizations create to inform their customers about their billing, their products, etc., not to mention all kinds of "self-service" options. This is influencing customer data on the supply side as well as customer data on the demand side.

Using the different data sources in the era of big data

To assess and to make maximum use of the added value of every data source, we use the 5 "W"s (see Figure 3.10):

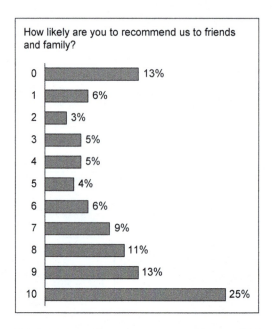

Figure 3.9 Illustration of customer demand data (NPS)

- Who is the customer?
- What is the customer doing/using?
- Where is the customer using (or buying) the product?
- When is the product bought or used?
- Why is the product used?

From a commercial perspective, these are the questions that always pop up. It shows that every data source has its specific strength in answering certain "W" questions, depicted by the colour in Figure 3.10. So survey data, for example, is very strong in answering the "Why" of customer behavior as well as in "What" the customer is doing or intending to do. However, these "W" questions are often only answered from a single data source perspective. This can cause problems because the answers to the different "W"s might not be consistent, or they may even be contradictory. To solve this, we think that the data sources that might come from surveys, transactions, social media, or mobiles need to be combined with each other.

But combining these data sources is quite challenging from a technical, statistical, and legal perspective. From a technical perspective, because some data sources might be anonymous or do not have a unique key to link the sources. From a statistical perspective, because not all data sources have the same coverage of the population (this might, for example, be a population sample or only data on customers and not on the total market). To deal with this, extrapolation

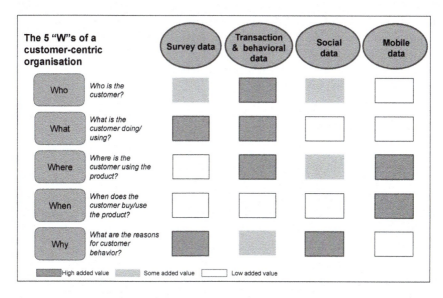

Figure 3.10 The 5 "W"s model for assessment of data sources

techniques will be necessary. From a legal perspective, because combining sources on the individual level might create conflicts with privacy policies, professional codes (such as that of market researchers), or legislation on privacy. In Chapter 3.1 we will go into more depth on how to solve merging datasets from different origins, with different coverage and/or legal hurdles for merging, using techniques such as data fusion.

Data warehouse

The data warehouse is often considered to be the central element of the commercial data environment. Data sources from inside and outside the firm provide data to the data warehouse. Through a data gathering system, the data are transformed into an electronic medium. The data warehouse functions to:

1 prepare the data for storage
2 store the data
3 literally describe the data
4 manage and control the data.

From the data warehouse, analytical databases or data marts are provided to customer intelligence specialists, data scientists, and database analysts (Zikmund, McLeod, & Gilbert, 2003). The data warehouse can be enriched with a software-based information delivery system. This information delivery system transforms data into information. This information is mainly descriptive in nature, and may include metrics, such as the number of active customers, the churn percentage in the last month, or the average sales per customer. However, the information delivery module may be enriched with standard modules for more advanced analytical purposes. Most frequently used are campaign management tools, in which standardized and often automated analytical tools are used to select customers for marketing campaigns.

Database structures

Within a firm, several databases with relevant commercial data are usually present. Firms may have databases on point-of-sales information (e.g. store sales; sales through sales persons), products, invoicing, customer contacts, etc. In a data warehouse all these data sources are integrated into one large customer database. The central focus of this database is the customer. However, from this database should not only customer information be retrieved, but also other information, for example information on sales person performance.

An important element of good databases is that the data are arranged in such a way that they can easily be retrieved by users. The database structure may, however, depend on the user. A sales manager is probably most interested in the performance of the sales reps, while a product manager most likely wants to know the performance of the products. A customer manager is most likely interested in customer metrics, such as customer profitability. To overcome this hurdle, relational database structures are currently standard. Relational databases use different key-variables which link several databases to each other. For example, in an insurance context the customer id and the product id are usually key variables. In a B2B context the customer id can again be a key variable, while the sales rep id can be too. Based on the type of information required, a primary key variable, a secondary key variable, etc. can be distinguished. In a sales database, the sales person id would be the primary key variable, while in a customer database the customer id is the primary key variable.

Figure 3.11 shows an example of the structure of a customer database. In this example the customer id is the primary key variable. For CVM purposes the customer as primary key variable is of essential importance. The customer name provides further information on that customer. The type of product is a secondary key variable, and the transaction channel is another. One can easily add more key variables, such as membership of a loyalty program, time, etc. From this database, one can in principle derive a database with the other non-primary key variables as key variables. For example, if one wanted to take the type of product as a key variable, a database could be created through aggregation and transformation procedures which shows per product the number of customers and the most frequently used transaction channels (see Figure 3.12)

Having multiple key variables, the database can be treated in a multi-dimensional way. For example, one can have two dimensions per customer, by

Customer id	Customer name	Type of products purchased (product ID)	Transaction channel
1001	A. Johnson	80	Internet
2002	P. van Hoof	07	Store
2004	George Hull	15	Direct mail
2008	Barack Thomas	05	Store
3028	Ismael Buunk	20	Catalog

Figure 3.11 Example of simple data table with customer as central element

Product ID	Number of customers	Most frequently used transaction channel
80	80,000	Catalog
07	100,000	Store
15	15,125	Store
05	5,000	Internet
20	200,040	Store

Figure 3.12 Example of product data table derived from customer database

knowing which product in which year (time) they purchased. Working with more dimensions quickly becomes more complicated. Customer information users generally find analyses at a high dimensional level difficult to understand, although software vendors have developed multi-dimensional databases in an effort to overcome this (Zikmund, McLeod, & Gilbert, 2003).

Data quality

Data quality consists of several dimensions:

- Completeness of data
- Data being up to date
- No mistakes in data

Completeness of data refers to whether all available data are present for all customers. For example, a data acquisition channel may be present for only a sample of customers (e.g. Verhoef & Donkers, 2005). Mistakes frequently occur, especially with regard to customer descriptors, such as name and address. These mistakes may arise as customers write down unclear names etc. on forms, perhaps on purpose, or when typographical errors mean that data entry is not done correctly.

The data being up to date concerns whether the data are being updated on a very frequent basis. A database that is not up to date can easily contain mistakes on all kinds of variables. For example, if customers have moved to another address, the address in the database will be wrong if it has not been updated. Or if integration of databases is not done frequently, a recent product purchase or a recent defection might not have been included yet, leading to unreliable information.

Mistakes can potentially have strong negative reputational consequences for a firm. For example, a firm may continue sending mail to someone who has recently passed away. Moreover, data being not up to date may also cause wrong predictions to be made on future customer value, which might lead to less than optimal strategies.

Data quality is thus important for shaping performance in CVM strategies (Zablah, Bellenger, & Johnston, 2004). However, the question is whether firms should have an extremely high level of data quality with perfectly complete data, no data mistakes and 100% up-to-date data. Neslin et al. (2006) propose that there might an optimum level (see Figure 3.13). Achieving good data quality comes at a cost. However, these costs rise in a non-linear fashion when higher levels of data quality are achieved, while the return in terms of increased customer value from this data quality may actually decrease in a non-linear fashion. This implies that firms should assess the optimum level of data quality and not pursue a 100% score.

There are several options available to solve problems with data quality. One option is to use reference databases for cleaning historical data quality issues in the databases; they can also be used as a reference table during data entry. Another option is to use a software approach for data cleaning, for example, by using tools to recognize duplicates within a dataset, or to recognize different options for registering a specific address.

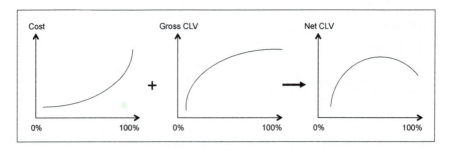

Figure 3.13 Net benefits of investing in data quality

Source: Adapted from Neslin et al. (2006)

Missing values and data fusion

Unfortunately, data will never be perfect. One of the important problems researchers may face is that there are missing values in the data. For example, there is no information on gender and age for some customers. One easy way to deal with these missing data is to throw away observations with missing values. This may, however, cause sample problems, especially when these missing values occur very frequently in a non-random fashion. For example, mainly for customers in a Northern geographic area, socio-demographic data may be missing because customers were not asked to provide these data. Missing values may also have a meaning. For example, customers may on purpose not provide data, because they distrust an organization or they are not very loyal customers (Vroomen, Donkers, Verhoef, & Franses, 2005). In the latter case missing values can potentially be predictors of behavior. For example, one might assume that customers with missing values are more likely to defect, as they distrust the firm. Thus in general one should carefully analyze the reason for multiple missing values, and consider whether these missing values occur in a random or non-random fashion. If it is a random event, one could probably delete observations with missing values or replace the missing values with, for example, the mean value.

A related problem is that many firms have specific data for only a subset of the sample. For example, suppose satisfaction data are only present for 10% of the customer database. For the other 90% no satisfaction data are available. Still, one might like to know the satisfaction scores for these customers as well. In the same vein one could have a share of wallet data for a sample of the customer base. Fortunately, methods have been developed by which the information in the sample can be used to estimate the missing data in the rest of the customer base. These techniques are called data fusion techniques (Kamakura & Wedel, 1997). A rather simple form of these techniques is reported in Donkers and Verhoef (2001). They use a regression model to predict the total number of insurance products a customer purchases. This includes purchases at both the focal firm and outside it—i.e. at competitors. For more information on advanced data fusion techniques we refer to Kamakura and Wedel (2003) and Kamakura et al. (2005).

Conclusions

In this chapter we started with making the distinction between different data sources, grouping them in different ways: structured versus unstructured and internal versus external. We stressed that big data are not just about the external unstructured sources, but also have to deal with the other sources. In line with the other chapters in this book, we distinguished three types of data: market data, brand/product data, and customer data. For every type there is a demand side type of data and a supply side type of data. Further, we discussed the added value of every source of data, by analyzing the different "W"s (Who, What, When, Why, Where). The description of database structures and possible issues with data quality and missing values should help in tackling practical issues around working with data.

Notes

1 See www.claritas.com/MyBestSegments/Default.jsp?ID=20&menuOption=ziplookup&pageName=ZIP%2BCode%2BLookup# (accessed September 18, 2015).
2 See http://meteorpublicrelations.com/wp-content/uploads/2014/09/Supermarket-sales-growths-show-improvement-for-first-time-this-year.pdf (accessed September 18, 2015).
3 For more information on mentality groups: www.motivaction.nl/en/mentality/the-mentality-groups/ (accessed September 18, 2015).
4 See http://appleinsider.com/articles/14/12/01/ubs-survey-finds-10-of-consumers-want-a-smartwatch-expects-24m-apple-watch-sales-in-fiscal-2015 (accessed September 18, 2015).

References

Donkers, B., & Verhoef, P. C. (2001). Predicting customer potential value: An application in the insurance industry. *Decision Support Systems*, 32(2), 189–99.
Kamakura, W. A., & Wedel M. (1997). Statistical data fusion for cross-tabulation. *Journal of Marketing Research*, 3(4), 485–98.
Kamakura, W. A., & Wedel, M. (2003). List augmentation with model based multiple imputation: A case study using a mixed-outcome factor model. *Statistica Neerlandica*, 57(1), 46–57.
Kamakura, W., Mela, C. F., Ansari, A., Bodapati, A., Fader, P., Iyengar, R., Naik, P., Neslin, S. A., Sun, B., Verhoef, P.C., Wedel, M., & Wilcox, R. (2005). Choice models and customer relationship management. *Marketing Letters*, 16(3/4), 279–91.
Nair, R., & Narayayan, A. (2012). Getting Results from Big Data: A Capabilities-Driven Approach to the Strategic Use of Unstructured Information, Booz&Hamilton. www.strategyand.pwc.com/media/file/Strategyand_Getting-Results-from-Big-Data.pdf (accessed November 26, 2015).
Neslin, S. A., Grewal, D., Leghorn, R., Shankar, V., Teeling, M. L., Thomas, J. S., & Verhoef, P. C. (2006). Challenges and opportunities in multichannel customer management. *Journal of Service Research*, 9(2), 95–112.
Prins, R., & Verhoef, P. C. (2007). Marketing communication drivers of adoption timing of a new e-service among existing customers. *Journal of Marketing*, 71(2), 169–83.
Venkatesan, R., & Kumar, V. (2004). A customer lifetime value framework for customer selection and resource allocation strategy. *Journal of Marketing*, 68(4), 106–215.
Verhoef, P. C., & Donkers, B. (2005). The effect of acquisition channels on customer loyalty and cross-buying. *Journal of Interactive Marketing*, 19(2), 31–43.
Verhoef, P. C., & Langerak, F. (2002). Eleven misconceptions about customer relationship management. *Business Strategy Review*, 13(4), 70–6.
Verhoef, P. C., Spring, P. N., Hoekstra, J. C., & Leeflang, P. S. H. (2002). The commercial use of segmentation and predictive modelling techniques for database marketing in the Netherlands. *Decision Support System*, 34(4), 471–81.
Vroomen, B., Donkers, B., Verhoef, P. C., & Franses, P. H. (2005). Selecting profitable customers for complex services on the Internet. *Journal of Service Research*, 8(1), 37–47.
Zablah, A. R., Bellenger, D. N., & Johnston, W. J. (2004). An evaluation of divergent perspectives on customer relationship management: Towards a common understanding of an emerging phenomenon. *Industrial Marketing Management*, 33(6), 475–89.
Zikmund, W. G., McLeod, Jr. R., & Gilbert, F. W. (2003). *Customer relationship management: Integrating marketing strategy and information technology.* New Jersey: Wiley & Sons.

3.1 Data integration

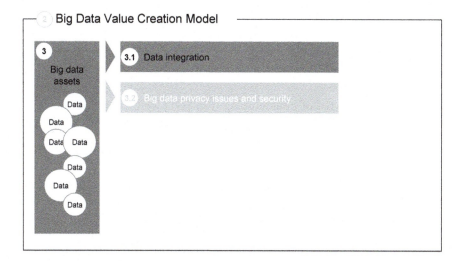

Introduction

Although the biggest challenges in the big data era seem to lie in collecting and storing data, we believe the real challenge is the integration of all kinds of data sources to realize successful big data value creation. This is because many of these data sources are not meant or built up for the purpose of integration with other data sources, and also because the data sources (integrated or not) often contain data variables that need further processing to create useful information. In this chapter we will discuss the different steps that are necessary for data integration as well as the process of creating marketing variables out of the different available data items within the commercial data environment.

Integrating data sources

The first step in the process of data integration is also called ETL (see Figure 3.1.1), the process of extraction, transformation and loading the input data sources into the data warehouse. This process of ETL can either be done by hand, or

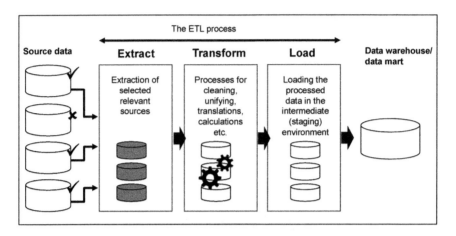

Figure 3.1.1 The ETL process

by using different types of programming (e.g. SQL), or by using off-the-shelf software tools (e.g. Informatica).

Extraction

The crucial part of the extraction stage is the selection of the relevant data sources to be included in the data environment. Part of this process is validation: checking whether the data sources extracted are the right ones that are needed and were specified initially. This validation is necessary since time changes might occur in the input of data sources that might affect the further processing of the input data and even the possible relevance of the specific data source. Another aspect of the extraction step is how the data are extracted. This can be done via an automated query that runs at a specified fixed moment in time or it can be performed manually (not preferred because of possible human errors being introduced, and the time it takes). However, in the first phase of setting up an integrated data environment and building up a sort of a "proof-of-concept" where the data still need to be extracted or are not yet fully stable, it may be preferable to perform several iterations by hand. The frequency of extraction of new datasets is also something that should be considered when organizing the loading process. Typically, for marketing information a monthly refreshment should be suitable, although especially in highly dynamic environments a higher frequency should be considered. Real-time refreshment does not seem feasible, from a technical perspective (there will always be a delay from data processing) and also from a business perspective. Analysts should ask the question of whether the extra benefit gained from having more up-to-date data is worth the cost of collection (e.g. Neslin et al., 2006). Those insights that are needed in real time can be triggered in an operational environment by implementing business rules and/or algorithms to make maximum use of collected insights.

Transformation

After extracting the data, the next step is transforming the different data sources to fit them into the commercial data environment, by applying all kinds of business logics. The transformation of the data during the transformation phase is often designed to make the data easier to handle (more storage efficient and more robust in data quality). Typical transformations are selecting certain data attributes, replacing values in the data (e.g. "M" instead of "Male"), translating values from character into numeric (e.g. "1" instead of "active customer"), calculating values (revenue excluding VAT = revenue divided by 1.21), or extracting and splitting variables into different variables (e.g. taking out the house number and street name of the address field and putting it into two new variables). All steps in the transformation stage are designed to make the data easier to handle during the analysis, make storage easier, and make integration with other data sources more straightforward (by making the data sources uniform).

Load

After transforming the data they will be further processed by loading them into the desired data environment. This will normally be done with an intermediate step called staging. During staging all data sources are loaded in an intermediate environment before being loaded into the tables of the desired data environment. The benefit of this is that it makes it possible to do final checks before publishing the data into the environment where users actually start working with the data or where reports are generated. The staging area also serves as sort of a backup in case something goes wrong by loading in the final tables. Most of the time the data in the staging area is intermediate and will be erased when it is no longer needed. There are two ways by which the data can be loaded into the final data environment. The first is by overwriting the earlier dataset in the commercial data environment. However, this could mean losing all kinds of historical data and is not the preferred option. Another way is to append the new data during the loading process to the existing data in the commercial data environment. In this way historical data can be kept and new data points are added each time the data are refreshed.

Dealing with different data types

Data sources vary in terms of content, scaling, source, and presence within the commercial data environment. It is our strong belief that instead of focusing on the "V" (volume) of big data, the real challenge is addressing the "V" (variety) of data sources, especially as we believe that every source adds a specific dimension to the commercial data environment. We broadly distinguish between four data types (see also Figure 3.1.2):

96 *Data integration*

- Declared data (customer descriptors)
- Appended data (transaction and billing data, customer contact data, marketing contact data, customer characteristics, customer attitudes, brand performance data)
- Overlaid data (zip-code, household data and research data like brand performance, customer attitudes, market and competitor data)
- Implied data (segmentation, scoring models, share of wallet, recency frequency monetary value (RFM) classification etc.).

Declared data: Customer descriptors

Customer descriptors involve all characteristics required for contacting customers, such as name, address, zip-code, phone-number, and email address. Using this information marketing actions can be directed at individual customers and invoices can be sent to customers.

Appended data

Transaction data concern all data on customers' (financial) transactions with the firm and may involve variables such as the last time of purchase, the type of product purchased, the monetary value of the purchase, transaction channel, and product

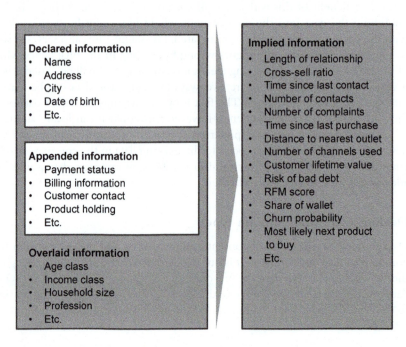

Figure 3.1.2 The different data types

returns. Customer contact data (contact history) are customer-initiated and may, for example, involve information requests, complaints, clarifications on invoices, website visits, and contact channel (i.e. phone, email etc.). Marketing contacts are firm-initiated contacts and may involve the number of mailings sent, timing of mailings, and details of loyalty program membership. Customer characteristics concern additional information on the customer related to socio-demographics, psychographics, lifestyle etc. Part of this data may arise from internal sources. For example, for health insurance customers have to provide their sex, age, household size etc.

Overlaid data

External data suppliers also provide information, at different levels of aggregation. One specific external profiling analysis is the incorporation of Zip-codes. External data providers, such as Axciom and Experian, have specific Zip-code level (or even household) information. Using this information firms can gain an understanding about which Zip-codes (and thus local/regional areas) over- or underrepresent their customers. Along with this Zip-code/household information, these external data suppliers have also developed information on specific segments, such as "rural families" and "single households." In Figure 3.1.3 we provide an overview of the segments that are used by Experian UK. Firms can use this information to further externally profile their customers and customer groups. For example, an online retailer may find that "rural families" are over-represented in their customer base, while the "single household" is almost completely absent. Indexing the data (further discussed in Chapter 4.1) can be very useful.

In Figure 3.1.4 we show an actual example of a clothing retailer that has many stores in larger villages outside the city. This retailer aims to compare his clientele with the population. As can be observed from the analysis, the "prestige

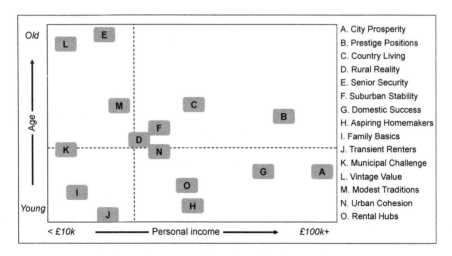

Figure 3.1.3 Overview of segmentation scheme used by Experian UK

MOSAIC Segment	Customers	%	Total pop.	%	Index
A. City Prosperity	1,781	1	733,402	4	35
B. Prestige Positions	23,113	18	1,332,251	7	250
C. Country Living	2,525	2	627,460	3	58
D. Rural Reality	11,083	9	3,714,825	20	43
E. Senior Security	4,006	3	524,909	3	110
F. Suburban Stability	9,378	7	901,103	5	150
G. Domestic Success	1,492	1	430,100	2	50
H. Aspiring Homemakers	6,329	5	506,810	3	180
I. Family Basics	51,453	40	4,120,614	22	180
J. Transient Renters	5,990	5	411,100	2	210
K. Municipal Challenge	894	1	322,113	2	40
L. Vintage Value	6,484	5	849,614	5	110
M. Modest Traditions	2,713	2	3,555,299	19	11
N. Urban Cohesion	1,361	1	490,589	3	40
O. Rental Hubs	1,132	1	217,521	1	75
Total	129,733	100	18,737,710	100	100

Figure 3.1.4 External profiling using ZIP-code segmentation for clothing retailer

Source: Adapted from Experian, UK[1]

positions," and "transient renters" have the highest over-representation in the customer base. The stores do not attract segments such as "modest traditions."

Customer attitude data are data on customer satisfaction and other attitudes, such as commitment or net promoter score (NPS). These data are usually collected by carrying out surveys among samples of the customer base. As a consequence, these data are usually not present for all customers. Brand performance data (i.e. data on brand awareness, brand preference etc.) are measured for customers and non-customers and are only available for a subset or sample of the customer base. Market and competitor data are data on market share, market volume, volume share, as well as information on the performance and market position of competitors.

Implied data

Finally, firms can derive data from combining all these other data. Important derived variables are share of wallet, propensity to buy scores, credit scoring,

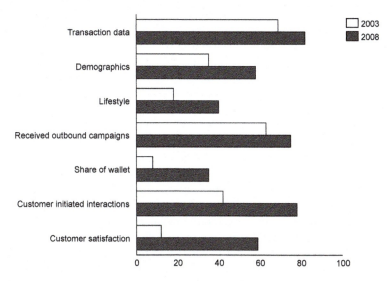

Figure 3.1.5 Presence of data types for Dutch firms

Sources: Verhoef et al. (2002) and Verhoef et al. (2009)

churn probability, and customer lifetime value (CLV). In fact derived data can also be considered as implicit information. The created variables are based on calculations, assumptions, and combinations of data sources. Here, the creativity and capabilities of data-scientists are crucial in creating a competitive edge on the use of data.

Verhoef, Spring, Hoekstra, & Leeflang (2002) and a replication study (Verhoef, Hoekstra, & Van der Scheer, 2009) have investigated the presence of data types for Dutch firms. Customer descriptors and transaction data are the types of data most frequently stored in customer databases. Between 2003 and 2008 a strong increase in the presence of all types of variables is observed (see Figure 3.1.5). This reflects the fact that firms have been successful in setting up complete data warehouses, in which information for all kinds of databases can now be integrated.

An important element of the commercial data environment is the customer database. Nowadays, firms have very large databases of customer data at their disposal. These data arise from all kind of sources. In the past firms usually had several databases with different kinds of contents, which were used in business processes such as sending out invoices and handling of inbound phone calls. Moreover, usually the data were structured around products instead of around customers. These databases were not integrated. Instead, individual customer data were fragmented over many databases. As a consequence firms did not have detailed individual customer information and could not have the full picture of what was actually happening with each customer over time. Due to the integration of databases in many large-scale CRM projects, one integrated customer database is now frequently available.

Data integration in the era of big data

The steps described above are typical for a conventional data warehouse in a commercial setting. The data in a typical data warehouse often have a customer/prospect-centric approach, where all data are being collected with the purpose of linking it to individual customers or to prospects at the individual or household level. Each table in the data warehouse contains a key data field that ultimately links them to the customer level. By combining all this data from the data warehouse—ideally into one single table or flat file—with still rather raw data added into the data warehouse, the dataset becomes richer, especially if (as described above) new variables are created. The next step is to deal with all kinds of data sources that also can be stored in the commercial data environment but either have information of only a subset of customers or were collected with another aggregation level in mind (as was the case for the market and product data described in Chapter 3). However, the technical challenge of dealing with the different aggregation levels is not the only challenge for making good use of these combined sources that are not integrated. In this section, as well as discussing how these data sources with different aggregation levels can be technically integrated, we will also discuss other challenges. We intend to look at a new way of analyzing these sources with a view to working out how to integrate them.

Non-integrated customer, market, and product data are typically used by different departments in the organization making analyses and reports on these data, everyone from the perspective of their own "silo." This often results in a lot of confusion and annoyance with the end-users of the outputs. End-users make comments like: "We have tons of data, so why is it taking so much time to create the right insights when we need them?" or "Why do we have to gather our crucial marketing insights from so many different departments within the organization?" or "We are overloaded with reports and overviews, but they don't give us input on how to improve our business performance" or "Although I now understand what has happened, please tell me also how to act."

Underlying these comments there are in fact three challenges organizations have to deal with in order to make maximum use of integrated data (see Figure 3.1.6):

- Technical challenges: Scattered and fragmented datasets
- Analytical challenges: Lack of a similar and synchronized customer/consumer perspective and consistent segmentation; explaining the past instead of predicting the future and; how to analyze with datasets at different aggregation levels
- Business challenges: No link with metrics of the P&L to realize alignment and acceptance from the financial department.

A simplified example might illustrate this best. Let's assume we are an insurance company selling car insurance. The management needs insights that help to explain the current performance of the organization and its competitive

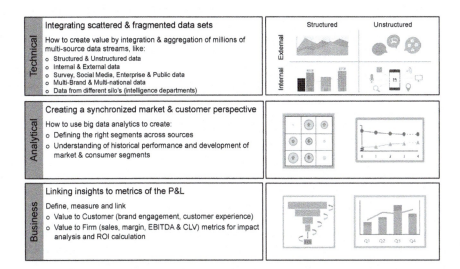

Figure 3.1.6 The challenges of data integration

strength, including the levers for performance improvement and actionable initiatives. The customer data is available at the individual customer level, with a customer-id and name and address of the customer indicating the product and brand the customer bought, when it was bought, where it was bought and at what price, and how the customer is using the product. For this same example we also have market data available per brand for all market players per moment in time, indicating the average value per brand per customer and the number of customers per brand. The market data have been collected by market research through a random sample of the population of consumers with car insurance. The third relevant data environment is online data stored on the webserver.

The technical challenges of integrated data

The technical challenge of data integration is mainly caused by different aggregation levels of data sources, but also by the fact that, as in our example above, the customer data is likely to be stored in the CRM data warehouse, accessible by analysts from the customer intelligence department, while the market data is stored by the research agency (only distributing a report to its client) or within the market research department. So in fact there are two technical challenges. The first challenge is to realize a centralized storage environment for the different data sources from different departments, the integrated environment that we call the commercial data environment. The second challenge is to physically integrate the data sources to enable analysis across all these data sources.

The first technical challenge can easily be solved by specifying the desired data extracts and downloading them into a dedicated storage environment. This can be a dedicated server or a stand-alone piece of hardware, like a powerful pc. Especially in the phase where proof is needed for a big data approach, the last option can be an affordable alternative to a fully fledged new commercial data environment.

The second challenge is the physical integration of the data sources. There are several ways of tackling this, each with its advantages and disadvantages. The different options are mainly driven by the aggregation level of the data source: the data source at the highest aggregation level can be considered "the weakest link," because it determines the aggregation level all other data sources have to align with. In our example above for the insurance company, it is very likely that the market data typically analyzed at the market player level is the highest aggregated data source.

Integration at the individual level

The first option for technical integration of the data sources is what we call "integration at the individual level." This means that the individual (or read "household" for "individual") is identified in every data source and that we start linking the different data sources using the keys identifying the individual: the keys for combining two sources should correspond. Integrating the sources will usually start with the largest database at the individual level. The first step is thus integrating this database (often the customer database) with the next largest database. Let's assume in our example that we want to integrate the customer data with the online data. In the customer data the individual can be identified by a customer id, or for example a combination of address plus birth data. The next step is to identify in our online data the right key for integrating individual online users to the customer base. In our online data we will often find the data stored at the visit level. So the first thing to do is to identify unique visitors. This should result in a unique visitor id resulting from a combination of a cookie id, and an ip number (and for registered users that are customers this could be the customer id). The registered users should be integrated with the customer database by using the customer id. The non-matching customers should be stored with the customer id as the unique identifier and the non-matching website visitors should be stored with the unique visitor id. Since integration at the individual level involves privacy issues and sensitive information, one should consider specific measures (for example pseudonymizing, as described in Chapter 3.2).

Integration at the intermediate level

The second option, integration at an intermediate aggregation level, uses a segmentation based on dimensions that can be identified in all sources to be integrated. The segmentation then becomes the common denominator to which all data should be aggregated for every time period. In our example of the insurance company, we could define the dimensions as age and income. Classifying each of these two dimensions in 5 classes would result in 25 segments to be identified in every data source per time period. If a data source does not have this information, this problem could be solved by first adding external data based on Zip-code or household level (e.g. from somewhere like Experian).

Integration at the time level

The third option for data integration is the least advanced. In this option data will be aggregated to the time period that can be identified in the data sources and the time axis will be the dimension on which to compare the different data sources.

Mixture of integration options

The fourth option is perhaps the one that will be used most—a combination of options 1, 2 and 3. In this option every data source to be integrated will first be checked for available possible unique identifiers. Based on this assessment it will become clear which will be the best of the above three options to use per data source.

The analytical challenges of integrated data

As well as the technical challenges to be addressed, we also see four analytical challenges. The first is the synchronization of the customer and consumer perspectives to be used in the integrated dataset and in the segmentation to be used across and within the different datasets. Defining the customer level and the consumer level can be difficult. One important decision to be made is whether to define this at the household level or the individual level. Once that is decided the next problem is how to identify this level consistently across the different data sources. This asks for internal alignment within the organization and departments and clear business logics to apply the final choices. Assuming this to be the case, the next analytical challenge to be dealt with is the choice of the dimensions and calculation of the segmentation to be used. The source to be integrated could already have a segmentation applied by which results are presented, and they may be very specifically tailored to the information in that specific database. When using segmentation in the integrated data, either for the integration itself or for analyzing across segments across the data sources, a uniform way of segmenting the data is needed. This requires a generic approach to the dimensions of segmentation applied within a specific data source. Just as with the decision on what customer/consumer definition should be used, segmentation is also a topic that should be aligned, discussed, and applied in the right way within the organization. The third analytical challenge around integrated data is the type of insights to be generated. Since integrated data, combining customer, market, and brand input, should offer an extra benefit over reporting on the different data sources in isolation, we think that the ultimate goal should be not trying to explain what has happened. The real benefit should be in being able to make a prediction on what will happen, by creating a holistic view of the marketing performance and identifying the levers that explain historical, current, and future performance.

104 *Data integration*

The fourth analytical challenge lies in the way integrated data can be used for modeling purposes, especially since in the aggregations necessary for physical data integration part of the modeling power of data might be lost. We will go into more depth on this in Chapter 4.2, when we discuss specific big data analytics.

The business challenges of integrated data

We see two different challenges around integrated data from the business perspective. An important business challenge is to define the right key performance indicators (KPIs) within and across the different data sources. The KPIs to be defined should reflect the marketing performance around customers, brand, and market, and should point up opportunities for improvement. The next challenge is to link the KPIs to the company's P&L.

Conclusions

In this chapter we have discussed three subjects around data integration: the ETL process, the process of creating all kinds of new variables from combining datasets, and the different challenges around the integration of data sources with different aggregation levels. Although all three subjects are crucial for making big data integration a success, we consider the last subject (and then especially the technical challenge of dealing with different aggregation levels) as driven by all developments around big data. Solving the challenges around different aggregation levels is the way to deal with the 'V' of variety in big data and so is a key success factor in realizing the potential of big data. In Chapter 6 we will discuss the case of an insurance company to give a pragmatic example of how the challenges around data integration can be dealt with.

Note

1 See www.experian.co.uk/marketing-services/products/mosaic-uk.html (accessed September 20, 2015).

References

Neslin, S. A., Grewal, D., Leghorn, R., Shankar, V., Teeling, M. L., Thomas, J. S., & Verhoef, P. C. (2006). Challenges and opportunities in multichannel customer management. *Journal of Service Research*, 9(2), 95–112.
Verhoef, P. C., Hoekstra, J. C., & Van der Scheer, H. R. (2009). *Competing on analytics: Status quo van customer intelligence in Nederland*. Report of Customer Insights Center (RUGCIC-2009-02), University of Groningen.
Verhoef, P. C., Spring, P. N., Hoekstra, J. C., & Leeflang, P. S. H. (2002). The commercial use of segmentation and predictive modelling techniques for database marketing in the Netherlands. *Decision Support System*, 34(4), 471–481.

3.2 Customer privacy and data security

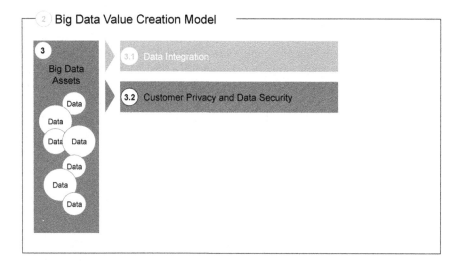

Introduction

So far in this book we have mainly discussed the value opportunities of big data and big data analytics. Indeed, these value opportunities can be considerable. However, in an era of big data firms are confronted with concerns about the storage and usage of data. This specifically concerns customer data. If customers have used digital and mobile devices, they will probably never be anonymous again. Their behavior is likely to be traced online, but also offline. For example, if customers with a mobile device enter a store, retailers using WiFi-based tracking tools can follow customers in the store and how they shop. On a more global level there are continuous debates about customers' data being analyzed by governments. This has become high profile news as a result of documents leaked by Edward Snowden, which revealed numerous global surveillance programs, many of them apparently run by the US National Security Agency (NSA) with the cooperation of telecommunication companies and European governments. This has raised a high level of concern globally on the information privacy of individual global citizens. Can firms like Google, Facebook,

Microsoft, and Amazon be trusted with regard to their privacy policies? And is the information contained in emails sent in Gmail, Microsoft Outlook, or Yahoo observable and available for analysis by governments?

The big data movement has thus created a stronger debate on privacy. The counsellor of the US President, John Podesta, suggests that big data raises serious questions on how we protect our privacy. The German Prime Minister Angela Merkel also considers privacy a big issue, but believes that despite the rising privacy concern, we must be able to use big data to our advantage. Unfortunately, this is not so straightforward. Recently, the Dutch Bank ING Retail announced a test that involved sharing payment data with other firms, with the objective of improving the value delivered to customers through providing attractive and relevant offers to ING customers. This resulted in strong reactions from customers, stakeholders, and politicians. Even the president of the Dutch National Bank actively communicated that he was not in favor of this big data initiative. ING had to retract this initiative and reduce their big data ambitions substantially. This case only emphasizes the struggle that firms are having with the privacy aspect of big data, although the prevalence of privacy issues may vary between firms and sectors. However, it is not only privacy that is an issue. Data security also deserves close attention, as data could become accessible to other parties with mischievous or criminal motives through hacking of computer systems and unsecured data transport.

In this chapter we will mainly focus on privacy. We will discuss what privacy actually is and how customers consider privacy issues. We will also discuss the role of governments and specifically legislation. Big data privacy policies will be elaborated on. Data security will be considered in the last sections of this chapter.

Why is privacy a big issue?[1]

As discussed above, big data has stirred up the privacy discussion. Privacy has been an issue for decades, but the big data development has put privacy back on the agenda of top management and governments. According to Jones (2003) big data are considered to be a threat to privacy for several reasons:

- Big data are permanently available
- Big data involve large volumes of data
- Big data on customers are collected invisibly
- There is no good assessment of the privacy sensitivity of data
- Due to the large volume of data, it is no longer accessible and understandable by customers
- Data from multiple sources are being fused
- Customers perceive a lack of control on big data collection.

If the privacy debate, particularly in Western societies, receives growing attention and if more restrictive policies are developed, the consequences for big data analytics and value creation are likely to be considerable. The Boston Consulting Group (2012)[2] has calculated that the so-called digital identity of customers has a value of approximately 330 billion euros for firms, while for customers the value is doubled, with a value of approximately 670 billion euros. They also estimate that a lack of trust and privacy can destroy 440 billion euros in the value of customers. Of course one can debate about the exact figures of the estimated value consequences. However, these calculations clearly show that there is much at stake for both firms and customers. Firms can become more restricted in what they can do with big data, which may, for example, result in less efficient and effective advertising. Customers can be worse off, because they get less attractive personalized offers and personalized services may be reduced. Despite this, governments are rightfully worried about privacy issues and the use of data. The key issue is probably that there is societal trade-off between what we deem as important data- and privacy requirements and the associated benefits from a lack of privacy.

What is privacy?

We talk a lot about privacy, but what is it actually? Privacy is a concept that has a strong philosophical background. In essence, it implies the right to be left alone (Warren & Brandeis, 1890). This almost suggests the fact that one should be able to live anonymously without being disturbed by anyone from any institution. This is of course rather unrealistic for the vast majority of consumers. However, it clearly suggests the fact that individuals should be able to make the trade-off between seclusion and interaction (Westin, 1967). This discussion is still rather philosophical. Bringing it more into the context of data Goodwin (1991) suggests that an individual should be conscious about which data and information are being shared and to what extent they control this sharing. Two concepts are rather crucial here: consciousness and control.

A concept that is frequently discussed is "privacy concern." Privacy concern usually focuses on six aspects of data:

1   Data collection: "Too much data and information is being collected"
2   Data usage: "Data is being used for other purposes than serving the consumer"
3   Data mistakes: "Mistakes in data can have negative consequences"
4   Data infringement: "Unauthorized access and usage of data"
5   Data control: "Insufficient control over own data"
6   Data consciousness: "Not sufficiently informed on data policies."

Research on privacy has mainly considered privacy concern as the main topic of investigation and considered drivers of privacy concern and the consequences of privacy concerns. We will elaborate on this in the next section.

Customers and privacy

Customers can thus be concerned about the privacy consequences of big data. Concerns and fears are mainly related to the re-usage of data, reputation losses due to the use of data, and the wrong interpretation of data and information. Research also suggests that customers are unconscious or not aware of the usage and collection of information and they actually seem to be worried that they do not have sufficient knowledge on data usage (Hong & Thong, 2013). However, market research has also shown that there are different segments of customers with different views on privacy concerns (Market Response, 2014; Fletcher, 2003; Ackerman, Cranor, & Reagle, 1999):

- Fundamentalist: Fundamentally against the collection and usage of data by firms and governments
- Pragmatist: Willing to share information as long as benefits are received
- Unconcerned: Do not consider sharing information as a problem and consider it as part of daily life.

Recent research in the Netherlands suggests that the majority of customers are pragmatist, although a substantial minority are fundamentalist. Unconcerned customers represent the smallest group (Market Response, 2014). Substantial research has devoted attention to specific drivers of privacy concerns. These studies suggest that, for example, older people are less likely to share information, and females are more concerned about their privacy (Youn, 2009).

An important question is whether privacy concern also leads to less sharing of information by customers. The relationship between privacy concerns and actual data sharing behavior is not so obvious, and the correlation between privacy concern and behavior is low. Only when customers have very strong concerns about their privacy do they change their behavior (Van Doorn, Verhoef, & Bijmolt, 2007). You could actually argue that customers do not behave very consistently. Customers seem to be worried about their privacy, but billions of customers around the globe constantly share very personal information on Facebook, and leave digital traces behind online. The strong disconnect between privacy concern and actual behavior is referred to as the "privacy paradox."

Governments and privacy legislation

Governments across the globe develop their own legislation. There is a good deal of fragmentation on privacy regulation. The most severe laws are found in the EU and Canada. The USA and Australia have less severe privacy legislation. In emerging countries (i.e. Brazil, Russia, India, and China, known as BRIC) legislation is relatively limited (see Figure 3.2.1).

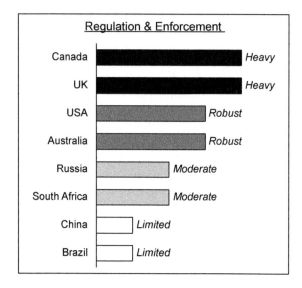

Figure 3.2.1 Data protection laws around the globe

Source: Adapted from DLA Piper, Data protection laws of the world[3]

Within the European Union, the membership states have developed Data Projection Directives, leading to EU general data protection regulation. There is an official EU institution that oversees the implementation of this legislation by firms that has the authority to provide official warnings, audits, and finally fines with a maximum of 100 million euros or 5% of the company's worldwide turnover. Indeed, the EU has started up privacy trajectories with important players, such as Google. There are some principles in the EU legislation that should be emphasized:

1   Right to be forgotten: Customers have the right that their information can be deleted if they require it
2   Right of portability: Customers have the right to view their collected personal information
3   Informed consent: Privacy is default for customers. Data are only collected if a customer opts for that (opt-in)
4   Clear notice: There is an official save time of contact information
5   Privacy by design: Protection of privacy should be part of the whole design or engineering process of new product and service innovations.

As noted, the legislation in the USA is not as strong as it is in the EU. One of the largest differences lie in the approach. Whereas the EU is rather proactive in its legislation, the USA is rather passive. Beyond that, the legislation in the USA differs between states. In the USA the Federal Trade Committee (FTC) is responsible for general privacy laws. The FTC wrote a large privacy report in 2012. They concluded that industry efforts to address privacy through self-regulation "have been too slow, and up to now have failed to provide adequate and meaningful protection." The report recommended many actions. Some of them would bring US regulation more in line with that of the EU. For example, they recommend a privacy by design approach. Furthermore, they emphasize that customers should have a choice. Customers should be presented with choices about the collection and sharing of their data at the time and in the context in which they are making decisions—not after having to read long, complicated disclosures that they often cannot find. FTC also recommends a "do not track" mechanism, which governs the collection of information about consumers' Internet activity to deliver targeted advertisements and for other purposes.[4] So far, the report has only resulted in recommendations for firms, which are not yet implemented in USA legislation.

Beyond data legislation, firms should be aware that the resulting policies from their data usage are also affected by laws. For example, if firms target personal characteristics, such as religion, gender and race, this could result in discrimination. Although the firm could act in accordance with specific privacy legislation, its resulting policies could be in conflict with regulations on discrimination. Hence firms should look beyond the privacy legislation, and should also consider regulation related to specific marketing actions.

Privacy and ethics

On a higher level one could debate whether firms should mainly focus on legislation and take that as the rule on how far they will go with data collection or whether they should take a broader perspective. The latter leads to a discussion on how firms make "moral" decisions. One could advocate an approach in which firms are allowed to collect data as long as the law allows them to do so. However, one could also adopt a more ethical perspective that goes beyond laws, where firms consider that they have an ethical responsibility. De Bruin (2015) distinguishes two important dimensions in this respect: ethical decision making and moral intensity. Ethical decision making applied to privacy involves four stages:

1. Firms have to recognize that privacy decisions have a moral dimension
2. Firms then have to form an ethical judgment concerning what ought to be done with regard to privacy
3. Firms have to establish the moral intention to act in conformity with what they have judged to be the right type of behavior with regard to privacy issues
4. Firms have to engage in that behavior.

The "moral intensity" of an ethical issue such as privacy refers to the magnitude of the consequences of the actions and the probability of it arising, as well as whether the consequences are concentrated on a group of people or dispersed among them. Importantly, it also depends on whether there is any social consensus about the fact that particular actions are good or evil (De Bruin 2015).[5] De Bruin (2015) explicitly states that, roughly speaking, when evil consequences are likely or severe, affect people in close proximity or a large number of people, and when the firm perceives this to be the case, the issue's moral intensity is high. The moral intensity of an issue determines how firms proceed through each of the four ethical decision-making stages. If moral intensity is high, then an issue is considered as a moral issue and elaborative ethical decision making is required.

The above discussion is rather theoretical. Taking a privacy perspective, in practice firms should put consideration of the moral intensity of privacy issues high on their agenda. It is our contention that the big data development has created a wider acknowledgement of privacy issues in society. It is probably too much to say that big data may result in wrong or evil consequences. However, when data are accessible to criminals "evil" things may actually happen to customers. Overall, we believe that privacy is an ethical issue that requires more attention than only considering the law. This would also be in line with a more customer-centric approach, as firms caring for customers and the interest of customers should strongly consider their views on privacy and how they should deal with data. Moreover, recent discussions have shown that big data initiatives can potentially harm a firm's reputation. In sum, privacy issues surrounding big data should be a very important discussion issue within firms, and they should go through more intensive decision making than only considering available legislation.

So in general we recommend that firms should strongly consider the ethical and reputational consequences of their big data and privacy policies. Specifically, they should adopt stakeholder management and consider reactions from customers, the government (including politics), and the media.

Privacy policies

There has been extensive research on privacy and specifically privacy policies. Based on this research we also have some recommendations on how to deal with specific data and privacy issues:

- Only collect data that are relevant and congruent. Relevant data means data that are considered useful in servicing the customer. Congruency of data means data should be related to the product or service provided. For example, for financial services, data on ownership of insurance products or financial transactions are congruent with the service. However, data on medical issues would not be considered congruent.

112 *Customer privacy and data security*

- From a privacy perspective the rule "more is less" holds. The more information is asked for, the less customers provide! So firms should limit themselves in what they ask customers to provide.
- Give something back to customers. Data has value for firms as well as for customers. Rewards (monetary and non-monetary) can inhibit the customer's willingness to share information. However, this does not work for irrelevant information. Moreover, there are differences between customer segments.
- Be transparent on data usage. Providing a clear privacy statement positively influences data sharing. It may reduce customers' lack of awareness on data usage, which may reduce privacy concern.
- Communicate the specific benefits of sharing data. If customers perceive the benefits of sharing data, they are more likely to share. Privacy mainly becomes a problem when the advantages of sharing data are not clear.
- Invest in brand trust. Customers are more likely to share information with firms they trust, as they believe the risks involved are lower. Trust particularly becomes an issue when customers are asked to share personal and sensitive information. Even trusted firms that wrongly use the provided data can find that their use of data backfires on them.
- One final recommendation is that firms should give customers control! According to the Boston Consulting Group, 82% of customers want to have control of the collection and usage of their information. Customers who feel in control have more positive views on sharing information and share more information as well. This can strongly increase the effectiveness of marketing. Giving control to customers implies the use of opt-in and opt-out options and the use of permission-based marketing.

The power of giving control to customers is excellently shown in a study by Catherine Tucker (2014) of MIT. She reports results of a study among Facebook users, where a simple control button on privacy was added. Privacy became standard and friends were no longer visible to everyone. Moreover, opting-out for the use of data was made more convenient. Tucker (2014) reports that the effectiveness of targeted and personalized advertising in particular was more than doubled (see Figure 3.2.2).

Privacy and internal data analytics

Privacy also has consequences for how data is analyzed, as the analysis of data on an individual customer level might not be allowed due to legislation. We consider the following specific solutions (see Figure 3.2.3):

- If individual data are really problematic to analyze from a privacy perspective, one could aim to analyze data on higher aggregation levels. For example, specific market segments could be studied or aggregated analyses could be done. All these analyses can provide customer insights.

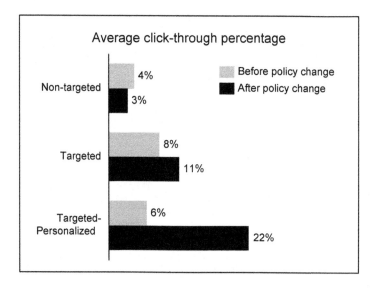

Figure 3.2.2 Effectiveness increase of Facebook advertising campaigns after addition of privacy button

Source: Adapted from Tucker (2014)

- When analyzing data, individual data can be anonymized. This is typically done when one only requires customer insights. Anonymizing of data is usually the standard in traditional market research. If one aims to include the results of the analysis in the database, the model results (e.g. churn model) can be used to create the model outcome in the data (e.g. churn probability).
- A specific form of anonymizing the data is what we call pseudomyzing the data. With a specific key data are anonymized. This anonymization is done by a trusted party (e.g. external IT firm, external law-firm). Only this trusted party knows the key. The analysts execute the analyses and the results can be input into the normal customer database. Again, the external trusted party takes care of de-anonymizing of the data.
- A final technique is linked to the already discussed permission-based marketing approach (Godin, 1999). A subsample of not anonymous data on customers who have given permission to analyze and use their data is analyzed. For the customers granting permission, the results of the analyses can be included in the database. For the remaining part of the data the outcomes of the analysis can be included by using the model estimations to predict the specific values. One concern here is that the permission-based sample will typically not be a random sample and hence the analytical results could be biased due to some self-selection issues.

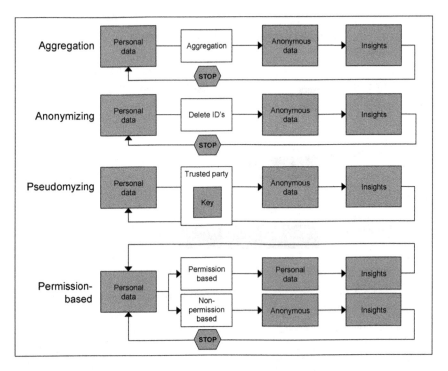

Figure 3.2.3 Different ways of handling privacy sensitive data

One final concern is that, although we nowadays have considerable discussion on big data developments, European firms in particular hesitate to collect long histories of customer data. For example, telecom firms in Western countries keep historical data for only one month and then throw the data away. This limits the possibilities of carrying out more dynamic analyses that involve panel data (Prins & Verhoef, 2007; Ascarza & Hardie, 2013). Some new methods are being developed that aim to benefit from historical data, but by using earlier analytical results. Specifically, Holtrop, Weiringa, Gijsenberg and Verhoef (2014) have developed the so-called GMOK (generalized mixture of Kalman filters) model. This is still in its infancy however and requires advanced methodologies.

Data security

A subject closely related to privacy is data security. The risk of data infringement (the unauthorized access and usage of data) discussed in the previous section can seriously impact on an individual's financial and/or personal safety, and also on the continuity of the firm with a security breach. Remember, for example, the hacking of LinkedIn passwords some years ago, or the Apple iCloud hack where nude pictures of celebrities were spread all around the Internet. These examples show that even renowned major companies can have data security problems, and highlight the need for every firm working with privacy or company sensitive information to take the right measures to secure their data.

We distinguish between three elements of data security. The first is the people element, people that use or have access to the data. The second is the system element, dealing with the physical data storage and the environment where the data are stored. The third is the processes, meaning the procedures and policies (including penalties) as defined by the organization, that define the rules for access, continuity, steering, and monitoring of security performance.

People

Not surprisingly, people are often the weakest link in data security. Very often employees of the firm are (at least partly) responsible for security issues. Everybody knows examples of sensitive data on a USB stick being left in a public place or on a non-company computer, or email attachments being sent outside the organization to the wrong person. These are only examples of data security failures that are not intentional. Even bigger are the security threats from people both inside and outside the firm who have malicious or criminal intentions. This means that firms should protect themselves from human failure or misbehavior. They should screen their employees' credentials and make employees aware of the compliance policies in place—even let them (some of them at least) take an exam on the compliance and security rules of the organization. Another way of dealing with the risk is to grant access to only those data sources that someone really needs to do his or her job.

Systems

By systems we mean the physical and technical environment where data are stored. These days the "cloud" is booming and more and more firms are putting crucial data sources in the cloud—which means that it is sometimes not clear where the data are physically located. Especially due to legal implications (i.e. under which law the data should be treated) firms should be aware of where their data are at the geographical level. In many firms there are many systems for which data are stored, sometimes even redundantly, meaning that all these systems should be in scope when considering the necessary measures for data security. Every system will have its own criteria on how critical the data in that system are for the daily operations of the firm, and what that implies for data security. Typical measures regarding systems are measures such as physical access to systems and computers (e.g. protocols for entering the rooms where the systems are located) or how often and when backups are made, and for how long it is acceptable that a system is "down."

Processes

We define three types of processes: (1) processes for access; (2) processes for continuity; and (3) processes for steering and monitoring. Processes for access define when and who has access to what data and for which purposes. This means defining, for each user, the different rights to work with or use data, and ensuring that every user has a strong username/password combination that will be updated at prescribed times. Processes for continuity define the firm's policies on how to deal with calamities, how and where to back up, what fall back options are available, and having a disaster recovery plan in place. The last processes are about steering and monitoring. These processes make sure that a data security baseline is in place within the organization, defining the critical performance indicators, including the standards for these indicators. Reporting on these indicators makes sure that the security measures are monitored and that the firm is aware of possible incidents, including the actions taken.

Conclusions

Privacy and security have become important issues within big data analytics. Privacy, in a sense, directly links analytics to the customer. Hence it is very important when executing big data analytics to take privacy issues into account. In this chapter, we have tried to give a comprehensive overview of what privacy actually is and why it is important. We discussed some important privacy policies. We also considered how privacy actually impacts analytics and mentioned specific solutions to circumvent this. Finally, we discussed some important issues surrounding data security. In sum, we believe that privacy and security should be primary issues when doing big data analytics. It is no longer only the law department of the firm that should worry about this. Privacy and security actually impact marketing, marketing analytics, and even the board.

Notes

1 This chapter is based on the report of the Customer Insights Center by Beke and Verhoef (2015).
2 See www.bcgperspectives.com/content/articles/digital_economy_consumer_insight_value_of_our_digital_identity/ (accessed September 18, 2015).
3 See www.dlapiperdataprotection.com (accessed September 17, 2015).
4 See www.ftc.gov/news-events/press-releases/2010/12/ftc-staff-issues-privacy-report-offers-framework-consumers (accessed September 17, 2015). The report can be downloaded from this website.
5 We refer to De Bruin (2015) for a more extensive discussion on ethical decision making.

References

Ackerman, M. S., Cranor, L. F., & Reagle, J. (1999). *Privacy in e-commerce: Examining user scenarios and privacy preferences.* ACM Conference on Electronic Commerce, 1–8.

Ascarza, E., & Hardie, B. G. S. (2013). A joint model of usage and churn in contractual settings. *Marketing Science*, 32(4), 570–90.

Beke, F. T., & Verhoef, P. C. (2015). *Privacy: Bedreigingen en kansen voor bedrijven en consumenten*. Report of Customer Insights Center (RUGCIC-2015-01), University of Groningen.

De Bruin, B. (2015). *Ethics and the global financial crisis: Why incompetence is worse than greed*. Cambridge, UK: Cambridge University Press.

Fletcher, K. (2003). Consumer power and privacy: the changing nature of CRM. *International Journal of Advertising*, 22(2), 249–72.

FTC (2012). *Protecting consumer privacy in an era of rapid change: Recommendations for businesses and policymakers*. Retrieved from FTC.gov. Retrieved September 18, 2015 from www.ftc.gov/sites/default/files/documents/reports/federal-trade-commission-report-protecting-consumer-privacy-era-rapid-change-recommendations/120326privacyreport.pdf

Godin, S. (1999). *Permission marketing: Turning strangers into friends and friends into customers*. New York: Simon and Schuster.

Goodwin, C. (1991). Privacy: Recognition of a consumer right. *Journal of Public Policy & Marketing*, 10(1), 149–66.

Holtrop, N., Wieringa, J. E., Gijsenberg, M. J., & Verhoef, P. C. (2014). *No future without the past? Predicting customer churn with limited past data*. Working Paper, University of Gronigen.

Hong, W., & Thong, J. Y. L. (2013). Internet privacy concerns: An integrated conceptualization and four empirical studies. *MIS Quarterly*, 37(1), 275–98.

Jones, K. (2003). Privacy: What's different now? *Interdisciplinary Science Reviews*, 28(4), 287–92.

Market Response (2014). *Privacy hoog in het vaandel, Market Response, Amersfoort*. Retrieved September 8, 2015 from https://ddma.nl/kennisbank/privacy-hoog-het-vaandel/

Prins, R., & Verhoef, P. C. (2007). Marketing communication drivers of adoption timing of a new e-service among existing customers. *Journal of Marketing*, 71(2), 169–83.

The Boston Consulting Group. (2012). The value of our digital identity. Retrieved from slideshare.net. Retrieved September 11, 2015 from www.slideshare.net/fred.zimny/boston-consulting-group-the-valueofourdigitalidentity.

Tucker, C. (2014). Social networks, personalized advertising, and privacy controls. *Journal of Marketing Research*, 51(5), 546–62.

Van Doorn, J., Verhoef, P. C., & Bijmolt, T. H. A. (2007). The importance of non-linear relationships between attitude and behaviour in policy research. *Journal of Consumer Policy*, 30(2), 75–90.

Warren, S. D., & Brandeis, L. D. (1890). The right to privacy. *Harvard Law Review*, 4(5), 193–220.

Westin, A. F. (1967). *Privacy and freedom*. New York: Atheneum.

Youn, S. (2009). Determinants of online privacy concern and its influence on privacy protection behaviors among young adolescents. *Journal of Consumer Affairs*, 43(3), 389–418.

4 How big data are changing analytics

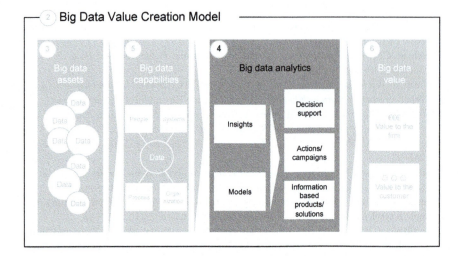

Introduction

Analytics is a major element of creating value from big data. Statistical analytics of marketing data have been around for decades. The revolutions of scanner data and customer relationship management (CRM) have considerably increased the importance of analytics in marketing: it creates strong market and customer insights and models that can be used for decision support, campaigns, and information-based products. However, the emerging presence of big data is changing analytics. Taking a more historical lens, we can observe certain developments in analytics. We will first describe the role of analytics and general types of marketing analysis. Subsequently, we discuss the different strategies for analyzing big data. We end with a discussion on how big data is changing analytics in specific marketing decision areas and in general (generic trends). In this chapter we do not discuss details of specific analytical techniques—we do that in the in-depth Chapters 4.1 and 4.2. We discuss how to have a greater impact with analytical results, through story-telling and visualization, in the in-depth Chapter 4.3.

The power of analytics

In an era of big data, firms heavily rely on the analytical function. Davenport and Harris (2007) argue that firms can gain a competitive advantage if they build up strong and effective analytical capabilities: "Analytics is then defined as the extensive use of data, statistical and quantitative analysis, explanatory and predictive models, and fact-based management to drive decisions and actions" (Davenport & Harris, 2007). These analytical capabilities can be used in different kinds of functions, such as human resource management, logistics, finance, and marketing. The use of these capabilities may, for example, lead to less waste in all kinds of processes and may optimize certain decisions. For example, retailers may create an assortment in such a way that category profitability is optimized (e.g. Van Nierop, Fok, & Franses, 2008). Several firms, such as Annheuser-Busch, Google, Tesco, Wall-Mart, Fed-Ex and Harrah's Entertainment, have adopted strategies that rely heavily on the analytical function. Davenport and Harris (2007) argue that customer analytics is one of the more important fields where firms can compete. For example, Capital One has achieved growth through a more effective analytical-based targeting of new and current customers. The performance implications of stronger marketing analytics have been shown in several studies (e.g. Hoekstra & Verhoef, 2011; Germann, Lilien, & Rangaswamy, 2012). The positive and significant effects of analytical capabilities on performance have been reported in many industries (Germann, Lilien, Fiedler, & Kraus, 2014), as shown in Figure 4.1. The largest effects are found within retail: the smallest within the banking and securities sector.

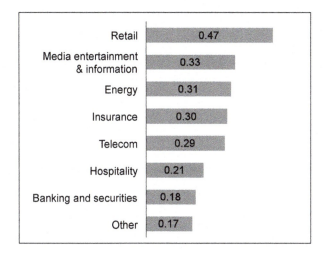

Figure 4.1 Associations between customer analytics deployment and performance per industry

Source: Adapted from Germann et al. (2014: 591)

Different sophistication levels

Davenport and Harris (2007) also distinguish several sophistication levels of analytics. A higher sophistication level should lead to larger competitive advantage (see Figure 4.2).

On a broad level they distinguish between access, reporting, and analytics. Access and reporting is frequently a standardized tool—for example by online analytical processing (OLAP)—within firms and is mainly descriptive in nature. One could also refer to this as market or customer knowledge-focused analysis. This analysis focuses on gaining market and customer insights from descriptive statistical analyses. The main objectives are to learn more about markets and customers and to provide management with information on marketing and customer metrics, such as market shares, brand awareness, retention rates, and customer profitability. These types of analyses focus on what has happened (past) instead of what will or could happen (future). Usually, simple statistical techniques are used, such as calculating averages. Access and reporting is pretty standard and is often included in management dashboards provided by software suppliers such as Business Objects, Cognos, etc. Analytics involve more sophisticated statistical techniques and answer more complicated business problems. It also focuses more on the future than on the past and is more prescriptive in nature. Analyses here may answer questions such as, "What is the optimal product assortment to offer in a store?" or "What would be the optimal price level?" (see Figure 4.3). Yet other questions could be, "What is the optimal number of mailers to be sent to a customer?" (e.g. Rust & Verhoef, 2005) and "Through which channels should we contact a customer in order to optimize customer value?" According to Davenport and Harris (2007) firms using these types of analytics should be the winners in tomorrow's business landscape.

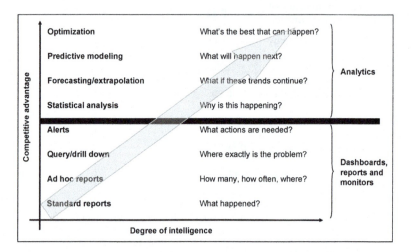

Figure 4.2 Different levels of statistical sophistication

Source: Adapted from Davenport and Harris (2007)

How big data are changing analytics   121

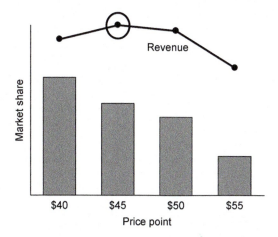

Figure 4.3 Optimization of market share vs. revenue per price level

General types of marketing analysis

We classify more sophisticated analyses going beyond the market and customer knowledge analyses on two dimensions (see Figure 4.4):

1. Explanatory vs. predictive analyses
2. Static vs. dynamic analyses.

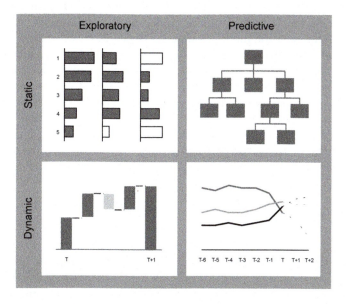

Figure 4.4 Classification of analysis types

The distinction between explanatory and predictive analyses is quite well known and is rather important. Explanatory analyses focus on the "Why?" question. A researcher aims to know why specific phenomena happen. For example, when running customer analyses, one would like to know why, for example, specific customers spend more. Then one could look for differences between customers with a high and low profitability. This could be done with different analyses with differing levels of statistical complexity and rigor. Predictive analyses focus on forecasting marketing- and customer metrics. Market forecasting typically focuses on sales forecasting of new products, and forecasting market share. At the customer level this may involve forecasting response to marketing actions, such as direct mails, emails, but also forecasting churn, product returns, and lifetime value (e.g. Donkers, Verhoef, & De Jong, 2007; Risselada, Verhoef, & Bijmolt, 2010). Again, predictive analyses can be done rather simply, perhaps by using a kind of weighted average to predict future sales, or in a more sophisticated fashion by using forecast models, such as time-series models or choice models. Interestingly, simple models sometimes perform as well as more complicated models. Donkers et al. (2007) show that a simple model to predict customer lifetime value (CLV) with past profitability as an estimate for future profitability predicts just as well as a much more complicated choice model.

Both explanatory analyses and predictive analyses can be executed in a static way or a more dynamic way. With static analyses, one typically analyzes cross-sectional data. That is, at a specific point in time (t) one has data on, for example, brands or customers, and one then analyzes these data. Specifically, one can then observe how brands differ or how customers differ and why they differ. One can even develop a predictive model to predict a specific event, such as churn at that point in time using the available data. This model can then be used to predict this event in the future. Static models dominate practice, as cross-sectional data are more common. In a dynamic analysis, data over time (t, t-1, t-2,… t-n) are analyzed. As an analyst one can then observe how specific metrics change over time and how this can be explained, and whether these changes can be forecast. Dynamic models are generally preferred to gain insights into the effectiveness of marketing metrics and how changes in the environment affect marketing outcomes (Leeflang et al., 2009). Some recent research has put forward an advanced dynamic model that holds out the promise of strong predictive power, and takes into account differences between customers (e.g. Holtrop, Wieringa, Gijsenberg, & Verhoef, 2014).

Strategies for analyzing big data

The presence of big data provides huge opportunities for analytical teams. One of the easiest ways of taking advantage of big data is probably just to start up analyses and start digging into the available data. By digging into the data one might gain very interesting insights, which can guide marketing decisions. The most famous example in this respect is that of UK-based retailer Tesco: when analyzing data of their loyalty card, they discovered that consumers buying diapers also frequently buy beer and chips (Humby, Hunt, & Philips, 2008). Although such an example can be inspiring, we posit that before starting up an analytical exercise one should clearly understand the benefits and disadvantages of the specific analysis strategy—as well as that of other strategies.

In our two-by-two matrix we distinguish between four basic analysis strategies (see Figure 4.5). We take into account two dimensions. First, analyses can be started based on whether or not a problem is pre-defined. A pre-defined problem can arise from:

- Marketing challenges (e.g. decreasing loyalty, eroding prices, lower acquisition rates)
- Marketing growth objectives (e.g. achieve sales growth of 20%, improve customer satisfaction).

Analytics can be done on the pre-defined data (e.g. a CRM database on customer transactions), but one may also aim to look for available data and combine these data based on the arising needs in the data analysis. This is the second dimension of our analysis strategy framework. Based on these two dimensions we distinguish four analytical strategies:

1. Problem solving
2. Data modeling
3. Data mining
4. Collateral catch

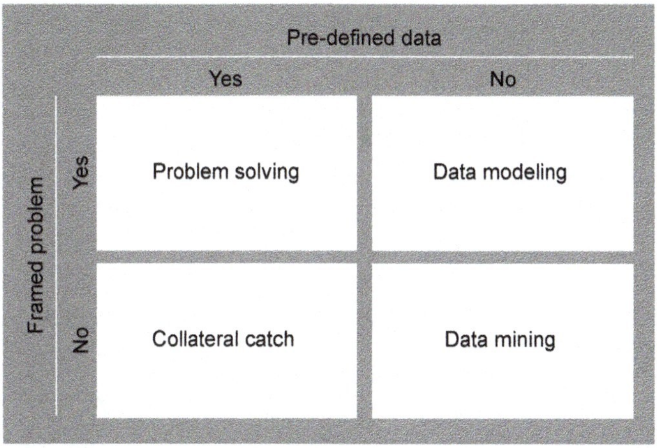

		Pre-defined data	
		Yes	No
Framed problem	Yes	Problem solving	Data modeling
	No	Collateral catch	Data mining

Figure 4.5 Big data analysis strategies

Problem solving

From a scientific perspective a problem-solving analytical strategy is deductive. Usually, the analyst starts with a managerial problem or issue. Problems may involve: "How can we increase the value of our customers?" or "How can we improve the net promoter score (NPS)?" or "Which pricing strategy should I use to attract more profitable customers?" After defining the problem hypotheses, assumptions could be defined, explicitly or implicitly, about potential solutions of the problem. For example, when studying drivers of NPS, analysts could develop a list of potential determinants of NPS, such as advertising, social media messages, the service experience, etc. The specific process, from defining the problem to developing a list of hypotheses, guides the selection of data to be analyzed (see Figure 4.6). Following up on the drivers of NPS, for example, researchers would probably look for data that includes NPS and combine that with data on potential drivers, or alternatively researchers might collect new data. A big difference between this approach and the data mining approach is that researchers do not start with the data. Big data can be used to solve the problem, but it is not a necessity to solve the problem. The problem can also be solved with limited data drawn from existing available data (e.g. a CRM database) or resulting from a new data collection effort (e.g. a survey).

Data modeling

There is also a problem that needs to be solved in the data modeling approach. For example, one objective could be to predict churn (see Figure 4.7). The difference with the problem-solving approach is that the focus is more on data and especially on the use of new data sources. Using new data sources one could, for example, aim to find new potential predictors of churn. One potential pitfall with this approach is that analysts focus too much on the data and lack strong conceptualizations on why specific relationships in the data are found. Outcomes may easily be spurious correlations in which the association is based on an underlying, unobserved variable. The approach may also lead to undesirable outcomes, such as the famous example in which a father of a teenager was offered baby products, because his apparently pregnant daughter purchased baby products using his loyalty program. This is clearly relevant to

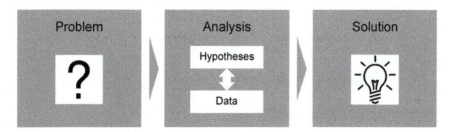

Figure 4.6 Problem-solving process

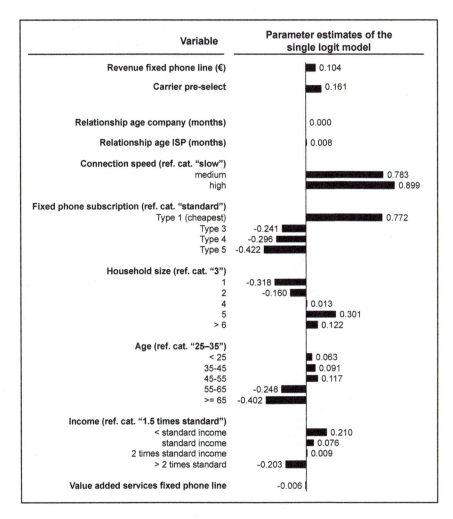

Figure 4.7 Churn model results for telecom firm

Source: Adapted from Risselada et al. (2010)

the privacy and behavioral targeting discussion put forward in Chapter 3.3. The approach can become overly data-driven instead of problem-driven, easily turning into a data-mining exercise. However, an advantage over the problem-solving approach is that the data-modeling approach is more flexible in terms of data usage. This may result in more innovative model solutions.

Data mining

This is a much more explorative analytical strategy. Typically data are not pre-defined and a defined problem does not guide the analysis. Also, no hypotheses are implicitly or explicitly stated. From a scientific perspective it is a typical inductive analysis. The key belief is that the widely available data can provide valuable insights just by digging into the data. In doing so, relevant new relationships can be discovered that can potentially be valuable. The classic data mining example, as mentioned earlier, is that when analyzing the Tesco Club Card data, analysts discovered that customers buying diapers also frequently purchased beer and chips on a Friday night (see Figure 4.8). This finding could be used to target promotions. The discovery of these patterns can create innovations. However, one major potential pitfall is that the analyses are unguided and may result in all kinds of associations that are difficult to interpret. Furthermore, as no specific problems are solved, many of these analyses are of little use, and may not offer any impact.

Collateral catch

The last analytical strategy is not an explicit strategy. It is rather a by-product of a problem focused analysis. When analyzing pre-defined data, analysts may sometimes discover new relationships, which can be very valuable. For example, when analyzing the impact of different touchpoints on conversion rates for an online retailer, we found differences in conversion rates for different devices (e.g. mobile, tablet, desktop), which we were not looking for in our analysis (see Figure 4.9). This induced us to study conversion rates in more depth, and specifically how device switching in the purchase funnel would impact conversion rates. These relationships are called "collateral catches" because they are not sought initially, and only become available as a result of some unusual feature of the research, or through some exploratory analysis being executed next to the more structured problem-solving analysis. One thing we have learned is that analysts should be open to these collateral catches. They may provide a deeper understanding of the phenomenon studied. Furthermore, these catches may be valuable in guiding new directions for solving the defined problem, or in providing new innovations for executing marketing.

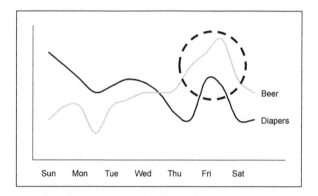

Figure 4.8 Tesco's beer and diaper data

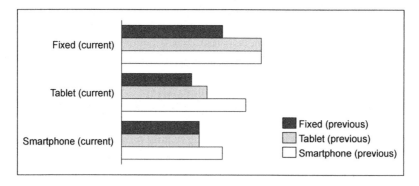

Figure 4.9 Different conversion rates after device switching

Source: Adapted from De Haan, Kannan, Verhoef, & Wiesel (2015)

How big data changes analytics

The growth of big data is changing how analyses will be executed. It will also change the scope of analytical questions to be answered, as more data are available. In our discussion we again focus on three areas of marketing analytics: (1) market; (2) brand and product; and (3) customers. We have noticed that these areas are, as already shown, interrelated, but our experience is that they are treated differently. Moreover, some industries—for example, fast-moving consumer goods (FMCGs)—usually have a typical brand/product focus due to the nature of their markets and product/brand offerings, while other industries (e.g. financial services, telecoms) have a stronger customer focus in their analytics. In these latter industries, firms also typically have more customer data (CRM databases) than the product/brand-focused industries. Market analytics are equally relevant for all firms, as they focus on how markets develop, and what that implies for firm strategies—for example, for allocation of resources across strategic business units (SBUs), brand and product management decisions, and customer strategies.

As already discussed in Chapter 3 one of the major challenges with big data is that data is changing (see for example the 3V model). A very important development with regard to data is that we are moving from single source data to multiple sources of data. This has considerable consequences, as with multi-source data you have to connect data in a smart way. This is not always obvious: connecting can seem easy but one needs a common variable that can be linked (see Chapter 3.1). Connecting data may also involve data connecting at multiple levels. For example, customer data can be linked to time-series data such as that arising from advertising (Prins & Verhoef, 2007); one then has data at different aggregation levels. The challenge here is that there is much variation in data between customers, but that the variation of time (i.e. in advertising or distribution) may be limited, while the number of data points at that level is also small compared to the number of data points at the customer level. This may also induce the use of more complicated models, such as multi-level models. Another important development is that data is becoming more unstructured, with text data being the most important example. But also social network data can be included, especially at the customer level. These data are also inherently complex (e.g. Risselada, Verhoef, & Bijmolt, 2014).

We show how big data is changing the data, analytics, and the relevance/scope of the analytics in Figure 4.10. Based on this schematic overview we discuss some of these developments, focusing mainly on changes in analytics.

Market level changes

At the market level, time series analyses are the most common way of forecasting market developments. However, in the presence of big data, we observe that firms want to assess the impact of specific changes in the environment. This is not impossible with traditional time-series analysis, as in these models explanatory X variables can be included, in models such as VARX and ARMAX (Franses & Van Dijk, 2000). However, the dominating impact of lagged variables and/or trend effects might reduce the effects of explanatory variables such as a changing environment. Moreover, at the aggregated level, environmental changes might not be observed, given that it only impacts a specific customer segment. This may especially hold for disruptive changes (Sood & Tellis, 2011). More specifically, disruptive innovations may be targeted at a relatively small segment in the

		Traditional analytics	Big data analytics
Market	Relevance	• Stable environments	• Turbulent environments with disrupting events
	Data	• Single source time series on forecast variables	• Multi-source time series on multiple variables • Additional unstructured data
	Analytics	• Aggregated analysis (time series) • Trend focused	• Aggregated + disaggregated analysis • Focus on changes in environment • Adaptive forecasting
Brand/product	Relevance	• Brand focus	• Brand accountability focus
	Data	• Single source survey attitude data	• Multi source: sales data, survey data, social data
	Analytics	• Descriptives and profiling • Product attribute analysis	• Text analyses • Linking brand metrics to performance metrics – big data integrated models
Customer	Relevance	• Customer focus	• Customer Engagement Focus
	Data	• Single source CRM data	• Multi source: CRM data, survey data (e.g. NPS), social data, contact data, advertising data
	Analytics	• Descriptives and profiling • Segmentation and migration analysis • Predictive models	• Linking marketing actions to customer performance • Customer journey analysis and dynamic targeting • Social network analysis and sentiment analysis

Figure 4.10 How big data are changing analytics

market, but may be adopted by the majority of the market when it takes off. The early adoption and increasing relevance of this innovation is likely not observed when analyzing aggregate-level data just because the change is too small and the trend is still upwards. To illustrate this we discuss the case of the Dutch telecom industry around 2010. The telecom market had developed strongly in the previous decade, but as the adoption of mobile telephones was reaching maturity, growth was declining. Moreover, the adoption of smartphones such as the iPhone, Blackberry, and the Samsung Galaxy increased the usage of Internet services on mobiles. One of the revenue drivers for telecom firms was the usage of text messages (i.e. SMS). Customers frequently used more text messages than their contract provided for, resulting in higher revenues as usage above the contract levels was priced higher. Hence, this service was really a cash cow. In 2010 a new independent service entered the market: WhatsApp. Through an app on the smartphone, customers could chat with each other for free. The fee for using this app was zero in the first year and after that it cost around 0.70 euro per year. The app was first adopted mainly by young customers. These young customers mainly used a brand focusing on young consumers. On the aggregate level no changes in text usage were found. However, strong changes could be found in a small, but influential segment in the market. The diffusion of WhatsApp was very rapid, and after a few months aggregated sales figures showed decreases in text usage (see Figure 4.11). These changes could, however, not have been predicted with traditional time-series analysis. More deep-diving into segment-level data

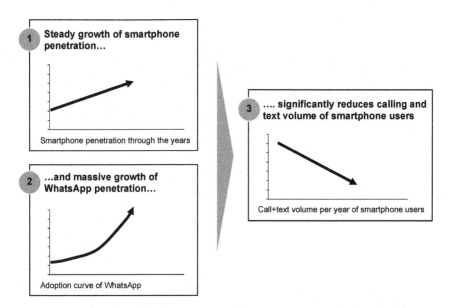

Figure 4.11 Impact of WhatsApp usage on the smartphone usage of a Dutch telecom company

was required to forecast these changes. Unfortunately in many telecom providers, the myopic top management found it hard to believe that these changes at the segment level could actually finally affect the whole customer base. Studying text analyses of online forum discussions could probably have helped to really understand what was happening.[1]

Brand and product changes

Brand and product management analytics traditionally have been rather descriptive, mainly using survey data on brand awareness and/or panel level sales data. These latter data were mainly available at a weekly level for FMCGs as a consequence of the scanner data revolution. Primarily in the academic community, researchers have considered the impact of marketing mix instruments on sales and/or market share (Leeflang, Wittink, Wedel, & Naert, 2000; Nijs, Dekimpe, Steenkamp, & Hanssens, 2001). Similarly, market research agencies have developed models such as ScanPro by AC Nielsen, to assess the impact of promotions on brand sales. The big data development is, however, also affecting brand and product management. Specifically, the use of multi-source data allows brand managers to assess the impact of the marketing mix on attitudinal brand metrics (brand share of mind metrics, i.e. preferences) and their simultaneous impact on sales (e.g. Hanssens, Pauwels, Srinivasan, Vanhuele, & Yildirim, 2014).

The changing nature of big data analytics for brands becomes rather clear in the following example. As a challenger, a Dutch telecom operator has gained a serious market share in a highly competitive market over a period of two years. In order to realize further growth, they wanted to re-position their brand. The company therefore has a strong need for a fact-based approach to underpin their market development strategy. An important insight that made them feel comfortable investing in their brand communication was gained from a multi-source data analysis that showed a positive relation between development of their brand performance (in terms of awareness, consideration, and preference) and their current market position in terms of sales share/ market penetration (see Figure 4.12).

Another development is that digital text analytics results in new metrics, such as digital brand sentiment indices, which can be measured over time without having any surveys. These metrics can be linked to sales, and also to stock prices (e.g. Tirunillai & Tellis, 2012). In specific markets, such as movies, these metrics seem highly relevant for predicting product success (e.g. Onishi & Manchanda, 2012). In general we expect big data to allow for a better assessment of several accountability issues: the effect of investment in brands, share of mind brand metrics, and market performance. New data collection methods, such as a mobile survey, may be used to understand the impact of different touch-points on brand preference (Macdonald, Wilson, & Konuş, 2012; Baxendale, Macdonald, & Wilson, 2015).

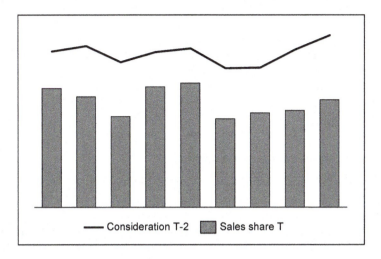

Figure 4.12 Case example of multi-source data analysis of relation between brand performance and sales share

Customer level changes

Major changes are expected at the customer level. Compared with market level and brand/product level data, customer data have already been relatively rich due to the developments in CRM. This increasing presence of data has especially accelerated developments in individual-level models designed to predict individual-level behaviors (e.g. Blattberg, Kim, & Neslin, 2008; Risselada et al., 2010). It also stirred up the development of new metrics, such as CLV (Venkatesan & Kumar, 2004). The big data revolution has pushed single source data of individual customers to one side, to be replaced by multi-source data. Hence, individual data will be enriched with other sources of data. For example, for a European public transport company we enriched individual-level survey data on satisfaction with operations data to fully understand the drivers of customer satisfaction. This provided interesting insights. For example, operations data on punctuality are an important driver of satisfaction (Gijsenberg, Van Heerde, & Verhoef, 2015).

We have already mentioned that individual-level data can be combined with aggregated level marketing data. Similarly social network data can be added. One of the major difficulties of this is that customers interact at different touchpoints online and offline, and similarly with online and offline advertising media. Big data analytics are required for online firms aiming to assess the importance of different online and offline advertising investments on online conversion rates (e.g. De Haan, Wiesel, & Pauwels, 2013).

Another major change is the extension of the customer management paradigm, by focusing more on customer engagement. Customer engagement goes beyond traditional customer transactions; it also focuses on non-transactional behavior of customers, such as word-of-mouth, likes on social media, blog posts etc. (e.g. Van Doorn et al., 2010). Hence models nowadays include social media data, such as individual customer online posts and likes, to account for customer engagement activities (De Vries, Gensler, & Leeflang, 2012). The increasing presence of communities also induces a stronger focus on social networks and the importance of these networks in creating value for firms (e.g. Hennig-Thurau et al., 2010; Libai et al., 2010). This creates a stronger demand for social network analyses.

Generic big data changes in analytics

As discussed in Chapter 2, big data is frequently characterized by the three Vs: Volume, Velocity, and Variety. Sometimes two other Vs are added: Veracity and Value. These changes in data may suggest that analytics will change dramatically, and it is sometimes even referred to as kind of disruptive event (e.g. Sathi, 2012). We have already discussed some changes, such as the movement to more unstructured data, in the previous section. But there are some additional changes, and our views on these changes are described below.

From analyzing samples to analyzing the full population

The increasing volume of data in a big data era suggests that we now can analyze very large databases with millions of observations. We are moving from studying a small sample to studying the full population. The rising computer power of the last few years has facilitated this, while also data storage capacity seems unlimited with sufficient space in the cloud. Indeed, it sounds very cool and convincing when an analyst can report that millions of observations have been analyzed. The advantages of analyzing very large databases is, however, relatively small. Actually, the outcomes of analysis of a true random sample of observations of a population of millions should not differ substantially from the analysis of the full population. It is not the volume that is important, it is important whether the analyzed sample is representative of the population studied. Volume is only important in order to get more reliable answers at a higher significance level. An analyst should, however, be more concerned about biases due to a wrong representation of customers, brands etc. in their data, rather than the volume of the data. This is not to say that the size of the analyzed sample is not relevant. Increases in lower numbers of sample size (e.g. moving from 400 to 2,000 observations) can be especially valuable, as reliability may increase and also specific econometric issues, such as collinear independent variables, may become less of an issue. However, moving from 20,000 to 50,000 observations or to 100,000 observations will become less rewarding for analytical purposes. In general we provide the following simple rules for when larger samples become more valuable:

- If more variables are studied in an analysis and specifically when studying the effects of multiple variables on an outcome variable
- If one needs to study different sub-samples. The sub-sample should be of sufficient size to analyze
- If there is much heterogeneity. For example, customers may differ strongly in how they behave, and how they respond to marketing actions
- If the studied variable occurs very rarely (e.g. conversion on an email campaign) and a sufficient number of data points is required to understand the drivers of this event
- If there is strong collinearity between the independent variables used to predict or explain a dependent variable, such as sales or churn.

Importantly, although the volume of available data is indeed increasing, we observe that it is not happening for all types of data. At the individual customer level, data volumes have indeed become huge and can be enriched with many others. Especially in the online environment, data can become massive. However, brand-level data on, for example, brand sales, brand preferences, and advertising are frequently still limited. For example, for a European public transport company we analyzed the effects of advertising on travelled kilometers per month, and while having three years of data this only resulted in 31 data points (Gijsenberg & Verhoef, 2015).

From significance to substantive and size effects

Analyzing large samples frequently leads to many highly significant effects. Small p-values seem the norm rather than the exception. However, in a big data era with these large samples, we argue that we should move away from significance and focus more on the size of these effects. With effect size we look for whether the found effects are substantial or small. For example, there might be a difference of one year in the average age between switching and loyal customers (e.g. 43 vs. 42 years), which is highly significant in a big data analysis. However, one might question the size of this difference. Should a firm then focus more on younger customers to prevent switching, as these customers are less loyal? Similarly, the addition of variables in an explanatory model will certainly frequently increase the explained variance of a model. The key focus should then be on the size of this additional explanatory power—is it really substantial or is it only incremental? Further, it is not only the size of the effect that should matter, but also the substantive and managerial meaning of a found effect. Going back to the loyalty example, one might question the managerial implication of such an effect. Should a firm develop different specific strategies for younger customers than they do for older customers, as young customers are more likely to switch? We have some specific recommendations for actions that an analyst should take when interpreting big data results:

- Focus on the size of the significant effects instead of significance only
- Visualize the found effects and consider the effect sizes
- Compare the found effects with existing benchmarks (e.g. when assessing the effectiveness of social media, one could compare it with the effect of traditional advertising)
- Develop marketing implications for found effects and challenge them.

From ad hoc data collection to continuous data collection

We have moved from ad hoc projects with data to continuous data collection. We consider four types of research-based data designs on two characteristics (see Figure 4.13):

1 Repetitions of respondents
2 Repetition of measures.

Ad hoc data projects frequently involve survey data collection efforts to answer specific questions such as, "What are customers looking for in a new product?" or "How can my brand best be positioned?" Ad hoc data for specific issues can also be collected among the same sample of respondents using a panel. This will frequently occur if a firm works with a marketing research agency applying an online panel, and if it does happen, there might be opportunities for a big data analyst to link the specific data collection efforts. What we now observe very frequently is data collection in which different samples are used to collect these data, which typically will be data on value-to-customer (V2C) metrics. This can involve monthly tracking of brand evaluations using an online marketing research panel and continuous survey research on satisfaction and NPS and other customer feedback metrics. In these kinds of studies different customers provide answers on the same measure, which allows firms to track their performance

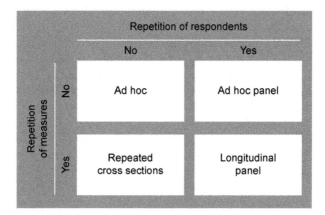

Figure 4.13 Different types of data approaches

on these metrics. However, customers cannot be followed over time, and this therefore leads to repeated cross-sections. The average performance of these studies can be linked to input variables, such as service performance affecting service quality perceptions (Gijsenberg et al., 2015) or brand preference metrics explaining brand sales (Srinivasan, Vanhuele, & Pauwels, 2010). However, customers are not easily followed. Here smart data fusion techniques, in which look-a-likes are being looked for in the different samples, might be a solution. Due to the larger number of individuals in a segment, these variations cancel out, so to speak, and the observed patterns become more reliable. Longitudinal panel data are readily available in good customer databases in which customer behavior is tracked over time. The longitudinal behavior of visitors can also be followed, in an online environment, by using cookies. Longitudinal measuring of V2C metrics among the same group of respondents is possible, but a huge challenge, as customers will drop out just by not responding to the next survey (e.g. Verhoef, 2003). Longitudinal data do, however, have the advantage that one can study how changes at the customer level affect their behavior (Verhoef, Franses & Donkers, 2002). We have the following recommendations:

- Set up continuous research on key (V2C) metrics
- Be aware that cross-sections do have similar sample characteristics over time
- Be consistent in the measurement of your important metrics. Consistency allows the big data analysts to report and analyze these metrics over time
- A longitudinal panel is not the holy grail! Repeated cross-sections can work rather effectively for many purposes.

From standard to computer science models

The development of big data is partially embraced by IT and computer science. This is of course not illogical, as IT developments have been a driving force behind big data developments. Computer scientists have developed various methods of analyzing data over the last few decades: one of the most famous early examples was the so-called "neural networks." More recently, different machine-learning techniques have been added, some of which have gained attention in the marketing literature. Probably the most important one is the "bagging-boosting" technique, which estimates specific more standard models on a large number of sub-samples, aiming to come up with the best prediction (e.g Lemmens & Croux, 2006; Risselada et al., 2010). One of the main problems that many people face with computer-science-based models is that it is frequently considered a "black box." That is, it is not clear to analysts what the model actually does and how it is specified. Models in marketing typically have an econometric background and can be specified (e.g. Leeflang et al., 2000). An advantage of these models is that they are more strongly based on ex-ante set expectations of effects, whereas computer science models may easily lead to data mining, without a strong theoretical and practical base.

The evidence of a stronger performance of computer science models is mixed. In general it seems difficult to come up with the best model across applications. Studying around 14 different databases, Donkers, Lemmens and Verhoef (2014) report that there is no method that is consistently winning. The probability that a method performs best seems to highly depend on the data being analyzed. They therefore propose that the best way to get good results is to combine the different methods, taking advantage of the strength of each of the methods. Some recommendations for analysts to follow when applying models are:

- Understand the backgrounds and pitfalls of (new) models before applying them
- Be inherently skeptical about the communicated performance of (new) models by software providers
- Test the performance of different methods on data being analyzed
- Select a method that can be communicated to marketing managers and has a good performance. That is, find optimal balance between performance and managerial insightfulness
- Use visual aids to communicate findings of specifically computer-science-based methods.

From ad hoc models to real-time models

In an environment where data become easily available, we move to a trend where models can be updated much more frequently. The need for model updates is clearly shown in extant research. Especially in more turbulent environments models can easily become outdated and as a consequence their findings are no longer valid and their prediction quality decreases. For example, in a telecom setting Risselada et al. (2010) show that the predictive performance of models decreases substantially in periods further away from the time when the model was developed (see Figure 4.14).

Luckily data is now available much more quickly, so that updating models is much easier. Especially in the online environment, data can be available in real time. This provides opportunities for constantly updating models with new data in constantly changing (online) environments. These models can then be used in online targeting. This move to constantly updated models probably won't happen in offline environments. However, here also we advocate more model updating, as it is unlikely that model results hold for a long time. The dynamics of today's market, with frequently changing market environments and changing customer behaviors, require a constant updating of models. We have some recommendations:

- Assess the stability of a developed model and the predictive performance of a model over time

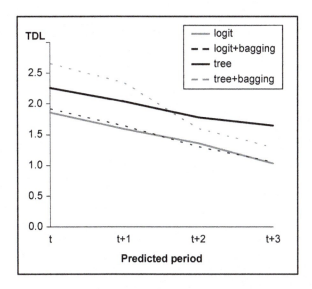

Figure 4.14 Average top-decile lifts of model estimated at time

Source: Adapted from Risselada et al. (2010)

- Do not expect your model-results, resulting insights and predictive performance to have eternal life
- In online environments base models can be updated to real-time models for targeting purposes with real-time data as input.

Conclusions

In this chapter we have focused on analytics. We specifically discussed the power of analytics. We strongly believe that analytics can improve the quality of marketing decisions and induce smarter marketing decisions. Analytics can focus on building insights, (predictive) models, and optimization models. It is important to distinguish between static and dynamic analyses, as well as between predictive and explanatory analyses. We clearly have laid out different analysis methods. We have a strong preference for approaches that are more problem-solving in nature. The big data environment is changing analytics in every marketing decision. We have discussed these changes and specifically focused on some frequently stated developments, such as the need for larger analysis samples. In the in-depth chapters we will discuss existing analytical classics (Chapter 4.1) and new big data analytics (Chapter 4.2), while we also describe how story-telling and visualization can be effective in creating analytics that have more impact.

Note

1 More about this classic case in telecom can be read in www.telecompaper.com/pressrelease/dutch-consumers-turn-to-mobile-apps-for-communication-needs-43-of-smartphone-users-has-whatsapp-installed--813359 (retrieved on October 30 2015).

References

Baxendale, S., Macdonald, E. K., & Wilson, H. N. (2015). Impact of different touchpoints on brand consideration. *Journal of Retailing*, 91(2), 235–53.

Blattberg, R. C., Kim, B.-D., & Neslin, S. A. (2008). *Database marketing – Analyzing and managing customers.* New York: Springer Science & Business Media.

Davenport, T., & Harris, J. (2007). *Competing on analytics – The new science of winning.* Boston, MA: Harvard Business School Press.

De Haan, E., Kannan, P. K., Verhoef P. C., & Wiesel T. (2015), *The impact of device switching on conversion rates.* Working Paper, University of Groningen.

De Haan, E., Wiesel, T., & Pauwels, K. (2013). Which advertising forms make a difference in online path to purchase? *MSI working paper series*, Boston.

De Vries, L., Gensler, S., & Leeflang, P. S. H. (2012). Popularity of brand posts on brand fan pages: An investigation of the effects of social media marketing. *Journal of Interactive Marketing*, 26(2), 83–91.

Donkers, B., Lemmens, A., & Verhoef, P. C. (2014). *The predictive power of churn models.* Working Paper, Erasmus University Rotterdam.

Donkers, B., Verhoef, P. C., & De Jong, M. G. (2007). Predicting CLV: A test of competing models in the insurance industry. *Quantitative Marketing and Economics*, 5(2), 163–90.

Franses, P. H., & Van Dijk, D. (2000). *Non-linear time series models in empirical finance.* Cambridge: Cambridge University Press.

Germann, F., Lilien, G. L., & Rangaswamy, A. (2012). Performance implications of deploying marketing analytics. *International Journal of Research in Marketing*, 30(2), 114–28.

Germann, F., Lilien, G., Fiedler, L., & Kraus, M. (2014). Do retailers benefit from deploying customer analytics? *Journal of Retailing*, 90(4), 587–93.

Gijsenberg, M. J., Van Heerde, H. J., & Verhoef, P. C. (2015). Losses loom longer than gains: Modeling the impact of service crises on customer satisfaction over time. *Journal of Marketing Research*, 52(5), 642–56.

Gijsenberg, M. J. & Verhoef, P. C. (2015). Moving Forward: The Role of Marketing in Fostering Public Transport Usage, *Working Paper*, University of Groningen.

Hanssens, D. M., Pauwels, K. H., Srinivasan, S., Vanhuele, M., & Yildirim, G. (2014). Consumer attitude metrics for guiding marketing mix decisions. *Marketing Science*, 33(4), 534–50.

Hennig-Thurau, T., Malthouse, E. C., Friege, C., Gensler, S., Lobschat, L., & Rangaswamy, A. (2010). The impact of new media on customer relationships. *Journal of Service Research*, 1(3), 311–30.

Hoekstra, J. C., & Verhoef, P. C. (2011). *The customer intelligence–marketing interface: Its effect on firm performance.* Working Paper, University of Groningen.

Holtrop, N., Wieringa, J. E., Gijsenberg, M. J., & Verhoef, P. C. (2014). *No future without the past? Predicting customer churn with limited past data.* Working Paper, University of Gronigen.

Humby, C., Hunt, T., & Phillips, T. (2008). *Scoring points: How Tesco is winning customer loyalty.* Philadelphia: Kogan Page Publishers.

Leeflang, P. S. H., Bijmolt, T. H. A., Doorn, J., Hanssens, D. M., Van Heerde, H. J., Verhoef, P. C., & Wieringa, J. E. (2009). Creating lift versus building the base: Current trends in marketing dynamics. *International Journal of Research in Marketing*, 26(1), 13–20.

Leeflang, P. S. H., Wittink, D. R., Wedel, M., & Naert, P. A. (2000). *Building Models for Marketing Decisions*. Dordrecht, the Netherlands: Kluwer Academic Publishers.

Lemmens, A., & Croux, C. (2006). Bagging and boosting classification trees to predict churn. *Journal of Marketing Research*, 43(2), 276–86.

Libai, B., Bolton, R., Bügel, M. S., De Ruyter, K., Götz, O., Risselada, H., & Stephen, A. T. (2010). Customer-to-customer interactions: Broadening the scope of word of mouth research. *Journal of Service Research*, 13(3), 267–82.

Macdonald, E. K., Wilson, H. N., & Konuş, U. (2012). Better customer insight – in real time. *Harvard Business Review*, 90(9), 102–8.

Nijs, V. R., Dekimpe, M. G., Steenkamp, J.-B. E. M., & Hanssens, D. M. (2001). The category-demand effects of price promotions. *Marketing Science*, 20(1), 1–22.

Onishi, H., & Manchanda, P. (2012). Marketing activity, blogging and sales. *International Journal of Research in Marketing*, 2(3), 221–34.

Prins, R., & Verhoef, P. C. (2007). Marketing communication drivers of adoption timing of a new e-service among existing customers. *Journal of Marketing*, 71(2), 169–83.

Risselada, H., Verhoef, P. C., & Bijmolt, T. H. A. (2010). Staying power of churn prediction models. *Journal of Interactive Marketing*, 24(3), 198–208.

Risselada, H., Verhoef, P. C., & Bijmolt, T. H. A. (2014). Dynamic effects of social influence and direct marketing on the adoption of high-technology products. *Journal of Marketing*, 78(2), 52–68.

Rust, R. T, & Verhoef, P. C. (2005). Optimizing the marketing interventions mix in intermediate-term CRM. *Marketing Science*, 24(3), 477–89.

Sathi, A. (2012). *Big Data Analytics – Disruptive technologies for changing the game*. Boise: MC Press Online.

Sood, A., & Tellis, G. J. (2011). Demystifying disruption: A new model for understanding and predicting disruptive technologies. *Marketing Science*, 30(2), 339–54.

Srinivasan, S., Vanhuele, M., & Pauwels, K. (2010). Mindset metrics in market response models: An integrative approach. *Journal of Marketing Research*, 47(4), 672–84.

Tirunillai, S., & Tellis, G. J. (2012). Does chatter really matter? Dynamics of user-generated content and stock performance. *Marketing Science*, 31(2), 198–215.

Van Doorn, J., Lemon, K. E., Mittal, V., Naβ, S., Pick, D., Pirner, P., Verhoef, P. C. (2010). Customer engagement behavior: Theoretical foundations and research directions. *Journal of Service Research*, 13(3), 253–66.

Van Nierop, E., Fok, D., & Franses, P. H. (2008). Interaction between shelf layout and marketing effectiveness and its impact on optimizing shelf arrangements. *Marketing Science*, 27(6), 1065–82.

Venkatesan, R., & Kumar, V. (2004). A customer lifetime value framework for customer selection and resource allocation strategy. *Journal of Marketing*, 68(4), 106–215.

Verhoef, P.C. (2003). Understanding the effect of customer relationship management efforts on customer retention and customer share development. *Journal of Marketing*, 67(4), 30–45.

Verhoef, P. C., Franses, P. H., & Donkers, B. (2002). Changing perceptions and changing behavior in customer relationships. *Marketing Letters*, 13(2), 121–34.

4.1 Classic data analytics

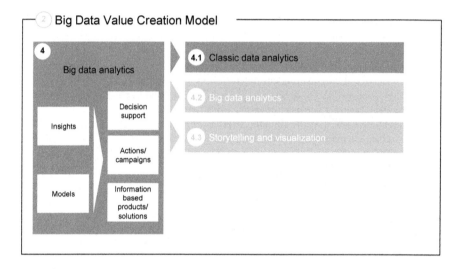

Introduction

Marketing analytics have been around for decades. Especially since the 1960s, marketing scientists and market research and consulting agencies have developed several models and techniques to analyze data. In particular, as early as the 1970s, econometric models were becoming popular. Leeflang and Naert (1978) published an influential book on the application of econometric models in marketing, and marketing scholars such as Philip Kotler and Gary Lilien, produced handbooks on marketing models (e.g. Lilien, Kotler, & Moorthy, 1992; Lilien & Rangaswamy, 2006). These models were mainly used for market and brand analytics. Several models have been applied and market researchers such as AC Nielsen advocated the use of specific models to, for example, predict the effects of promotions on sales, for example by using the SCANPRO model (Wittink, Addona, Hawkes, & Porter, 2011; Leeflang et al., 2015). A model frequently cited for its enormous success in business is Conjoint Analysis, used to measure customer preferences for specific attributes (Roberts, Kayandé, & Stremersch, 2014). By the 1990s David Shepard and Associates successfully demonstrated the use of analytics in direct marketing to increase profits (David Shepard Associates, 1999). Early in 2000 a limited number of firms adopted prediction models for customer behavior. With the growth of customer relationship management (CRM), the attention on and application of individual models predicting individual customer behavior increased sharply (Blattberg, Kim, & Neslin, 2008; Verhoef, Spring, Hoekstra, & Leeflang, 2002; Verhoef, Hoekstra, & Van der Scheer, 2009).

Overview of analytics

In this chapter we will discuss a selection of classic data analytics. Based on our discussion in Chapter 4, we will classify these analytics based on their:

- application area (market, brand, customer)
- whether they are descriptive or predictive; and
- whether they are a static or dynamic method.

In Table 4.1.1 we show our selection of seven classic techniques. We in no way claim that this is an exhaustive list; we solely base our discussion on what we observe as important techniques in marketing practice. We start with descriptives as in many cases these are still very important given that they are frequently used for management reporting in, for example, marketing dashboards. Also, profiling is still rather descriptive in nature, as it usually reports descriptives on specific variables of different brands/customer groups. The next classics involve more complicated and frequently multivariate analytical techniques, such as cluster analysis and regression. We will continue with a discussion of each of these seven "classics."

Classic 1: Reporting

With reporting, analysts aim to provide management information on some relevant descriptive statistics on specific KPIs, such as market share, customer satisfaction, and/or customer profitability. Reporting is especially important in marketing dashboards and specific tooling to facilitate them has been developed in business intelligence software such as IBM Cognos and SAP Business Objects. Averages or means are probably most frequently reported (e.g. average satisfaction score). It is not our objective here to discuss all these statistics in depth, as we assume they are rather basic and should be known to readers of this book. If not, we refer to basic statistics books and marketing research books (see Malhotra, 2010). However, we still observe some common mistakes when reporting KPIs:

- Be aware of the measurement scale: Multiple variables are measured using non-metric scales—for instance churn might be measured by a simple yes/no. Averages can then not be calculated. In these instances percentages should be reported (i.e. churn rate).

Table 4.1.1 Seven classic data analytics

Classics	Description	Application area	Method/techniques	Focus	Method
1 Reporting	Descriptive statistics provided that are used to summarize and describe data.	Management information on relevant KPIs for all application area's	Counts, percentages, central tendency, variability, dispersion	De	St
2 Profiling	A description of a customer or a group of customers that includes demographic, geographic, and psychographic characteristics, as well as buying patterns, creditworthiness, and purchase history.	Brand: profiling target groups. Customer: understanding differences in customer needs and behavior, identifying look-alikes	Frequencies, cross tabs, indices, variance analysis, decile analysis, gain chart analysis	De	St
3 Migration analysis	Analyzing the movement of individual customers over time in terms of behavior product usage, or value.	Customer: In/outflow analysis, up/down sell, customer value development	L4L, cohort analysis, survival analysis	De	Dy
4 (Customer) Segmentation	Dividing a market or customer base into groups of individuals that are similar in specific ways relevant to marketing, such as age, gender, interests, spending habits, and so on.	Brand: for positioning, developing product differentiation strategies. Customer: differentiation in offering services, pricing, etc.	Cluster analysis, principle component analysis (PCA), latent class analysis	De	St

(Continued)

Table 4.1.1 (Continued)

Classics	Description	Application area	Method/techniques	Focus	Method
5 Trend analysis & market forecasting	Analysis that aims to explain and predict marketing metrics (e.g. sales, market share) over time using time series data. Based on these analyses the effects of marketing instruments can be assessed.	Market/brand: market size forecasting, product diffusion, brand sales forecasting, marketing mix elasticities	Trend analysis, regression models, time series analysis, VAR models	Pr	St
6 Product attribute analysis	Collection of methods and techniques that aims to understand the importance of impact of product and service attributes. Specifically the contribution of each attribute to the product utility is assessed.	Product/brand: new product development	Stated importance, regression analysis, conjoint analysis	De Pr	Dy
7 Predictive modeling	Collection of techniques having in common the goal of finding a relationship between a customer response, variable and various predictor or "independent" variables with the goal in mind of measuring future values of those predictors and inserting them into the mathematical relationship to predict future values of the target variable.	Customer response prediction, churn Prediction, Cross-selling predictions, lifetime value calculations	Answer trees, regression/logit, bagging-boosting, hazard models	Pr	Dy

De: Descriptive; Pr: Predictive; St: Static; Dy: Dynamic

- Averages can be misleading: Only looking at the average can be misleading, especially when there is much heterogeneity. Therefore, we strongly recommend not only looking at overarching statistics, but also at the distribution of variables. In this regard, descriptives such as the standard deviation can be useful. Graphically, box plots can be shown. A histogram is also very useful. A histogram can, for example, show that there are two segments of customers when considering a customer feedback metric: haters and lovers. Inventing some numbers for this metric (see Figure 4.1.1), an average might then report a score around 6, and this average is not very informative, as apparently there are very unsatisfied customers (scoring around 4) and very satisfied customers (scoring around 8).
- Focus on extremes: To outperform competition an average performance is frequently no longer sufficient. Firms need to delight customers and have extremely well evaluated brands to successfully compete. Marketing metric reporting should therefore go beyond only reporting averages, and also consider extreme responses. This is specifically important for customer feedback metrics, in which top2-boxes or specific transformations such as the net promoter score (NPS) can be very valuable (see also our discussion in Chapter 2.1).
- Report trends: Reporting on the current status can be informative, but managers will be more interested in the trend. Is the churn rate going down? Are customers becoming more satisfied? Does our brand image improve? Does the market grow? In that sense, specific trend metrics such as growth rates can be very informative descriptors. Static descriptors then become more dynamic and will raise specific questions (see Figure 4.1.2 for a sales trend).

Finally, we note that descriptive analyses can be very valuable as the first step in an analysis. The analyst gets more knowledge about the different data and their development over time. Moreover, a descriptive analysis may show whether

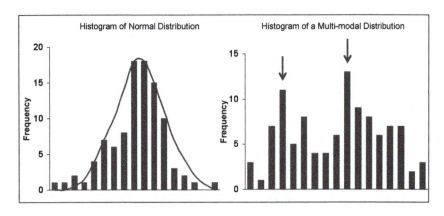

Figure 4.1.1 Different distributions causing similar averages

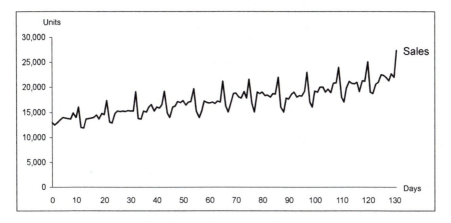

Figure 4.1.2 Example of time series for sales

there are specific mistakes in the data and/or specific outliers (abnormal observations). We therefore strongly recommend analysts to first do some descriptive analyses before executing more complicated techniques.

Classic 2: Profiling

With profiling, analysts aim to provide a description of brands and customer segments. For example, researchers may want to compare Apple vs. Samsung vs. Blackberry users on specific variables, such as age, education, and gender. Similarly, customer segments can be compared in terms of response to marketing offers, churn, customer lifetime value (CLV), etc. These analyses may help firms to improve their understanding of characteristics of subgroups and segments, which in turn may be useful for tailoring propositions. In customer management it can be useful to identify look-alikes for acquisition campaigns. To achieve this, crossings should be made. This just means that per brand or customer segment descriptive information is provided. For simplicity we will discuss these techniques for customer level analyses.

Customer crossings

Depending on the measurement scale of the customer characteristic, different descriptive statistics are provided. For continuous and interval scales averages are usually reported. Using analysis of variance, an F-test can assess the existence of significant differences between customer groups. For ordinal and nominal scales percentages, reflecting the percentage occurrence of a specific characteristic in a customer group, is calculated. To assess the presence of significant differences between groups Chi-square tests can be used. These tests are frequently significant with large samples, and one should be careful by only looking at significance levels here (see also Chapter 4). In this book we assume some basic knowledge of these tests, and we refer to the basic marketing textbook of Malhotra (2010) for a more in-depth discussion for interested readers.

One important issue is how to present the outcomes of customer crossings in a way which allows readers to quickly understand differences between customer groups. One useful way is to index the value for each group, where the index is the value of the descriptive (e.g. average) within a group divided by the average for the whole customer base multiplied by one hundred. In Figure 4.1.3 we show this indexation for profiling of new customers on age classification. As a kind of rule of thumb analysts typically consider an index larger than 110 or smaller than 90 as "substantial." However, one should be careful with small cell sizes, as in these instances differences can be very large in terms of indices, while they are not actually significant.

Decile analysis

A frequently used technique to divide customers based on their value is decile analysis. With this method customers are divided into ten equal sized groups, each consisting of 10% of the customer database. These groups are ranked, where the segment with the lowest average value gets rank 10 and the segment with the highest average value is ranked as 1. In a subsequent analysis, ranked segments can be characterized by specific variables. These variables may include customer characteristics such as customer revenues, margins, or responses to marketing activities. For example, for each customer profitability decile the average age can be calculated, or the average retention rate (see Figure 4.1.4). We carried out a decile analysis for a book club, based on the monetary value of each customer. In a subsequent analysis, we calculated the average retention rate in test mailing. As can be observed from Figure 4.1.4, the average retention rate is highest in decile 6, which does not have the highest monetary value. Actually the retention rate is relatively low for the most valuable segment.

Age	Total Base		New Customers		
	#	%	#	%	Index
younger then 25 years	60,000	5	6,000	7	149
25–35 years	150,000	12	14,000	17	139
35–45 years	280,000	22	23,000	27	122
45–55 years	310,000	25	18,000	21	86
55–65 years	250,000	20	15,000	18	89
65 years or older	200,000	16	8,000	10	60
Total	1,250,000	100	84,000	100	100

Figure 4.1.3 Profiling new customers on age classification

Deciles	Average monetary value (x 1000)	Average retention rate %	Index
1	385	78	91
2	314	81	94
3	283	80	93
4	253	95	110
5	223	96	112
6	192	97	113
7	160	95	110
8	127	93	108
9	90	75	87
10	46	70	81
Total	207	86	100

Figure 4.1.4 Decile analysis for monetary value and retention rates

A decile analysis is often referred to as a gains chart analysis for customer response analysis. This gains chart is actually very similar to decile analysis. The deciles are ranked based on their response probability. Some subsequent calculations can be done to calculate the margin per decile and the deciles with a positive margin can be selected for targeting (see Figure 4.1.5).

External profiling

So far, we have mainly discussed analyses where we compare customer segments with other segments. One could label this an internal customer profiling analysis. However, managers are also interested in the profile of their customers (segments) in comparison with the rest of the market. For this purpose, firms use external profiling analyses. In this analysis, characteristics of a firm's customers (groups) are compared with customer characteristics in the market or population. Again, indexing is frequently used to make these comparisons. Using these indices, one could for example say that customers of a private bank are two times as wealthy as the average bank customer.

Decile	Mail	Response	Response rate %	Response index	Revenue €	Cost of response €	Margin €	Average margin €
1	10,000	3,300	33	**266**	49,500	15,000	**34,500**	**10.45**
2	10,000	1,500	15	**121**	22,500	15,000	**7,500**	**5.00**
3	10,000	1,300	13	**105**	19,500	15,000	**4,500**	**3.46**
4	10,000	1,300	13	**105**	19,500	15,000	**4,500**	**3.46**
5	10,000	1,200	12	97	18,000	15,000	**3,000**	**2.50**
6	10,000	1,200	12	97	18,000	15,000	**3,000**	**2.50**
7	10,000	900	9	73	13,500	15,000	−1,500	1.67
8	10,000	900	9	73	13,500	15,000	−1,500	1.67
9	10,000	600	6	48	9,000	15,000	−6,000	10.00
10	10,000	200	2	16	3,000	15,000	−12,000	60.00
Total	100,000	12,400	12	100	186,000	150,000	36,000	2.90

Figure 4.1.5 Gain chart analysis for book club

Zip code analysis

One specific external profiling analysis is the incorporation of zip codes. External data providers, such as Acxiom and Experian, have specific zip-code-level information (see Chapter 3). Using this information firms can gain an understanding about which zip codes and thus local/regional areas, over- or underrepresent their customers. Along with this zip code information, these external data suppliers also have developed specific segments, such as "rural families" and "single households." For example, an online retailer may find that rural families are over-represented in their customer base, while the single household is almost not represented at all. Again indexing can be very useful. To calculate the index, one needs to divide the frequency percentage of zip code segments within the customer base/group by the frequency percentage of these zip code segments within the population.

In Figure 4.1.6 we show an actual example of a clothing retailer. This company aims to compare its clientele with the population. As can be observed from the analysis, the Prestige Positions, Aspiring Homemakers, Family Basics and Transient Renters are overrepresented in the customer base.

Similar analyses can be done at the brand level. In Figure 4.1.7 we show how each segment contributes to the sales of fair trade and total coffee. As one can observe, the demanding segment takes care of 24% of total coffee sales and 40% of fair trade coffee sales. This implies that the demanding segment is a very interesting segment for fair trade coffee with an above fair share of 167 [(40/24) × 100].

Some practical guidelines

There are some specific issues an analyst can encounter when running a profiling analysis:

Classic data analytics 149

MOSAIC Segment	Customers	%	Total pop.	%	Index
A. City Prosperity	1,781	1	733,402	4	35
B. Prestige Positions	23,113	18	1,332,251	7	250
C. Country Living	2,525	2	627,460	3	58
D. Rural Reality	11,083	9	3,714,825	20	43
E. Senior Security	4,006	3	524,909	3	110
F. Suburban Stability	9,378	7	901,103	5	150
G. Domestic Success	1,492	1	430,100	2	50
H. Aspiring Homemakers	6,329	5	506,810	3	180
I. Family Basics	51,453	40	4,120,614	22	180
J. Transient Renters	5,990	5	411,100	2	210
K. Municipal Challenge	894	1	322,113	2	40
L. Vintage Value	6.484	5	849,614	5	110
M. Modest Traditions	2,713	2	3,555,299	19	11
N. Urban Cohesion	1,361	1	490,589	3	40
O. Rental Hubs	1,132	1	217,521	1	75
Total	129,733	100	18,737,710	100	100

Figure 4.1.6 External profiling for a clothing retailer using Zip code segmentation

- The number of variables can be large. Profiling becomes then rather difficult, as the number of comparisons on specific variables becomes too much. We therefore strongly recommend to either focus on a limited number of pre-selected variables or to reduce the number of profiling variables by using principal components analysis (PCA), as explained in Box 4.1.1 later in this chapter.
- One should be careful with over-interpreting differences between groups. One common mistake is that the analysis reveals that a firm is overrepresented in a specific lifestyle segment. Firms may then only want to target this segment. However, this segment can be rather small. So one should look beyond the profiles, but also consider factors such as segment size.
- Differences in profile analyses can become easily significant, especially when analyzing large data. As already discussed in Chapter 4, one should not only focus on significance but also on the size of the found differences.
- Profiling is a univariate analysis in which one considers studies with a maximum of two variables. In essence, these are just associations and one should be very careful in interpreting these associations, as there can be spurious correlations. Causal inferences cannot be made!

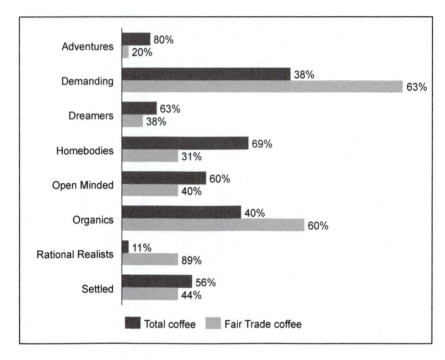

Figure 4.1.7 Sales share per customer segment for total coffee and fair trade coffee

Source: adapted from GfK panel services[1]

- Crossings with continuous variables are not very insightful given the large number of possible cells. One way to overcome this is to create sub-groups in the continuous variable. Actually the decile analysis is a way to do this (and it can be done with fewer subgroups—e.g. quartiles—as well. This may help analysts to gain more insights on how a variable is associated with other variables.

Classic 3: Migration analysis

Migration analysis can be used to investigate the development of customers and brand or product usage over time. This migration analysis is frequently required to understand changes in aggregate sales figures over time. Changes in numbers of transactions, number of customers, turnover etc. are often reported, especially in financial reports, but many of the changes are not major, and this tends to suggest that everything is stable. However, there are multiple behaviors hidden under the surface of these aggregate figures. Important value drivers may change: new customers are being acquired, customers may churn, cross-selling and down-selling and product and brand switches may occur (e.g. Verhoef, Van Doorn, & Dorotić, 2007). To capture value development over time, analysts need to gain insights into how customer status (e.g. churn) and behavior is

Classic data analytics 151

changing over time. Although on a year-by-year basis changes may be limited, over a longer time period structural changes in the underlying value drivers (e.g. lower acquisition rates, continued down sell), can have dramatic effects. In Figure 4.1.8 we provide an example for a telecom provider. In Figures 4.1.8 to 4.1.12 we provide fictive figures to illustrate the Like-4-Like (L4L) analysis.

On a yearly basis there are changes, but they are not very dramatic. However, over five years, 5% of the customers are lost. The question is: what happened? A first analysis of the underlying value drivers, in which the base is decomposed in churners and new acquired customers, shows that the number of acquired customers is not sufficient in size to overcome the loss of customers due to churn (see Figure 4.1.9).

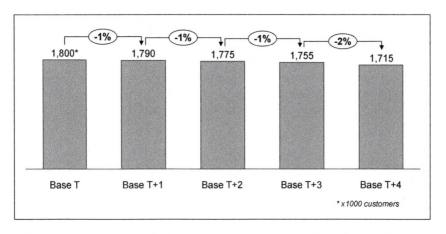

Figure 4.1.8 Falling subscription base for a telecom provider

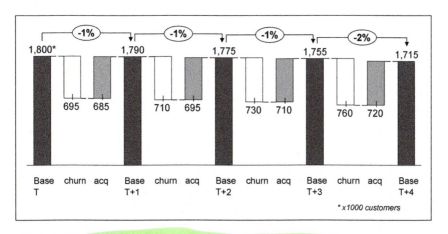

Figure 4.1.9 Decomposing subscription base in acquisition and churn

Migration matrix

A classical way to show migrations within the customer base is to use a migration matrix. These migration matrices show how customers change from one period (t) to the next period (t+1). In Figure 4.1.10, we show how the customers at time t, purchasing different services from a telecom firm, move in terms of their purchase behavior. For example, of the 72,500 customers purchasing products A, B, and C, 15,000 churned, while 26,000 customers kept the same product bundle. However, some customers also have a down sell. In this figure we could also have chosen to show percentage values. Although the migration matrix has its advantages, it also has two disadvantages that make it hard for managers to understand:

1. The large number of combinations in these migration matrices means that the matrix is difficult to interpret. Although Figure 4.1.10 seems insightful, it already has 64 combinations (8 × 8). If in these tables percentages are also added, the number of figures to be processed becomes enormous.
2. Using a migration matrix only one KPI can be shown. For example in Figure 4.1.10 we only show number of customers in a group. However, one might also like to know the revenues and the CLV.

Product combination & migration		Base T+1							Outfow	Total
		A&B&C	A&B	A&C	B&C	A	B	C		
Base T	A&B&C	26,000	9,000	12,000	5,000	2,000	3,000	500	15,000	57,500
	A&B	15,000	48,000	500	1,000	22,000	18,000	1,000	50,000	105,500
	A&C	12,000	4,000	95,000	2,000	30,000	2,000	8,000	95,000	153,000
	B&C	500	500	1,000	12,000	500	1,000	1,000	5,000	16,500
	A	8,000	20,000	12,000	1,000	445,000	18,000	5,000	450,000	509,000
	B	2,000	5,000	500	3,000	2,000	105,000	500	120,000	118,000
	C	500	500	2,000	500	500	500	31,000	25,000	35,500
	Inflow	20,000	45,000	90,000	10,000	420,000	105,000	30,000	-	720,000
	Total	64,000	87,000	123,000	24,500	502,500	147,500	47,000	760,000	1,715,000

Figure 4.1.10 Migration matrix of customers of a telecom firm

Like-4-like analysis

To overcome these issues, the so-called L4L analysis is frequently used, particularly in retailing, where management aim to understand the net turnover development accounting for closing and opening of a new store. Within customer management a L4L-analysis aims to insightfully show the customer flow accounting for different value drivers, such as cross-selling, up-selling, down-selling etc. Further, it can combine volume and value KPIs. In Figure 4.1.11 we show an example of the value development decomposed by value driver. As can be observed, strong value is created with up-selling customers, whereas value is lost through, for example, outflow of customers (churn) and down-selling. Note that inflow also has a negative value effect on the customer base, probably because acquisition costs are rather high. Creating a L4L analysis seems rather easy, but it is more difficult than frequently initially considered. We consider the following steps to create a L4L-analysis for period t and t+1:

1. Calculate the number of customers at period t
2. Determine the total value of customers at period t and period t+1 per value-driver. For outflow value is zero at t+1 and for inflow value is zero at t
3. Determine the differences between the two time periods t and t+1
4. Determine the relative contribution in % of what each group has on the total value of the base
5. Determine the weighted value impact by multiplying the percentage by the value difference.

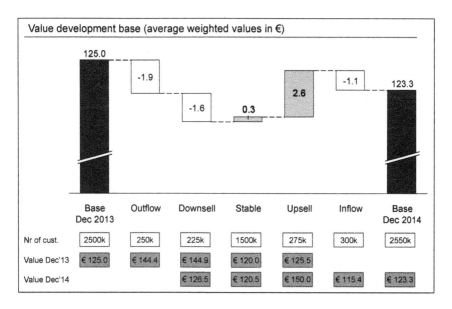

Figure 4.1.11 Like-4-like analysis for value development of the customer base of a phone operator

In Figure 4.1.12 we display the steps on how to execute an L4L analysis, which clearly shows the execution of the five steps discussed above.

More in-depth analyses

An L4L-analysis provides insights into the changes of the value-drivers over time. A next step is to execute a more in-depth analysis, an in-depth analysis per value driver. One example is the so-called "cohort analysis," in which acquired customers (inflow) are followed over time. In Figure 4.1.13, we show the results of such a cohort-analysis, revealing that first month churn has improved and churn is stabilizing in the fourth month.

A simple survival analysis can also be done to observe the churn over time of customers in specific customer groups (see Figure 4.1.14). In this survival analysis, one observes how customer groups A, B, and C develop over time, and specifically what percentage of customers have remained customers after a specific time period.

More advanced analytics

The analytics discussed so far in this chapter are mainly descriptive in nature and do not require extensive modeling. These methods mainly concern analyzing the data in a smart way to understand migration patterns and subsequent value consequences in a customer base. But within marketing science more advanced models are being used to model and predict migration patterns. Specifically, Markov models have been used. Hidden Markov models have become very

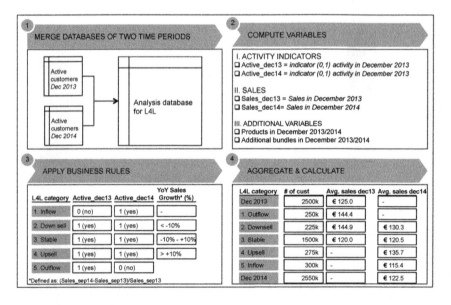

Figure 4.1.12 Steps for execution of an L4L analysis

popular. These models assume that there are some hidden unobservable states in which customers move in their relationship with a company. Using a hidden Markov model, these states can be uncovered and customers can be classified to the found state in each period. Netzer, Lattin and Srinivasan (2008) were the first to apply this methodology, when analyzing gift-giving behavior of alumni of a US-based university (see also Mark, Lemon, Vandenbosch, Bulla, & Maruotti, 2013). One can also use these models to assess potential effects of marketing instruments (e.g. direct marketing) on moving customers between states. Typically, a low active state is found for customers who have infrequent transactions with the company, while also a state for loyal, frequently interacting customers is usually found.

Classic 4: Customer segmentation

In our previous discussion on customer profiling, we explained some simple methods to segment the customer base. There are also more advanced methods that can be used to segment the customer base, which use statistical algorithms to find customer segments. In the above analyses, database analysts usually define their own segmentations and usually only segment on a limited set of variables (e.g. monetary value in the decile analysis given as an example). Statistical segmentation techniques allow researchers to segment on multiple variables and to base the segmentation on statistical criteria, such as statistics on model fit (Wedel & Kamakura, 2000). Researchers have several methods at their disposal to execute a segmentation analysis. Methods available in software packages such as SPSS/IBM include K-Means, two-step cluster analysis, and hierarchical cluster analysis. Researchers face several decisions in this analysis, of which deciding the number of segments is the most important. This decision can be made on

Cohort		Months after start					
		1	2	3	4	5	6
	Jan	85%	75%	65%	64%	63%	58%
	Feb	85%	76%	70%	67%	65%	
	Mar	87%	80%	75%	73%		
	Apr	88%	81%	75%			
	May	92%	82%	76%			
	Jun	93%	85%				
	Jul	95%					

% = percentage of active customers

Figure 4.1.13 Example of a cohort analysis

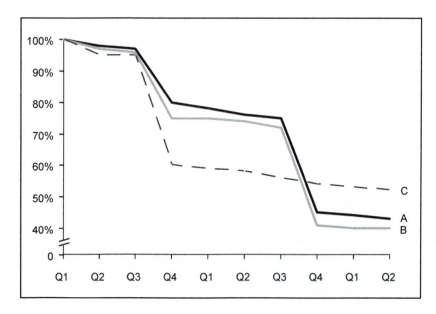

Figure 4.1.14 Example of a survival analysis

statistical fit-indices and/or more subjective grounds, such as the interpretation of the several cluster solutions.

Execution of cluster analysis

For now, we assume that most analysts still rely on the available cluster methods in statistical packages, such as K-Means. We consider five important steps when executing such an analysis:[2]

1. Selection of cluster variables
2. Data preparation
3. Running the analysis
4. Selecting number of clusters
5. Profiling the clusters.

Selection of cluster variables

Typically two general types of variables are distinguished: internal (segmentation) variables and external (profiling) variables. Segmentation variables are used for creating segments, whereas profiling variables are used to describe the segments. The selection of segmentation variables should ideally be based on some underlying idea of which segments could be present and, more specifically, on which bases one aims to segment the market. Segmentation can be done using, for example, socio-demographic variables, values, lifestyles, perceived benefits, brand and product usage, or customer profitability. If one aims to develop benefit segmentation, the segmentation variables should measure benefits of products.

Data preparation

For cluster analysis there are two main problems. First, the number of segmentation variables is frequently large. Second, the measurement scale frequently does not fit. We will first discuss the second problem. Although cluster analysis is rather flexible, more continuous scales are preferred. Scales with multiple non-ordered categories create problems. However, binary variables (e.g. gender) can, if required, be included. The first problem leads to massive interpretation problems of clusters. We therefore frequently first use a data-reduction technique, such as PCA, to end up with a lower number of cluster variables (see Box 4.1.1). The component scores can subsequently be included in the cluster analysis. Note that one should be careful when using this technique, because the derived principal components only explain limited variance in the underlying variables. The variables should then be included in the analysis.

Box 4.1.1 Short explanation of principal components analysis

Principal components analysis

The main use of principal components analysis (PCA) within the analyses we discuss is as a data-reduction technique. Analysts typically analyse a large number of variables, which frequently strongly correlate. Although analyzing this large number of variables is in principle possible, it creates problems. The number may just become so large that interpreting the different outcomes for the different variables, becomes too complex. Especially in regression-type models, the large number of variables can create problems in the estimation due to multi-collinearity. As a consequence, the estimated coefficients and accompanied significance levels are no longer reliable. One solution for this problem is to use PCA (also referred to as "factor analysis"). This technique reduces the number of variables into a lower number of uncorrelated principal components (PCs) or factors, which represent an underlying dimension. For example, if one has variables on Internet usage, mobile usage, and tablet usage, these variables could end up in one PC, representing the digital level of customers. The resulting PCs can, for example, be used to profile or as input in a cluster analysis. The use of PCs in a regression model reduces multi-collinearity problems, as the PCs are uncorrelated. PCA is not solely used for data reductions: it can also be used substantively in survey scale development and brand positioning research (e.g., Lilien & Rangaswamy, 2006). The key challenge is to find the right number of interpretable PCs.

Execution
Execution of PCA requires four main steps:

- Variable selection, preparation, and analysis
- Selection of the number of PCs
- Interpretation of the PCs with rotation
- Saving the PCs.

Variable selection and preparation
First the set of variables to be analyzed should be selected. These variables should at a minimum be interval-scaled. In some cases, binary variables can also be included, but this is generally not preferred. Nominal variables cannot be used. If one focuses on data reduction, there is no other selection criterion, as one just aims to analyse a lower number of variables. To prepare the data the variables need to be standardized, meaning that they get a mean of 0 and a standard deviation of 1. Most software packages will automatically execute this standardization. The analysis can then be executed in standard packages.

Selection of the number of PCs
One key challenge is to select the right number of PCs. The main and default criterion used is that of the eigen value being larger than one. This criterion clearly focuses on data reduction as the eigen value measures the part of the explained variance of a PC. If the eigen value is smaller than one, the PC explains less variance than a single variable. A more substantive method is to focus on the interpretation of PCs.

Interpret PCs
The interpretation of PCs considers the variables grouped together and the importance of these variables. For the interpretation, rotation techniques are used. The most important and frequently used technique on the interpretability of the PCs is to use Varimax rotation. PCs can be difficult to interpret when the variables grouped into a PC do not seem related. One could then consider solutions for different numbers of PCs. The importance of each variable in the PC can be learned from the rotated factor loading, which varies between 0 and 1. Typically only variables with loadings larger than 0.30 or 0.40 are considered. The larger the loading, the more important the variable in the PC. If variables do not contribute to any PCs (only low loadings), they are excluded

from the analysis. Typically analysts also do not prefer variables to have high loadings in multiple PCs, as that creates interpretation problems. One frequently would then try different solutions. In the table below we show the outcome of a PCA for the perceptions of attributes of supermarkets.

Saving PCs

If the analyst has come to a final number of PCs and has a final solution, the PC scores can be saved in the database. Importantly, these scores have an average of 0 and a standard deviation of 1. The scores are difficult to interpret. A higher score on, for example, a PC measuring digital customer behavior only suggests that customers are showing more of this behavior. However, no exact values can be linked to this. To do so, transformation back to the original variables is required.

Survey elements – specific attributes	Factor loadings		
	Price	Service	Convenience
Low prices	.899		
Attractive offers	.602		
Product quality		.681	
Customer friendly personnel		.747	
Good supply of fresh products		.732	
Large assortment		.790	
Long opening hours		.573	
Store attractiveness		.857	
Fast checkout		.713	
Good supply of additional services		.624	
Child friendliness of the store		.644	
Tidy store		.852	
Spacious store		.766	
Knowledgeable personnel		.769	
Much attention for new products		.768	
The store is nearby			.749
Sufficient supply of other stores close to the focal store			.671

Source: Hunneman et al. (2015)

Running the analysis

Many cluster methods are available within the standard software packages, and within these methods also specific options are available. An analyst should have sufficient knowledge about each of these methods and their options to make an informed choice. Typically, analysts also combine specific methods. For example, the hierarchical cluster analysis on a small sample is very useful as a first step in an analysis (hierarchical cluster analysis is less able to analyze large datasets, and also the selection of clusters is more difficult with larger number of data). Based on this hierarchical cluster analysis, the number or the range of clusters can be determined. These clusters and their average values can then be used as input into a K-means analysis, which can handle larger datasets more easily.

Classic data analytics

Selection of number of clusters

A dendrogram can be used to select the number of clusters. A dendrogram shows how specific cases are combined into clusters (see Figure 4.1.15). Based on a subjective assessment of the dendrogram a range of cluster solutions can be considered.[3] When running the subsequent K-means analysis, several solutions for this range of clusters can be achieved. A definite selection should then be based on segmentation criteria, such as size of the clusters and interpretability. This will probably be done simultaneously with the next step, as profiling the cluster solutions helps in interpreting the clusters.

Profiling clusters

The profiling of clusters can be done on the internal cluster variables and the external (profiling) variables not included in the cluster analysis. This helps to gain a further understanding of the found segments, as profiling variables such as socio-demographic characteristics, media usage, channel usage, and brand purchase behavior are being used. One way to profile the clusters is to use discriminant-analysis,[4] which can be used to show which variables explain specific

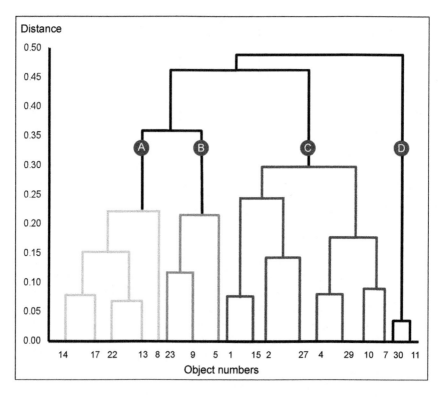

Figure 4.1.15 Example of a dendrogram

cluster memberships. One can also use this technique to classify customers in a cluster. Based on profiling, target segments can be chosen and target-marketing strategies can be developed. A smart way to understand differences between segments is to use a scatterplot in which the segments are related to the most discriminating profile variables (see Figure 4.1.16).

Advanced cluster techniques

More advanced statistical cluster methods are available in specialized software packages, such as Latent Gold. Among marketing academics, latent-class cluster analysis in particular has received considerable attention (Wedel & Kamakura, 2000). This method has been applied to derive customer segments in different areas, such as multi-channel usage and financial service buying behavior (e.g. Konuş, Verhoef, & Neslin, 2008; Paas, Bijmolt, & Vermunt, 2007). One important advantage of this technique is that it provides fit-statistics on which the optimal number of segments can be more objectively determined. Furthermore, it easily allows the linking of covariates to a segment solution, making it relatively easy to detect how segments differ in terms of background characteristics. A detailed discussion of these techniques goes beyond the scope of this textbook. We refer to Wedel and Kamakura (2000) for a more detailed discussion. In Figure 4.1.17 we show the study of Konuş et al. (2008) on multi-channel usage as an example of this technique.

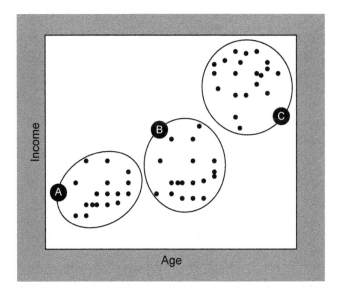

Figure 4.1.16 Visualization clusters

162 *Classic data analytics*

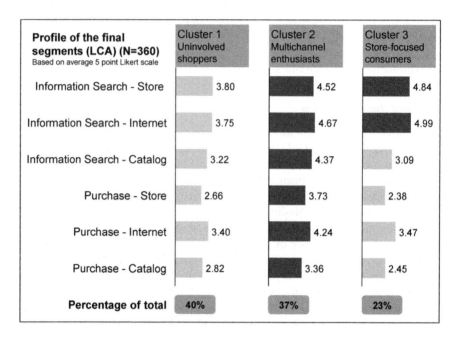

Figure 4.1.17 Example of a cluster analysis of shoppers
Source: Adapted from Konuş et al. (2008)

Some practical guidelines

When executing cluster analysis in practice, we encountered some practical issues and considerations requiring attention:

- The above discussion of doing two separate cluster analyses (hierarchical and K-Means) is considered rather complicated and time-consuming. Furthermore, the large size of current datasets means that K-Means becomes more useful. Another common way of running the analysis is for the analyst to execute a K-Means cluster analysis for a number of cluster solutions (e.g. 3–6 clusters) and then compare the different solutions and select the one that performs best on interpretability and usefulness.
- One way to reduce computation time can be to execute the cluster analysis on a smaller sample and subsequently use a discriminant analysis to classify customers into a segment.
- To create more impact with cluster analysis, we strongly recommend reflecting on the found clusters with marketing executives. This will be a first test for the usefulness of the segmentation.
- Although customers may principally belong in many segments (e.g. Wedel & Kamakura 2000), we recommend assigning them to one cluster to create more simple business rules.

Classic 5: Trend analysis market and sales forecasting

Firms are frequently interested in how a market develops or how brand sales will grow. For them this is important so that they can constantly monitor market attractiveness, and for planning purposes they aim to know which level of brand sales they can realistically expect. For this purpose, firms might be interested in trends (e.g. is the market growing?), but also in actual forecasts. Notably, trends can be used in forecasting models as well. Although forecasting can be done with other techniques, such as subjective forecasting and through conjoint studies (see Classic 6), we focus here on models that use time series on the forecasted variable and predictor variables. Note that forecasts are not only done for market or brand sales, but can also be used to predict, for example, satisfaction scores over time (e.g. Gijsenberg et al., 2015). Typically linear regression models with continuous dependent variables are used. The basics of regression models are discussed in Box 4.1.2.

Box 4.1.2 Basics of linear regression models

The linear regression model is probably the most frequently used multivariate technique. It seems very easy to use, but there are many pitfalls that require some understanding. There are multiple crucial steps when building a model, where we specifically focus on the phases where the purpose and scope of the model is clear and data are available, and the focus is achieving model results. The crucial steps are:

1. Model specification
2. Estimation
3. Testing and validation

Model specification
The linear regression model is usually defined for a continuous dependent variable Y which is observed over time and a set of explanatory variables X as:

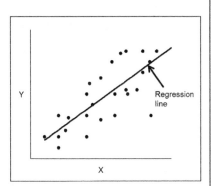

$$Y_t = \alpha + \beta_1 X_{(1+t)} + \beta_2 X_{2t} + \cdots + \beta_k X_{kt} + \varepsilon_t$$

As a researcher, one would be interested in the estimations of the β parameters, the respective standard errors, and significance levels. This model assumes linear relationships between the dependent variable and the independent variable(s). This is, however, not always the case. For

---

example, for advertising there could be decreasing returns on increased advertising. Or satisfaction could have a non-linear effect on purchase behavior (e.g., Van Doorn & Verhoef, 2008). To account for this, the X variables should be transformed using, for example, a log-transformation (decreasing effect) or a quadratic effect. Other possible transformations are a square root and a reciprocal relationship. These models are then referred to as non-linear additive models. The estimation is still done in a linear way; one accounts for non-linearities by transformation of the X-variables. There is a second set of models, multiplicative models, in which the relationship between the dependent and independent variable(s) are all very non-linear. Frequently, analysts will then do a log-log transformation (i.e. both the dependent variable Y and the independent variables X are log-transformed). The advantage of this method is that the estimated parameters for marketing variables, such as price and advertising, can be interpreted as elasticities.

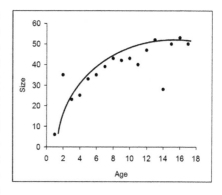

Estimation

The standard linear regression model is estimated using ordinary least squares (OLS). The basic underlying idea of OLS is that the estimation method aims to minimize the difference between the estimated value of Y and the true value of Y (referred to as residual value or disturbance term ε). This implies practically that the objective of the estimation is to minimize the squared sum of all these differences. The OLS model has several assumptions. They mainly concern the residual value. One important assumption is that the residuals should be normally distributed. The model quality is further assessed by considering the explanatory power. The most important measure for this is R^2, which can take the value between 0 and 1, with 0 having no explanatory power and 1 having perfect explanatory power. The R^2 measure is a relative measure and its value depends on how well the regression line fits the data and the amount of dispersion in the values of the dependent variable. Researchers would like to have high values for R^2. However, one should be careful with this. High values can be achieved with wrongly specified models, for example when part of the Y-values are included in the X-variables (e.g. prices are set based on expected sales). Moreover, some data have such a large dispersion that it is just difficult to explain. High values can also be achieved by using more explanatory variables. To account for this effect, the so-called "adjusted R^2" can be calculated, which will be lower than the value of R^2.

Testing and Validation
Before interpreting the model results, specific model issues need to be checked. This specifically concerns the assumptions underlying the linear regression model. Important issues that require attention are:

- The expected value of the disturbance term is non-zero
- The normality of the disturbance terms
- The error terms are proportional to the values of the dependent variable (also referred to as heteroscedasticity)
- The presence of multi-collinearity (strong correlations between independent variables)
- The presence of auto-correlation, implying that the error terms over time are correlated (only relevant for models with time series)
- The independent variable is correlated with the disturbance term (also referred to as endogeneity).

If one of these specific issues happen, specific problems such as biased, unreliable parameter estimates and non-trusted p-values occur. In practice, strong attention is given to multi-collinearity. However, the other assumptions are also important. Leeflang et al. (2015) heavily emphasize the important assumption that the expected value of the disturbance term is non-zero. This occurs when the model is not well specified and specifically when not all relevant predictors are included. They therefore strongly emphasize the importance of a well-specified model. Recently, we have observed considerable attention being paid to endogeneity. This occurs, for example, when managers base their used marketing mix on the expected effects and sales levels. Another cause for this could be that there is self-selection. For example, customers become a member of a loyalty program because they believe they will buy more in the future (e.g., Leenheer, Bijmolt, Van Heerde & Smidts, 2007). For predictive purposes endogeneity seems less of an issue than for more descriptive purposes of a model (Ebbes, Papies & Van Heerde, 2011). If the model does not violate these criteria, the estimated parameters could be interpreted with the respective p-values. An important aspect here is to consider the face validity of the findings. For example, a positive effect of price on sales generally does not have face validity and if it occurs the alarm bells of an analyst should start to ring! Ultimate validation of the model and specifically for predictive models is the predictive quality.

166 *Classic data analytics*

> We recommend the use of hold-out samples and plotting the predictive value and the actual value in the estimation sample and the hold-out sample. Beyond that several prediction metrics can be calculated:
>
> - Average prediction error (APE)
> - Mean squared error (MSE) (with this metric large errors are weighted more heavily than smaller ones)
> - Mean absolute percentage error (MAPE) (this is a more relative measure as the error's terms are corrected for the actual value).

In the next sections, we will discuss several versions of the regression model that can be used for prediction. In essence, these models are similar in terms of how they are estimated. However, the model specification is different. In our example, we focus on sales predictions, but we note that similar approaches can be used for many other continuous dependent variables. We assume that time series data are present.

Trend analysis

With trend analysis, the main underlying idea is that sales follow a specific trend. For example, for a new product the sales figures might rise over time. A first step in trend analysis is just to plot the sales development over time (see Figure 4.1.18). This plotting immediately provides the analyst information on the presence (or absence) of a trend in the data. It may also hint at specific

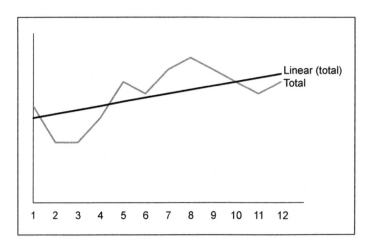

Figure 4.1.18 Trend analysis

trends. If it is a linear trend, there might be a straight-line development in sales. However, if it is non-linear sales might, for example, grow exponentially over time. The specification of the model should account for these non-linear effects, by including non-linear trend variables. The basic specification of the regression model including a linear trend is as follows:

$$Sales_t = \alpha + \beta_1 \times t + \varepsilon_t \qquad (4.1.1)$$

Usually an analyst will be mainly interested in the β coefficient and its significance level. A positive and significant coefficient implies a positive linear trend, whereas a negative and significant coefficient implies a negative linear trend. As noted the trend can be non-linear, something which can deduced from a plot of sales over time. To account for this, specifications might include a quadratic trend (t^2) or exponential trend (e^t) if the sales grow more strongly over time, or a square root trend ($\sqrt{t}$) or a log trend (ln t) if the sales grow less strongly over time. We strongly recommend analysts to consider different trend operationalizations.

An important issue is that trends should not be interchanged with seasonality patterns. With seasonal patterns sales follow a specific shape during the year, because demand depends on specific developments during the year (e.g. beer sales might go up during summer). To account for these effects seasonal dummy variables (variables set at value 1 if a specific season occurs) should be included in the models. These variables pick up the specific seasonal effect.

Regression models

One problem with trend analysis is that it only considers the effects of time on sales, while a firm's marketing of course also influences marketing metrics such as sales. Typically the trend models will have a relatively low explanatory power. This will especially hold in stable markets with existing products and brands. For new products and/or growing/declining markets trend variables may have a reasonable explanatory power. Models have been developed to assess the effects of specific instruments and to predict the impact of changes in marketing instruments on sales. We note that these models are typically not used to predict sales as such over time. Researchers have been more interested in what happens with sales if, for example, the advertising budget is increased by 10%. In a rather basic form these models are formulated as a regression model in which sales depend on the value of the included instruments. In these models one can also account for trend and seasonal effects if required. The typical form of this regression model including three marketing instruments and a trend is as follows:

$$Sales_t = \alpha + \beta_1 \times Advertising_t + \beta_2 \times Price_t + \beta_3 \times Distribution_t + \beta_4 \times t + \varepsilon_t \qquad (4.1.2)$$

This model can be formulated in such a way that both sales and the marketing instruments are log-transformed, but for now we assume linear effects with non-transformed variables. Generally, one would expect positive β coefficients for advertising and distribution and a negative β coefficient for price. One important problem is that the true effect of these variables is not the estimated effect, because of the endogeneity problem arising from the fact that managers may change their marketing based on expected sales. Typically, the estimated effect is larger than the true effect. The challenge is, however, to find the true effect. Analysts should be aware of these problems. One solution is to correct for this. Econometricians have proposed several methods, including the use of so-called "instrumental variables" (see Leeflang, Wieringa, Bijmolt and Pauwels (2015) for discussion). A problem arising is that sometimes the remedy is worse than the problem, especially if bad instruments are used (Rossi, 2014). Another practical solution is to account for endogeneity by assuming somewhat lower coefficients, based on experience combined with the estimated findings.

A more complicated model specification is needed to account for dynamic effects. These dynamic effects are required in order to take into account potential delayed response effects on marketing instruments. For example, advertising in t-1 can still have an effect on sales at time t. In its simplest form this model is specified as follows:

$$Sales_t = \alpha + \beta_1 \times Advertising_{t-s} + \beta_2 \times Price_{t-s} + \beta_3 \times Distribution_{t-s} + \beta_4 \times t + \varepsilon_t \quad (4.1.3)$$

where s is the number of time periods between the time a marketing instrument is used (i.e. advertising spending) and the sales that result from the use of that marketing instrument. In Figure 4.1.19 we show an example of a model explaining sales for a chocolate brand (Leeflang et al. 2015). In this example own price has a strong expected negative coefficient, whereas different types of promotions for that brand generally have positive effects. There are also some seasonal effects, as in Spring other types of chocolate (e.g. Easter eggs) are purchased. There are many more complicated versions of these models, such as the geometric lag model and the Koyck model. We refer to Leeflang et al. (2015: Chapter 2) for a detailed discussion.

Time series models

Time series models are a specific form of regression models. In their most simple form these models include the lag of a dependent variable as an explanatory variable. However, this is not necessary. If sales time series follow a very stable pattern and the values seem to vary around an average model, a moving average process can be modeled in which sales at time t solely depend on disturbance terms at t–s.

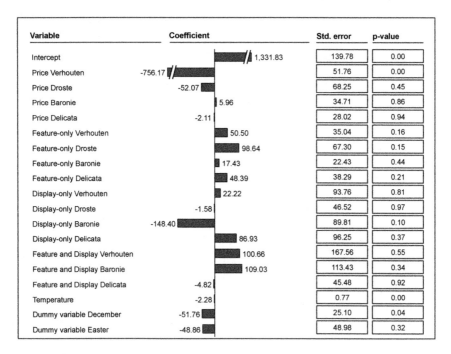

Figure 4.1.19 Effects of different marketing instruments on sales for a chocolate brand
Source: Adapted from Leeflang et al. (2015: 113)

In many cases, however, time series do not follow a stable pattern. In these cases it is common to include trends, lagged variables, and also explanatory variables. The lagged variable is sometimes also referred to as an autoregressive term and models can have multiple lags of the sales variable in the model. Typically, models with lagged sales variables have a strong explanatory power and their predictive ability can also be strong. In its most simple specification a linear model with lagged sales and marketing instruments is specified as follows:

$$Sales_t = \alpha + \beta_1 \times Sales_{t-1} + \beta_2 \times Advertising_t \\ + \beta_3 \times Price_t + \beta_4 \times Distribution_t + \varepsilon_t \quad (4.1.4)$$

By including this lag variable of sales a regression model accounts for the fact that marketing instruments can have a long-term effect. Time series models seem relatively easy to grasp. However, there are many pitfalls, not least because time series can be non-stationary. A stationary process is a stochastic process whose joint probability distribution does not change when shifted in time. Consequently, parameters such as the mean and variance, if they are present, also do not change over time and do not follow any trends. If the time series parameters in the model are non-stationary then any results cannot be interpreted, and researchers should transform the data to make them stationary. If a trend is causing t non-stationary series, the time-series data should be detrended. A way to do this is to include a trend variable in the model. If the data are then stationary they are considered as trend-stationary. However, frequently this is not sufficient. A frequently applied method is then to take first differences. This implies that the non-stationary variables are transformed as follows (example sales):

$$\text{First Difference Sales}_t = \text{Sales}_t - \text{Sales}_{t-1}. \quad (4.1.5)$$

If the data are stationary after first-differencing they are said to be difference-stationary. The data can then be analyzed. It is thus crucial when studying time series data that researchers assess the stationarity of the data: several tests are available to do this (e.g. the augmented Dicky-Fuller test). We strongly warn against just estimating all kinds of times series without a solid understanding of time series analysis, as there are many pitfalls.[5]

Time-series models have been extended and specifically so with the introduction of so-called vector-autoregressive (VAR) models. These VAR models are now frequently used in marketing science to estimate short- and long-term effects of marketing instruments (e.g. Pauwels, 2004; Dekimpe, & Hanssens, 1995; Nijs, Dekimpe, Steenkamp, & Hanssens, 2001). In these models a system of equations is formulated in such a way that each included variable is influenced by the lags of other included variables. So in its simplest form, with sales and two marketing instruments, price and advertising, there are three equations estimated simultaneously in which one also allows the disturbance terms to be correlated. In a rather simplistic form this model can be specified as follows, assuming stationary series:

$$\text{Sales}_t = \alpha + \beta_{s1} \times \text{Sales}_{t-1} + \beta_{s2} \times \text{Advertising}_{t-1} + \beta_{s3} \times \text{Price}_{t-1} + u_{st}$$
$$\text{Avertising}_t = \alpha + \beta_{a1} \times \text{Sales}_{t-1} + \beta_{a2} \times \text{Advertising}_{t-1} + \beta_{a3} \times \text{Price}_{t-1} + u_{at}$$
$$\text{Price}_t = \alpha + \beta_{p1} \times \text{Sales}_{t-1} + \beta_{p2} \times \text{Advertising}_{t-1} + \beta_{p3} \times \text{Price}_{t-1} + u_{pt} \quad (4.1.6)$$

The above model can be extended by including some control variables (X), turning it into a VARX model. Several other variants of these models have been developed. To understand the short- and long-term effect, impulse response functions have to be estimated. VAR models gain in popularity as more time series data become available.

In general it is believed that time series models will gain in popularity. Dekimpe and Hanssens (2010) specifically consider the expanding amount of available data, the increasing dynamics in the marketing environment, the greater need for marketing accountability, and the emergence of online data, as important drivers. They specifically state that they are confident that the importance of time series models in marketing will continue to grow (Dekimpe &

Hanssens, 2010: 27). Despite this development we observe that marketers are still reluctant to use these models, whereas they have become very common in, for example, finance and economics (i.e. for forecasting economic growth). One main problem with VAR models is that they could easily become a kind of black box in which every variable is influenced by many other variables, and the analyst may not have a sufficient understanding of what is actually occurring. We have already mentioned the many pitfalls in using time-series models, but training in their use is so far limited to business schools and marketing programs. In Figure 4.1.20 we show the predicted values of a VAR type model (DASVAR) explaining perceived service quality (PSQ) for a European railway company. We used an estimation sample to estimate our model and predicted the PSQ (predicted PSQ asymmetric Lag SVAR in graph) for both the estimation sample and the hold-out sample The model predicts the satisfaction series pretty well, both in-sample and out-of-sample.

Practical considerations

In general there are some practical considerations to take into account when using regression models:

- When estimating models researchers should carefully investigate the different assumptions (see Box 4.1.2).
- We strongly recommend carrying out robustness checks in which different versions of models are estimated to assess whether model parameters remain rather similar or not. If they remain similar the model is usually considered robust.

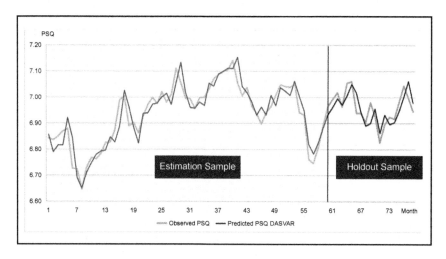

Figure 4.1.20 Predictions for service quality time series of a European public transport firm

Source: Adapted from Gijsenberg, Van Heerde, & Verhoef (2015)

- Do not over-value the explanatory power of models, and do have realistic expectations. A time series model will typically have high R^2, but this may also depend on the data. Regression models using cross-sections typically have lower R^2. However, when using survey data R^2 might be higher due to common method variance issues.
- We strongly recommend the plotting of data to identify patterns in the data and possible (non)-linear relationships.
- A frequent question concerns the sample size required to estimate regression models. A general rule of thumb we frequently use is that per independent variables around 5 observations should be present (Leeflang et al., 2015). Having sufficient data points is important, as results may easily become instable and unreliable.
- Be aware of the fact that when analyzing aggregated data, the analyst ignores underlying segments or brands or customers. Hence parameter estimates could be different for different segments or brands. The question here is whether one should pool the data over these segments or brands, or estimate per segment or per brand, called "unpooled analysis" (see Leeflang et al., 2015). If data cannot be pooled, the aggregated pooled analysis will lead to wrong estimates.

Classic 6: Attribute importance analysis

Especially in new product development, firms aim to understand the importance of specific attributes. For a digital camera one would like to know the importance of attributes such as number of pixels, size, and price. For hotels the destination, the size of rooms, additional services etc. could be important attributes. Attributes are not only important for new product development, but also for creating satisfied customers. Firms would like to know the contribution of each service attribute towards customer satisfaction. For example, hotels would like to know how an improvement in the service at the reception desk could improve satisfaction. Typically, we distinguish between three methods that can be used to assess the importance of attributes:

1. Stated importance measurement
2. Regression-based approach
3. Conjoint analysis.

Stated importance measurement

A rather simple approach is to ask customers which attributes they believe are important. Typically customers are asked to rate the importance of specific attributes on, for example, a 5-point scale (1 = absolutely not important attribute, 5 = very important attribute). Analysts will report the average scores, as well as top-2 scores. Of course a higher average score means a higher importance. One problem with this type of method is that customers do not make a trade-off between attributes. Frequently, customers state that many attributes are very important and there are not many differences between attributes. One solution is to use different survey questions, such as ranking of a list of attributes, where the most important attribute is ranked as first. Ranking induces customers to at least make some trade-offs. Note that in this process descriptive statistics are being used.

Regression-based approach

The regression-based approach is mainly used in service research. The common approach is to measure overall customer satisfaction (or another feedback metric, such as NPS) and to link this satisfaction score to evaluations on service attributes (e.g. on a 7 or 10 point scale). Usually these evaluations and the satisfaction score are measured in the same survey. As a step in between a PCA can be executed on the scores on each of these service attributes to reduce the number of attributes in the regression analysis and solve multi-collinearity problems. Running the regression analysis, one can then observe the importance of each of the attributes by looking at the estimated standardized coefficients. A larger standardized coefficient implies that the attribute is more important. Hunneman, Verhoef and Sloot (2015) show that for Dutch retailers, the service attributes are most important for creating customer satisfaction (see Figure 4.1.21 for the main effects in their model).

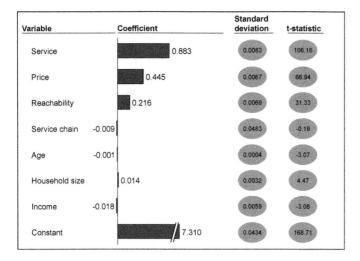

Figure 4.1.21 Effects of store attributes on store satisfaction

Source: Adapted from Hunneman et al (2015)

One problem with the regression-based approach is that the used survey method induces a strong correlation between the independent and dependent variables, which is known as "common-method variance." Part of the explained variance in the dependent variable is then due to the fact that the dependent variables and independent variable are measured in the same survey, frequently using a similar attitude scale (Podaskoff, MacKenzie, Lee, & Podaskoff, 2003; Lindell & Whitney, 2001). As a result the estimated coefficients are too high. The explained variance is also typically high, with values of, for example, around 0.40 or 0.50. Probably the importance of different attributes can be gathered from these data, if one assumes that this bias affects all variables and their respective coefficients in much the same way. However, using these estimated coefficients to predict how changes in service attribute evaluations affects satisfaction should be done with great care. One solution is to use a number of surveys in which the evaluations and the satisfaction score are measured separately. Another solution is to measure independent variables more objectively—asking not for an evaluation but rather whether a specific event has been experienced.

Conjoint analysis

Conjoint analysis was developed in the 1970s and is considered to be one of the techniques that has successfully transferred from marketing science into practice (Roberts et al., 2014). Specific software packages have been developed by, for example, Sawtooth Software to execute conjoint analysis, but it is also available as a standard technique in standard packages. In essence the conjoint method involves an experimental design in which preferences for specific products are measured and the resulting data are analyzed with a regression or logit model. The conjoint experiment is a within-subjects design in which respondents are exposed to a set of artificial constructed products that vary in terms of specific attribute levels. The basic idea of conjoint analysis is that each product or service consists of a bundle of j attributes that jointly results in a product utility:

$$\text{Product Utility} = a + \text{Utility Attribute}_1 + \text{Utility Attribute}_2 + \cdots + \text{Utility Attribute}_j \qquad (4.1.7)$$

For each artificial product a utility or preference is measured using several kinds of methods. In conjoint analysis, a model dependent on the preference measurement method is estimated, aiming to assess the importance of specific attributes. One of the key advantages of conjoint analysis is that respondents see the full product and thus have to trade off specific attributes (e.g. a low price for airline tickets vs. more leg room). The conjoint model can be used for specific information-based products or services in which—based on derived individual customer preferences—recommendations are given to customers. The conjoint model then functions as an algorithm underlying a specific recommendation website or app. The typical steps in conjoint analysis are the following:

1   Study design: Choice of attributes and levels
2   Choice of conjoint design
3   Collecting the data
4   Analyzing the data and interpretation of results.

Study design

The first step in setting up a study is probably the most important. For the studied product, the relevant attributes and level should be chosen. For choosing a flight from Paris to New York, the following attributes and levels could be important: airline (Air France, United, Delta); leg room (small, large); price ($750; $900); and indirect flight (via London Heathrow) or direct. In Figure 4.1.22 we show the selection of attributes for a conjoint study in which customers should evaluate different cab services.[6] There are some specific issues to consider when choosing the attributes and the accompanying levels (Eggers & Sattler, 2011):

- It is generally advised to keep the number of attributes low, to decrease the complexity for respondents when evaluating the respective products. Six attributes are considered as a kind of maximum. If other attributes are relevant, but they are, for example, standard available for all products, it is advised to include them but not to vary them in the experimental study.
- The chosen levels should be realistic. For example, suggesting a very low price of $250 for a direct flight from Paris to New York is not very realistic.

Conjoint attribute	Levels
Service provider	Uber
	Robocab
	Service provided by the city
Car brand	Toyota
	Tesla Motors
	Google
Waiting time until the taxi arrives	No waiting time
	3 minutes
	5 minutes
Driving time to the hotel	15 minutes
	20 minutes
	25 minutes
Price	10 Euro
	15 Euro
	20 Euro

Figure 4.1.22 Attributes chosen for study on cab services

- The number of levels per attribute should be limited. More levels require a larger experiment and larger samples. As a general rule of thumb Eggers and Sattler (2011) advise not to use more than 7 levels. In general fewer levels with more reliable estimates is preferred over less precise estimates of attributes with more levels.
- One specific issue concerns the "number of levels effect." This effect arises when the number of levels is not equally distributed over the attributes. Attributes with more levels than the other attributes (e.g. 5 for price and 2 for leg room) leads to a higher relative importance of an attribute with more levels. Hence, the parameters for these attributes are biased upwards. This typically happens with the price attribute. As a consequence the price attribute is considered as too important. The advice to try to avoid this effect is to keep the number of levels similar across attributes.
- A second important bias could arise due to the "range effect." If the range between two levels is too large the effect of the attribute becomes too strong. For example, if a price range of $500 to $900 is used instead of a range from $750 to $900 the effect of price will be larger for the first range. It is generally advised to use a range that is realistic within the market which is not too large.

Choice of conjoint design

The choice of the design first concerns how preferences will be measured. There are three methods to measure preferences:

- Rating-based conjoint
- Ranking-based conjoint
- Choice-based conjoint

With rating-based conjoint analysis the respondents are asked to evaluate each of several products with different attributes on a rating scale (e.g. 0 = very unattractive to 10 = very attractive). These tasks are rather simple for respondents. The disadvantage of this method is that there is no explicit trade-off between different product options. With ranking-based conjoint analysis the respondent is shown several product options and is asked to rank them from very unattractive (lowest rank) to very attractive (highest rank). With this method a trade-off is being made, but the disadvantage is that this task can only reasonably be done with a low number of product options, thereby creating only a low number of attributes and levels. It is virtually impossible to rank 20 options. With choice-based conjoint the respondent is repeatedly shown a number of product options (e.g. 3) and then has to choose the most attractive product from the choice set (see Figure 4.1.23 for choice design of a cab study). Choice-based conjoint analysis has become rather popular among marketing scientists; they believe it to be effective, because choices are an integral part of people's everyday life (Eggers & Sattler, 2011). Furthermore, rating scales in particular

	Option 1	Option 2	Option 3
Service provider:	Service provided by the city	Robocab	Robocab
Car brand:	Google	Toyota	Conventional taxi service with a driver
Waiting time until the taxi arrives:	3 minutes	5 minutes	No waiting time
Driving time to hotel:	25 minutes	15 minutes	20 minutes
Price:	20 euro	10 Euro	20 euro (excl. tip)

Please consider the options below. These are different transportation possibilities that you will have to get from the airport to your hotel (according to the scenario). Option 1 and Option 2 are autonomous taxi services. Option 3 is a conventional taxi service with a driver. Which of these options do you prefer?

Figure 4.1.23 Example of a choice-based conjoint design for a cab study

become problematic in multi-cultural studies, as respondents in different cultures may use these scales differently.

If the conjoint method is chosen the research design then has to be set up. One specific issue is that especially with many attributes and levels, the number of possible products increases dramatically. It would be very unreasonable to ask respondents to evaluate each potential product. Hence, more efficient designs should be developed that show respondents a much lower number of products, but which is still is able to produce reliable parameter estimates. Eggers and Sattler (2011) refer to four important criteria for choice-based conjoint studies:

- Balance: All attribute levels appear an equal number of times.
- Orthogonality: Each attribute level pair appears an equal number of times.
- Minimal overlap: The alternatives within a choice set are maximally different from one another, i.e. avoid equal levels within one attribute.
- Utility balance: The alternatives within a choice set are equally attractive to the respondent, so that choice sets avoid dominating or dominated alternatives.

Collecting the data

Data are now frequently collected using online surveys in which respondents are shown realistic products. There are some considerations to take into account when collecting the data. First, the sample size should be sufficiently large. Larger sample sizes are required when more attributes and levels are tested. Samples should also be representative of the market. Second, in this within-subject design respondents can become fatigued when confronted with multiple choice options. Researchers should keep respondents engaged during the conjoint task. One way to do so is to give the respondent an incentive-aligned procedure. For example, they can get a fictive budget which they can use to spend during the choice task (e.g. for spending for a specific alternative). A lottery can be used to reward respondents. One specific issue for choice-based conjoint analysis is that researchers could choose to include the non-choice option. This is more realistic, as in real life customers can also choose not to buy a product if their preferred option is not available.

Analyzing the data and interpretation

The data are analyzed using regression-based techniques. The type of analysis depends on the chosen design. For rating-based conjoint analysis regression models are used, while for choice-based conjoint analysis logit models are used (see the sections on Classics 5 and 7). In principle, a model can be estimated for each respondent. Hence, for each respondent the importance of each attribute can be estimated. The average values of these individual parameters would then be the average importance of each attribute. Conjoint estimation in, for example, the SPSS software saves the individual estimates and also shows the aggregate results. However, analysts can estimate aggregate models themselves. As multiple observations per respondent are available, panel models should be used (e.g. Wuyts, Verhoef, & Prins, 2009). To improve the predictive ability of the models, interaction effects between attributes can also be added. For example, price may reduce the importance of brands. Importantly, the predictive ability can be tested with a hold-out product that is not included in the analysis. Interaction effects may indeed occur.

Conjoint analysis can also be combined with cluster analysis to derive a benefit segmentation. The most simple way to do this is to use the estimated individual utilities saved in the analytical database. These utilities can be used as input into a cluster analysis (see the section on Classic 4). Another way is to use more advanced methods in which latent class analysis is used to derive segments with specific utilities per attribute. For the cab study a latent-class study was executed (see Figure 4.1.24). The resulting classes or segments of this analysis can be interpreted as follows. Segment 1 seems to be a fan of Tesla and tends to slightly prefer city services over other services. Segment 2, however, is a strong believer in the Uber and Toyota brands, and values a low price. Segment 3 values city services and prefers Google over the other brands. They put less value on driving time than the other segments.

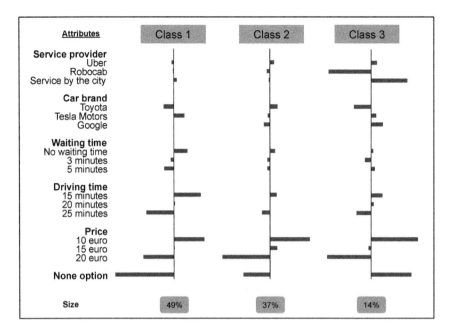

Figure 4.1.24 Segmentation analysis for conjoint study on cab services

Advanced methods and market forecasting

A relatively recent method that is gaining in popularity because of the increased use of computer-aided surveys is adaptive conjoint analysis. In adaptive conjoint analysis surveys can react directly to the answers given by each respondent. As a consequence, unimportant or unacceptable features can be excluded during the survey. The main advantage is that more attributes can be used in this kind of method. Moreover, it makes the conjoint task more engaging for respondents.

One final issue is that conjoint studies can also be used for market forecasting purposes of different alternative products. Based on the chosen product attributes different scenarios on the percentage of potential customers interested in such a product can be calculated. More specifically, preference shares can be calculated. However, these preference shares are not similar to market shares, given the fact that the conjoint study does not fully mimic market conditions due to its experimental nature. It is therefore strongly advised to work with different scenarios that mimic the market situation and do simulations with these scenarios. This will provide the analyst with a potential set of preference shares, that might be closer to actual market shares. Still, one should be very careful, as competitors might react, customer preferences may change etc.

Classic data analytics

Practical considerations

In the above discussion we have already been rather elaborate. Despite that, there are some additional practical tips when executing attribute importance studies:

- When including attributes in the study, one should preferably take attributes into account that marketing can influence.
- We strongly advise not to focus solely on the aggregate findings, in which the attribute importance for the total sample is calculated. In fact there is sufficient heterogeneity between customers and customer segments on attribute preferences. Hence, a more individual or segment-level approach is warranted.
- Simulation studies using the outcomes of the conjoint study to predict the potential future market shares of new products can be very useful to create more impact.

Classic 7: Individual prediction models

One important task for customer analysts is to predict future individual customer behavior. For that purpose, analysts have several methods and statistical techniques at their disposal. A naive way of predicting would be to assume that behavior does not differ between customers and one assumes that the average behavior (e.g. average response rate on a mailing) is the same for all customers. This is, however, not a reasonable assumption. Making it a bit more complicated one could assume that behavior differs between segments. For that purpose, customer crossings with behavioral outcomes could be made. If one then knows the segment membership (e.g. decile 1), we can predict future behavior (see Classic 2 on profiling and specifically decile analysis/gain chart analysis). A specific method assuming this is the recency, frequency and monetary value (RFM) method. Finally, one can use different statistical models to predict customer behavior. We will first discuss RFM and then move on to statistical methods such as decision trees and logit.

RFM model

RFM stands for recency, frequency and monetary value. Recency refers to the time since the last transaction. Frequency concerns the number of transactions in a considered time period and monetary refers to the average or total monetary value of all transactions in a specific time period. The RFM model originates from direct marketing and has been frequently applied by firms (Verhoef et al., 2002) such as Readers Digest. It is considered a very powerful model for predicting responses to mailings and may also be used to gain insights on the expected lifetime value of customers (e.g. Fader, Hardie, & Lee, 2005).

To execute RFM analysis, analysts should calculate an RFM-index. A standard way of forming the RFM index is to provide importance weights a_i

counting up to one for each of the RFM components. RFM is then calculated as follows:

$$\text{RFM} = a_1 \times R + a_2 \times F + a_3 \times M., \tag{4.1.8}$$

where a_1, a_2, and $a_3 \geq 0$, and $a_1 + a_2 + a_3 = 1$

In this formula, the standardized (mean value = 0, standard deviation = 1) R, F and M scores are used to account for scale differences. The weights can be based on intuition and experience. For example, marketers might know that frequency is the most important determinant of response to a mailing, while monetary value is less important. Based on this insight, monetary value is assigned a lower importance weight than frequency. A second way of calculating the importance weights is to formally estimate a model in which one estimates the effect of each of R, F and M on past mail response or response on a test mailing. From the results one can gain detailed insights on the importance of each of these variables.

Another way of calculating the RFM-index is the execution of PCA. PCA is frequently used to calculate indices (e.g. price index). The RFM variables are included in the PCA, where one can choose the option of a single principal component (or factor). If a proper solution can be retrieved, the PCA scores can be saved, reflecting the RFM index (see Box 4.1.1).

The RFM index can be used as a segmentation variable and, using for example decile analysis, customers can be divided into different RFM segments. For each RFM segment the average response rate etc. can be calculated. Figure 4.1.25 shows how we divided the customer base of a book club into five segments for the separate RFM variables and the formed RFM index. The latter was based on a PCA. The RFM segmentation is clearly linked to response. The segment with the highest RFM has the highest response rate. Segmenting on recency only does not result in strong differences in response rates. This indicates that recency is not a good predictor of response.

Decision trees

Decision trees can be used in a broad range of statistical techniques. Based on the found associations between one independent binary variable (e.g. response) and usually multiple predictors, a tree structure with different customer segments can be drawn.[7] In a statistical sense one could argue that this technique involves both segmentation and prediction. However, in customer value management (CVM) practice it is mainly used for predictive purposes. Several names for these techniques are found in literature and software programs such as CHAID, Cart, and Answer Tree can be used.

The big advantage of using a decision tree is that it is quite a user-friendly technique. Computer programs have developed user-friendly interfaces. Moreover, the outcomes of the analysis are easy to explain to managers graphically. In practice, outcomes of decision tree analyses on customer churn are

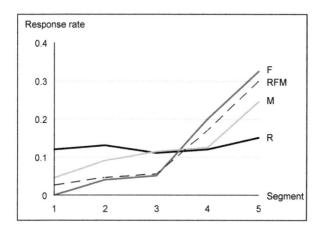

Figure 4.1.25 Response rate for different RFM-segments

often presented to boardroom members. Another advantage is that one gets more insights into different relationships in the data. Especially, one gets insights into potential interaction effects and non-linear effects. For example, one may observe that in especially large households living in urban areas churn or response is higher. One disadvantage is that the technique can be considered something of a black box. It is not clear to analysts what is actually happening. In an extreme sense the analyst puts variables in the program and the decision tree pops out. Still, its usefulness is generally highly valued. Some researchers use CHAID as a method to get more insights into the data and the interdependencies between variables. The outcomes of CHAID are subsequently used for fine tuning other analytical models, such as regression-based models (e.g. Neslin, Gupta, Kamakura, Lu, & Mason, 2006).

Figure 4.1.26 shows the outcome of a CHAID analysis for the response to a shop mailing. The average response is 1.16%. In a subsequent node of the tree, household size is the most discriminating variable. Household sizes from 2 to 5 have the highest response. There is still some heterogeneity in response within this segment. Therefore, a second node is added, with distance to the shop as a discriminating variable. Especially for households living close to the store, response is even higher, with an average response rate of 1.89%.

Logit models

Within customer management and branding research, analysts frequently have to predict binary events such as churn or brand choice. Analysts sometimes use well-known regression models to predict this kind of event. The ordinary regression model, however, assumes that the dependent variable is continuous and therefore it is not perfectly suited for the prediction of these binary events.

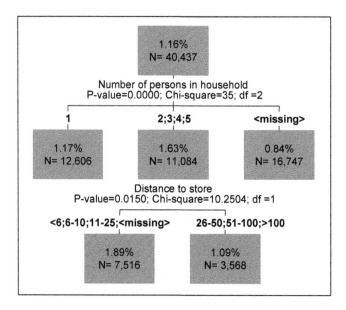

Figure 4.1.26 Example of a decision tree using CHAID

For this reason logistic regression has been developed. In this regression-type model the dependent variable is binary. In literature the model is often referred to as the logit model. This type of model has been extensively used in the brand loyalty literature. Logistic regression and decision trees are the models most commonly used to predict churn; together they accounted for 68% of the entries of a churn modeling contest[8] in which both practitioners and academics participated (Neslin et al., 2006). Neslin et al. (2006) concluded that logistic regression and tree approaches perform best in terms of prediction and that the differences between the models in predictive accuracy are "managerially meaningful."

The objectives of the logistic regression model are twofold. First, one aims to assess the impact of predictors on the occurrence of an event. Second, one aims to predict the probability of occurrence of the event. This probability p varies between 0 and 1 (or, multiplied by 100, between 0% and 100%). In the logistic regression model the binary dependent variable Y (e.g. churn) is econometrically transformed in a latent continuous variable Y^*. In our example we considered response to the mailing of a store and included variables such as distance to the store (DISTANCE), and household size. If we work with these two variables we get the following equation:

$$Y^* = \ln \frac{p}{1-p} = \beta_0 + \beta_1 \times DISTANCE \times \beta_2 \times HHSIZE \qquad (4.1.9)$$

This latent continuous variable can then be explained by the independent variables. For each of these variables, coefficients and accompanying significant levels are derived. The coefficient (β) shows the impact of that variable on the latent continuous variable Y^*. These coefficients should be interpreted in a different way as in the regression model. For example, assume that a coefficient is 0.5 household size. A rise of 1 in household size does imply that the latent variable Y^* increases by 0.5. However, it does not imply that the probability of the occurrence of an event rises by 0.5. To assess this probability a logistic transformation should be used, which can be formulated as follows:

$$p = \frac{1}{1+e^{-(\beta_0 + \beta_1 \times DISTANCE \times \beta_2 \times HHSIZE)}} \qquad (4.1.10)$$

This probability can subsequently be used in all kinds of calculations. In this case the expected revenue/margin per customer of a mailing can be calculated. If churn is explained one can assess the lifetime value of a customer as one knows the average margin on a customer and the churn probability (e.g. Donkers, Verhoef, & De Jong, 2007). The quality of the model can be evaluated in terms of its explanatory power and the hit rate. The most commonly used statistic is the Chi-square test, which assesses whether the predictors have some explanatory power. Programs also frequently report R^2 types of measures, which show how good the model is at explaining the event. High R^2 are frequently considered better. One cautionary note is that the statistics for the logistic regression have different meanings than they do in the standard regression model. Moreover, in this type of model, and especially in a CVM context, these measures tend to be low. Finally, one frequently uses the hit rate, which is calculated as the percentage of events predicted in the right group. One should also be careful with evaluating this statistic, especially if events occur infrequently. All cases tend to be classified automatically in the most frequently occurring event group. For more detailed information on the logistic regression model we refer to Franses and Paap (2001) and Blattberg et al. (2008).

Fortunately, statistical programs such as SPSS provide standard procedures to execute logistic regression procedures. These programs also calculate the probability, so analysts do not have to execute the shown transformation themselves. Figure 4.1.27 shows the logistic regression output for the response on a mailing example (as discussed in the CHAID section). The model output shows some significant coefficients (B) (sig. < .05): distance to the store, type of bank, and household size. It appears that customers who are further away from the store are less likely to respond to the mailing. However, large households are more likely to respond. The output also reports the standard error and the Wald statistic. The size of the Wald statistic also shows which variable has the largest impact on an event. In this case distance to the store has the largest impact, with a Wald statistic of 6.837.

		B	S.E.	Wald	df	Sig.	Exp(B)
Step 1a	DISTANCE TO STORE	-.142	.054	6.837	1	.009	.868
	GENDER	-.214	.220	.942	1	.332	.808
	AVERAGE SPEND/M	-.027	.039	.504	1	.478	.973
	BANK	.444	.203	4.766	1	.029	1.559
	HHSIZE	.138	.065	4.466	1	.035	1.148
	Constant	-3.883	.336	133.694	1	.000	.021

Figure 4.1.27 Output of logistic regression mailing example in SPSS

Computer science models

In computer science also several models have been developed aiming to improve predictions of the models discussed above. One problem with these models is that the results might be affected by the specific composition of a sample. Therefore so-called aggregation methods are used. The key idea behind these models is that improved predictions could be obtained by averaging the results of a large number of models. The intuition behind aggregating multiple model results is that the quality of a single predictor might depend heavily on the specific sample (Breiman, 1996b) and is not known beforehand. Averaging predictors of varying quality will result in more stable predictors (Breiman, 1996a, Malthouse & Derenthal, 2008).

An aggregation method that originated in the machine-learning field is bootstrap aggregation, or "bagging" (Lemmens & Croux, 2006). In the bagging procedure a model is estimated on a number of bootstrap samples of the original estimation sample, resulting in a number of predictions for every customer. The final prediction is obtained by taking the average of all predictions (Breiman, 1996a). The bagging procedure seems especially useful for improving the performance of decision trees. The performance of logistic regression models is not substantially improved by using the bagging procedure, as the logistic regression model results are less affected by sample composition (Risselada, Verhoef, & Bijmolt, 2010). For more specific details on bagging we refer to Lemmens and Croux (2006). We also note that standard bagging has not been implemented yet in standard software packages such as SPSS and SAS.

Predictive performance measures

The literature proposes several metrics that can be used to assess the predictive performance of prediction models. The most important are:

- Hit rate
- Top-decile lift
- Gini coefficient.

Hit rate

The hit rate is defined as the percentage of customers that is correctly predicted. It can be formally expressed as:

$$\text{hit rate} = \frac{\text{number of customers correctly classified}}{\text{number of customers}} \times 100\% \qquad (4.1.11)$$

The hit rate is a fairly easy metric to interpret, and is also a standard calculation. An important problem, however, is that especially in many customer prediction models it is less informative due to the infrequent occurrence of events. In many models customers become mainly classified in the most occurring event. As a consequence it is almost impossible to compare different competing models and to assess their predictive quality.

Top-decile lift

"Lift" is the most common measure for model performance (Blattberg et al., 2008). Intuitively, lift measures whether the model is better able to distinguish between, for example, responders and non-responders, or churners and non-churners. For the calculation of top-decile lift a gains-table needs to be developed. Customers are assigned to deciles based on their predicted event (e.g. churn) probability. For each decile the average predicted event probability is calculated. The lift is subsequently calculated as:

$$\text{lift decile}_j = \frac{\text{average predicted event probability of decile}_j}{\text{average event probability}} \qquad (4.1.12)$$

In Table 4.1.2 we provide an example of such a calculation for a model predicting direct mail response. The top-decile lift is the lift in decile 1. The top-decile lift is substantial, as the response rate is 6%, while the average response rate is only 1.60%. Based on the calculations of the lifts in each decile, the cumulative lift can be computed. The cumulative lift of the kth decile is defined by the percentage of all responders accounted for by the first k deciles (Blattberg et al., 2008: 319). In Table 4.1.2 the top two deciles account for 59.4% of all responders. The higher the cumulative lift for a specific decile, the better the model.

Gini coefficient

The Gini coefficient is related to the lift model performance measures, in that it is essentially the area between the model's cumulative lift curve and the lift curve that would result from a random prediction. For this purpose one should create a gains chart. In this gains chart the percentage of customers, ordered by their event probability, is plotted along the x-axis, and the cumulative number

Table 4.1.2 Gains and lift scale

Decile	Predicted Response Rate	Lift	Cumulative Lift (in %)
1	6.00	3.75	37.5
2	3.50	2.19	59.4
3	2.50	1.56	75.0
4	1.50	0.94	84.4
5	1.00	0.63	90.6
6	0.65	0.41	94.7
7	0.50	0.31	97.8
8	0.19	0.12	99.0
9	0.12	0.08	99.8
10	0.04	0.03	100.0
Total	**1.60**	**0.03**	

Source: Adapted from Blattberg et al. (2008)

of customers experiencing the event is plotted along the y-axis (compare with cumulative lift). An example is shown in Figure 4.1.28. The straight line or the perfect equality line is the line representing a model with random predictions (no information). The curve results from predictions. A larger distance between the curve and the perfect equality line means a stronger model performance.

The Gini coefficient can be calculated from the gains chart as shown in Figure 4.1.28. We mainly consider the area (A) between the perfect equality

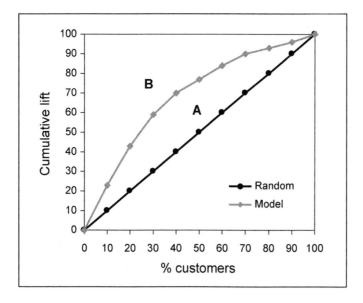

Figure 4.1.28 Gains chart

line and the model curve. The coefficient is calculated by dividing A by the area above the perfect equality line (A+B). The Gini coefficient can have a value between 0 and 1. A value of 0 implies that the model predicts just as well as a random predictor. If the model has a value of 1 it principally means that there is only one customer and that customer is classified as the customer with the highest event probability. This is a very rare case. In general, one would chose models that have coefficients closer to 1.

Practical Issues

When executing a database analysis one can encounter many issues that can make the life of a database analyst pretty tough and challenging. Below we discuss some of these issues, which include problems with infrequent events, multi-faceted behavior, self-hidden findings, and sample selection.

- Occurrence of Infrequent observations: In database marketing it often happens that specific events occur infrequently. For example, only 2% of customers may respond to a mailing or only 1% adopt a new service. To predict this event large databases are required. A rule of thumb is that an analyst requires around 100 customers for whom the event occurs. This would imply a database of, at a minimum, 10,000 customers for an event probability of 1%. This should not be too problematic nowadays. However, large databases are more difficult to handle and usually also require more time for calculations to be carried out on them. One solution to overcome these hurdles is to create a balanced sample, in which the customers with an infrequently occurring event are over-sampled and the customers with no event are under-sampled. For the logit model this implies that only the constant in the model is affected, while the other coefficients of the predictor variables should not be affected. The advantage of oversampling is that smaller databases can be analyzed. One must be careful to note that oversampling leads to biased estimates when it is done in a non-random fashion and the sample consists of relatively many customers experiencing the event (e.g. churn) with a certain (influential) characteristic (e.g. many young customers). Donkers, Franses and Verhoef (2003) have reflected on this issue and have provided details on how to correct for over-sampling.
- Multi-faceted customer behavior: In many instances the modeled behavior is not a single event. For example, if a charity institution aims to predict response to a mailing, they are also interested in the donation amount, as this also drives the revenue on the mailing. In the same vein, catalogers might not only be interested in the prediction of a purchase, but also in the subsequent product return probability (Petersen & Kumar, 2009). In many instances behavior is multi-faceted. Fortunately, one can apply models to predict these different though related behaviors jointly. For example, to model both response to a charity mailing and the donation amount, one can use a Tobit(2) model or one can model the purchase probability

and the subsequent order size (e.g. Konuş, Verhoef, & Neslin, 2014). In this model a logit model is used to predict response or purchase, while a regression model is used for predicting the donation amount (for responders) or order size (for buyers). In the second analysis one accounts for the selection effect of responding and the potential interdependence between these two events.

- Churn is not observed: In contractual relationships churn and many other behaviors are typically observed in the database, as customers have to renew their contract. However, for many retailers one only observes buying behavior. Logit models are then less suitable for customer analysis. Instead, duration models can be used to model the time to next purchase. These models can also be useful when analysts aim to model the time until a customer churns or adopts a new product (e.g. Prins & Verhoef, 2007; Polo, Sesé, & Verhoef, 2011). These models are also referred to as hazard models, but go beyond the scope of this book. We refer to Franses and Paap (2001) for a detailed discussion on these models.

- Self-hidden Easter eggs and more: The interactions between firms and their customers are often continuously recorded in a database. As a consequence, one can observe the consequences of the interactions in real time. However, one important issue is that this also may impact the findings. Let's assume for example that customers with a high purchase volume usually receive a mailing. In a subsequent analysis, the researcher finds a link between purchase volume in the past and purchase propensity. The question is whether this relationship occurs because of the high volume or because of the selective mailing strategy. In a sense the finding of this relationship could be labeled a self-hidden Easter egg in the database. A related issue is that found relationships occur due to specific underlying mechanisms which might cause the found relationship to appear strong when it is actually smaller or even absent. This problem occurs, for example, when analyzing the effect of loyalty programs (LPs) on customer loyalty. This effect is overestimated, as one does not account for the fact that loyal customers are more inclined to use an LP. In econometric terms one calls this an endogeneity problem (see also Box 4.1.2).

Conclusions

This chapter has discussed seven analytical classics. These classics vary in application area, use different methods and techniques that can be divided into the descriptive vs. predictive nature and the static vs. dynamic focus. These methods do, however, have in common that they are frequently used within marketing intelligence functions. Moreover, many of these methods will also play a role in big data environments. We believe it is therefore very important to master these methods before immediately doing all kinds of big data analytics. In this chapter we have aimed to provide a combination of a theoretical sound discussion of the different methods and important practical applications and insights of these methods. If readers are more interested in specific details, we refer to suggested readings cited in the text. Especially for analysts aiming to be an expert in specific methods, understanding the detail can be very useful. However, one warning is warranted here. In some cases analysts may become too expert, with the potential danger of ignoring the practical implications of their (advanced) modeling efforts. In sum, the analyst should be use-oriented when applying the different models.

Notes

1 We thank Marcel Temminghof from GfK for sharing these data.
2 We refer to Wedel and Kamakura (2000) for an extensive discussion on cluster analysis. See also Hair, Black, Babin, Anderson and Tatham (2006) for more on multivariate data analysis.
3 The number of clusters can also be determined with some statistical criteria, such as the fusion coefficient. However, this subject goes beyond the scope of this book. In any case, the dendrogram is typically rather insightful.
4 Discriminant analysis is a multivariate technique used to explain and predict group membership. This technique is available in packages, such as IBM/SPSS. We refer to Hair et al. (2006) for a more in-depth discussion.
5 We refer to Franses, van Dijk and Opschoor (2014) for an extensive discussion on time-series models. For readers interested in marketing the work of Koen Pauwels with multiple applications of several variants of the VAR model could be especially relevant. For an overview of time series models in marketing we refer to DeKimpe and Hanssens (2010).
6 We thank Felix Eggers for sharing this example.
7 The level association is usually assessed with the Chi-square statistic, which you can find in a CHAID (Chi-square automatic interaction detection) analysis.
8 This contest was organized by the Teradata Center for Customer Relationship Management at the Fuqua School of Business at Duke University in 2003.

References

Blattberg, R. C., Kim, B.-D., & Neslin, S. A. (2008). *Database marketing – Analyzing and managing customers*. New York: Springer Science & Business Media.
Breiman, L. (1996a). Bagging predictors. *Machine Learning*, 24(2), 123–40.
Breiman, L. (1996b). The heuristics of instability in model selection. *The Annals of Statistics*, 24(6), 2350–83.
David Shepard Associates. (1999). *The new direct marketing: How to implement a profit-driven database marketing strategy*. Europe: Mcgraw-Hill Education.
Dekimpe, M. G., & Hanssens, D. M. (1995). The persistence of marketing effects on sales. *Marketing Science*, 14(1), 1–21.
Dekimpe, M. G., & Hanssens, D. M. (2010). Time-series models in marketing: some recent developments. *Marketing Journal of Research and Management*, 1(1), 93–8.
Donkers, B., Franses, P. H., & Verhoef, P. C. (2003). Using selective sampling for binary choice models. *Journal of Marketing Research*, 40(4), 492–7.
Donkers, B., Verhoef, P. C., & De Jong, M. G. (2007). Predicting CLV: A test of competing models in the insurance industry. *Quantitative Marketing and Economics*, 5(2), 163–90.
Ebbes, P., Papies, D., & Van Heerde, H. J. (2011). The sense and non-sense of holdout sample validation in the presence of endogeneity. *Marketing Science*, 30(6), 1115–22.

Eggers, F., & Sattler, H. (2011). Preference measurement with conjoint analysis. Overview of state-of-the-art approaches and recent developments. *GfK Marketing Intelligence Review*, 3(1), 36–47.

Fader, P. S., Hardie, B. G., & Lee, K. L. (2005). RFM and CLV: Using iso-value curves for customer base analysis. *Journal of Marketing Research*, 42(4), 415–30.

Franses, P. H., & Paap, R. (2001). *Quantitative models in marketing research*. Cambridge, UK: Cambridge University Press.

Franses, P. H., van Dijk, D., & Opschoor, A. (2014). *Time series models for business and economic forecasting*. Cambridge UK: Cambridge University Press.

Gijsenberg, M. J., Van Heerde, H. J., & Verhoef, P. C. (2015). Losses loom longer than gains: Modeling the impact of service crises on customer satisfaction over time. *Journal of Marketing Research*, 52(5), 642–56.

Hair, J. F., Black, W. C., Babin, B. J., Anderson, R. E., & Tatham, R. L. (4th ed.). (2006). *Multivariate data analysis*. New Jersey: Prentice Hall.

Hunneman, A., Verhoef, P. C., & Sloot, L. M. (2015). The impact of consumer confidence on store satisfaction and share of wallet formation. *Journal of Retailing*, 91(3), 516–32.

Konuş, U., Verhoef, P. C., & Neslin, S. A. (2008). Multichannel shopper segments and their antecedents. *Journal of Retailing*, 84(4), 398–413.

Konuş, U., Verhoef, P. C., & Neslin, S. A. (2014). The effect of search channel elimination on purchase incidence, order size and channel choice. *International Journal of Research in Marketing*, 3(1), 49–64.

Leeflang, P. S. H, Wieringa, J. E., Bijmolt, T. H. A., & Pauwels, K. H. (2015). *Modeling markets*. New York: Springer.

Leeflang, P. S. H., & Naert, P. A. (1978). *Building implementable marketing models*. Dordrecht: Kluwer.

Leenheer, J., Bijmolt, T. H. A., Van Heerde, H. J., & Smidts, A. (2007). Do loyalty programs really enhance behavioral loyalty? An empirical analysis accounting for self-selecting members. *International Journal of Research in Marketing*, 24(1), 31–47.

Lemmens, A., & Croux, C. (2006). Bagging and boosting classification trees to predict churn. *Journal of Marketing Research*, 43(2), 276–86.

Lilien, G. L., & Rangaswamy, A. (2nd ed.). (2006). *Marketing engineering: Computer-assisted marketing analysis and planning*. Victoria, BC, Canada: Trafford Publishing.

Lilien, G. L., Kotler, P., & Moorthy, S. (1992). *Marketing models*. Prentice Hall PTR.

Lindell, M. K., & Whitney, D. J. (2001). Accounting for common method variance in cross-sectional designs. *Journal of Applied Psychology*, 86(1), 114–21.

Malhotra, N. K. (2010), *Marketing research: An applied orientation*. New York: Prentice Hall.

Malthouse, E. C., & Derenthal, K. M. (2008). Improving predictive scoring models through model aggregation. *Journal of Interactive Marketing*, 22(3), 51–68

Mark, T., Lemon, K. N., Vandenbosch, M., Bulla, J., & Maruotti, A. (2013). Capturing the evolution of customer–firm relationships: How customers become more (or less) valuable over time. *Journal of Retailing*, 89(3), 231–45.

Neslin, S. A., Gupta S., Kamakura, W. A., Lu, J. X., & Mason, C. H. (2006). Defection detection: Measuring and understanding the predictive accuracy of customer churn models. *Journal of Marketing Research*, 43(2), 204–11.

Netzer, O., Lattin, J. M., & Srinivasan, V. (2008). A hidden Markov model of customer relationship dynamics. *Marketing Science*, 27(2), 185–204.

Nijs, V. R., Dekimpe, M. G., Steenkamp, J.-B. E. M., & Hanssens, D. M. (2001). The category-demand effects of price promotions. *Marketing Science*, 20(1), 1–22.

Paas, L. J., Bijmolt, T. H. A., & Vermunt, J. K. (2007). Acquisition patterns of financial products: A longitudinal investigation. *Journal of Economic Psychology*, 28(2), 229–41.

Pauwels, K. H. (2004). How dynamic consumer response, competitor response, company support and company inertia shape long-term marketing effectiveness. *Marketing Science*, 23(4), 596–610.

Petersen, J. A., & Kumar, V. (2009). Are product returns a necessary evil? Antecedents and consequences. *Journal of Marketing*, 73(3), 35–51.

Podsakoff, P. M., MacKenzie, S. B., Lee, J. Y., & Podsakoff, N. P. (2003). Method biases in behavioral research: A critical review of the literature and recommended remedies. *Journal of Applied Psychology*, 88(5), 879–903.

Polo, Y., Sesé, F. J., & Verhoef, P. C. (2011). The effect of pricing and advertising on customer retention in a liberalizing market. *Journal of Interactive Marketing*, 25(4), 201–14.

Prins, R., & Verhoef, P. C. (2007). Marketing communication drivers of adoption timing of a new e-service among existing customers. *Journal of Marketing*, 71(2), 169–83.

Risselada, H., Verhoef, P. C., & Bijmolt, T. H. A. (2010). Staying power of churn prediction models. *Journal of Interactive Marketing*, 24(3), 198–208.

Roberts, J. H., Kayandé, U., & Stremersch, S. (2014). From academic research to marketing practice: Exploring the marketing science value chain. *International Journal of Research in Marketing*, 3(2), 127–40.

Rossi, P. E. (2014). Even the rich can make themselves poor: A critical examination of IV methods in marketing applications. *Marketing Science*, 34, 655–72.

Van Doorn, J., & Verhoef, P. C. (2008). Critical incidents and the impact of satisfaction on customer share. *Journal of Marketing*, 72(4), 123–42.

Verhoef, P. C., Hoekstra, J. C., & Van der Scheer, H. R. (2009). *Competing on analytics: Status quo van customer intelligence in Nederland*. Report of Customer Insights Center (RUGCIC–2009–02), University of Groningen.

Verhoef, P. C., Spring, P. N., Hoekstra, J. C., & Leeflang, P. S. H. (2002). The commercial use of segmentation and predictive modelling techniques for database marketing in the Netherlands. *Decision Support System*, 34(4), 471–81.

Verhoef, P. C., Van Doorn, J., & Dorotić, M. (2007). Customer value management: an overview and research agenda. *Marketing Journal of Research and Management*, 3(2), 105–20.

Wedel, M., & Kamakura, W. A. (2000). *Market segmentation: Concepts and methodological foundations*. Boston: Kluwer Academic Publishers.

Wittink, D. R., Addona, M. J., Hawkes, W. J., & Porter J. C. (2011). SCAN*PRO®: The estimation, validation, and use of promotional effects scanner data. In Wieringa, J.E., Verhoef, P.C., & Hoekstra J.C. (Eds), *Liber Amicorum in honor of Peter S.H. Leeflang*, University of Groningen.

Wuyts, S., Verhoef, P. C., & Prins, R. (2009). Partner selection in B2B information service markets. *International Journal of Research in Marketing*, 26(1), 41–51.

4.2 Big data analytics

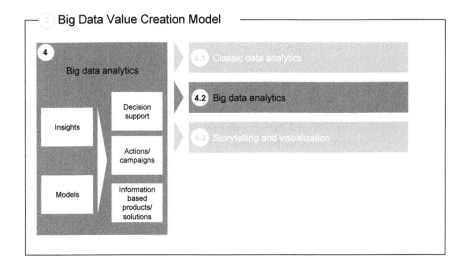

Introduction

The developments in big data are changing analytics. There are three major developments underlying these changes. First, new data types and specifically non-structured data are being analyzed. Traditional data analysts typically do not always have the skills to analyze these data, as totally new methods are required. Further, new data may require more computer science techniques. Second, in this new big data and digital environment, new challenges and questions arise. An important challenge, for example, is how to evaluate investments in new online advertising tools such as search engine advertising and affiliates. Third, new analytical techniques are being developed that can account for the huge continuous data inflow. As a consequence, a total new playing field for analysts has unfolded. This implies that traditional analysts have to adapt to these new circumstances and have to understand and be able to apply these new techniques. Fortunately, some of these big data analytics still use some of the classics as discussed in Chapter 4.1. However, some techniques are rather new and are not included in the statistical toolkit of traditional analysts. In this chapter we aim to discuss seven new big data analyses. These big data analyses are a combination of new techniques, specific marketing applications and specific types of data. Not all of them involve very sophisticated models. In Table 4.2.1 we provide an overview of seven new big data analytical areas, their importance for marketing decisions at the market, brand, or customer level and the statistical methods they use, and we will go on to discuss each of these areas in more detail.

Big data area 1: Web analytics

Web analytics can be viewed as a new big data application area of standard descriptive techniques, as it involves new data sources, which are typically more massive than standard data sources. Web analytics gained attention early in 2000, as early online marketers tried to understand how consumers use websites and visit online stores. This behavior is different from how, for example, customers visit supermarkets (see Table 4.2.2).

Analysis of clickstream data

To analyze behavior on websites, so-called "clickstream data" are used. Clickstream data are defined as the electronic record of Internet usage collected by web servers or third-party servers. Two types of clickstream data can be distinguished (Bucklin & Sismeiro, 2009):

- Site-centric: detailed records of what visitors do when navigating and interacting with a specific site (offline: compare to loyalty card information of one specific store)
- User-centric: detailed records of online behavior tracing across sites (offline: scanner data of specific consumer products).

Basic analyses of clickstream data focus on the purchase funnel on the website. Website analytics aim to collect metrics on the phase of the purchase funnel (see Figure 4.2.1). In this online funnel different steps are being made, and online markets aim to improve the usability of the website and use other marketing instruments to increase the performance on each of these steps to finally end up with a high conversion rate. In the end, these analyses are fairly descriptive and focus on counting.

One could go beyond counting and consider what drives specific behavior on websites. For example, one could model the duration of a visit on the website and its effect on conversion (e.g. Johnson, Bellman, & Lohse, 2003; Bucklin & Sismeiro, 2003). Or the evolution of purchase behavior on websites can be considered (Shi & Zhang, 2014). For online retailers also market-basket analysis can be done, which focuses on what is being purchased during a visit and how the basket can be filled through personalized offers. Going beyond website analytics, online and offline marketers have become very interested in the customer journey and how that affects purchase behavior—something which we will discuss in the next section.

Table 4.2.1 Seven big data analytics

Big Data Analytics	Description	Application area	Method/techniques	Focus	Method
1 Web analytics	Web-analytics aim to understand how consumers use websites and visit online stores.	Customer: online purchase behavior, market basket analysis, AB testing	Descriptive analytics	De	St
2 Customer journey analysis	Businesses interact with their users and potential clients across multiple channels and touchpoints, including television, telephones, the Internet, mobile phones, and retail stores. Customer journey analytics allow businesses to take data from all these sources and where possible make sense of it. This allows them to better understand customer journeys and the effects of touchpoints on purchase behavior.	Customer: innovation/development/optimizing customer service & contact models	Channel switching matrix, attribution models, VAR models	De	St
3 Attribution modeling	Customers are influenced by several touchpoints in their purchase decision process. To assess the effects of customer touchpoints on conversion and sales, attribution modeling is used. Sometimes this is also referred to as the development of "path to purchase" models.	Customer: allocating resources among touchpoints. Pricing/contracting third partners, such as Google or comparison websites etc.	Attribution models, VAR models	Pr	Dy

(Continued)

Table 4.2.1 (Continued)

Big Data Analytics	Description	Application area	Method/techniques	Focus		Method
4 Dynamic targeting	A more focused form of market segmentation that groups consumers based on specific behavioral patterns they display when making purchasing decisions, enabling producers to adapt their marketing approach to specific groups. Instead of using static lists, rules are generated to create dynamic segments based on any demographic, behavioral criteria, or cross-channel interaction, such as a customer's profile, behavior, location, when they last interacted, campaigns or goals triggered, and more.	Customer: real-time offering, recommendation, personalization	Collaborative filtering, latent class models (finite mixture), hierarchical Bayes models, Markov chains		Pr	Dy
5 Big Data integrated models	Big data developments result in more data availability from different sources. These data are integrated and as a consequence data with different aggregation levels will exist. This creates challenges for analysts and may induce the use of complicated models, such as Bayesian models.	Multi-source data predictions and forecasting models in/for all application areas	Regression models, multi-level models, adaptive forecasting models, Bayesian models	De	Pr	Dy

(Continued)

Table 4.2.1 (Continued)

Big Data Analytics	Description	Application area	Method/techniques	Focus	Method
6 Social listening	Active monitoring of social media channels for information about a company or organization, usually tracking content of various social media such as blogs, wikis, news sites, micro-blogs such as Twitter, social networking sites, video/photo sharing websites, forums, message boards, blogs and user-generated content in general as a way to determine the volume and sentiment of online conversation about a brand or topic.	Market: trend watching, product innovations Brand: experience, pos/neg emotions	Text analytics	De	Dy
7 Social network analysis	Social network analysis views social relationships in terms of network theory, consisting of nodes, representing individual actors within the network, and ties or edges which represent relationships between the individuals, such as friendship, kinship, organizations and sexual relationships. These networks are often depicted in a social network diagram, where nodes are represented as points and ties are represented as lines.	Identification of influencers (i.e. Hubs) and customer engagement value	Social network metrics	De	St

De: Descriptive; Pr: Predictive; St: Static; Dy: Dynamic

198 *Big data analytics*

Table 4.2.2 How Internet choice differs from supermarket choice

Internet choice	Supermarket choice
• Intent unclear at outset Browse? Search? Buy?	• Store visit reveals purchase intent
• Active/Interactive Visitor participates in creating choice context	• Passive

• Addressable
  Choice context is personalizable
	• Fixed
	  Choice context common

• Dynamic Marketers can intervene at low cost	• Static

Source: Bucklin et al. (2002)

Large scale experimentation: A/B testing

Having gained an understanding of the purchase funnel and any specific issues connected with it, firms will want to go on and solve these issues. This could be done by, for example, improving search engine optimization (SEO). Another way is to improve the website. Firms nowadays use large-scale experimentation to test changes in website design. For example, Booking.com changed specific wordings in offers and observed how this improved (or failed to improve) conversion rates. This large-scale experimentation is also known as A/B testing (see Figure 4.2.2). This A/B testing is nothing more than a randomized field experiment among a large number of visitors of the website. Typically, a new website is tested among a group of visitors and the results are compared with a control group who still use the old version of the website. One can extend this testing by using more complicated experimental designs, such as factorial designs. If the

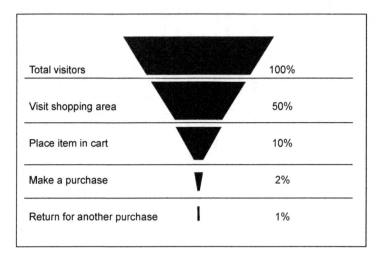

Figure 4.2.1 Online purchase funnel

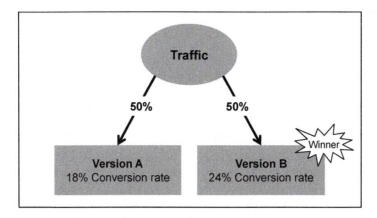

Figure 4.2.2 A/B testing

experiment is fully randomized, an analysis of variance (ANOVA) can be used to test for significant effects on outcomes. To account for potential customer specific effects, such as age and loyalty, covariates can be included in an analysis of covariance (ANCOVA). Note that given the large scale of these experiments, not only the significance of these effects should be considered, but also the size of the found differences (see Chapter 4). In general A/B testing is not much different from the testing of marketing tactics used in previous years, such as testing different versions of direct mailings (e.g. David Shepard Associates, 1999). Probably the only difference is that A/B testing usually involves very large samples.

Big data area 2: Customer journey analysis

Customer journey analysis considers how customers interact with multiple touchpoints moving from consideration, search, and purchase to consumption and after-sales. The research is interested in describing this journey and understanding the choices for touchpoints in multiple purchase phases.

The extended customer journey analysis typically uses qualitative interviews, survey data or observations. In service marketing blue printing has been developed to assess the importance of several touchpoints in the service delivery (e.g. Bitner, Ostrom, & Morgan, 2008). It has also become an important topic in multi-channel research (Verhoef, Kannan, & Inman, 2015). Customer journey analysis is frequently executed using qualitative techniques in which customers are asked to describe their channels and touchpoints used and which channel they prefer to use. Based on these qualitative insights firms may develop strategies on how customers can optimally be steered through their channels.

A more quantitative analysis aims to describe the used channels in different phases of the purchase process. Typically, one makes a distinction between (Neslin et al., 2006):

- Channels/touchpoints used for search
- Channels/touchpoints used for purchase
- Channels/touchpoints used for after-sales.

The channels can be both offline and online. Channel behavior online can be tracked more easily (using cookies) than tracking channel usage offline. Only when customers can be identified offline (e.g. through a loyalty card) might one be able to observe their behavior and store that in a database. Note that even in this case one only observes the channel usage for customers that visited the offline channel of the firm and purchased. This means that, for example, a visit to a store to search (but not purchase) is not observed, while a purchase linked to, for example, a loyalty card is observed. Hence to get a full picture of the channel of usage of customers firms frequently have to rely on survey data which asks which channels have been used for search, purchase, and after-sales (e.g. Verhoef, Neslin, & Vroomen, 2007; Gensler, Verhoef, & Böhm, 2012). Survey data mainly recall channel usage and/or channel preferences.

Specific household panels of firms like GfK may also observe this behavior, but then frequently only purchase data are recorded (e.g. Melis, Campo, Breugelmans, & Lamey, 2015). A relatively new method is real-time tracking using mobile technologies. Customers can use a mobile app to record their interactions with multiple brand touchpoints (MacDonald, Wilson, & Konuş, 2012). It is likely that this technique will develop further and that based on location data and a mobile app, visits to stores etc. will be recorded automatically. Still, this will only occur for a sample of customers—those who allow research firms to observe their behavior. In Figure 4.2.3 we report a survey study on the effects of different touchpoints that customers have been exposed to and their effects on advertising recall and brand consideration. Digital and television jointly have a strong effect on brand consideration and thus jointly contribute to the effectiveness of the campaign.

The analysis of these channel usage data typically results in a description of channel usage patterns. Reports might also discuss the use of mobile phones when shopping offline etc. So in essence most of these analyses are fairly descriptive and cannot be labeled as big data analytics. In Figure 4.2.4 we provide some of these statistics as an example and specifically on the showrooming vs. webrooming behavior. Showrooming involves visiting the store for search and subsequently switching to the online channel for purchase, whereas with webrooming the online channel is used for search and the store is used for purchase (e.g. Rapp, Baker, Bachrach, Ogilvie, & Beitelspache, 2015; Verhoef et al., 2015).

Customer segments on channel usage can also be distinguished. For example, Konuş, Verhoef and Neslin (2008) distinguish between enthusiastic multi-channel shoppers, store-shoppers, and unenthusiastic multi-channel shoppers, using latent class analysis as a segmentation technique (see Figure 4.2.5). These segments, however, differ between the studied product categories.

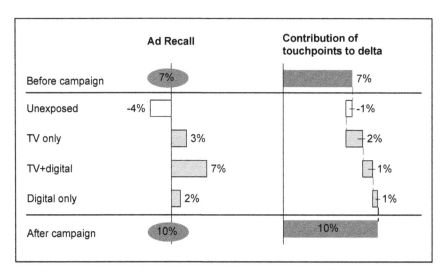

Figure 4.2.3 Effect of different touchpoints on advertising recall and brand consideration

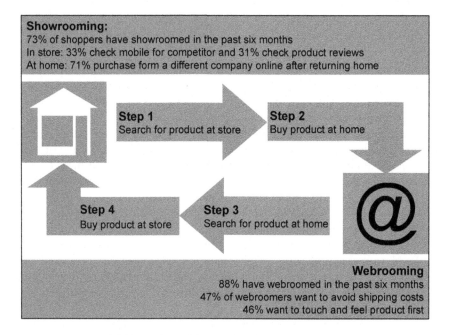

Figure 4.2.4 Use of different channel for search and purchase: Webrooming vs. showrooming

Source: Adapted from Edwards (2014)

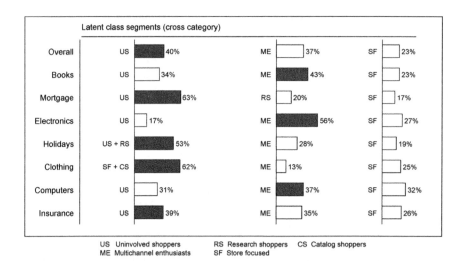

Figure 4.2.5 Latent class segmentation based on customer channel usage

Source: Adapted from Konuş et al. (2008)

As a next step one might aim to explain and/or predict channel choices in the different phases. To explain channel usage in different phases, one could include customer characteristics (e.g. age, income), customer buying behavior (e.g. customer value, purchase frequency), attitudes towards channels and prior channel usage (e.g. Verhoef et al., 2007; Konuş, Neslin, & Verhoef, 2014). Typically choice models are used. This becomes more complicated when multiple channels can be used simultaneously, which typically occurs for the search phase (i.e. online and store for search). Multivariate probit models can then be applied, as these models allow for many choices to be made. In the purchase phase a single channel should be chosen and then logit or probit models can be used. Channel choices also depend on each other, through, for example, channel lock-in. Channel choices in the search phase may affect channel choices in the purchase phase, and vice versa (e.g. Gensler et al., 2012). In principle the usage of channels can be considered as a kind of switching process between channels during different phases. In that sense, Markov switching models could be useful. However, so far we are not aware of studies using this method.

As a next step, channel choices can also be linked to purchase behavior. For example, one question might be whether a channel migration (e.g. moving from catalog to online) increases the purchase probability (e.g. Ansari, Mela, & Neslin, 2008), or whether channel elimination reduces the revenues from customers (see Figure 4.2.6, and for more extensive model results see Konuş et al., 2014).

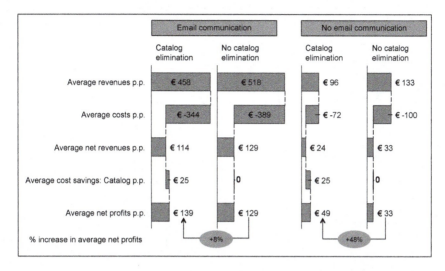

Figure 4.2.6 Revenues, costs, and profit per group with and without search channel catalog
Source: Adapted from Konuş et al. (2014)

Big data area 3: Attribution modeling

When purchasing online, customers go through many stages according to the purchase funnel approach. Customers are influenced by several touchpoints. These touchpoints can be firm initiated—for example via emails—or customer initiated—for example, via search engines (De Haan, Wiesel, & Pauwels, 2013) and may occur at different phases of the purchase funnel. Customers may thus vary in their readiness to purchase (see Figure 4.2.7). Firms will typically only have limited information on the total usage of touchpoints in this "path to purchase" and will typically only observe the ones that are used to visit the retailer's website. Consequently, the question is whether the sale can be attributed to this last-used touchpoint or to other touchpoints, which are generally not observed. It is essential to know this, for allocating resources among touchpoints. It is also important to make deals with partners, such as Google or comparison websites. To assess the effects of customer touchpoints on conversion and sales, attribution modeling can be used. Sometimes this is also referred to as the development of "path to purchase" models.

Methods

The most common method for attributing sales is "last-click." In this rather naive way the sale is attributed to the last used touchpoint. This is a rather simple approach and does not require any modeling. To assess the performance of each touchpoint one can calculate metrics such as the number of websites visited

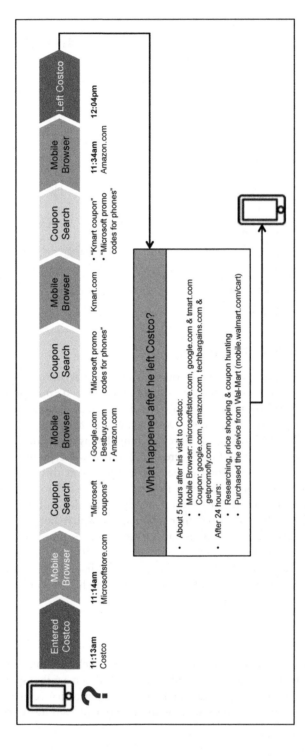

Figure 4.2.7 Purchase funnel: Path to purchase on mobile handset

through this touchpoint, and the conversion rate per touchpoint. It is questionable whether this is a right approach, as the touchpoints used before the last one contributed as well. So last click will typically overestimate the contribution of the touchpoint. There are other methods available. "First-click" attribution is used: the purchase is attributed to the first-used touchpoint. Average attribution methods assume that every used touchpoint contributes equally to the sale: this can be adjusted by using time-decay attribution by assuming that the latest used touchpoints contribute more strongly to the sale. Some adjustments can also be made by using other weighting scores. This is referred to as "customer attribution" (Van der Heijden, De Haan, & Hoving-Wesselius, 2014).

A more complicated method of attributing sales involves creating a dataset in which the purchase (or not) is recorded, along with the used touchpoints, and if possible other customer characteristics. A logistic regression model is then used to estimate the effect of each touchpoint on purchase. However, one concern here is that in some channels some customers have a higher inherent readiness to purchase. This would imply endogeneity of the touchpoints, and one should correct for this (see Chapter 4.1). This is not straightforward, as more information is required and this information is frequently not available. In a case study on attribution modeling presented in Chapter 6 we show how touchpoint usage in the last purchase occasion can function as a way to correct for the endogeneity in touchpoint usage. And indeed the contributions to purchase of specific touchpoints such as search engines are corrected downwards. Interestingly, this study also shows that the results of correcting are rather similar to a model that accounts for the effects of touchpoints and some customer characteristics, such as customer loyalty. In Figure 4.2.8 we provide the estimated effects of a "correct" attribution model and a model in which the last click assumption is being used. As one can observe, there are relatively large differences between the found effects.

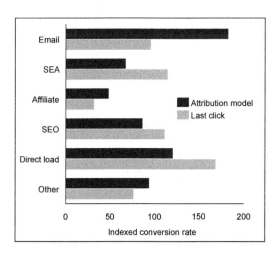

Figure 4.2.8 Comparison of effects estimated by attribution model and last click method

These attribution modeling methods involve an individual level approach to assessing the contribution of specific touchpoints. This implies that individual-level data of touchpoints are required. As noted earlier, these data are available for online retailers of the last-used touchpoint. More elaborate searches could be available if cookies are used. But offline touchpoints are not available. Measuring the effects of offline touchpoints at the individual level requires that customers are constantly monitored in what they see and do. Panels are now being developed to collate this information for a sample of customers. We have already discussed specific methods using mobile panels (MacDonald et al., 2012). Another solution is to use aggregated daily data, in which for an online retailer the daily spending in offline (e.g. advertising) and online (e.g. search engine) media is monitored and linked to the daily online website metrics (i.e. website traffic, sales). De Haan et al. (2013) describe how they use these data to assess the effects of online and offline media spending on these metrics. They use a specific version of the VAR model (see Chapter 4.1). Although with this approach both offline and online media spending can be considered, online marketers consider this aggregate approach to be rather difficult as they are so much used to analyzing individual-level data when doing web analytics.

Big data area 4: Dynamic targeting[1]

Targeting customers with the right offers has been around for a long time. In particular, direct marketing models have been developed to select those customers who are most responsive to direct mailings (e.g. Bult & Wansbeek, 1995). The arrival and growth of the Internet and digital devices with apps have moved targeting to higher levels. Using real-time behavioral data firms aim to provide personalized offers to customers visiting the website or logging on to an app. Given the relatively low costs of approaching customers online, personalization strategies have become economically more attractive (e.g. Zhang & Wedel, 2009). Successful personalization can be a way to gain a competitive advantage, as it could result in more satisfied customers and more effective marketing. As a consequence, closed loop marketing (CLM) has become popular. CLM consists of a cycle in which customer information is continuously collected and updated, and advanced analytics are used to forecast customer behavior and used to redesign and personalize products, services, and marketing effort, in short cycles (Chung & Wedel, 2014), as shown in Figure 4.2.9.

We distinguish between two major types of dynamic targeting approaches that differ with respect to the methods they use (Chung & Wedel, 2014):

- Recommendation systems
- Personalization systems.

Big data analytics 207

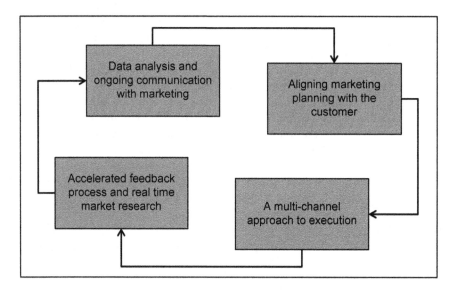

Figure 4.2.9 Closed-loop marketing process
Source: Adapted from Chung & Wedel (2014)

Recommendation systems

Recommendation systems have been around since the start of Internet retailing and are used extensively by firms such as Amazon and Netflix. The key idea of recommendation systems is that based on a customer's characteristics and characteristics of other customers, specific recommendations can be given to customers (e.g. "this book might be something for you"). Three types of recommendation systems can be distinguished (Chung & Wedel, 2014):

- Content filtering systems
- Collaborative filtering systems
- Hybrid forms of content and collaborative filtering systems.

Content filtering systems involve digital agents that produce recommendations based on the target customer's past preferences for products/services and the similarities between those products/services. Hence products or services are offered that are rather similar to the ones purchased before. For example, if one frequently buys fantasy books, it is likely that the next recommendation will be for a fantasy book as well. Collaborative filtering aims to make a recommendation using the preferences of other, similar customers. In practice, frequently so-called memory-based systems are being used here. These systems use measures of similarity between customers' preferences or behaviors. These systems are simple to implement, easily scalable, and robust (Chung & Wedel, 2014).

However, when it involves billions of recommendations for millions of products, more advanced technology, such as map reducing, could be needed. In Chapter 6 we describe the case of an online retailer actually using this technology to achieve their business and marketing objectives with their recommendations. Another technique often adopted is the nearest neighbour algorithm. Because of reported problems with the more simple memory-based systems, model-based systems have been developed in the marketing literature (e.g. Bodapati, 2008). Model-based systems using, for example, stochastic, Bayesian, and/or latent-class type of models tend to outperform the memory-based systems, but are computationally intensive (Chung & Wedel, 2014).

Ansari, Essegaier and Kohli (2000) suggest that recommendation systems should not only be based on customers' revealed preferences and the revealed preferences of other customers, but should also involve preferences for product attributes, expert judgments, and specific customer characteristics. Recommendation systems are therefore sometimes updated with preferences for attributes. Firms can use conjoint analysis to derive individual estimates of attribute utilities (see Chapter 4.1). The problem with attribute utilities is that they are likely to be collected only for a limited number of customers. For new customers these attribute utilities are not available and thus they should be combined with behavioral patterns of customers. For example, a combined algorithm using both conjoint utilities and behavioral patterns could be developed, thereby also considering the behavior of other similar customers, for a website selling hotel breaks. In Figure 4.2.10 we provide an overview of this algorithm. Importantly, this algorithm also accounts for the reviews written about the hotel. This is actually an ongoing trend in recommendation agents. Many recommendation agents nowadays use reviews written by customers, as many customers write reviews. The popularity of social networks such as Facebook, where customers can *like* products and brands, stimulates the use of reviews in these agents as well.

Personalization

The key difference between recommendation systems and personalization systems is that recommendation systems recommend existing products or services, whereas personalization systems adapt the offering to customers' needs. Note that it not only involves product or service offerings—how the website is displayed (looks and feels) to customers can also be personalized. In that sense, personalization systems are more customer-driven than recommendation systems. Customization is a term that is also used frequently in the context of personalization. Customization involves the firm facilitating the customer by tailoring products and services to his or her preferences (Arora et al., 2008). A famous example is Dell.com, where customers can combine specific attributes to customize their preferred computer. Car manufacturers such as BMW also allow customers to customize. The firms thus provide an interface to customers to customize a product: the customer is making decisions. With personalization the firm tailors the marketing mix to the customer, based on available customer

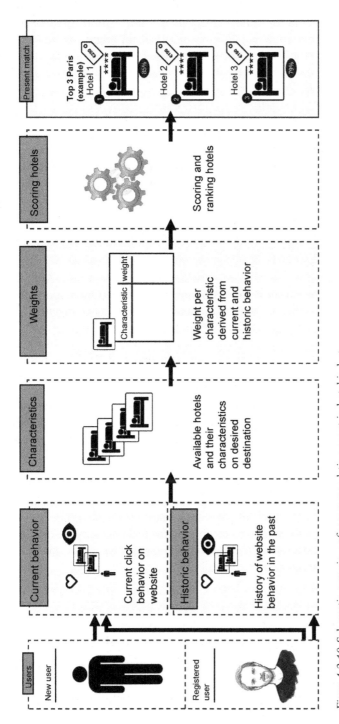

Figure 4.2.10 Schematic overview of recommendation agent in hotel industry

information (Arora et al., 2008). Examples of personalization can be found in many industries and for some—especially for information-based services—personalization has become key. For example, Last.fm might play music based on a customer's prior selection of songs and likes/dislikes of songs. Pandora suggests songs on these prior selections as well as on similarities between song attributes (Chung & Wedel, 2014).

For personalization systems it is very important to learn consumer preferences. This can be done using a short survey on consumer preferences. Based on the results of this exercise, a personalized offer can be provided. And based on the outcome of this offer (i.e. accept or reject offer) a consumer's preferences can be updated (see CLM approach). Especially in more mobile environments, adaptive personalization systems (APS) have been developed. APS takes full advantage of unobtrusively obtained customer information to provide personalized services in real time (Rust & Chung, 2006; Chung, Rust, & Wedel, 2009). These systems require very limited or no input from the customer and rely heavily on purchase data. Importantly, APS can learn from small pieces of information over time and pick up changes in consumer preferences.

In the marketing literature there are many applications of these APS, which vary in their use of statistical and econometric methods. One important issue in personalization is that one aims to account for customer heterogeneity in the used model. Several personalization systems use a latent-class type of models, for example a finite mixture model (e.g. Zhang & Wedel, 2009), in which parameters for specific customer segments are estimated (e.g. Wedel & Kamakura, 2000; see also Chapter 4.1). For other purposes specific algorithms are used that frequently have their background in artificial intelligence. For example, Chung, Rust, & Wedel (2009) use a dynamic Markov Chain Monte Carlo method as a filtering mechanism and also use a combination of model-based and collaborative personalization approaches. Other algorithms are used in other studies. The details of these methods go beyond the scope of this book and we refer to some of the cited articles published in top marketing journals. One method to develop more individual estimates that has gained attention is hierarchical Bayesian model estimation (e.g. Rust & Verhoef, 2005). With Bayesian model estimation individual regression parameters can be estimated. The very basic and intuitive principles of models accounting for heterogeneity are discussed in Box 4.2.1. It is worth noting that this modeling approach is not only used for personalization purposes.

Box 4.2.1 The essence of modeling customer heterogeneity: Moving to hierarchical Bayesian models

Traditional regression and choice models in marketing assume similar effects for all included variables in the models. Assume for simplicity that we aim to explain a choice (i.e. response to an offer, new product etc.). This choice for individual i is represented in a logit model using an observed latent variable Y_i^* and we explain this choice by one variable price. In principle the simple logit model is then formulated as follows:

$$Y_i^* = \beta_0 + \beta_1 \times Price + \varepsilon_i$$

As noted, both the constant and coefficient of price are similar for all considered individuals. This assumption is, however, not so plausible. Customers will respond differently to marketing mix instruments, including price. Moreover, the inherent probability of choosing a brand or product may differ between customers. In principle some heterogeneity could be captured by including additional customer characteristics, such as age, income, usage, etc. Heterogeneity can also be accounted for by using interactions. For example, an interaction between price and income could be included, as high-income customers could be less price sensitive. A next step is to allow the parameters to vary between segments (s = 1..S). This is actually what finite mixture models do. The basic model is then formulated as follows:

$$Y_i^* = \beta_{0s} + \beta_{1s} \times Price + \varepsilon_i$$

The parameters now differ between segments. The number of segments is determined by considering fit-criteria and typically differs between applications. In their study on personalized promotions Zhang & Wedel (2009) find two segments.

Hierarchical Bayesian models allow research to estimate individual parameters. These parameters have a distribution, and can subsequently be explained by specific other variables Z (i.e., age, income, usage, relationship duration). Formally, this can be written down in a hierarchical way as follows:

$$Y_i^* = \beta_{i0} + \beta_{i1} \times Price + \varepsilon_i$$
$$\beta_{ik} = \alpha \times Z_i + \delta_i$$

To estimate this in a Bayesian way, simulations (e.g. Markov Chain Monte Carlo (MCMC)) should be done and specific samplers (i.e. Gibbs) should be used. This results in more complicated equations than written down here. The results of these analyses can be used in personalization and can be used to develop optimal one-to-one personalized marketing strategies (e.g. Rust & Verhoef, 2005). For very interested readers we refer to work by Ohio State professor Greg Allenby and UCLA professor Peter Rossi, who are the leading experts in Bayesian models in marketing (www.econ.umn.edu/~bajari/iosp07/rossi1.pdf; see also Allenby, Rossi, and McCulloch (2005)).

Big data area 5: Integrated big data models

One of the key-characteristics of big data is that it involves multiple data sources that can be combined to predict market phenomena. A well-known example is that the number of individuals with flu can be predicted by looking at the number of specific searchers on Google (see Figure 4.2.11). With this the flu activity around the globe can be estimated.[2]

We derived this graph in Spring 2015. Google has since decided to no longer publish current estimates of flu and dengue based on search patterns. Some bloggers seem to attribute this decision to criticism of flu estimates.[3]

Overall in a big data era we move from single data sources to multiple data sources, and this may also involve new data sources. This may enrich models and in turn induce a stronger predictive power. However, one should also be careful! Specifically, the Google flu predictions sometimes overestimated flu activity. Lazer, Kennedy, King, & Vespignani (2014) warn about the use of these new data sources.[4] One of their concerns is over what they call "big data hubris." They warn analysts not to just replace existing data and models with new social and online data. Instead of substituting for old data and methods, new data and models should complement them. Moreover, they warn that big data sources have measurement problems and should be considered in a similar way to old data. What is the validity of the new data? How is it measured and what is the measurement error? (See Chapters 3 and 3.1). And so on. For example, with the flu search data, one might be concerned about endogeneity and causality. The fact that people are searching probably goes hand-in-hand with them having the flu.

Having made these very important caveats on new data sources, it is still undeniable that big data allows more data sources to be integrated to develop richer models that are likely to lead to a better understanding of marketing

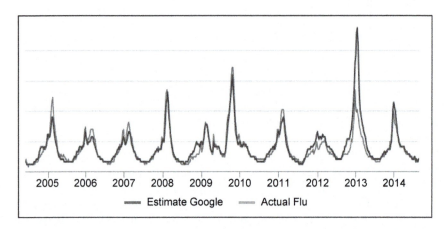

Figure 4.2.11 Flu activity USA predicted by Google

Source: Adapted from www.google.org/flutrends/about/how.html

phenomena and predictions. This requires a deeper understanding of the analytical challenges encountered with integrated models. However, it may also provide opportunities for the application of new techniques.

If one starts combining data sources, one encounters many problems, such as missing values. In Chapters 3.1 and 3.2 we discussed many of these issues, including missing values, and solutions such as data fusion. For now, we assume that we have solved these issues and sufficient data are available. Before analyzing the data, it is important to assess the aggregation level of multiple data sources. Is there the same aggregation level in terms of analyzed entity (e.g. market, brand, customer) and time (e.g. daily, weekly, monthly, yearly)? If aggregation levels are similar, which could be the case when predicting weekly sales of aspirin using past sales of aspirin, trends, and weekly Google trends on flu search key words, the standard models (see Chapter 4.1) can be used without any complications.

Combining different aggregation levels

Challenges may occur when firms start collecting data of multiple entities, for example:

- One aims to explain individual monthly customer retention for mobile phone operator using individual variables (e.g. age, usage, relationship duration), but also monthly brand advertising data and weekly Google searches on mobile phone plans.
- One aims to explain individual monthly customer satisfaction over time for a public transport organization, using data on individuals public, transport usage, weekly punctuality of used train-connections, and available services on visited train stations.
- One aims to explain weekly brand sales using data on (competitive) brand advertising, pricing, and promotions, individual daily brand likes and individual monthly measured brand attitudes.

Some general solutions are as follows:

- Aim to aggregate the data to one (single) aggregation level and analyze the data at that aggregation level. A simple rule is that the aggregation level of the dependent variable is decisive in such a way that one cannot have explanatory variables with lower aggregation levels than the aggregation level of the dependent variable (e.g. a brand level dependent variable cannot be explained by individual level variables). In the brand sales example, one would aggregate the data at the brand level. Individual brand likes and attitudes would then be aggregated to average weekly brand likes and monthly brand attitudes.
- The time aggregation problem can also be solved by making assumptions. For example, for monthly brand attitudes, one might assume that

the attitudes are similar for every underlying week in that month. Or one might assume some transitions between the different months. The brand attitudes in the first week of a month are then partially based on the attitudes of past month and the current month.

Multi-level models

One potential model solution to consider is the use of a multi-level model. In a multi-level model one acknowledges that there are specific aggregation levels in the data analyzed. The classic example is the analysis of a children's school performance. Children (lowest aggregation level) are part of a class or school and are living in a specific region (highest aggregation level). In a marketing context individual customers might buy different brands in many stores. In a multi-level model at different aggregation levels equations are formulated. Here we aim to discuss the basics of multi-level models. We assume we have two levels in the data: brands (j) and customers (i). In our example we aim to explain the loyalty of customers to multiple brands and the role of brand attitudes (BrAtt) and some customer characteristics (X). In a multi-level model one first starts with a model at the first level (customer level).

$$Loyalty_{ij} = \beta_{0j} + \beta_{1j} \times BrAtt_j + \beta_2 \times X + \varepsilon_{ij} \qquad (4.2.1)$$

At a second level one might assume that the constant (base brand loyalty) and the effect of brand attitudes is affected by some brand level variables, such as average brand advertising (Adv). The following equations are then formulated to account for this:

$$\beta_{0j} = \gamma_{01} + \gamma_{01} \times Adv_j + \delta_{0j} \qquad (4.2.2)$$

$$\beta_{1j} = \gamma_{10} + \gamma_{11} \times Adv_j + \delta_{1j} \qquad (4.2.3)$$

Note that we do not assume that the effects of some customer characteristics are influenced by advertising, as this parameter β_2 is similar for all brands. To apply a multi-level model it is crucial to have multiple entities (i.e. brands) per level. A multi-level model is not useful if only one brand is studied—in that case there is simply no variation in advertising. For more technical details on multi-level models we refer to Snijders and Bosker (2012).

We have also applied multi-level analysis in customer management applications. Specifically, when considering the effects of multiple customer feedback metrics (CFM) on retention (see Chapter 4.1), we used multi-level models, as we had observations of customers of multiple brands in multiple industries (De Haan, Verhoef, & Wiesel, 2015). Hence, we used a multi-level model with three levels. This also allowed us to investigate the effects of CFMs at three levels. At the customer level (CFM cust.) we studied whether a higher CFM score resulted in higher customer loyalty. At the firm level (CFM firm) we investigated

Big data analytics   215

whether a higher CFM than other brands resulted in a higher average loyalty to a firm. At the industry level we considered whether industries with higher CFM scores have a higher average loyalty. We estimated models per CFM. We also allowed for correlations between the different equations in the model. The results for the customer satisfaction metric and the NPS metric are displayed in Figure 4.2.12 (see De Haan et al. (2015) for more details). The major significant effects are typically found at the customer and firm-level.

Adaptive forecasting techniques

In a broader sense, big data developments have also stirred up interest in adaptive forecasting techniques, as they have enriched the understanding of the idea that estimated effects might be affected by events. Moreover, in a dynamic world it is unlikely to be right to assume that parameters of models are stable. Especially for forecasting purposes, accounting for these dynamics is crucial. Adaptive forecasting in time-series analysis had already been developed in the 1960s to account for regular events, such as seasons (e.g. Mincer, 1969). Thereby, they assume that coefficients and error structures may vary between these events. For example, a very simple assumption might be that during thanksgiving or Christmas sales are expected to be higher, and as a consequence in that period the relevant constant in a model should be adjusted.

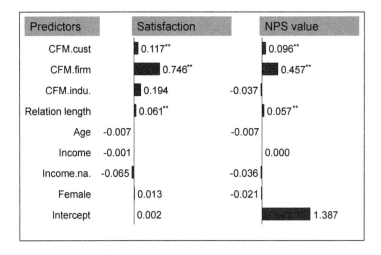

Predictors	Satisfaction	NPS value
CFM.cust	0.117**	0.096**
CFM.firm	0.746**	0.457**
CFM.indu.	0.194	-0.037
Relation length	0.061**	0.057**
Age	-0.007	-0.007
Income	-0.001	0.000
Income.na.	-0.065	-0.036
Female	0.013	-0.021
Intercept	0.002	1.387

Figure 4.2.12 Estimation results of multi-level model to assess performance of CFMs

Source: Adapted from De Haan et al. (2015)
**$p<0.01$,
*$p>0.05$ (one-tailed for the CFMs, two tailed for the rest
* Significantly (p0<.05) smaller than the firm-level effect

Another way to account for changing events is using so-called "regime switching" models (Hamilton, 2008). Under specific regimes (e.g. expansion of economy) specific parameters are estimated, while under other conditions (e.g. economic recession) other parameters are estimated. It is of course crucial to understand when these event changes occur. For forecasting purposes, one might develop predictions under different scenarios (regimes), which allows, for example, the prediction of how sales would develop under bad and good economic times.

Bayesian models can also be used to account for changes in the environment (see Box 4.2.1). One way would be to allow parameters in the model to change over time. For example, the effects of marketing spending may depend on the competition in the market or the growth rate in the market. If the dataset is sufficiently large and sufficient variation occurs, the effects of marketing spending may depend on these variables and thus time-varying marketing effects can be estimated. An example can be found in Ataman, Mela, & Van Heerde (2008) where time-varying effects of different marketing mix variables are estimated for newly introduced products for which it is reasonable to assume varying parameter estimates (see Figure 4.2.13). They come up with the effects of different instruments for achieving growth and building market potential. As can be observed, achieving distribution is of utmost importance.

Big data area 6: Social listening

Social listening has become one of the most popular new analysis tools, as in this big data era unstructured and specifically text data has become omnipresent

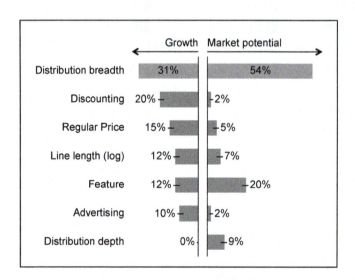

Figure 4.2.13 Effects of marketing mix variables on brand performance using time-varying parameter models

Source: Adapted from Ataman et al. (2008)

in online communities, social media like Facebook and Twitter, as well as in reviews on websites such as TripAdvisor, and retailers such as Amazon. These data are accessible to multiple parties and research agencies have specialized in providing firms with information on how customers view their firms and brands. There are also some standard tools available, such as Radian6 for social media monitoring. Text analytics is used for the analysis of social data. Text analytics has been around for years, but it has now been automated and firms like IBM and SAS offer tools to analyze these data. A famous application is Dr. Watson, developed by IBM. Beyond text analytics, pictures and videos can also be analyzed. We will mainly focus on text analytics in our discussion, as this is most widely adopted now and is considered an important big data analytics technique (Chen, Chiang, & Storey, 2012). According to Chen et al. (2012) text analytics have their academic roots in information retrieval and computational linguistics. In information retrieval, document representation and query processing are the foundations for developing a vector-space model, Boolean retrieval model, and probabilistic retrieval model, which in turn became the basis for the modern digital libraries, search engines, and enterprise search systems (Salton, 1989). In computational linguistics, statistical natural language processing (NLP) techniques for lexical acquisition, word sense disambiguation, part-of-speech-tagging (POST), and probabilistic context-free grammars are of huge importance for representing text (Manning & Schütze, 1999).

Marketing research agencies have also specialized in text analytics. It is mainly used to understand opinions of customers, something which is often called "opinion mining." Opinion mining refers to the computational techniques for extracting, classifying, understanding, and assessing the opinions expressed in various online news sources, social media comments, and other user-generated contents. A specific form of opinion analysis is sentiment analysis, which is often used in opinion mining to identify sentiment, affect, subjectivity, and other emotional states in online texts (Chen et al, 2012: 1176). Sentiment analysis can also be considered a specific step in opinion analysis. In our discussion we will first focus on opinion analysis in general: we will subsequently discuss sentiment analysis as a specific step in opinion analysis. We also refer to our discussion on digital sentiment indices in Chapter 2.1.

Execution of opinion analysis

To execute opinion analysis the following steps are required.

1 Social data collection and set up databases
2 Feature generation and pruning
3 Opinion word extraction
4 Assessment of orientation of opinion words (sentiment)
5 Summary generation (using visualization)

In Figure 4.2.14 we display these steps of text analytics approaches adapted from Hu and Liu (2004). Similar schemas can be found in other studies as well.

218 *Big data analytics*

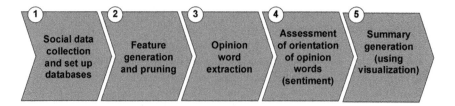

Figure 4.2.14 Text analytics approach
Source: Adapted from Hu & Liu (2004)

Social data collection and database set up

As a first step the researcher has to decide what text they want to analyze. This starts with a clear research objective. For example, if firms want to gain insights from customer reviews of a brand or product, raw data of reviews should be selected. However, if firms want to measure the sentiment about a specific brand, data on what is being written about brands in multiple social fora should be collected. These examples already imply that the collection of data is not an obvious step. There are issues surrounding where to collect data, the included time period, and which brands and/or products data will be collected for. If the data are being collected a database for text data should be set up, which can be used for analysis. To set up this database POS-tagging (part-of-speech tagging) is used, which assigns or "tags" information to each word in a sentence. Tags mainly involve the characteristics of the word in a sentence. A tag could be whether the word is a noun, or whether it is a verb or an adjective, etc. (see example in Figure 4.2.15).

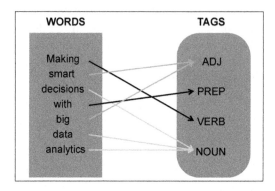

Figure 4.2.15 Illustration of POS tagging

Big data analytics 219

This raw database is usually pre-processed, which might include the removal of stop words, stemming, and fuzzy matching. Fuzzy matching is used to deal with word variants and misspellings (Hu & Liu, 2004). An outcome of this step can be a "word cloud" (see Figure 4.2.16).

Feature generation and pruning

The second step involves the identification of relevant product or brand features which people have expressed in their opinions. Sometimes this can be rather easy. For example, if a review for a digital camera involves a sentence like: "The size of the camera is good," it is clear that the feature "camera size" is meant. However, if the sentence was: "This camera would not easily fit in your pocket," it is much more difficult for text analytics to pick up that this customer is also hinting at camera size. Explicit features are thus easy to find, whereas more implicit mentions of features are more difficult to find. Text analytical packages have tended to focus on explicit features. Researchers would probably mainly be interested in the most frequently mentioned features. Another problem is that customers may use different words for similar features (e.g. size and largeness). Associative mining can be used to find a frequent items set, which is a set of words (or a phrase) that occur together in some sentences (e.g. Hu & Liu, 2004). This approach will not lead to a perfect set of features. To achieve a final and hopefully good set of features, pruning techniques are used. Hu and Liu (2004) describe the use of two pruning techniques: compactness pruning and redundancy pruning. Compactness pruning checks features with two or more words and removes those features that are likely to be meaningless. Redundancy pruning focuses on removing redundant features. For example, for mobile phones "life" is not a useful feature, whereas "battery life" could be meaningful. This step can be done using computer programs. However, in many cases a human text analyst is still required to execute parts of these steps.

Figure 4.2.16 Illustration of a word cloud

One important issue is the fact that as well as frequent features, infrequent features are also mentioned. It would be easy to ignore these infrequent features. However, these features can be interesting for a specific customer segment. And perhaps these features may indicate some important, not widely spread developments in the market, which may become dominant. So it might be dangerous to ignore them. One way to find these figures is to make matches between infrequent features and frequently used opinion words.

Opinion word extraction

In the next step, words in the sentences that provide a customers opinion about a product feature or brand are identified. Usually, opinions in sentences are given through the use of adjectives (e.g., nice, bad, etc.). A sentence can be considered an opinion sentence when it includes adjectives. Researchers could decide whether they include only those sentences that are linked to the product features or brands being studied. Typically one would like to include only sentences in the analysis in which opinion words are linked to product features or brands.

Assessment of orientation of opinion words

When the opinion words have been identified, it is important to understand their semantic orientation. This basically means whether the word deviates from the norm for its semantic group. And one can also distinguish between words having a desirable state that have a positive orientation, and words having undesirable state that have a negative orientation. Examples of words having a positive orientation are awesome, good, fantastic, etc. Words having a negative orientation could be sad, disappointed, awkward, etc. Some words can also be neutral. In marketing research this orientation is frequently referred to as the valence. Words can have a negative valence, a neutral valence or a positive valence. Others have referred to this as the "affective content" (e.g. Ludwig et al., 2013). The assessment of this valence or affective state is typically done in (brand) sentiment analysis and is the basis for calculating digital sentiment indices (see Chapter 2.1). Based on this orientation, text analytics can also lead to some quantitative outcomes. The words in a sentence could get a score (e.g. −1 negative, 0 neutral, 1 positive). One could also seek ways to assess the valence strength. For example, while fantastic and good both have a positive valence, fantastic is considered as much more positive than good. In a quantitative way "fantastic" could get a score of +2 and "good" a score of +1. Standard dictionaries can be used to assess the valence. For example, researchers have used the dictionary of affect in language as developed by Sweeney and Whissel (1984)—see for example Verhoef, Antonides, & De Hoog (2004) but also other dictionaries can be used—see for example Ludwig et al. (2013).

Summary generation

The final step is to create a summary of the results. This can be a simple frequency table. For example, one could report the frequency of each mentioned feature. Subsequently, these features can be linked to opinions. Here the occurring frequency of negative, neutral and positive valence can be reported. These descriptive analyses are the norm in text analytics in marketing. Further analyses can, however, also be executed. For example, linked brand features or associations can be used to create a visual brand association map (Gensler, Völckner, Egger, Fischbach, & Schoder 2015; see also Figure 4.2.17). Input from text analytics (i.e. the valence scores) can also be used as input in predicting, for example, brand sales, brand acquisition, and other metrics (e.g. De Vries, 2015; Srinivasan, Rutz, & Pauwels, 2015).

Big data area 7: Social network analysis

In today's digital environment social networks have become prominent as a result of a growing number of social communities: Facebook, LinkedIn, and in China, Renren, are probably the most prominent more general communities. Beyond these general communities, there are also many smaller specialized communities that focus on specific themes such as music, sports, cooking, and lifestyle. In many apps hybrid forms of services are combined with social communities. For example, the running and cycling app Strava has services on running and cycling performance, but users are also connected to other users.

Social networks are of course not a new phenomenon. They have been around for years; for example almost twenty years ago Achrol and Kotler (1999) mentioned the growing importance of networks in marketing and specifically business-to-business marketing. Within sociology the importance of social networks has also been stressed (e.g. Burt 1987). The increasing presence of

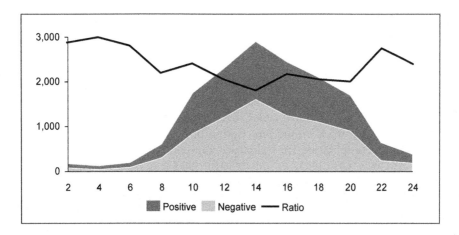

Figure 4.2.17 Number of tweets by time and sentiment

social communities has stirred up a huge amount of attention for networks: we are now considered to live in the era of the connected customer (Wuyts, Dekimpe, Gijsbrechts, & Pieters, 2010). As a consequence, customer-to-customer (C2C) interactions have become very important in marketing, and it is generally accepted that customers influence each other. This idea is not new. In his famous diffusion model, Bass (1969) introduced the notion of social contagion capturing this social influence through multiple mechanisms (Van den Bulte & Stremersch, 2004). Social communities have also increased the availability of network data, which in turn has led to more studies on social network data within marketing.

Analyzing social networks

We consider the following steps in network data analytics:

1 Creation of network data
2 Description of the network using network metrics
3 Social network targeting and valuation.

Social network data[5]

The way the network is defined is an important issue. There are three general ways to collect network data:

1 Self-reports on networks
2 Zip code level as a proxy for a network
3 Use of actual networks using digital and mobile technologies.

Thus far, most studies have used either self-reported data or geographical data (Zip codes) to build a network. Although the use of surveys is common (Wasserman & Faust, 1994), they have several drawbacks, including dependence on respondents' memories, differences across respondents' interpretations, and self-report biases (Bertrand & Mullainathan, 2001), all of which can lead to erroneous descriptions of the network. Geographical data are also commonly used because most customer and marketing databases contain Zip code information (Bell & Song, 2007; Nam, Manchanda, & Chintagunta, 2010). The idea is that if individuals live closer together they can be in a social network. In his influential work on the prescription of pharmaceutical drugs, Wharton professor Christophe van den Bulte used Zip-code data to create networks of physicians who were likely to impact each other (e.g. Iyengar, Van den Bulte, & Valente, 2011). However, social interaction is not measured directly, and so the use of these data requires the assumption that people living close to each other influence each other (Choi, Hui, & Bell, 2010; Iyengar, Van den Bulte, & Choi, 2011). It is unlikely to be an accurate description since social interaction is becoming less and less dependent on spatial proximity (Haenlein, 2011).

As an alternative, online social networks are a potentially rich source of network data. The number of people in these networks is typically large, and data are relatively easy to obtain (Godes & Mayzlin, 2004; Stephen & Galak, 2010). A disadvantage of this method is the difficulty in combining network information and behavioral and transactional data for the same person. Furthermore, people are typically connected in an online network to many others who are not relevant from a social influence perspective since it requires only very little effort to establish and maintain a 'friendship' tie (Ackland, 2009; Trusov, Bodapati, & Bucklin, 2010).

Another alternative is the use of direct communication data from email or (mobile) telephony. In the latter case so-called call detail records (CDR) can be used to create networks. In CDR data, all phone calls and text messages are recorded individually. A person's mobile phone network is a good proxy for his or her social network (Eagle, Pentland, & Lazer, 2009; Haythornthwaite, 2005) and has been used to model retention (Nitzan & Libai, 2011) and adoption (Hill, Provost, & Volinsky, 2006; Risselada, Verhoef, & Bijmolt, 2014). The analysis of these networks is, however, not trivial because of the potential for privacy infringements (see Chapter 3.3).

Social network metrics

Social networks in marketing are mainly used to identify those networks or specifically those individuals that have an overly strong influence on other customers, and thus can help to diffuse ideas, opinions, and new products in the market. Social marketing campaigns such as viral marketing and referral campaigns aim to focus on these customers. These influential customers are typically the first customers approached by the firm in a social campaign, and are considered the seeds of a campaign. These seeds will influence others and thereby spread the message (in the case of a viral campaign) or convince others to act (in the case of a referral campaign).

An important question is how to identify these influential customers. A traditional way has always been to use a survey measure: opinion leadership (e.g. Kratzer & Lettl, 2009). Customers report on their beliefs on their influence on other customers. Recent research suggests that this measure is actually not very good and has no direct impact on actual influence (Risselada, Verhoef, & Bijmolt, 2015). There is thus a discrepancy between self-reported influence and actual influence, which should not come as a surprise, as similar discrepancies between other self-reporting measures and behavior have been found (e.g. between purchase intention and purchase behavior).

Actual network characteristics do, however, make a difference. These network metrics all focus on the centrality of customers in a network, and specifically the following metrics are proposed (Van den Bulte & Wuyts, 2007):

- Degree centrality
- Betweenness centrality
- Closeness centrality.

224 Big data analytics

Degree centrality (see Figure 4.2.18) measures the number of contacts an individual has in a network. Customers with a high degree centrality are called hubs, as through these customers many other customers can be reached (similar to airport hubs, where from an airport hub like Atlanta or Amsterdam many destinations can be reached). One concern is that these hubs have many contacts, but their effort per contact could be lower. Several studies have, however, shown that these hubs work pretty well (e.g. Hinz, Skiera, Barrot, & Becker, 2011), and degree centrality predicts influence (Risselada et al., 2015). Degree centrality only considers direct contacts, and does not consider the position of the customers in a more extended network.

The other two metrics have a more extended network perspective (see Figure 4.2.19). Betweenness centrality measures the extent to which an individual is in the shortest route or path between customers in a network. The underlying idea is that customers with a low betweenness centrality have more power

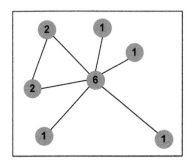

Figure 4.2.18 Degree centrality

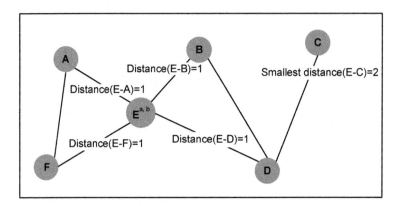

Figure 4.2.19 Betweenness centrality and closeness centrality[6]

Notes:
a Betweenness centrality for E = 6
b Closeness centrality for E = 1.2

in a network. Closeness centrality measures the average number of steps in a network it takes to reach all other customers in a network. It basically measures how easy it is for customers to reach all other customers in a network. A low closeness centrality suggests that this should be more easy. While these metrics provide useful information and indeed matter (e.g. Katona, Zubcsek, & Sarvary, 2011), they are usually more difficult to measure, as a complete network is required. Degree centrality does not require a full network structure, as one only has to count the number of contacts.

As well as looking at network characteristics, contacts between individual customers in a network can also be characterized. Two key variables are tie strength and homophily. Tie strength reflects the intensity of the contact between customers. When a tie is strong the intensity of communication is stronger and thus it is likely that customers have a stronger influence on each other (Nitzan & Libai, 2011). It can be measured by, for example, the number of contacts (e.g. calls, Whatsapp messages) or the distance between individuals. Homophily reflects the degree to which customers in a network are similar. It is generally accepted that similar individuals tend to behave in a similar way, because customers tend to associate more with similar people (McPherson, Smith-Lovin, & Cook, 2001). One way of measuring homophily is by scoring two individuals on whether they have similar characteristics, such as age, education, gender etc. (e.g. Risselada et al., 2014).

Social targeting and network valuation

In many cases firms will be happy with being able to identify influential customers. As noted earlier, these customers can then be used as seeds in social campaigns. In an online environment this approach is referred to as a viral marketing campaign. Subsequently these campaigns have to be evaluated and firms might be interested in measuring the effect of these campaigns and to assess the resulting network value of customers. The response of customers to viral marketing campaigns can be modeled. Van der Lans, Van Bruggen, Eliashberg & Wierenga, (2010) developed a viral branching model. Hinz et al. (2011) report that seeding indeed works and creates more value. As a next step customer engagement metrics such as customer referral value (CRV) and customer influence value (CIV) can be calculated (Kumar et al., 2010; see also Chapter 2.2).

Network variables for each customer can also be used to predict behavior. Several studies have shown that similar customers with strong ties influence one another. So if a firm knows that a customer has defected, they could identify customers in the network of that customer who are also at risk for defecting (Nitzan & Libai, 2011). If a customer has adopted a new product, individuals in his/her network can be identified and contacted to induce new product adoption as well. We warn, however, that the social influence effects are less simple than usually considered, as social influence not only operates at the customer level but also at the market level through, for example, social norms (Risselada et al., 2014).

Emerging techniques

As a result of digital developments new techniques to analyze data will emerge. Text analytics have improved considerably over the last decade. Nowadays, customers constantly upload photos and videos using, for example, mobile phones, and this new data can also provide information about brands and customer experiences. Photo and video analytics will emerge to help get relevant marketing information from these new sources of data. Established firms, such as Microsoft, but also new firms, are developing techniques to analyze videos.[7]

Advances in mobile phone usage will also induce more attention for mobile analytics. Mobiles can be used to follow customers in stores, for example. Mobile analytics provide technological solutions for retailers by developing aggregate reports used to reduce waiting times at checkouts, optimize store layouts, and to understand consumer shopping patterns. The reports are generated by recognizing the Wi-Fi or Bluetooth MAC addresses of cell phones as they interact with store Wi-Fi networks. Mobile data can probably become very powerful. So far knowledge of this is limited. However, in five years from now the situation might have dramatically changed, as firms are starting to experiment with these data and many studies will be executed using these data.

Conclusions

Big data have an impact on analytics as new data became available and new application areas became prominent. In this in-depth chapter we have discussed seven new big data areas, some of which have been there for a while already (e.g. web analytics), while others are rather new (e.g. attribution modeling, social listening). We have aimed to discuss each of these areas in sufficient depth to enable the reader to understand the basics of the area and the many available techniques. We note that some of the techniques build on existing traditional techniques. For example, in the case of attribution modeling logit models are proposed as a way to study the contribution of each touchpoint to conversion. Finally, we discussed some emerging areas, which are yet not sufficiently developed to extensively discuss in this book. In five years from now this situation might, however, be totally different.

Notes

1. This section benefited strongly from the excellent overview provided by Chung & Wedel (2014) on personalization in services.
2. See www.google.org/flutrends/about/how.html (accessed September 23, 2015).
3. See http://bits.blogs.nytimes.com/2014/03/28/google-flu-trends-the-limits-of-big-data/?_r=0).
4. See http://gking.harvard.edu/files/gking/files/0314policyforumff.pdf (accessed September 22, 2015) This article makes very insightful reading on problems with big data.
5. This section is based on Beckers, Risselada and Verhoef (2014: 97–120).
6. We thank Hans Risselada for sharing these figures.
7. See http://techcrunch.com/2015/05/04/video-to-data/ (accessed September 24, 2015).

References

Achrol, R. S., & Kotler, P. (1999). Marketing in the network economy. *Journal of Marketing*, 63(4), 146–63.
Ackland, R. (2009). Social network services as data sources and platforms for e-researching social networks. *Social Science Computer Review*, 27(4), 481–92.
Allenby, G. M., Rossi, P. E., & McCulloch, R. E. (2005). *Hierarchical Bayes models: a practitioners guide*. SSR Working Paper Series. Retrieved from Social Science Research Network. Retrieved October 1, 2015 from http://ssrn.com/abstract=655541.
Ansari, A., Essegaier, S., & Kohli, R. (2000). Internet recommendation systems. *Journal of Marketing Research*, 37(3), 363–75.
Ansari, A., Mela, C. F., & Neslin, S. A. (2008). Customer channel migration. *Journal of Marketing Research*, 45(1), 60–76.
Arora, N., Dreze, X., Ghose, A., Hess, J. D., Iyengar, R., Jing, B., Joshi, Y., Kumar, V., Lurie, N., Neslin, S., Sajeesh, S., Su, M., Syam, N., Thomas, J., & Zhang, Z. J. (2008). Putting one-to-one marketing to work: Personalization, customization, and choice. *Marketing Letters*, 19(3–4), 305–21.
Ataman, M. B., Mela, C. F., & Van Heerde, H. J. (2008). Building brands. *Marketing Science*, 27(6), 1036–54.
Bass, F. M. (1969). A new product growth for model consumer durables. *Management science*, 15(5). 215–27.
Beckers, S. F. M., Risselada, H., & Verhoef, P. C. (2014). Customer engagement: a new frontier in customer value management. In R. T. Rust, & M. H. Huang, (Eds), *Handbook of Service Marketing Research* (pp. 97–120). Cheltenham UK: Edward Elgar Pub.
Bell, D. R., & Song, S. (2007). Neighborhood effects and trial on the Internet: Evidence from online grocery retailing. *Quantitative Marketing and Economics*, 5(4), 361–400.
Bertrand, M., & Mullainathan, S. (2001). Do people mean what they say? Implications for subjective survey data. *The American Economic Review*, 91(2), 67–72.
Bitner, M. J., Ostrom, A. L., & Morgan, F. N. (2008). Service blueprinting: A practical technique for service innovation. *California Management Review*, 50(3), 66–94.
Bodapati, A. V. (2008). Recommendation systems with purchase data. *Journal of Marketing Research*, 45(1), 77–93.
Bucklin, R. E., & Sismeiro, C. (2003). A model of web site browsing behavior estimated on clickstream data. *Journal of Marketing Research*, 40(3), 249–67.
Bucklin, R. E., & Sismeiro, C. (2009). Click here for internet insight: Advances in clickstream data analysis in marketing. *Journal of Interactive Marketing*, 23(1), 35–48.
Bucklin, R. E., Lattin, J. M., Ansari, A., Gupta, S., Bell, D., Coupey, E., Little, J.D.C., Mela, C., Montgomery, A., & Steckel, J. (2002). Choice and the Internet: From clickstream to research stream. *Marketing Letters*, 13(3), 245–58.
Bult, J. R., & Wansbeek, T. (1995). Optimal selection for direct mail. *Marketing Science*, 14(4), 378–94.
Burt, R. S. (1987). Social contagion and innovation: Cohesion versus structural equivalence. *American Journal of Sociology*, 92(6), 1287–335.
Chen, H., Chiang, R. H. L., & Storey, V. C. (2012). Business intelligence and analytics: From big data to big impact. *MIS Quarterly*, 36(4), 1165–88.
Choi, J., Hui, S. K., & Bell, D. R. (2010). Spatiotemporal analysis of imitation behavior across new buyers at an online grocery retailer. *Journal of Marketing Research*, 47(1), 75–89.
Chung, T. S., & Wedel, M. (2014). Adaptive personalization of mobile information services. In R. T. Rust, & M. H. Huang, (Eds), *Handbook of Service Marketing Research* (pp. 395–412). Cheltenham: Edward Elgar Pub.

Chung, T. S., Rust, R. T., & Wedel, M. (2009). My mobile music: An adaptive personalization system for digital audio players. *Marketing Science*, 28(1), 52–68.

David Shepard Associates. (1999). *The new direct marketing: How to implement a profit-driven database marketing strategy*. Europe: Mcgraw-Hill Education.

De Haan, E., Verhoef, P. C., & Wiesel, T. (2015). The predictive ability of different customer feedback metrics for retention. *International Journal of Research in Marketing*, 32(2), 195–206.

De Haan, E., Wiesel, T., & Pauwels, K. (2013). Which advertising forms make a difference in online path to purchase. *MSI Working Paper Series*, 13(104), Boston.

De Vries, L. (2015). *Impact of Social Media on Consumers and Firms*. Doctoral dissertation, University of Groningen.

Eagle, N., Pentland, A. S., & Lazer, D. L. (2009). Inferring friendship network structure by using mobile phone data. *Proceedings of the National Academy of Sciences*, 106(36), 15, 274–78.

Edwards, G. (2014). How to embrace retail's newest trend: Webrooming. Retrieved from Retail TouchPoints Blog. Retrieved September 11, 2015 from http://retailtouchpoints.tumblr.com/post/59107311088/how-to-embrace-retails-newest-trend-webrooming

Gensler, S., Verhoef, P. C., & Böhm, M. (2012). Understanding consumers' multichannel choices across the different stages of the buying process. *Marketing Letters*, 23(4), 987–1003.

Gensler, S., Völckner, F., Egger, M., Fischbach, K., & Schoder, D. (2015). Listen to your customers: insights into brand image using online consumer-generated product reviews. *International Journal of Electronic Commerce*, 20(1), 112–41.

Godes, D., & Mayzlin, D. (2004). Using online conversations to study word-of-mouth communication. *Marketing Science*, 23(4), 545–60.

Haenlein, M. (2011). A social network analysis of customer-level revenue distribution. *Marketing Letters*, 22(1), 15–29.

Hamilton, J. D. (2008). Regime switching models. In Durlauf S. & Blume L., (Eds), *Palgrave Dictionary of Economics*. London: Palgrave McMillan.

Haythornthwaite, C. (2005). Social networks and Internet connectivity effects. *Information Communication & Society*, 8(2), 125–47.

Hill, S., Provost, F., & and Volinsky, C. (2006). Network-based marketing: identifying likely adopters via consumer networks. *Statistical Science*, 21(2), 256–76.

Hinz, O., Skiera, B., Barrot, C., & Becker, J. U. (2011). Seeding strategies for viral marketing: An empirical comparison. *Journal of Marketing*, 75(6), 55–71.

Hu, M., & Liu, B. (2004). Mining opinion features in customer reviews. *American Association for Artificial Intelligence*, 755–60.

Iyengar, R., Van den Bulte, C., & Choi, J. (2011). *Distinguishing among multiple mechanisms of social contagion: Social learning versus normative legitimation in new product adoption*. Working paper. The Wharton School, University of Pennsylvania.

Iyengar, R., Van den Bulte, C., & Valente, T. W. (2011). Rejoinder – further reflections on studying social influence in new product diffusion. *Marketing Science*, 30(2), 230–2.

Johnson, E. J., Bellman, S., & Lohse, G. L. (2003). Cognitive lock-in and the power law of practice. *Journal of Marketing*, 67(2), 62–75.

Katona, Z., Zubcsek, P. P., & Sarvary, M. (2011). Network effects and personal influences: The diffusion of an online social network. *Journal of Marketing Research*, 48(3), 425–43.

Konuş, U., Neslin, S. A., & Verhoef, P. C. (2014). The effect of search channel elimination on purchase incidence, order size and channel choice. *International Journal of Research in Marketing*, 3(1), 49–64.

Konuş, U., Verhoef, P. C., & Neslin, S. A. (2008). Multichannel shopper segments and their antecedents. *Journal of Retailing*, 84(4), 398–413.

Kratzer, J., & Lettl, C. (2009). Distinctive roles of lead users and opinion leaders in the social networks of schoolchildren. *Journal of Consumer Research*, 36(4), 646–59.

Kumar, V., Aksoy, L., Donkers, B., Venkatesan, R., Wiesel, T., & Tillmanns, S. (2010). Undervalued or overvalued customers: Capturing total customer engagement value. *Journal of Service Research*, 13(3), 297–310.

Lazer, D., Kennedy, R., King, G., & Vespignani, A. (2014). The parable of Google flu: Traps in big data analysis. *Science*, 343(6176), 1203–5.

Ludwig, S., De Ruyter, K., Friedman, M., Brüggen, E. C., Wetzels, M., & Pfann, G. (2013). More than words: The influence of affective content and linguistic style matches in online reviews on conversion rates. *Journal of Marketing*, 77(1), 87–103.

Macdonald, E. K., Wilson, H. N., & Konuş, U. (2012). Better customer insight – in real time. *Harvard Business Review*, 90(9), 102–8.

Manning, C., & Schütze, H. (1999). *Foundations of statistical natural language processing*. Cambridge: MIT Press.

McPherson, M., Smith-Lovin, L., & Cook, J. M. (2001). Birds of a feather: Homophily in social networks. *Annual Review of Sociology*, 27(1), 415–44.

Melis, K., Campo, K., Breugelmans, E., & Lamey, L. (2015). The impact of the multi-channel retail mix on online store choice: Does online experience matter? *Journal of Retailing*, 9(2), 272–88.

Mincer, J. (1969). *Economic forecasts and expectations: Analysis of forecasting behavior and performance*. New York: National Bureau of Economic Research.

Nam, S., Manchanda, P., & Chintagunta, P. K. (2010). The effect of signal quality and contiguous word of mouth on customer acquisition for a video-on demand service. *Marketing Science*, 29(4), 690–700.

Neslin, S. A., Grewal, D., Leghorn, R., Shankar, V., Teeling, M. L., Thomas, J. S., & Verhoef, P. C. (2006). Challenges and opportunities in multichannel customer management. *Journal of Service Research*, 9(2), 95–112.

Nitzan, I., & Libai, B. (2011). Social effects on customer retention. *Journal of Marketing*, 75(6), 24–38.

Rapp, A., Baker, T. L., Bachrach, D. G., Ogilvie, J., & Beitelspacher, L. S. (2015). Perceived customer showrooming behavior and the effect on retail salesperson self-efficacy and performance. *Journal of Retailing*, 91(2), 358–69.

Risselada, H., Verhoef, P. C., & Bijmolt, T. H. A. (2014). Dynamic effects of social influence and direct marketing on the adoption of high-technology products. *Journal of Marketing*, 78(2), 52–68.

Risselada, H., Verhoef, P. C., & Bijmolt, T. H. A. (2015). Indicators of opinion leadership in customer networks: Self reports and degree centrality. *Marketing Letters*. Forthcoming.

Rust, R. T., & Chung, T. S. (2006). Marketing models of service and relationships. *Marketing Science*, 25(6), 560–80.

Rust, R. T., & Verhoef, P. C. (2005). Optimizing the marketing interventions mix in intermediate-term CRM. *Marketing Science*, 24(3), 477–89.

Salton, G. (1989). *Automatic text processing: the transformation, analysis, and retrieval of information by computer*. Boston, USA: Addison-Wesley Longman Publishing.

Shi, S. W., & Zhang, J. (2014). Usage experience with decision aids and evolution of online purchase behavior. *Marketing Science*, 33(6), 871–82.

Snijders, T. A. B., & Bosker, R. J. (2012). *Multilevel analysis: An introduction to basic and advanced multilevel modeling*. London: Sage Publishers.

Srinivasan, S., Rutz, O., & Pauwels, K. (2015). Paths to and off purchase: Quantifying the impact of traditional marketing and online customer activity. *Journal of the Academy of Marketing Science*. Forthcoming.

Stephen, A. T., & Galak, J. (2010). *The complementary roles of traditional and social media in driving marketing performance.* Working paper, Carnegie Mellon.

Sweeney, K., & Whissel, C. (1984). A dictionary of affect in language: I. Establishment and preliminary validation. *Perceptual and Motor Skills*, 59, 695–8.

Trusov, M., Bodapati, A. V., & Bucklin, R. E. (2010). Determining influential users in Internet social networks. *Journal of Marketing Research*, 47(4), 643–58.

Van den Bulte, C., & Stremersch, S. (2004). Social contagion and income heterogeneity in new product diffusion: A meta-analytic test. *Marketing Science*, 23(4), 530–44.

Van den Bulte, C., & Wuyts, S. H. K. (2007). *Social networks in marketing.* Boston: MSI Relevant Knowledge Series.

Van der Heijden, M., De Haan, E., & Hoving-Wesselius, T. (2014). Een modelmatige aanpak om het effect van online adverteren op conversie te achterhalen. In A. E. Bronner (Ed.), *Jaarboek MarktOnderzoekAssociatie.* Haarlem: Spaar en Hout.

Van der Lans, R., Van Bruggen, G., Eliashberg, J., & Wierenga, B. (2010). Viral branching model for predicting the spread of electronic word of mouth. *Marketing Science*, 29(2), 348–65.

Verhoef, P. C., Antonides, G., & De Hoog, A. N. (2004). Service encounters as a sequence of events: The importance of peak experiences. *Journal of Service Research*, 7(1), 53–64.

Verhoef, P. C., Kannan, P. K., & Inman, J. (2015). From multi-channel retailing to omni-channel retailing: Introduction to the special issue on multi-channel retailing. *Journal of Retailing*, 9(2), 174–81.

Verhoef, P. C., Neslin, S. A., & Vroomen, B. (2007). Multichannel customer management: Understanding the research-shopper phenomenon. *International Journal of Research in Marketing*, 24(2), 129–48.

Wasserman, S., & Faust, K. (1994). *Social network analysis – Methods and applications.* UK: Cambridge University Press.

Wedel, M., & Kamakura, W. A. (2000). Market segmentation: conceptual and methodological foundations. In *International series in quantitative marketing.* Boston: Kluwer.

Wuyts, S. H. K., Dekimpe, M. G., Gijsbrechts, E., & Pieters, R. (2010). *The connected customer: The changing nature of consumers and business markets.* New York: Routledge Academic.

Zhang, J., & Wedel, M. (2009). The effectiveness of customized promotions in online and offline stores. *Journal of Marketing Research*, 46(2), 190–206.

4.3 Creating impact with storytelling and visualization[1]

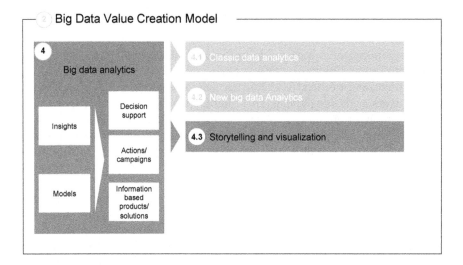

Introduction

In the preceding in-depth chapters we have discussed analytical techniques. In order for analysts to create impact with both traditional and big data analytics, how the analytical results are communicated is essential. One of the main dangers of analysis is that a report is not even presented, or ends up in the never-opened desks of managers and therefore never has any effect on management decisions. To have impact two issues are of crucial importance:

1. The presence of a clear storyline in which the message of the implications is concisely discussed
2. The use of powerful visualization of the analytical results (i.e. effective use of visual aids).

The importance of these two issues is increasingly present. The growth in the availability of continuous digital information results in people having less time available to attend to communications. Consumers as well as managers (being also consumers) switch between multiple devices continuously to read messages (e.g. on WhatsApp), emails, news apps, social media, etc. It is now very common that in meetings participants do not give their full attention to presentations because of being distracted by what else is being shown on their tablets or mobile phones. It is therefore very important that the presentations of research results are sufficiently clear and attract attention. Further, today's overload of digital information means that managers have to find ways of filtering the right information and interpreting the results. This information load is not new. Over the last two decades people have been addressing the growing importance of information stress. This arises because of the growing divergence between what information is available and what we can process (see Figure 4.3.1). It can be viewed as a black hole between data and knowledge that starts to exist when information is not telling us what we want and should know. For a long time, managers did not understand that they did not know. However, now they understand what they do not know and as a consequence they feel information stress (Wurman, 1989).

This increasing overload is calling for solutions. One of the solutions has been to work with infographics. These infographics are a typical way to make complex information more accessible for the reader. They exist in many forms. It might, however, be questionable whether infographics are effective. An infographic usually involves little structure and tells many facts in the form of text and figures. The graphs or pictures are mainly used as illustrations to make the information more attractive.

We strongly believe in the combination of data, storytelling, and visualization. These three elements should strengthen each other in such a way that the information has impact (see Figure 4.3.2). If analysts, based on the strengths of their data and analytics, are able to tell a strong story and provide strong visualizations, they should have a strong impact. A kind of "sweet spot" is achieved, as strong visualizations and good story telling combined with excellent data and analytics

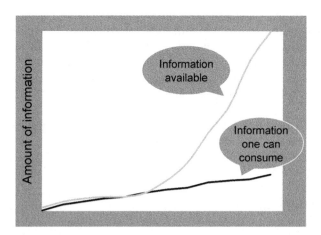

Figure 4.3.1 Information overload

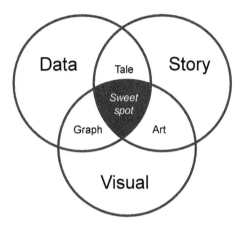

Figure 4.3.2 Sweet spot of data, story and visual

will be well received by managers in an era of information overload. To achieve this multi-disciplinary skills are required. This is not easy, as frequently the analyst focuses on numbers and may be unskilled at communicating a strong story. We will discuss this general issue in more detail in Chapter 5.

In this in-depth chapter we discuss how to build up a good storyline in analytical reports and presentations and how strong visualization can be achieved. Before doing so, we first focus on why many analytical projects with strong data and analytics fail to have impact.

Failure factors for creating impact

Many analysts have probably experienced carrying out a very nice study, but in the end their work did not change marketing strategies or tactics. Why does this occur? It is definitely not the analytical quality that is causing the problem. The numbers have been crunched in the right manner, the right research questions have been studied, but still impact is limited. This is probably the greatest frustration of many analysts. Having no impact will in the long run threaten the positon of the analytical function within firms. Creating impact is also strongly required to create value with big data analytics! It is therefore very important to understand why reports do not have an impact and what typically goes wrong. We have already emphasized the huge importance of storytelling and visualizations. Based on our experience in analytical functions in many firms, we can identify some specific issues that frequently go wrong and reduce the impact of analytical exercises:

- There is no structure to the report. One frequently reports independent analyses that are not strongly related and as a consequence many unrelated messages are being communicated instead of a few strongly related messages.

- There are no strong and clear conclusions or messages. The findings are nice to know, but it is unclear what the manager should do differently after reading the report. One easily gets the "So what?" response.
- The reports include too many pages or slides. Moreover, the conclusions are only reported at the end of the report. The attention of the reader has died out by the end of the report and conclusions and implications are not read or mentally processed! The consequence is no impact.
- The main findings are good and understood, but combined with nice-to-know irrelevant insights. These insights distract the reader and result in less focus on the main message of the study.
- There are inconsistencies in the report. This creates a discussion on the content and may create confusion, reducing the perceived reliability of the results.
- The report focuses too much on the statistical details and reporting on why specific methods have been chosen. Although this is highly valued in scientific publications, managers have no strong interest in the details. Instead of reporting this in the main text, it can be provided as an appendix.
- The slides (or pages) are packed with many messages and as a result look very crowded. Assuming that normal humans have only limited processing capacity and are easily distracted, they can usually process only a limited number of points.
- Analysts frequently only report many numbers instead of graphs. Numbers are less easily processed than visual graphs.
- And if graphs are being used, they are too complex and provide too much information. As a consequence it becomes a puzzle for managers to pick out the right information.

All these issues relate to weak communication. Improved communication can happen when analysts learn how to build a strong focused story for their results and are able to visualize them in the right way.

Storytelling

One of the basic principles of a good report or presentation is that it has a core message. This core message should be introduced with a specific situation and complication and should subsequently be underpinned with arguments. This approach is based on the pyramid principle as advocated by Barbara Minto (2009).[2] At the end of the 1960s she worked as a consultant at McKinsey & Company, where she focused on the development of methods to help their advisors to structure their presentations and reports. The pyramid refers to the principle that each advice should have a pyramid-like structure. At the top of the pyramid is the advice, and below the top structure, in different points or paragraphs, is the motivation. If the motivation is divided into multiple subpoints or issues a new pyramid starts to exist. Subsequently, one provides a powerful discussion (or description) of the complication to introduce the key-message.

In our experience of giving advice to companies based on analytics, we have observed that this pyramid principle is very powerful. It really strengthens the impact of analytics. Schematically this results in the structure as displayed in Figure 4.3.3.

To understand why this method can be powerful, we first consider what is frequently being done when reporting. Normally, analysts start to discuss what they have done in a kind of chronical order. They want to show the manager their analytical road trip from problem statement to end results. The analysts only end their presentation or report with the important conclusions. They also want to be as complete as possible and aim to tell every detail. This is very logical. Analysts have been trained like this in universities. When writing a thesis, they start with a problem statement, discuss the theory, the data collection, the analytical method, the results section and end with important conclusions. Similar structures can be found in many scientific papers, and this may potentially explain the limited impact of scientific papers on practice (Roberts, Kayandé, & Stremersch, 2014). However, when doing this, the manager with limited time and attention only gets to the most important results at the end of the report or when the session is almost finished.

A report has much more impact when its core message and the context are directly understood. By "directly" we mean that this should be set out at the beginning of each report or presentation. The core message can then be underpinned with a limited number of arguments—one frequently uses seven as a kind of rule of thumb, a kind of magical number based on Miller's law. The cognitive psychologist George A. Miller of Princeton University has shown that there are severe limits in our capacity to process information

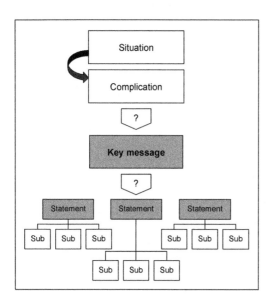

Figure 4.3.3 Building blocks for a clear storyline

(Miller, 1956). His work has been interpreted to mean that the average number of objects an average human can hold in memory is around 7. This strongly suggests limiting the volume of messages and arguments being discussed.

The above discussion clearly shows that there is a mismatch between how an analyst presents an analysis and how it should be presented. An analyst frequently solves the problem with a bottom-up type of approach. However, effective communication suggests a top-down approach (see Figure 4.3.4). It is essential for analysts to understand this difference. When finishing a project and preparing the report and/or presentation they should get out of the analytical mode and move to the effective communication mindset. We have observed that analysts typically find this difficult, given that they tend to focus on details and frequently forget the overall picture and why the analysis is being done. It is therefore important to work in analytical teams, where effective communication skills are embedded in the team (see also Chapter 5).

Checklist for a clear storyline

The above discussion probably seems rather intuitive, but how can its conclusions actually be implemented? We take the schema as shown in Figure 4.3.3 as a starting point, and briefly point to some issues requiring attention.

Situation

When describing the initial situation, the following issues require consideration:

- Is the discussed situation not controversial? Does the description in itself raise specific questions and/or a debate? If the latter occurs it will be more difficult to discuss the core message.

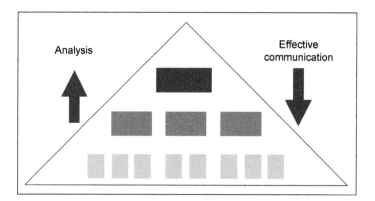

Figure 4.3.4 Analysis process vs. effective communication

- Does the audience recognize the described situation? If so, they will be more receptive.
- Is the situation description underpinned with figures and are these figures understood and believed in the organization? If the latter is not the case the situation description will be less effective. Still, figures showing specific problems in performance (e.g. decrease in net promoter score (NPS), or increase in churn rates) are very important to show the relevance of the report.
- Does the situation description create a complication and a specific research question?

Complication

The complication can be defined as describing the problem or challenge. This should be directly related to the situation description. There are some specific issues here to consider as well.

- Does the complication describe its potential impact for the organization? For example, in the case of decreasing churn rates, the impact could mean lower sales over time, decreasing market share, and lower profitability.
- Is the complication firmly underpinned with arguments and/or figures? Again we advise focusing on figures that can be directly linked to performance consequences. This will create a stronger belief in the relevance of the executed study.

Message

When discussing the message the following issues should be checked:

- Is there a single core message or are there many messages? We prefer to work with a single core message to have more impact of that single message.
- Does the core message create some curiosity or question? Curiosity will create attention and a desire to listen.
- Does the core message provide an answer to the complication?

Underpinning the message

When providing arguments for the message, it is important to assess what, why, and how the argument is being used. Does the argument really make sense and will it provide a strong underpinning of the message? Specific issues that require attention are:

- Do the arguments link with questions a reader will ask when reading the core message? It is thus very important to understand how managers will react and what questions will come up when the core message is being read.

- Are the arguments complete and mutually exclusive? A complete list of arguments will show that the analyst has seriously thought about the provided conclusion. Mutually exclusive arguments means that there is no overlap in the conclusions or in the opportunities you found.
- There should not be too few nor too many arguments. A general rule of thumb is that there should be a minimum of two arguments and a maximum of five.
- One should start with the most important and convincing argument and end with the least important one.
- Are the arguments compatible? For example, when having strategic arguments, one should not have arguments that are more tactical. Or if arguments are based on facts, it is probably not wise to use sentiments as well.

In Figure 4.3.5 we give some examples of storylines that differ in their purpose. In example one we show how one can come up with business opportunities that achieve the business target.

Visualization

Visualization is of utmost importance in creating impact with data analytics. The reason is actually rather simple: "A picture is worth a thousand words." The ability to understand and extract value from data is much easier when it is done through data visualization rather than from looking at the raw data or the simple statistics of the data. In 1973, the statistician Francis Anscombe demonstrated the importance of graphing data. Anscombe's Quartet shows how four sets of data with identical simple summary statistics can vary considerably when graphed (see Figure 4.3.6).

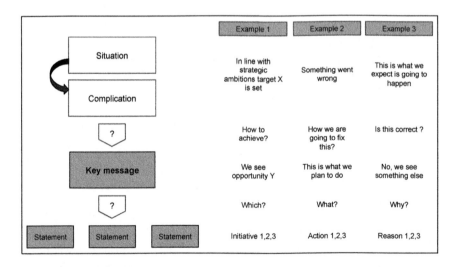

Figure 4.3.5 Examples of different storylines for different purposes

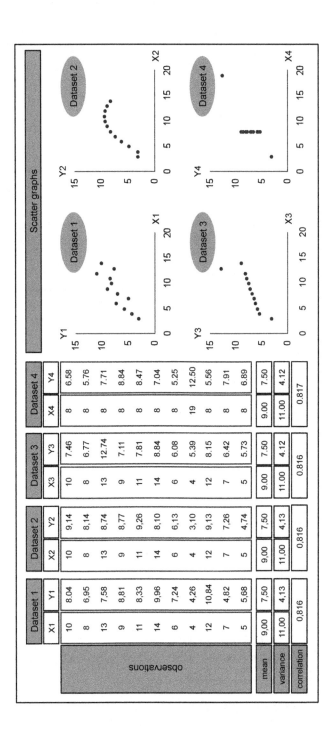

Figure 4.3.6 Graph of Anscombe's Quartet data table
Source: Adapted from Anscombe (1973)

240 *Creating impact with analytics*

There are also some statistics underlying these claims. For example, if information is transferred orally only 10% of the receivers can remember that information after 72 hours; this percentage rises to 65% if the information is visualized. This is called the "picture superiority effect" (Paivio & Csapo, 1973). So if you look at Figure 4.3.7 it is more likely that you will remember the right part (with the apple) than the left part.

Visualization in analytics is used for many purposes. Generally there are three objectives that can be achieved by visualizing data:

- Exploration of data
- Understand and make sense of the data
- Communicate the results of the analysis.

The first two objectives are generally parts of the analysis process. Before running all kinds of analyses it is wise to explore the data with visuals to help make sense of them. This can lead to immediate valuable insights and the understanding of potential relationships in the data. The last objective is clearly linked to the presentation of the results and creating impact. Of course in some cases visualization of data explorations can also be used in the presentation if it underpins the main message of the report. Visualizations in many forms can be used wherever results are presented, such as in reports, presentations, marketing dashboards, and websites. We will probably observe new trends in which apps will be used to visualize data.

In the next sections we aim to provide some practical guidelines on how to effectively visualize when communicating the results. We specifically focus on:

- Choosing the right chart type
- Design of the chart

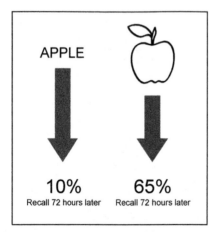

Figure 4.3.7 The picture superiority effect

We will also provide you with some practical tips and tricks to further improve the visualization.

Choosing the chart type

A common mistake when using a chart is to just choose a chart, for example a bar chart or a scatter plot, and assume that using such a chart in a report or presentation will be sufficient and it will be self-explanatory. However, this is frequently not the case. Choosing the right chart format to communicate the analytical results should be done carefully. The problem that researchers face is that there are many graph types, styles, and methods to present data. This makes it difficult to choose the right format. To find the right chart type, it is important to know that there are four core types to visualize data:

1 Showing a relationship between data points
2 Comparing data points
3 Showing the composition of data
4 Showing the distribution of data.

When choosing the right chart type it is first important to assess which graph type fits best with the message, the one aim to convey. In doing so, one has to consider the purpose of the graph. The above distinction in the various ways to visualize can be helpful in this respect. We will therefore discuss the different types of data visualization for each of these four types.

Relationship between data points

A graph displaying a relationship aims to show the association or correlation between two or more variables through the data presented, such as showing the relationship between in-store sales and holidays. The most common "relation charts" that do this are scatter plots and bubble charts. But you can also think about geographic or geospatial graphs or even network charts when you want to show the relation between objects (see Figure 4.3.8).

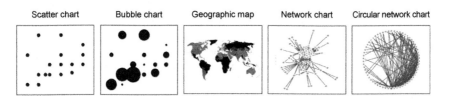

Figure 4.3.8 Relationship charts

- A scatter chart is used to show a relationship between two variables (X,Y) to determine if they tend to move in the same or opposite directions. An example might be plotting NPS (X) and retention (Y) for a sample of months.
- A bubble chart is an extension of the scatter chart, adding a third variable. This ends up being reflected in the size of the bubble. For example, when showing the relationship between NPS and retention, the size of the bubble might reflect the number of customers at a specific data point.
- A geographic map typically shows the relationship between geographic location and a variable. For example, one might aim to show the sales volume per region or country. Geographic units can be countries, regions, Zip code areas, etc.
- A network chart typically shows the relationships between objects (see Figure 2.1.6) or individuals. This last type of visualization can be used in social network analysis, which we discussed in Chapter 4.2.
- In a circular network chart, the network chart is extended by showing the position and the importance of the objects. One concern is that these network charts become less clear when many objects are involved, and may even become unreadable.

Comparing data points

The basic idea of comparison of data points is that one aims to compare scores for (a set of) variables across multiple subunits (e.g. groups, time). For example, one might aim to show the sales per category per quarter. Or one may aim to show the conversion rates for different websites over time. Again, different types of "comparison charts" can be chosen (see Figure 4.3.9).

If one has simple comparisons (e.g. sales per brand), then usually one of two rather similar chart types is used:

- A column chart is used when there is a limited number of subunits
- A bar chart is used when the number of subunits is larger, as more space is available in this graph.

For more complex comparisons, in which multiple measurements for multiple groups need to be compared, more complex graphs are required:

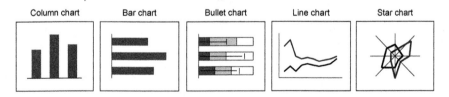

Figure 4.3.9 Comparison charts

- A radar chart (also known as web chart, spider chart, star chart) is a graphical method of displaying multivariate data in the form of a two-dimensional chart of three or more quantitative variables represented on axes starting from the same point (e.g. the allocated budget versus actual spending of different departments, or scoring on product attributes of different designs). Sometimes it is hard to visually compare lengths of different spokes, because radial distances are hard to judge, though concentric circles help as grid lines. Instead, one may use a simple line graph, particularly for time series.
- A bullet chart builds upon the bar chart and has been developed by Stephen Few (2006: 120–206). The bullet graph provides a primary measure unit (e.g. year-to-year revenues), and compares this measure with other measurement units (e.g. target). It also shows the context in terms of ranges of performance—for example, "good," "average," and "weak" (see Figure 4.3.10).

When comparing measurements over time, it is easy enough to use a column graph if only a limited number of categories for only a few periods (e.g. four quarters) is being considered. However, generally more categories and more time periods are considered. A line chart is especially useful if multiple time periods are being considered (e.g. sales development over the year by, say, weekly units).

Composition

When using a composition chart, the aim is to show how the data are being built up out of different subunits. In its most basic form this results from a frequency table. For example, one might like to show the distribution of the origin of website visitors over different touchpoints (e.g. Google, Banners, Affiliates, Direct Load). Again there are many "composition charts" that can be used (see Figure 4.3.11).

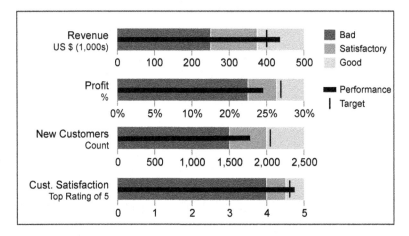

Figure 4.3.10 Example of a bullet chart

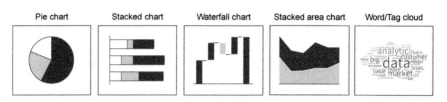

Figure 4.3.11 Composition charts

We would make the following observations about composition charts:

- The pie chart is very popular. It is very useful when a limited set of items or categories is being shown. A common mistake is to use it for many items. The pie chart quickly becomes unreadable and not informative! Some experts (e.g. Stephen Few) believe that one should never use a pie chart, as especially with multiple variables they require a lot of space. Moreover, the pie charts might be difficult to interpret without providing exact figures.
- A stacked chart is a stapled column or bar chart. It can, for example, be used to show the distribution of sales per product per region, where the regions are shown in each bar and each bar represents a product.
- A waterfall chart is good for showing the breakdown of a variable in components. In contrast with the pie chart, this chart provides a good visualization of the size of each of the components. Moreover, it is also possible to show negative values, which is frequently impossible in many other graphs. We recommend using different colours for positive (e.g. green) and negative values (e.g. red). An example of such a chart is a breakdown of churn effects (i.e. total churn decomposed into inevitable churn, price churn, bad service churn, etc.). Extensions can also show developments over time. We frequently also use this chart to show the explanatory power of each variable in a regression equation.
- Tag/word clouds have become increasingly popular, with the increasing usage of unstructured data. Using outcomes of text mining exercises, the importance of each word can be visualized in a word cloud. The larger and the more bold the word the more frequently the word is observed. Generating these clouds is now straightforward using free online tools like Tagul, Wordle, or Tagcloud.

Some of the above charts can also be used to show changes over time. We have already mentioned the waterfall graph, but this can also be done with other graphs:

- In the stacked column chart, stapled columns per period can be linked with small lines to graphically show the time element.
- The stacked area chart becomes increasingly popular, as this visualization can show more changes over time. In comparison with stacked column

chart many more time units (even continuous, e.g. sales per week/day over a year) can be shown, thereby even showing the development of multiple stacked subunits (e.g. brands in a category). This plot can be unclear, especially when there are a number of peak periods and down periods in the data. The ratios in the data can then become unclear.

Distribution

As the name suggests, a distribution chart (see Figure 4.3.12) is used to display how data is distributed and to understand outliers and categories that are outside the norm. One could, for example, consider the distribution of age groups of customers, distribution of revenues over all customers (is there an 80/20 rule?), or examine the power of a response prediction model.

The graphs used to show distribution are similar to those used for comparing variables. Graphs for a single variable are:

- A column histogram, which is a rather simple graph and is usable when there are a few categories per variable (e.g. age groups).
- A line histogram, which is similar to a column histogram but can handle many more categories (e.g. ages instead of age groups). In some cases plots can be used, but in general these are not recommended when there are large peaks and dips in the data (as discussed with the stacked area charts), because then they become hard to read.

If a researcher aims to display multiple variables and aims to show some distribution, the following graphs can be used:

- A double bar chart can be used if you want to compare, for example, the distribution of customers and distribution of revenues. This is also called a decile analysis.
- Lift and gain charts are a useful way to visualize how good a predictive model is. An example might be predicting direct mail response, where on the horizontal x-axis the number of customers is plotted, and on the vertical y-axis, the cumulative lift of the prediction model (see Chapter 4.1).

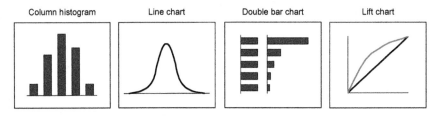

Figure 4.3.12 Distribution charts

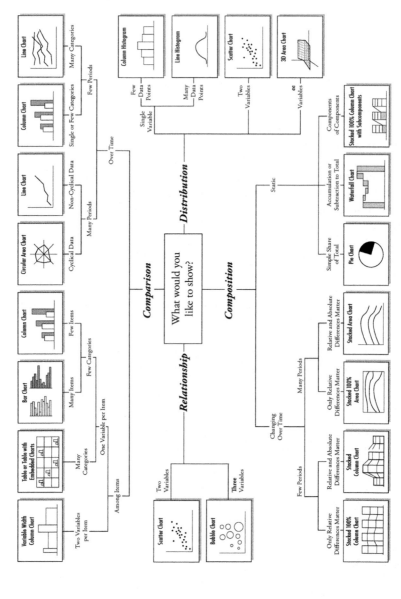

Figure 4.3.13 Chart suggestions—a thought starter

Source: Adapted from Abela (2008)

Creating impact with analytics 247

- The scatter chart provides a kind of cloud of points that have a position on the horizontal x-axis and the vertical y-axis. This may show something about the potential association between variables, as we already noted when discussing relation charts.

Andrew Abela (2008) has provided a nice choice process for the type of graph to be used (see Figure 4.3.13). Although not all the graphs that we discussed here are shown, this flow diagram can be very useful when searching for the right graph to use (see Figure 4.3.14).

Finally, we stress that our overview of graphs is not exhaustive. We have aimed to discuss the most important and most frequently used graphs. Although care has be taken when using these graphs, many of them can create more impact when incorporated into a report or presentation.

Graph Design[3]

After choosing the graph type one should consider the design of the graph. This is also essential, as the design will determine the attention the graph will get. Colin Ware, Director of the Data Visualization Research Lab at the University of New Hampshire, terms the basic building blocks of the visualization process as "pre-attentive attributes" (Ware, 2008). These attributes immediately catch our eye when we look at a visualization. They can be perceived in less than 10 milliseconds, even before we make a conscious effort to notice them. A list of pre-attentive attributes is given in Figure 4.3.14.

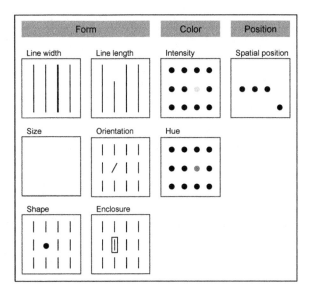

Figure 4.3.14 Pre-attentive attributes

Source: Adapted from Ware (2008)

248 *Creating impact with analytics*

These pre-attentive attributes can be useful when designing a graph, as they immediately identify a visual. These attributes are also the basis for patterns shown in a graph.

Analytical Patterns

Colin Ware (2008) states that:

> If pre-attentive attributes are the alphabets of visual language, analytical patterns are the words we form using them. We immediately identify the pre-attentive attributes in a visualization. We then combine the pre-attentive attributes to seek out analytical patterns in the visual.

The basic analytical patterns are displayed in Figure 4.3.15.

The basic attributes and patterns allow receivers to process visual information. However, it is not only the patterns that are useful. Beyond that one might want to highlight or emphasize specific patterns over others.

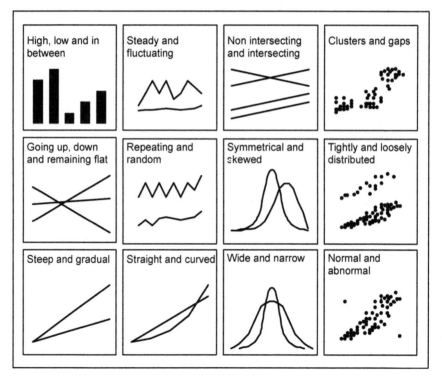

Figure 4.3.15 Basic analytical patterns

Source: Adapted from Ware (2008)

Tips and tricks

We have some tips and tricks to help the researcher working with graphs to do a much better job of creating them:

- Keep it simple! This is the golden rule. Always choose the simplest way to convey your information.
- Kill the grid lines unless they are absolutely necessary, or at least make them subtle so they do not distract from the information you're trying to present.
- Make sure your chart is centered on the data you want to present.
- Your axes should be clearly labeled, and should have units on them where necessary, so no one has to guess or infer what you're trying to say.
- Use colour, size, and position to help the reader to see what is important. Colour serves to highlight exceptions, not to enliven a dull dashboard.
- Remember, your goal is that anyone can pick up your chart, whether you're there to talk about it or not, and understand what information the data are trying to communicate.
- One frequently believes that outcomes of regression models should be put in tables. However, regression models can also be shown in graphs, for example by showing the standardized coefficients for the most important variables in a bar chart or by showing the explanatory power of each variable in a waterfall chart (see Figure 4.3.11 for examples).
- We recommend researchers should try out a number of graphs and learn to "play" with them. This way one immediately learns the pros and cons of each graph, and it becomes easier to pick the right one.
- Be aware of misleading with graphs. If different scales are used on, say, the y-axis, small effects can become visually large. Gaining attention is not the same as misinterpretation of effects.
- 3D graphs can be unnecessarily confusing. The perspective information in the background can give the impression that it is less important than information in the front. Use compelling headlines and decks to describe the take-away message of the visualization.

Trends

We conclude with a discussion of some trends in visualization. In practice and in line with the growth of big data development we observe a stronger focus on design. We also observe that more infographics are being used. David McCandless is taking infographics and data-visualization to the next level. In his book *Information is Beautiful* (2010) he visualizes captivating and intriguing patterns and connections across art, science, health, and pop. Analysts frequently lack the skill for this kind of work and professional design artists are being used. We also see an increasing use of text-based graphs, such as word-clouds.

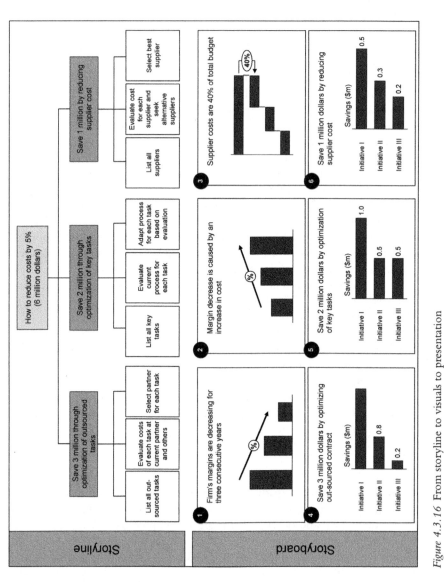

Figure 4.3.16 From storyline to visuals to presentation

We are probably aware of only some of the visualization trends. With the technological advances becoming available to help the display of visual effects, three-dimensional graphs will become more popular and insightful. Just watch the way Professor Hans Rosling handles a presentation, commentating on a moving hologram that illustrates the health, wealth, and population of 200 countries over 200 years in less than a minute (Rosling, 2007). We also believe that the growing importance of video means that presentations will also become more video-based.

Conclusions

In this chapter we have put forward the proposition that low impact is a general problem for many analytical studies. A very clear storyline and visualization are key-ingredients for creating more impact. In sum, we have the following clear recommendations for analysts; if they are followed, the result should be a storyboard in which the storyline and the visuals are integrated (see Figure 4.3.16).

- Start the presentation by creating a clear storyline.
- Write the storyline in full sentences:
  - What is the situation/complication?
  - What is the core message?
  - How can this message be underpinned?
- Continue by drawing some initial slides and visuals. Do not use a computer, but use a drawing board to stimulate creativity.
- Write out the headings of each slide in full sentences.
- Choose the right graphs to visualize the supporting insights.
- Using this basis, make a report/presentation.
- Use a critical counterpart to challenge the presentation.

Notes

1 Compared to other chapters, this chapter has a very strong "how to" focus. Attention to the creation of reports is very limited in the academic marketing literature. We have aimed to write a comprehensive chapter that provides the analyst with sufficient practical guidelines to set up an effective report or presentation. This is heavily based on our own combined experience of giving hundreds of presentations on our analytical studies for major companies.
2 There are other methods as well. However, we find that this method provides several advantages and focus on it in this chapter.
3 This section draws heavily on Colin Ware's study (2008).

References

Abela, A. (2008). *Advanced presentations by design: Creating communication that drives action.* San Francisco, CA: Pfeiffer.

Anscombe, F. J. (1973). Graphs in Statistical Analysis. *The American Statistician*, 27(1), 17–21.
Few, S. (2006). *Information dashboard design*. CA: O'Reilly.
McCandless, D. (2010). *Information is Beautiful*. UK: HarperCollins.
Miller, G. A. (1956). The magical number seven, plus or minus two: Some limits on our capacity for processing information. *Psychological Review*, 63, 81–97.
Minto, B. (2009). *The Pyramid Principle: Logic in writing and thinking*. Edinburgh Gate, Harlow, Essex: Pearson Education.
Paivio, A., & Csapo, K. (1973). Picture superiority in free recall: Imagery or dual coding? *Cognitive Psychology*, 5, 176–206.
Roberts, J. H., Kayandé, U., & Stremersch, S. (2014). From academic research to marketing practice: Exploring the marketing science value chain. *International Journal of Research in Marketing*, 3(2), 127–40.
Rosling, H. (2007). New insights on property. Retrieved fromTED.com. Retrieved September 11, 2015 from www.ted.com/talks/hans_rosling_reveals_new_insights_on_poverty?language=en
Ware, C. (2008). *Visual thinking: for design*. Morgan Kaufmann Series in Interactive Technologies. Amsterdam: Elsevier.
Wurman, R. S. (1989). *Information anxiety*. New York: Doubleday.

5 Building successful big data capabilities

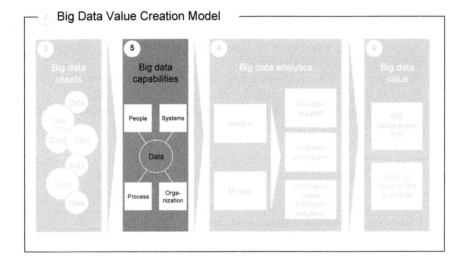

Introduction

Having big data is not sufficient of itself to develop a successful value-creating big data strategy. Firms need to invest in big data capabilities that transform the organization into a fact-based and more data-driven enterprise. At first blush this seems easy to achieve. Firms should just buy some software, hire some big data experts, and the big data initiatives can take-off. According to IDG (2014) the top five big data investments involve storage, servers, cloud infrastructure, discovery and analytics, and applications. However, many of these investments will certainly lead to serious disappointments. And indeed according to Cisco 60% of companies agree that big data will help improve decision making and increase their competitiveness,[1] but only 28% indicate that they are currently generating strategic value from their data. Probably some short-term successes can be achieved; however, for a long-term impact firms should invest in people, systems, processes, and the organization. Our experiences have shown that firms may face several hurdles to do so. For example, firms may be confronted with old systems and databases that are difficult to replace. Importantly, there is also a shortage of analytical talent (Manyika et al. 2011; Leeflang, Verhoef, Dahlström, & Freundt, 2014; see also Figure 5.1). Finding analytical people to hire can be a nightmare. Western European companies are now hiring talent from India and other Asian countries to fill analytical vacancies. Another hurdle is to change the culture to one in which analytical solutions are considered as very valuable input in marketing decision making, instead of only focusing on intuition.

In this chapter we will discuss the major ingredients from which firms can successfully build an analytical competence, one that fully allows them to benefit from big data opportunities. Based on our big data value creation model, we will structure our discussion mainly around four building blocks of a successful analytical competence:

1 Process: creating a common business-driven way of working that is underpinned by privacy and security
2 People: to recruit, to develop, and to maintain the right analytical talent
3 Systems: the platform and tools for an integrated data-ecosystem
4 Organization: taking the right role and place in the organization for the most impact.

However, we will start with our vision on what the transformation of an organization entails if it wishes to create strong analytical competences.

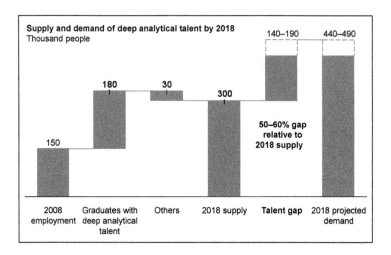

Figure 5.1 Shortage of supply in analytical talent

Source: Adapted from Manyika et al. (2011)

Transformation to create successful analytical competence

Over the past few decades marketing intelligence (MI) has become a more important function within many firms. We observe this especially in service industries, such as retailing, telecom, and financial services. Numerous examples have been discussed in literature and can be seen in practice, in which organizations such as Tesco, Capital One, O'Hara's, and KPN, have developed analytical functions to help them effectively compete (e.g. Verhoef & Lemon, 2013; Davenport & Harris, 2007; Humby, Hunt & Phillips, 2008). And as already discussed there is also ample scientific empirical evidence that firms investing in these analytical competences can actually outperform competition (e.g. Germann, Lilien, & Rangaswamy, 2012; Germann, Lilien, Fiedler, & Kraus, 2014). MI departments or functions perform an important role in creating these competences. In an era of big data this will become even more important.

However, we also observe that in many companies analytical competences have not been fully developed. In fact one could put forward the statement that many firms are not well-prepared internally for the presumed big data revolution. They simply lack a strong analytical competence. As a consequence, the MI department (if present at all), is not likely to play an important driving role in big data value creation. In many firms these departments stick to their traditional role, in which they frequently only deliver simple reports and customer selections on requests and do not actively participate in value-creation discussion lacking strong market and customer insight—all because of a lack of analytical capabilities. The MI department then mainly has a reactive supplier role.

Changing roles

In general we have observed a changing role in how MI operates in firms. These changing roles are displayed in Figure 5.2. MI departments frequently start in a supplier role in which the credo is: "We deliver what is being asked for." In a next phase they can become a challenger, in which they are also asked to provide input on specific marketing decisions based on their presumed market and customer knowledge. In the next phases, the function moves from an advisor role, to an initiator role, and finally an orchestrating role. These three phases can be considered as top-class MI roles. In the advisor role, the MI function gets a stronger say in marketing decision making and consults it as an important advisor, whose input is valued and strongly taken into account. As an initiator, the MI function develops independent marketing proposals in close cooperation with the marketing department. The orchestrating role is observed very infrequently, and basically implies that MI is embedded within marketing decision making and becomes a driving force responsible for orchestrating customer contacts over the multiple available channels.

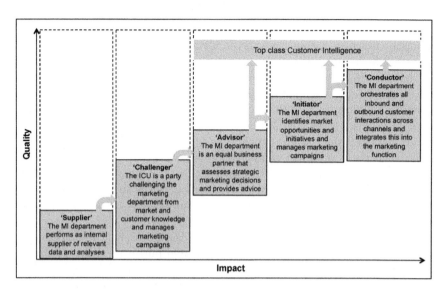

Figure 5.2 Changing role of the marketing intelligence department
Source: Adapted from Verhoef, Hoekstra, & Van der Scheer (2009)

Changing focus

The changing role of the MI department induces a changing focus, scope, and available capabilities within MI department. Based on our years of experience with organizations that have made a strategic choice to bring the intelligence function to a higher level, we state an outline of the desired changes and resulting outcomes these organizations often envision and experience (see Table 5.1). In sum, we observe that functions move from a tactical focus to a more strategic focus. As a consequence, their input in decision making is changing and they also use a different analytical approach. Instead of looking-back, a more forward-looking predictive approach is embraced. They also consider that an integrated view on customer and market data is required. In doing so, they will be a driving force within the organization to stimulate data integration developments. In terms of daily operations, we observe a shift from reactive analyses to more proactive agenda-setting analyses. This also induces a strong focus on clear reports and visualization of the results. Overall, these changes will result in an attractive place to work, where young, talented, and ambitious analysts are willing to work.

For a successful example we discuss the transformation of the MI department at Dutch Telco KPN (see Box 5.1). A main challenge for firms to achieve these transformations is in developing an intelligence team with the right skills. We will elaborate on that in the next sections.

Table 5.1 Shifting focus of the marketing intelligence function

Area	From	To
Strategic focus	Tactical and short-term focus on actions and campaigns	Strategic and long-term focus on V2C and V2F
Input marketing decision making	Provider of figures and queries	Fact-based and actionable advice that meets the business planning
Analytical approach	Looking back and explanatory insights	Forward-looking insights and concrete proposals for change
Intelligence role	Fragmented view of the customer base on scattered data, information, and knowledge across multiple departments/silos	One-intelligence approach and method with a single customer view that is accessible throughout the organization
Daily operations	Eliminating workload, which is filled by the daily operation, (reactive) is the norm	Proactively setting own agenda and priorities in line with the organizational KPIs
Output	Supply of raw output in Excel type of program	Clear and strong visualized presentations with clear message
Visibility within firm	Impact visible for the immediate area (i.e. marketing and sales)	Impact visible for the entire organization
Attractiveness of function	Department with limited growth prospects	Department influx of new talent with attractive career paths and a breeding site for talent
Attractiveness for employees	Obscurity as an attractive employer for its leading analytics	Preferred employer for analytical top talent

Box 5.1 Building up an analytical competence at KPN

The Dutch incumbent Telco KPN understood the necessity of building up an intelligence function several years ago. Confronted with suboptimal marketing campaigns, increasing competition, and high increasing churn, the firm began implementing customer management with a strong focus on fact-based marketing. The management of KPN also understood that a strong MI function was essential. However, the firm lacked strong analytical skills. Therefore, it set up the Marketing Intelligence (MI) Academy jointly with the marketing intelligence consulting agency MIcompany. Baptiest Coopmans, former member of KPN's board of directors, stated: "Our own education programs were not focused on customer intelligence, but focused on educating marketing managers and organizational leaders. With the MIacademy we aim to develop top talented specialists, which are able to fully understand customer needs." A three-year training program was developed for new young master graduates. In this program, they were trained in analytical techniques but were also trained in improving the interface between the MI function and marketing. Important skills included the effective presentation of marketing facts and interpersonal communication. Furthermore, MI trainees were trained in deriving growth opportunities from their analytical findings/insights to develop strong recommendations for marketing. The whole program has been evaluated (see figure below). The management of KPN is fully convinced of the success of building a strong MI with MIacademy. Marteyn Roose, at that time director of customer management at KPN, stated: "Statistical tooling, methods and central data warehousing are all beneficial, but it's our people that make the real difference. The benefits of attracting top talented graduates and training them to become top performing MI professionals have proven to be tremendous in all kinds of areas." KPN identified several of the benefits of the program shown below. Since then, the program has resulted in additional revenues and cost reductions. Direct revenues have occurred through improved marketing campaigns (overall improving net present value of orders by 132%) and the development of successful growth initiative opportunities (>€140 million in 2010). Indirect and more long-term revenues have also been realized, for example, through the strong development of the customer management function within KPN. There is an increasingly high demand throughout all departments and disciplines in KPN. This ensures that few MI professionals choose to leave KPN to look for challenging careers elsewhere. The traditional focus of MI was mainly the optimization of marketing campaigns. At KPN, that scope was broadened to all disciplines (e.g., marketing, sales, service, network) and on all levels (i.e., up to the board of directors). A strong MI function is a necessity. The program's strong focus on the interface between marketing and MI also resulted in greater acceptance of more accountable or fact-based marketing. Cost reductions mainly occurred from lower recruitment costs and short vacancy periods (>95% of new talent acquired without any recruitment aid). Moreover, the firm could pay lower salaries because it did not need to hire experienced MI specialists (20% saving, including educational costs). The firm also required less input from external dedicated marketing intelligence firms, as sufficient skills were now present internally.

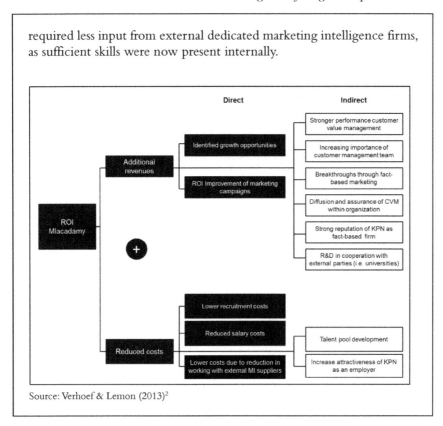

Source: Verhoef & Lemon (2013)[2]

Building block 1: Process

The "process" focuses mainly on how, within firms, analytical projects are defined and executed. We consider five important phases of the analysis (see Figure 5.3):

This process is driven by the business question and leads to output whose purpose is to answer that question. As outlined, this process seems rather straightforward and fits with our preferred analytical problem-solving analysis strategy. However, the most important hurdle is the cooperation of and

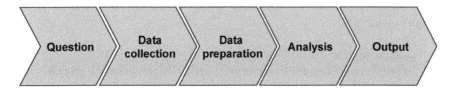

Figure 5.3 Phases of the standard analytical process

understanding between the different departments and the MI department. These departments can sometimes function as separate silos that do not understand each other (see Box 5.2). This may come with the risk that analyses lose their usefulness and the MI department becomes obsolete. It can become even more complicated when there are separate departments gaining market and customer insights.

Box 5.2 Views on the marketing intelligence process

Marketing Intelligence:

- *"Marketing does not understand that answering a simple question takes a lot of work for us"*
- *"We recently did a great analysis, but nothing is done with it"*

Marketing:

- *"Marketing Intelligence has written a wonderful extensive report, but the report does not really answer my question"*
- *"I am convinced that the results are significantly reliable, but I do not see how I can apply this in practice"*

Sales:

- *"Marketing Intelligence supports the Marketing department with its campaigns, but they totally do not understand what is going on in our field"*
- *"In addition, they do not have access to the relevant data for us"*

Finance:

- *"As long as the figures of Marketing Intelligence are not in line with our reporting, findings are unreliable and therefore not useful for control and policy"*

The opinions given in Box 5.2 reflect how the MI department functions within the organization, and how this may result in reduced impact. There are three main reasons why the intended impact and added value of analytics is frequently limited:

- Unclear starting point of the analysis
- Limited connection to the dynamics of the business planning process
- Unclear and not impactful presentation of analyses.

Starting point of the analysis

For decades, analysts were mainly used to provide information that focused on providing rather descriptive analyses giving explanations, making comparisons, and evaluating marketing campaigns. Typical questions for marketing analysts are:

- How many active customers do we have?
- What is the profile of new customers?
- Why has the outflow of customers increased over the past period?
- What segments can we distinguish in our customer database?
- What was the response to the last campaign?

There is nothing wrong with asking these questions. However, it is not clear what the underlying business challenge actually is. Focusing solely on the above questions would have some impact on marketing decisions, but would not have an impact that goes beyond marketing. In order to be more impactful the starting point of the analysis should always be related to a clear business challenge. This gives the right focus, the right priority for use of scarce resources (time, capacity, and budgets), and creates a common acknowledgement of the relevance and importance of the executed analyses. We observed one firm within which for years the marketing research department executed analyses on how to improve satisfaction—without having much impact. At some point, satisfaction became a key-metric requiring attention for the firm and its stakeholders. The intelligence department started to understand the relevance of the metric to the business challenge and started impactful projects, supported by top management, on reporting, explaining, and predicting satisfaction. It is thus important for analysts to understand the business challenge. Good business challenges should:

- Always be linked to objectives and KPIs and therefore measurable
- Should be linked to themes as market attractiveness, brand performance, and customer management (see also Chapter 2)
- Result in different actionable options for management.

Here are a number of examples of clear business questions which give the right focus for the analysis process:

- How can the churn of post-paid subscribers in the consumer market be reduced by 3% in the coming year?
- How can we increase the cross-sell ratio of our insurance products for the retail market from 1.2 to 1.8?
- How can we increase our market share by 5% through the acquisition of new customers in the business for small enterprises?
- How do we have to allocate our media budget to increase our brand preference from 10% to 15%?

To get a well-defined and to-the-point business question driving the analyses, we believe the following issues are crucial:

- Have a good initial discussion with relevant owners of the problem within the firm.
- Clearly determine on which level your analysis has the strongest impact: market, brand, or customer.
- Determine whether the project focuses on incremental improvement or optimizing of current business and marketing practices or aims to achieve strategic changes and growth opportunities;
- Determine which definitions of the analyzed KPIs are used within the firm.
- Assess the importance of the identified business challenge by quantifying the business impact of the problem (e.g. reducing churn could lead to an increase in EBITDA).
- Determine the intended change in the KPI of interest (i.e. reduce churn with 3%).
- Validate and set targets/objectives based on existing business plans, strategy papers, outlooks, and reports.
- Make sure that you have different propositions and or solutions for the identified business challenge that needs to tested or evaluated in such a way as to keep an open mind to perhaps unexpected opportunities, rather than immediately come up with a kind of standard and frequently expected advice.

Support during the analysis process

Once the business challenge is defined, the next step to ensure impact during the analysis is good management. We have found the following to be useful guidelines:

- Ensure consensus on the business demand (with business managers and finance & control).
- Make sure the right people are involved and informed during the analysis process.
- Provide a schedule and overview of the steps that you go through.
- Ask for active support during the analysis phase, including time and capacity for coordination, consultation, and feedback.
- Make sure that there is sufficient access to all necessary information.
- Make sure that there is budget for (unexpected) out-of-pocket expenses (insert external data, capacity, etc.).

Given where the MI function comes from, it is not so strange that many intelligence teams are not fully aware of what the most important topics for top management are. To help get a project rolling and to get more support from top management, knowing their agenda is of great importance. It will also help to ask the right questions. So we strongly recommend that MI specialists look beyond daily tasks and marketing challenges. A related recommendation is that analysts should be connected with finance. In many organizations finance have a strong say in setting KPIs and the definition of these KPIs, as they have to be reported to external stakeholders. Hence, when analyzing these metrics analysts should use the metrics as being used by finance. Analyses in which metrics differ from those used in finance are often interpreted as not reliable and therefore not useful. Always validate results based on existing outlooks, business plans, strategy documents, and management reports.

Building block 2: People

The transformation of the MI department also requires the attraction of employees who can work effectively in these departments. The largest challenge is that it is difficult to find good employees. There is a shortage of good analysts that can function well in this highly demanding job. Including this market challenge there are three people challenges:

1 Selection: What is the profile of the employees required?
2 Acquisition: How do I acquire the right analysts from the job market?
3 Retention: How do I keep the good analysts, given the shortage in the market?

Analyst profile

Although we are mainly emphasizing the function analyst, this seems like an old-fashioned term. In the era of big data, firms are no longer looking for analysts, but for data scientists. The data scientist is then considered as being the sexiest job in the world (Davenport & Patil, 2012). There are several descriptions of data scientists, for example:

> *A high ranking professional with training and curiosity to make discoveries in the world of big data*
>
> (Davenport & Patil, 2012: 71)

> *A data scientist is somebody who is inquisitive, who can stare at data and spot trends. It's almost like a Renaissance individual who really wants to learn and bring change to an organization*
>
> (Bhambhri IBM)[3]

In our view the descriptions are rather vague and do not sufficiently focus on what firms should actually look for and cannot be used to select and/or train people. We therefore focus on the skills an MI analyst or a big data scientist should have. These skills or individual capabilities can be divided into four areas (see Figure 5.4):

- Analytical capabilities
- Data and tools
- Business sense
- Communication and visualization.

All the skills listed in Figure 5.4 are important. However, unfortunately these skills are not often combined in a single person. For example a specialist with excellent analytical skills frequently lacks business sense and finds it very difficult to communicate effectively. This does not imply that one should not hire top analytical talent! These experts are needed, especially given today's strong big data challenges and the sophisticated analytical models required to solve them. Another strategy would be to go for someone scoring average on every dimension. However, it is unlikely that these people will move the organization forward, as there might be a lack of innovation on every dimension. In terms of building an analytical competence with the right people, firms should strive to develop a good team of professionals in which each of these capabilities is sufficiently provided at a high level. We have some specific recommendations:

Analytical capabilities	Business sense
• Above average score on capability tests: conceptual, analytical, numeric • Statistical modeling and experiment design • Supervised learning: decision trees, logistic regression • Unsupervised learning: clustering, dimensionality reduction	• Passionate about the business • Willingness to improve business performance • Deep industry specific knowledge • Organization sensitivity • Leadership qualities • Problem solver • Engage with senior management
Data and tools	Communication and visualization
• Curious about data and sources • Computer science fundamentals • Statistical computing package e.g. R, Matlab, SAS, IBM (SPSS) • Database tools like SQL and NoSQL • MapReduce/Hadoop concepts	• Translate data-driven insights into decisions and actions • Define and support your key message • Storytelling skills • Consistency and structure • Visual art design

Figure 5.4 Multi-disciplinary skills of an analyst

Building successful big data capabilities   265

- Do not aim to get the employee that has all these capabilities (you could call this the "sheep with five legs" syndrome).
- Instead build up a team in which each of the capabilities is present at a sufficiently high quality level.
- Do not aim to build a fully fledged analytical capability all at once but take a stepwise approach.

Team approach

To help set up the team approach, it can help to map MI employees on their specific profile. Based on the four capabilities, on a rather general level four profiles can be distinguished (see Figure 5.5):

1   The consultant: Strong business sense and communication & visualization skills
2   The data specialist: Strong analytical and data & tools skills
3   The data analyst: Strong analytical and specifically visualization skills
4   The IT professional: Strong data & tools and business sense skills.

Importantly, building up the analytical team should usually be done rather gradually, as shown in Figure 5.6. Frequently, firms start by using the services of some independent data analysts and/or specialized consulting agencies. At some point the need for their own analytical team becomes apparent and a small team is built up. This team should then be educated using specifically

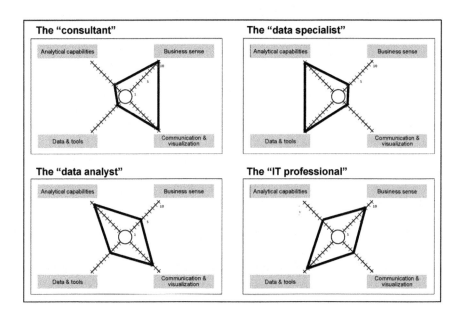

Figure 5.5 Possible big data staff profiles

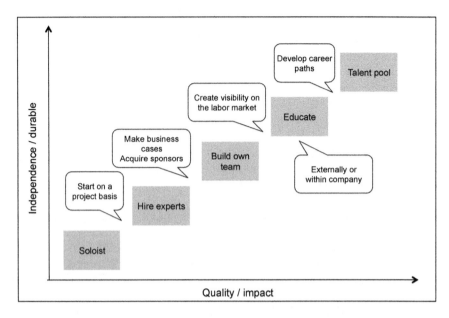

Figure 5.6 Stepwise development of analytical competence within the firm

developed internal programs or external programs of business schools and/or consulting agencies. At some point there should be sufficient knowledge and expertise within the firm, and firms should be able to independently build up their own analytical competences. At this stage it becomes important to develop career paths for the analysts in the team.

Acquiring good people

The supply of good analysts is much lower than the demand (see Figure 5.1). This creates a huge challenge for firms aiming to build an analytical competence. One can easily develop the ideal department in terms of required profiles. However, getting the right people is far from trivial. One of the problems is that MBA programs are not good at developing analytical skills as they mainly focus on managerial skills. We can find few MBA programs that seem to focus on big data. Also regular Master of Science programs in marketing typically focus on marketing management knowledge and provide limited opportunities for studying analytics. In a changing and more data-driven marketing environment a stronger focus on analytic courses within marketing programs becomes a necessity. The supply of students well trained in statistics is also limited in many Western countries, where many students prefer to study psychology, management, law etc.[4] We also observe that well-trained students with strong econometric skills frequently prefer to work in finance rather than in marketing. One of the reasons for this is that marketing is frequently considered as not being quantitative in nature; another is that salaries in quantitative finance are frequently higher. There is a job to do for firms as well as marketing departments within universities to convince these students that marketing is actually a very attractive working area. An example of good practice is Erasmus University, where the econometric department, on the instigation of Professor Philip Hans Franses (Professor in Econometrics and Marketing Research), started a marketing track for econometricians more than a decade ago. The following suggestions are helpful for attracting top analytical talent:

- An obvious suggestion is that firms aim to build up employee brand equity (BE) (Tavassoli, Sorescu, & Chandy, 2014). Young professionals prefer companies, like Google, that are innovative and have a strong BE.
- Providing an active education plan for young analysts may help as well. Companies providing these education programs in which young analysts are trained on the job have a unique selling point.
- Reach out to universities and business schools in which talented young people are educated. Companies could participate in analytical classes with data-based cases, in which they meet students, and students become familiar with companies and their analytical job prospects.

Beyond attracting young talent, firms also have some other solutions at their disposal to get around the shortage of analytical talent:

- One solution is to train existing employees in the area of marketing research and database marketing. Our experience, though, is that this is not as easy as it sounds. Knowledge of these employees has to some extent become obsolete in a big data era and a training of new work mentality with a stronger focus on business, communication and visualization is not straightforward.
- A second solution is to make sure effective work processes within organizations are in place and to automate specific processes. As a consequence less talent is needed. For example, customer selections could probably be automated. Also reporting can be automated, especially for continuous data collection.

Talent retention

Given the shortage of talent and the investments required in education of acquired talent, employee retention is of urgent importance for analytical functions. Furthermore, analysts build up tacit knowledge that is very valuable to keep. Hence analyst retention should be a top priority for firms building up an analytical competence. Holtom, Mitchell, Lee and Eberly (2008) warn that in industry the chronic shortages of qualified employees have driven up the costs of turnover much faster than the rate of inflation. This underlines the importance of the loyalty of talented people. Frequently, loyal analysts are not the top employees within the firm. So there is a danger that if firms do not invest in the loyalty of talented people, their MI function may slide down the ladder and the need to build up a fully fledged MI department starts all over again. We have seen that happen in many organizations. For example, within a service firm, at some point talented employees became unsatisfied and, as a consequence of a lack of support from top management and ongoing uncertainty, started looking around, and found jobs in other industries, such as online retailing and finance. For talent retention, several issues have been deemed important, such as salaries and atmosphere, but given the focus on young talent, the most important factor is probably personal development (e.g. De Vos & Meganck, 2009). We have the following suggestions for firms:

- Develop attractive future career opportunities within MI departments, but potentially also outside the department. If former MI employees become active in other functions (e.g. finance, marketing), they may become active ambassadors for big data approaches within the firm.
- Create sufficient opportunities for personal development and freedom to innovate. Data-scientists are looking for ways to use data to solve problems, and are less attracted by specific tasks, such as customer selections.
- Importantly, a corporate vision on big data usage and building up the analytical competence is an important ingredient for creating a working environment in which talented people feel they can contribute to the success of the organization and career opportunities are sufficiently warranted. Organization literature refers to this: there should be sufficient organizational support (Holtom et al., 2008).

Building block 3: Systems

One of the initial reactions of firms with regard to big data could be an immediate aim to build large systems in which all big data are integrated and analytical and support tools are included as well. In such a way one large big data system is created. This approach would be in line with what we have seen when firms were implementing customer relationship management. Firms invested millions in integrated software systems such as Oracle, Microsoft, Siebel, etc. One of the major lessons learned was that firms should not focus on the technology but should focus on what the technology can do for customers (Verhoef & Lemon, 2013; Rigby, 2014). This major lesson is easily forgotten in a big data environment where every IT-oriented consulting and tooling firm is communicating the impressive opportunities of big data. For firms there is a plethora of options to choose from different providers and software solutions. In the 2015 edition of marketing technology landscape supergraphic of chiefmartic.com[5] 1,876 vendors are represented across 43 categories. The number of vendors nearly doubled from the previous year's edition, which charted 947 companies. And the number of vendors is still growing (see Figure 5.7).

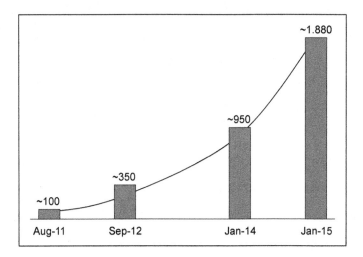

Figure 5.7 Number of vendors in marketing technology landscape represented in supergraphics of chiefmaric.com

As we have already discussed in earlier chapters, sound expectations should drive business decisions on big data. This also holds for system investments. So it is also true that with big data systems, technology should never lead the decisions here! With regard to big data marketing solutions, the systems should be user and customer-driven instead of technology-driven. In that sense marketing analysts should have a strong say in the development of big data systems and marketing should be an advocate of the customer in this process. Jointly with IT they should come up with workable and scalable solutions.

We observe many firms striving for a total new big data system which is frequently just not feasible and not necessary. Many firms already have good systems in place for different solutions (e.g. CRM or enterprise resource planning). The important thing about a big data environment is that systems can be linked. We advocate an approach in which old systems and new big data solutions (e.g. Hadoop) co-exist within an organization, loosely divided into four different 'layers' (see Figure 5.8):

1 Data sources
2 Data storing
3 Analytical data platform
4 Analytical applications.

It is thus very important to emphasize that the use of one big system is generally an illusion. Firms will use different systems in the different identified layers, but even within the layers (e.g. analytics), different software can be used depending on the objectives to be achieved.

270 *Building successful big data capabilities*

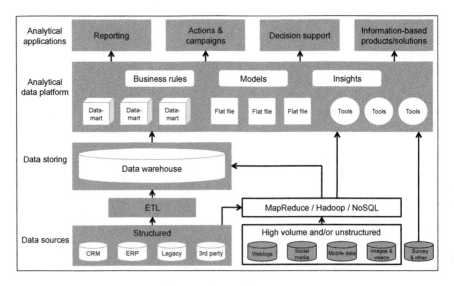

Figure 5.8 Different layers of a big data analytical system

Data sources

Within a firm there are multiple data sources. Many of these data sources function on their own. For example, a firm can have a good billing data system, which functions pretty well for billing purposes. Similarly, they could have databases in which operational data on customer service requests are stored. Before starting a big data system, firms first should make sure that the data in each of these internal databases is good and reliable. Big data analyses are useless when bad data are analyzed, despite the fact that the analyzed datasets are large. In this respect the old wisdom "garbage in is garbage out" holds in a big data era as well. In many firms there have been efforts to integrate databases having a similar main focus. Specifically firms have invested in CRM databases in which billing data, marketing data, customer service data etc. are integrated to create a total view on each single customer. Integrated customer databases are of essential importance for customer level analyses and are a key ingredient of successful predictions on churn, lifetime value, etc. Traditionally, these databases are then available in a data warehouse. Although these data warehouses could involve millions of data points depending on firm size, number of customers etc., they are relatively simple compared to the requirements of the new big data era currently confronting firms.

As already discussed, big data development leads to large data volumes, but probably more important is that there are very different data sources with different data structures and data types, which cannot be linked easily. For example, whereas service interactions in a call center can be linked to individual customers, interactions on websites with different devices are more difficult to link to an individual customer (see Chapter 3.1). Similarly, unstructured data on websites, blogs, and social media cannot be fully linked to individual customers. Furthermore, aggregation levels of data may differ (e.g. brand level vs. customer level). It is impossible to store these data in an integrated data system. We strongly advise that in a big data strategy, firms should not strive to integrate all different data sources. They should only integrate data that can easily be integrated because there are strong identifiers between the data sources (e.g. customer id for CRM database). Instead they should create a big data platform in which the several databases are available and can easily be accessed by analysts based on their respective analytical questions.

Data storage

Several data sources can be saved in a large data warehouse. This data warehouse is typically internal to the firm. We refer to Chapter 3 on the specifics of data storage. Importantly, many firms now also use the cloud to store data. The typical way of processing and integrating all data sources that have been assessed as relevant is called ETL (extract/transform/load): it handles all input data sources in order to save and use them in the data warehouse (see also Chapter 3.1).

Analytical big data platform

The big data platform thus involves a set of databases which should be accessible by analytical specialists. These databases can be the more traditional sort available in standard data warehouses, but for large volumes and/or unstructured data, specific big data solutions such as Hadoop clusters can be used. Firms should take care of security issues and should only provide authorization to access specific data to internally selected employees. We must emphasize that this big data platform is only a data platform. Using this big data platform a database specialist could aim to combine specific data sources through, for example, data fusion and SQL queries. For example, when studying the churn of customers, one could combine CRM data with data on social media (e.g. likes for specific customer segments). Or analysts, when doing longitudinal analyses of brand sales, could build a database consisting of weekly brand sales, weekly advertising efforts, weekly social media likes, and the digital sentiment index (DSI).

These datasets should be structured in such a way that they can be analyzed in the program being used. In practice the term "data mart" is used to refer to datasets derived from the big data warehouse. A data mart is the access layer of the data warehouse environment that is used to get data out to the users. Data marts are typically small subsets of the data warehouse and are usually oriented to a specific business line or team, in this case the MI team. Whereas data warehouses have an enterprise-wide depth, the information in data marts pertains to a single department. From this data mart flat files can be extracted which can be further integrated and processed to be used in analytical tools. Often these analytical tools also have functionalities for further data processing, such as creating all kind of new variables by classifying or combining the different input variables.

Analytical tools or packages focus on the statistical, econometric, and linguistic analysis of the data. In the past, firms typically chose a preferred analytical tool. This tool could be either (partially) specifically developed for the firm or a standard statistical software package, such as SPSS (nowadays part of IBM) or SAS. A specifically developed tool would consist of typical analyses being used in a firm presented in a user-friendly way. Data inflow to these programs is then frequently automated. However, this approach has limited scope and it is virtually impossible for an analyst to do additional analyses on data. Statistical packages have a full set of statistical analyses available that can be used for multiple analytical purposes. For example, in packages like SPSS and SAS standard available techniques include all descriptive analyses, such as regression techniques, cluster analysis, etc. Analysts are often trained in these packages in their bachelor and master programs at universities. In fact one of the strategies of SPSS has been to provide software to students at low prices. The use of these packages provides more freedom to analysts. However, a sufficient understanding of this software and the underlying techniques is required. One of the mistakes we frequently observe is that software users start analyzing data with (advanced) techniques without a sufficient understanding of the different pitfalls of doing so.

Despite their limitations, the discussed software packages have proved to be very useful and have become more user friendly over the years, with the introduction of windows-interfaces, help functions, etc. The big data development is changing the statistical analysis field dramatically. The statistical packages are not yet fully suited for big data analytics (see also Chapter 4.2). We specifically observe the following developments:

- Due to the presence of more unstructured data, new analysis techniques such as text mining are being used more often.
- Frequently, statistical packages are limited in terms of the data volume they can handle.
- New advanced techniques, such as Bayesian and extensive panel analyses, are not available in these packages.
- The big data development has attracted big data scientists, who are creating their own programs.
- Open source packages, such as R, that are being developed through a large knowledge base in the online community, can handle large databases and estimate the more complicated models needed when analyzing big data.

Because of these developments we urge firms not to limit themselves to only one analytical package. The danger of using only a single package is that one cannot exploit the richness of big data. Firms that have big data scientists in their analytical teams should be able to fully exploit the data—when they are not limited by using a single statistical package. The danger here is, of course, that analysts go for the most complicated model and keep digging into the data and ignore the managerial meaning of their analyses.

A specific disadvantage of the use of analytical software (either standard or open source) is that the output is frequently not user friendly. Furthermore, the models developed are not always easy for managers to apply. For example, if managers want to make sales forecasts using an estimated regression model, they will typically fail. A solution advocated by Wharton professor Pete Fader and London Business School professor Bruce Hardie is to use models that can be estimated and applied in Excel. They specifically developed forecast models with an underlying negative binomial distribution model to predict product sales and customer value (Fader & Hardie, 2001; 2009). Their models can be extremely useful, but there are not many other examples using such an Excel-based approach.

We have already discussed the role of models and insights in our big data value creation model. We will discuss the additional important role of business rules in the next section on linking analytics to operations and specifically to actions and campaigns.

Analytical applications

The fourth layer of big data systems involves analytical applications—that is, reporting, actions and campaigns, decision support, and information-based products and solutions. We have already discussed issues surrounding decision support and information-based products and services in Chapter 2. We will now mainly focus on reporting systems and actions and campaigns.

Reporting systems

Reporting systems aim to make the results available to management through, for example, marketing dashboards. Marketing dashboards have become rather popular and are defined by Pauwels et al. (2009: 3) as: "A relatively small collection of integrated key performance metrics and underlying performance drivers that reflects both short and long-term interests to be viewed in common throughout the organization". Pauwels et al. (2009) and Reibstein, Norton, Joshi and Farris (2005) propose five stages of dashboard development:

1. Selecting the key metrics
2. Populating the dashboard with data
3. Establishing relationships between the dashboard items
4. Forecasting and "what if" analysis
5. Connecting to financial consequences.

274 *Building successful big data capabilities*

Observing these steps, we generally derive two main functions of a marketing dashboard. First, it reports the results on some key metrics (e.g. retention rates or NPS) on a regular (e.g. monthly) basis. Second, results of models are included in such a way that managers can check what occurs if they take specific actions. For example, they might be keen to know what happens with customer equity if they improve their service (Rust, Lemon, & Zeithaml, 2004). Dashboards are thus filled with data and the final model results, which can be used to execute "what if" analyses.

The link with operations: actions and campaigns

In our discussion on the different layers of systems we mainly took a data and analytical perspective. However, it is important to notice that operational systems and processes are directly linked with analytical systems (see Figure 5.9). Operational systems involve, for example, software that links daily operations (e.g. a call center) to data and specific business rules or selection rules. Business rules and selection rules are the results of analytical exercise. These business rules could be that, for example, only customers that have a high customer lifetime value (CLV)—determined by the outcomes of analytics—get a reduction on the price they pay for a specific contract. In a call center the agent using an operational system will be able to observe the customer

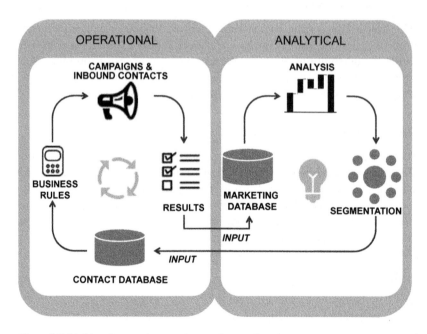

Figure 5.9 Linking data, analyses, actions and campaigns

information on a computer screen and using this system can then make offers to customers to renew a contract. Notably, although the interaction occurs in the operational environment, it is sourced back in databases. Building on the call center example, the interaction with a customer discussing the renewal of a contract can be included in the database, recording data on the offer, the outcome of the offer (renewal or not), and so on. In a big data environment the data can be enriched with the unstructured data on the conversation between the agent and the customer (e.g. Verhoef, Antonides, & De Hoog, 2004). Selection rules typically involve a rule on how to select customers who will receive a specific targeted offer (e.g. an email campaign with a target promotion). These selection rules are very common and used in many sectors, including retailing and financial services. They are mainly used in outbound campaigns.

In a digital environment operational systems become very important as interactions on websites can be customized based on automated analytical exercises, themselves based on different business rules which consider the browsing behavior of customers at websites, the CLV of customers etc. The most famous example of this technique is probably that of firms like Amazon, which suggest products to customers that have been purchased by other customers who have a similar choice behavior (also called "collaborative filtering"). However, in current digital analytical environments operations and analytics have become intertwined and the distinction between them has become blurred. With the millions of interactions occurring at websites, models can be developed that are constantly updated with relevant new information. The analyst first has to develop the "basic" model and its specific econometric specification. The estimation parameters can then be updated based on the constant digital interaction with customers on websites, apps etc., and based on that, constantly relevant and targeted offers can be provided to customers visiting these digital channels. In this context Chung, Rust and Wedel, (2009) have developed an "adaptive personalization system" and illustrate its implementation for digital audio players. The proposed system automatically downloads personalized playlists of MP3 songs into a consumer's mobile digital audio device and requires little proactive user effort (i.e. no explicit indication of preferences or ratings for songs). They show that their system works in real time and is scalable to the massive data typically encountered in personalization applications. Specifically, they develop a system consisting of (a) a personalized agenda, (b) an adaptive learning algorithm, (c) a collaborative customization model for all customers, and (d) a dynamic customization model for individual customers. For illustration we provide their model in Figure 5.10. For more details we refer to their paper published in *Marketing Science* (Chung et al., 2009). We expect that due to the development of these models the analytical system and the operational systems will become more integrated. In Chapter 4.2 we provided a more in-depth discussion on personalization.

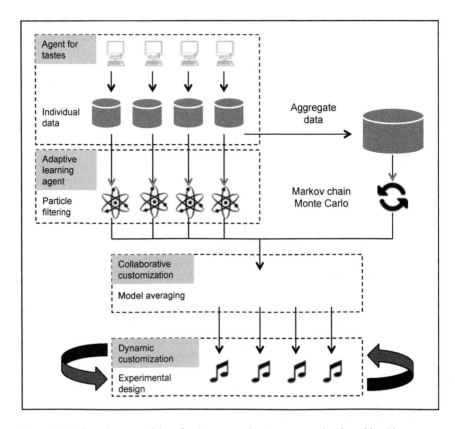

Figure 5.10 Flow diagram of the adaptive personalization system developed by Chung, Rust and Wedel (2009)

Source: Chung et al. (2009)

Building block 4: Organization

The organizational side of the big data development gets relatively less attention. There is a strong focus on attracting talented big data analysts and tooling. The organization of the analytical competence within the organization is, however, important as well. We observe three specific challenges:

1 Centralization of the analytical function
2 Cooperation with other departments/functions
3 Presence of a data-driven culture.

Centralization or decentralization

Firms building up a big data analytical competence face the challenge of where to locate this function. This is especially a challenge for firms active in multiple business units. For example, firms operating one business unit for the consumer market and another for the corporate market could have two analytical functions per business unit or one single analytical function serving both business units. Firms with global operations could have a global analytical function serving all separate country organizations or several functions serving local country organizations. Hagen et al. (2013) suggests that there are three models for organizing an analytical competence (see Figure 5.11). In the first option a decentralized organization is chosen, where for each strategic business unit (SBU) an analytical function is set up. The advantages of this setup are that the analytical competence can specifically be developed for each SBU, serving the specific needs of each SBU. The function is also likely to have a strong impact on decision making in each SBU. A strong disadvantage, however, is that that functions are relatively small and inefficiencies occur. Specific knowledge and capabilities are developed in each SBU and there are no economies of scale. Further, these separate functions lack an overall strategic view. In the second model, a more decentralized function is developed under the responsibility of one SBU that serves that SBU as well as other SBUs. This may create more efficiencies and standardize solutions. However, one problem is that there will be competition among SBUs for the analytical capacity and it is likely that the responsible SBU will benefit most. In a final model the analytical function becomes an independent centralized staff function serving multiple business units. As with the second model, this will lead to more standardization and less inefficiency. One large potential challenge with this organization format is that the function can become very independent and insufficiently connected with the different marketing departments for impactful analytical functions. This would indicate a need for analytical functions to be more closely linked to a SBU. However, there are some disadvantages to this as well, as it may, for example, lead to a lower overall analytical skill level.

In general several rules can be used to help decide between a more decentralized versus a more centralized approach. Decentralization is preferred over centralization when:

- There are strong analytical skills within the firm
- There is a large number of analysts
- The analyst team is mature and independent
- If there is a strong need for specialized knowledge in different SBUs
- If teams do not depend too much on data- and software suppliers.

Cooperation with other functions

One of the problems that analytical functions encounter is the level of cooperation they have with other departments and specifically the marketing department. Generally, cooperation between departments is considered

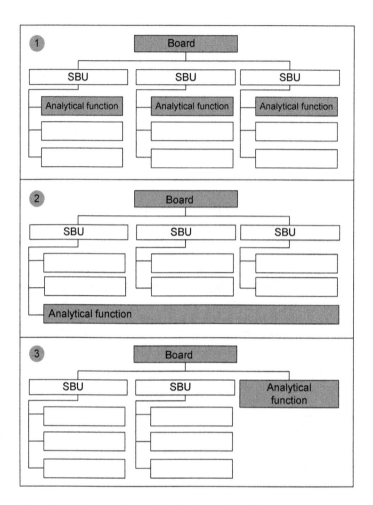

Figure 5.11 Organization models for the analytical function

Source: Adapted from Hagen et al. (2013)

good. This has been shown for cooperation between marketing & R&D, and between marketing and sales (e.g. Homburg & Jensen, 2007; Leenders & Wierenga, 2002). It has been suggested that some competition between departments can be good, as this competition may induce a stronger performance of the separate departments as they have to deliver a good performance in order to get sufficient support from the board. Still, the competition should be combined with cooperation. The term "coopetition" has been coined for this form of cooperation (Luo, Slotegraaf, & Pan, 2006).

Another problem is that marketing analysts and, for example, marketing managers, might have different thought worlds (Verhoef & Pennings, 2012),

Building successful big data capabilities 279

because of the different tasks they do and different personalities. In general analysts like to focus on the analysis itself and are less interested in its implications. Moreover, analysts will typically focus more on details of the applied methods. Marketing managers would move more easily to the next marketing action.

Inspired by the work of the psychologist Carl Jung, we have profiled both marketing analysts and members of marketing departments on specific personality traits (see Figure 5.12). It is interesting to observe that there are indeed strong differences. Analysts are interested in in-depth discussions about details and strongly value personal relationships in their working environment. In contrast, senior marketing department members and managers are more entrepreneurial and focus more on outcomes and making decisions, taking a stronger leadership role.

Thus there are clear differences between analysts and members of other departments. Still, for making smart marketing decisions strong cooperation is required. We have some suggestions how to achieve this:

- There should be a general willingness of departments to work effectively together, where both cooperation and some competition occurs.
- It is important that both functions understand the different thought worlds and personal orientations of the other; this may overcome communication problems and lead to more effective meetings.

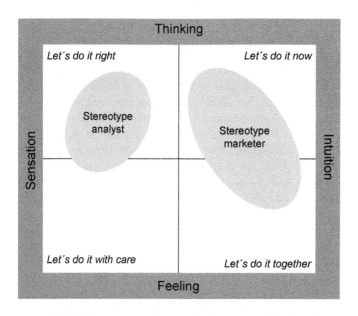

Figure 5.12 Different personality profiles of analysts and marketeers

- Both departments should have a sufficient understanding of each other's expertise areas. This implies that analysts should have sufficient marketing knowledge, and marketing department members should understand the basics of analytics.
- Analysts should focus more on what their analytic outcomes of (to be executed) analyses could imply for management.

Establishing a data-driven culture

A more overarching enabler of a successful implementation of big data analytics within firms is that firms should transform in such a way that they rely more on data in their (marketing-) decision making. This implies a more data-driven culture, which in turn implies that firms should base their decisions more on established data-based facts rather than intuition or gut feeling. The latter frequently occurs within marketing: marketing is frequently blamed for having nice creative ideas without understanding their implications for business and performance (Verhoef & Leeflang, 2011). As McGovern, Court, Quelch and Crawford (2004: 74) state: "The marketing field is chockablock with creative thinkers, yet it's short on people who lean toward an analytic, left-brain approach to the discipline."

A more data-driven culture within marketing is also frequently referred to as "fact-based marketing," clearly suggesting the difference from more intuition-based marketing. Facts are typically based on internal analytics, although they can also be based on some general laws in marketing arising from a meta-analysis of executed studies within marketing science, for example by summarizing a large number of studies on advertising effects. Sethuraman, Tellis and Briesch (2011) report an average short-term advertising elasticity of 0.12, suggesting that a 10% increase in advertising budgets increase sales by 1.2% in the short-run. A stronger focus on marketing accountability within firms will typically induce a stronger data-driven culture. Marketing accountability is generally considered as the extent to which marketing departments are able to show the effects of marketing actions on marketing and business performance metrics in their plans (ex-ante) or evaluations (ex-post)—see for example Verhoef and Leeflang (2009). Firms having a stronger marketing accountability have more influential marketing departments and also tend to perform better (Verhoef & Leeflang, 2010; O'Sullivan & Abela, 2007).

Despite this evidence of the benefits of marketing accountability, establishing a data-driven culture is not easy. This is partly because of the different thought worlds between MI and marketing. Frequently, marketers do not sufficiently embrace data initiatives and see it as threatening the way they have acted for years. Data and analytics belong to a separate department or function not belonging to the core of marketing. One of the most frequently stated comments is that a data-driven culture kills creativity and leads to enduring discussions on the bottom-line effects, resulting in many good plans never being implemented. We believe this comment is based on a wrong view of analytics. In very specific tactical tasks (e.g. mail selections, assortment optimization) relying heavily on analytics will for sure increase the productivity of marketing. There is sufficient evidence to show that using analytics improves firm performance, for example due to the fact that scarce resources are now allocated more efficiently between different customer segments (e.g. Kumar & Shah, 2009). However, for more strategic long-term decisions, big data analytics will play a different role. Here, analytics will provide insights on market development, brand developments, new unserved segments, innovation opportunities, etc., which should be used as input in developing more long-term oriented strategic marketing plans. Model outcomes and insights are then one of the inputs, but also other considerations, including managerial intuition, should be taken into account. As already noted, research does suggest that a combination of both model inputs and intuition leads to the best decisions (Blattberg & Hoch, 1990).

One final note is that we believe that due to the rapid developments in big data, big data are actually themselves a driving force behind many (service) innovations, which we refer to as information-based solutions or products. For example, Amazon filed for a US patent for a "method and system for anticipatory package shipping," which is based on predictive analytics. This move illustrates an increasing desire on the part of mass market retailers to draw on the latest technologies to anticipate consumers' needs before they express them or perhaps are even aware of them.[6] Similarly, agricultural Norwegian-based fertilizer supplier Yara uses data-based systems to adjust fertilizing to the needs of the crop. Also the web analytical solutions with adaptive forecasting techniques (Chung et al. 2009) mentioned earlier in the chapter can create innovative service and customer-interface solutions. In fact many commentators in the area of service marketing believe that big data will change how customers will be serviced in coming decades (Rust & Huang, 2014).

Top management support

Top management support is essential, in order to put in place a strong analytical marketing function that actually has something meaningful to say within the organization; it has frequently been shown to be a driver of the adoption and use of marketing decision support systems and data-based marketing (e.g. Wieringa & Oude Ophuis, 1997; Verhoef & Hoekstra, 1999). Actually, when requiring changes in culture, top management support is a prerequisite (e.g. Kirca, Jayachandran, & Bearden, 2005). It is required to arrange investments (i.e. acquiring talent, retention of talent, education, and systems) in the analytical functions and to induce a stronger data-driven culture. Although this is widely known, support for a strong role of analytics does not naturally occur. There are a couple of ways to achieve this. First, when discussing big data analytics, managers can focus on the benefits of increased accountability of marketing. This can be done by arranging support at the CFO level. It is also important to forge a strong connection between the intelligence function and finance. Our experience is that this link can be pretty successful, especially when there is agreement on which metrics to use. Second, a greater use of data can fuel a greater focus on the customer. Big data analytics can be used to improve customer experiences. In today's marketing environment we observe a greater focus on customers and their experience in multiple channels, and analytics can be an important ingredient for successfully delivering this experience (Rust & Huang, 2014). Third, as noted earlier, the increase in data provides opportunities to create innovations and growth by developing information-based solutions and products. Strong analytical functions can be part of this development process. So in sum, analytics can have a strong impact on firms and many functions of the firm (e.g. finance, marketing, R&D). If top management is aware of this, it is more likely they will provide support.

Conclusions

In this chapter we have discussed the building of successful big data analytical capabilities within firms. This is an important topic which is frequently neglected when discussing big data opportunities. However, in order to create value with big data, these capabilities are of essential importance. First, we considered the internal process for executing impactful analytics within firms. It is crucial that these analytics start with a business question or a business need. Analytics for the sake of analytics does not create value. Subsequently, we discussed the important challenges of acquiring and keeping big data analysts, and the development of an analytical function within firms. We provided an in-depth discussion of the different profiles looked for. We considered the systems required for applying successful analytics. Importantly, technology should not be leading. We discussed that the big data analytical system will consist of different layers. Finally, we elaborated on many organizational issues concerning the organizational structure, cooperation between MI and other functions, the presence of a data-driven culture, and the requirement for top management support. Probably most important here is that firms require a strong data-driven culture which should be supported by top management and should be sufficiently embedded within the organization structure to ensure successful cooperation between the analytical function and other (marketing) functions within the firm.

Notes

1 See www.cisco.com/c/dam/en/us/solutions/enterprise/connected-world-technology-report/Global-Data-CCWTR-Chapter3-Media-Briefing-Slides.pdf (accessed November 2, 2015).
2 This example is based on work Natasha Walk did for MIcompany, where she was responsible for the MIAcademy. At that time Peter Verhoef was member of the advisory board of MI Academy. It has been published as a case in Verhoef & Lemon (2013).
3 See www-01.ibm.com/software/data/infosphere/data-scientist/ (accessed September 27, 2015).
4 See for some details on education: https://nces.ed.gov/pubs2009/2009001.pdf; www.infoplease.com/ipa/A0934035.html and www.ara.cat/societat/Linforme-PISA-cinquena-part_ARAFIL20101207_0005.pdf (all accessed September 27, 2015).

5 See http://chiefmartec.com/2015/01/marketing-technology-landscape-supergraphic-2015/ (accessed September 27, 2015).
6 See www.atelier.net/en/trends/articles/e-commerce-amazon-hopes-anticipate-consumer-purchases-predictive-analytics_427319 (accessed September 28, 2015).

References

Blattberg, R. C., & Hoch, S. J. (1990). Database models and managerial intuition: 50% model + 50% manager. *Management Science*, 36(8), 887–99.
Chung, T. S., Rust, R. T., & Wedel, M. (2009). My mobile music: An adaptive personalization system for digital audio players. *Marketing Science*, 28(1), 52–68.
Davenport, T., & Harris, J. (2007). *Competing on analytics – The new science of winning*. Harvard Business School Press.
Davenport, T., & Patil, D. J. (2012). Data scientist: The sexiest job of the 21st century. *Harvard Business Review*, 90(10), 70–6.
De Vos, A., & Meganck, A. (2009). What HR managers do versus what employees value: Exploring both parties' views on retention management from a psychological contract perspective. *Personnel Review*, 38(1), 45–60.
Fader, P. S., & Hardie, B. G. S. (2001). Forecasting repeat sales at CDNOW: A case study. *Interfaces*, 31(3), 94–107.
Fader, P. S., & Hardie, B. G. S. (2009). Probability models for customer-base analysis. *Journal of Interactive Marketing*, 23(1), 61–9.
Germann, F., Lilien, G. L., & Rangaswamy, A. (2012). Performance implications of deploying marketing analytics. *International Journal of Research in Marketing*, 30(2), 114–28.
Germann, F., Lilien, G., Fiedler, L., & Kraus, M. (2014). Do retailers benefit from deploying customer analytics? *Journal of Retailing*, 90(4), 587–93.
Hagen, C., Khan, K., Ciobo, M., Miller, J., Wall, D., Evans, H., & Yaday, Y. (2013). Big data and the creative destruction of today's business models. *Holland Management Review*, 148(4), 25–37.
Holtom, B. C., Mitchell, T. R., Lee, T. W., & Eberly, M. B. (2008). Turnover and retention research: A glance at the past, a closer review of the present, and a venture into the future. *The Academy of Management Annals*, 2(1), 231–74.
Homburg, C., & Jensen, O. (2007). The thought worlds of marketing and sales: Which differences make a difference? *Journal of Marketing*, 71(3), 124–42.
Humby, C., Hunt, T., & Phillips, T. (2008). Scoring points: How Tesco is winning customer loyalty. Philadelphia: Kogan Page Publishers.
IDG. (2014). *Big Data research*. Retrieved from IDG Enterprise. Retrieved September 11, 2015 from www.idgenterprise.com/report/big-data-2
Kirca, A. H., Jayachandran, S., & Bearden, W. O. (2005). Market orientation: A meta-analytic review and assessment of Its antecedents and impact on performance. *Journal of Marketing*, 6(2), 24–41.
Kumar, V., & Shah, D. (2009). Expanding the role of marketing: From customer equity to market capitalization. *Journal of Marketing*, 73(6), 119–36.
Leeflang, P. S. H., Verhoef, P. C., Dahlström, P., & Freundt, T. (2014). Challenges and solutions for marketing in a digital era. *European Management Journal*, 32(1), 1–12.
Leenders, M. A. A. M., & Wierenga, B. (2002). The effectiveness of different mechanisms for integrating marketing and R&D. *Journal of Product Innovation Management*, 19(4), 305–17.
Luo, X., Slotegraaf, R. J., & Pan, X. (2006). Cross-functional "coopetition": The simultaneous role of cooperation and competition within firms. *Journal of Marketing*, 70(2), 67–80.

Manyika, J., Chui, M., Brown, B., Bughin J., Dobbs R., Roxburgh C., & Hung Byers, A. (2011). Big Data the next frontier for innovation, competition and productivity. Retrieved from McKinsey Global Institute. Retrieved October, 2015 from www.mckinsey.com/insights/business_technology/big_data_the_next_frontier_for_innovation.

McGovern, G. J., Court, D., Quelch, J. A., & Crawford, B. (2004). Bringing customers into the boardroom. *Harvard Business Review*, 82(11), 70–80.

O'Sullivan, D., & Abela, A. V. (2007). Marketing performance measurement ability and firm performance. *Journal of Marketing*, 71(2), 79–93.

Pauwels, K. H., Ambler, T., Clark, B., LaPointe, P., Reibstein, D., Skiera, B., Wieranga, B., & Wiesel, T. (2009). Dashboards & marketing: Why, what, how and what research is needed? *Journal of Service Research*, 12(2), 175–89.

Reibstein, D. J., Norton, D., Joshi, Y., & Farris, P. (2005). Marketing dashboard: A decision support system assessing marketing productivity. Marketing Science Conference. Atlanta.

Rigby, D. K. (2014). Digital-physical mashups. *Harvard Business Review*, 92(9), 84–92.

Rust, R. T., & Huang, M. H. (2014). The service revolution and the transformation of marketing science. *Marketing Science*, 33(2), 206–21.

Rust, R. T., Lemon, K. N., & Zeithaml, V. A. (2004). Return on marketing: Using customer equity to focus marketing strategy. *Journal of Marketing*, 68(1), 109–27.

Sethuraman, R., Tellis, G. J., & Briesch, R. A. (2011). How well does advertising work? Generalizations from meta-analysis of brand advertising elasticities. *Journal of Marketing Research*, 48(3), 457–71.

Tavassoli, N. T., Sorescu, A., & Chandy, R. (2014). Employee-based brand equity: Why firms with strong brands pay their executives less. *Journal of Marketing Research*, 51(6), 676–90.

Verhoef, P. C., & Hoekstra, J. C. (1999). Status of database marketing in the Dutch fast moving consumer goods industry. *Journal of Market-Focused Management*, 3(4), 313–31.

Verhoef, P. C., & Leeflang, P. S. H. (2009). Understanding the marketing department's influence within the firm. *Journal of Marketing*, 73(2), 14–37.

Verhoef, P. C., & Leeflang, P. S. H. (2010). Getting marketing back into the boardroom: The influence of the marketing department in companies today. *GfK-Marketing Intelligence Review*, 2(1), 34–41.

Verhoef, P. C., & Leeflang, P. S. H. (2011). Accountability as a main ingredient of getting marketing back in the board room. *Marketing Review St. Gallen*, 28(3), 26–31.

Verhoef, P. C., & Lemon, K. N. (2013). Successful customer value management: Key lessons and emerging trends. *European Management Journal*, 13(1), 1–15.

Verhoef, P. C., & Pennings, J. M. (2012). The marketing finance Interface: An organizational perspective. In S. Ganesan, & S. Bharadwaj, (Eds), *Handbook of Marketing and Finance* (pp. 225–43). Cheltenham, UK: Edward Elgar Publishing.

Verhoef, P. C., Antonides, G., & De Hoog, A. N. (2004). Service encounters as a sequence of events the importance of peak experiences. *Journal of Service Research*, 7(1), 53–64.

Verhoef, P. C., Hoekstra, J. C. & Van der Scheer, H., (2009). *Competing on analytics: Status quo van customer intelligence in Nederland*. Groningen: Customer Insights Center.

Wierenga, B., & Oude Ophuis, P. A. M. (1997). Marketing decision support systems: Adoption, use and satisfaction. *International Journal of Research in Marketing*, 14(3), 275–90.

6 Every business has (big) data; let's use them

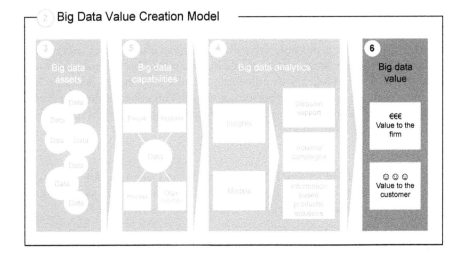

Introduction

So far, we have mainly discussed the different building blocks for creating value with big data analytics. In this chapter we aim to provide real-life examples on how big data analytics can be implemented to create value. We discuss five cases, which vary in sector, big data approach, and focus. The first case involves mainly traditional analytics, and focuses on a customer lifetime value (CLV) calculation. In the next cases, we move more to big data analytics. In Case 2 we present a data integration in which data from multiple sources are analyzed to improve marketing effectiveness among multiple customer groups. In Case 3 we discuss a case that focuses on the systems side of big data analytics in order to achieve more success with personalization efforts. Attribution modeling for an online-retailer is discussed in Case 4. Our final case focuses on social network analytics, where one of the key messages is that social hubs can be identified by looking at some available non-social network variables. When discussing these cases, we apply the storytelling method and visualization methods as discussed in Chapter 4.3, in line with the philosophy that one should practice what one preaches.

Case 1: CLV calculation for energy company[1]

Situation

The Dutch energy market has been liberalized and customers can now switch between energy companies. This has resulted in voluntary churn rates moving from 0% to much higher levels. New providers with a price focus have entered the market. As a consequence, the number of customers of the energy company has decreased and revenues are under pressure. The company realizes that competition has definitely changed and that they need to compete for customers and customer value.

Complication

Although churn seems to be the problem, this is not so clear. Customer value at energy companies is not only driven by churn, but also involves energy and other product usage, service costs, payment issues etc. The question is which value drivers they should try to influence and how they should do so. So far, the value components have not been studied well. This complication requires a strong conceptualization on the value drivers and gaining the right data.

Key message

The energy firm should not only look at revenues and retention. When managing customers and optimizing customer value, they should also consider how they can reduce inbound service costs and payment enforcement costs.

Data and model used

The CRM database of the firm was relatively rich and embedded the information on product possession, churn, margins, payment method, payment problems, etc. We were able to analyze data from 0.9 million customers. Before setting up the econometric model, we created a conceptual model on drivers of CLV. Based on this, logit models were estimated explaining each of the drivers and predicting the occurrence of an event. These predictions were used to predict the CLV. Next, the outcomes of the models were used, to understand how specific drivers can be influenced and which specific actions could increase CLV.

Results

Conceptually four drivers of CLV were identified (see Figure 6.1):

- Retention (1-churn)
- Revenues (electricity and gas)
- Credit losses (not paying, payment enforcement costs)
- Service costs (including inbound calls).

Every business has (big) data; let's use them 287

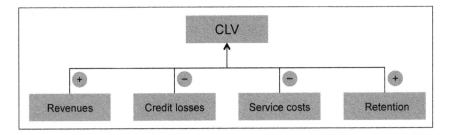

Figure 6.1 Value drivers for an energy company

The predictions were used to understand the contribution of each of the components and this showed that revenues and service costs are the most important value drivers in terms of their contribution to CLV. Retention has only a limited contribution (see Figure 6.2), whereas revenues per customer, bad debt (including payment enforcement), and service cost strongly contributed to CLV.

The next question asked was whether one could influence the drivers. Hence, specific actions were formulated, together with an idea of their potential success. An immediate reaction is that one would probably suggest that one should sell more energy. However, energy usage is largely defined by factors such as household size and the weather. Moreover, from a sustainability perspective energy firms are actually implementing measures to lower energy usage, for example through promoting energy saving light bulbs.

To define the success probability, the researcher talked with many marketing employees to understand which actions would be more likely to be successful.

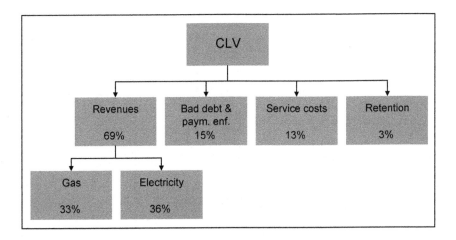

Figure 6.2 Contribution of each of the value drivers to CLV

This resulted in a qualitative assessment of a success probability. Next the numbers of customers that could be affected and which value gain could be achieved were assessed. Using the simulation results, it was found that especially lowering service contacts and stimulating a lower level of payment enforcement had the largest potential value impact (see Figure 6.3).

Additional insights

The analysis also showed that the value drivers differ significantly per value-segment. Service costs and bad debt become especially important in the low-value segment. These customers could become more valuable if service costs were lower.

Success factors

The model results helped the company base its marketing actions on customer value drivers. In summary:

- The analysis was executed in-house by a senior data analyst, who was very well aware of scientific studies on CLV and was able to estimate sophisticated models.
- The simulation of the model results involves both actual model results and qualitative assessments of success.
- There was a rich CRM database available: all the required data were available in that database and it was not necessary to collect data from multiple data silos. As such we were able to analyze a very large sample of customers.

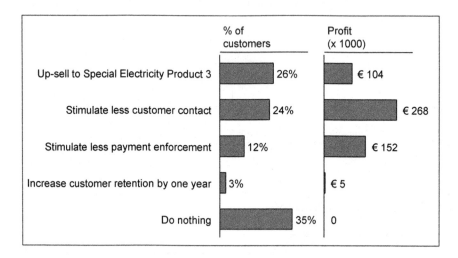

Figure 6.3 Impact of different value driver improvements on CLV

Case 2: Holistic marketing approach by big data integration at an insurance company

Situation

An insurance company with multiple brands has traditionally focused on a broad target group. Despite this broad focus, the customer base is not representative of the total market population, being overrepresented with elderly, high-income households. The insurance market is in decline and competition is fierce, with a move from traditional high-cost channels (via an intermediary or call center) to the lower cost online channels (comparison sites, direct conversion on website etc.). Competitors are spending substantially more on media than they used to. This puts pressure on the market share. To better face competition and to sustain or (even better) improve the market share there is a need to substantially increase the effectiveness of current marketing investments. To realize this, a holistic marketing approach in combination with a granular perspective of the market and customers is desired. Furthermore, insights are needed into the performance per customer profile on brand, proposition, distribution, and pricing of the current marketing mix.

Complication

In realizing the above, three complications came up that made this a big challenge for the organization. The first complication was organizational: the responsibilities for market, brand, pricing, and distribution were dealt with in different silos within the organization, not necessarily working closely together. Because of this, it was quite impossible to realize an aligned holistic and consistent marketing approach of the total marketing mix. The second challenge was with the data sources needed to measure and to improve performance. These data sources were collected and stored with the customer intelligence department and the pricing department within the organization and with several external market research agencies. Some of the data were not even available in a database format, but only in hard copy reports. Because of this, it may not come as a surprise to learn that a dataset integrating all these data sources was not available. Consequently, the necessary KPIs to measure and improve performance could not be created easily due to different data formats, definitions, aggregation levels, and measure periods/moments. The third complication was the lack of a framework or integral segmentation that could serve as a common denominator for all the data sources and KPIs in scope. Within the organization several breakdowns of the market and the customer base were available; however, they were not aligned.

Key message

As a solution for the complications described above an interactive, visually attractive big data dashboard was developed that was easy for both marketers and analysts to use (see Figure 6.4). This enabled a shift from separate measurements

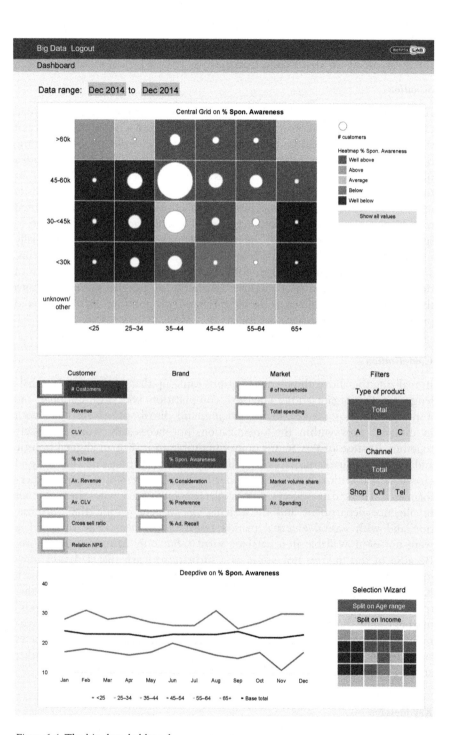

Figure 6.4 The big data dashboard

of the effect of marketing investments and value KPIs, to detailed and dynamic measuring, interpreting, and forecasting of the marketing performance. In this way, an increase of performance and thus return on investment with a granular perspective on customer profiles could be realized.

The solution consisted of several elements that were crucial for success. In the dashboard the central element was a heat map that showed a segmentation that was consistent for all KPIs in all data sources. The colours in the heat map were determined by the over- or underrepresentation of a specific KPI for a specific segment in the heat map. The different KPIs were clustered around customers, brand, and market. Furthermore, filters were added to make a deep dive possible on specific products and/or channels and/or time frames.

Results

The results created by realizing the big data dashboard approach were:

- An integrated database, where market data (including competitor performance), brand tracking data, customer data, and customer satisfaction data were integrated and presented per segment.
- Consensus on the set of KPIs to be measured, in order to measure the total marketing performance.
- A better understanding of total marketing performance and its effectiveness, per KPI, per segment, and also of the relationship between the KPIs.
- Substantial opportunities (multimillion euros) for initiatives to improve the marketing performance and marketing ROI.
- A roadmap for additional relevant data sources to be added.

Model used

At the start of the project, we developed a conceptual framework to visualize the shift to be made (see Figure 6.5). In this framework, we showed that ideally the effectiveness of the spending of the marketing budget would become visible in what we called the input KPIs. However, we also showed that the input KPIs are just an intermediary step. Linking the performance of the input KPIs to the defined output KPIs (measuring V2C and V2F metrics), by splitting them out across the segments in the heat map, should make the relationships visible.

Insights

Analyzing the performance using the dashboard in several interactive sessions with marketers and analysts showed that, for different reasons, different performance levels arose in the segments of the heat map. This suggests that different strategies are required to improve the performance for specific customer profiles. One of the key insights was that the performance with

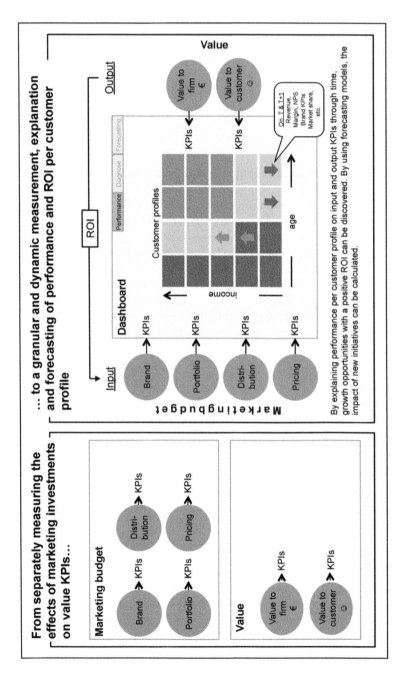

Figure 6.5 The conceptual model for the holistic approach

youngsters was low (low market share), due to branding issues. At the same time we saw high in- and outflow from this segment, mainly due to aggressive campaigning at this group in a certain time frame with only one specific product. The initiative aimed at this group was more selective targeting (only the potential loyal customers) and at the same time more focused on offering a broader product range in order to create a more sustainable relationship. Another insight was that due to delays in updates of the pricing module (used for making a calculation for a good offer to potential new customers) a lot of deals were lost, especially in the family high-income segment, as a result of too conservative pricing by the outdated pricing module. Because the segment at stake is high value and high volume a slight improvement would result in a significant (euro) potential.

Success factors

The key to success for the approach was not just by having a tool—the big data dashboard—in place. Other factors were much more important, such as:

- Using an agile approach, first creating a proof-of-concept within six weeks, and from there further implementing and refining the created solution;
- Involving all relevant marketing disciplines in defining the KPIs and in analyzing the results (i.e. using multidisciplinary teams)
- Focusing on execution: how do we translate the insights into action?
- Being pragmatic, starting with only these high impact data sources that could be extracted easily
- Aggregating the data sources to the defined dimensions of the segmentation, also preventing working with too sensitive data and/or privacy issues
- Making the solution scalable and implementable within the organization, preventing high IT impact.

Case 3: Implementation of big data analytics for relevant personalization at an online retailer

Situation

The retailer is active in a growing market with many strong competitors. To provide more value to their customers, they aim to inspire customers and provide more relevant recommendations to their customers when they visit the company's website. They strive to give customers fully automated suggestions of relevant product offers that may surprise customers. They can already provide customized offers based on some product recommendation systems (see Chapter 4.2). However, they now aim to give more relevant personalized offers in different settings that really make a difference and go beyond the "usual suspect" offers.

Complication

This retailer has millions of customers and offers an assortment of more than 8 million stock keeping units (SKUs). Moreover, online customers search, look for, and purchase multiple products, either at the same time or sequentially. Overall this leads to a very large number of customer/product interactions (two billion per year) and even more product relations, in terms of searches and/or purchases in the same category or multiple categories, for the same brand, for the different themes or occasions, etc. How to analyze these data is not obvious and requires lengthy computation times (i.e. 400 hours). Personalization based on all kinds of product relations can take so long to compute that it may not be effective. The challenge is to develop a scalable computation process, where instead of many weeks, a much shorter time period is required. This allows the retailer to come up with more real-time and relevant offers, which should lead to higher conversion rates.

Key message

The retailer implemented map-reducing technology through which, over a period of two years, the computation time was reduced to one day and the click through rate (CTR) was raised by 40%.

Approach

The retailer acquired limited hardware and started to use the open source software Hadoop. They trained a team of data experts to use the software. They first did a pilot for a pre-sale set and used A/B testing (see Chapter 4.2) to test differences in CTRs between the old method and the new method. After the first positive results they scaled up to other sets like sale and post-sale and sets around themes and product accessories.

Model used

To gain product recommendations and other added value propositions from customer interactions and behavior during a customer journey, an algorithm is needed. A customer searches and/or purchases different products during one or more visits. These products therefore have a relationship (see Figure 6.6). For many customers and a product range of over 8 million products, this will result in billions and billions of product relations.

To make sense of all these data, the retailer developed an algorithm by taking the following steps (see also Figure 6.7):

1. Cluster: The first step is to record all possible product relations and to cluster these to equals.
2. Aggregate: By aggregating on unique product relations the number of times that each relation appears is calculated (the product relation score).

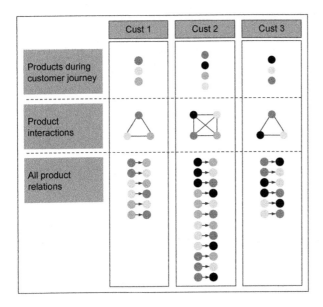

Figure 6.6 From search/purchase behavior to product combinations

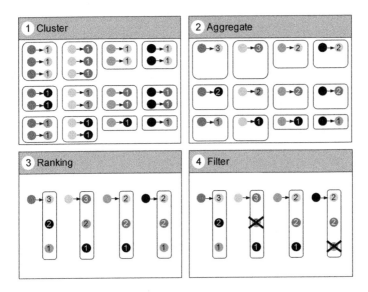

Figure 6.7 Algorithm for calculating product recommendations based on the product relation score

3 Rank: The next step is to rank each product by highest to lowest product relation scores.
4 Filter: The last step is to filter out undesirable relations. There are five sorts of filters:

- Noise: relations that are very rare
- Policy: unwanted relations such as medicines or eroticism
- Practical: relations with products that are out of stock or out of range
- Usual suspects: top five recommendations, which are already recommended in general
- Derivatives: relations with product variants (for example, silver and gold iPhones).

Executing the algorithm over billons of product relations requires a lot of computer time and working space. To manage this, the retailer used MapReduce programming technology (see Figure 6.8). The principles of MapReduce are actually quite simple.[2] MapReduce can process a lot of data in a short time because it splits a big task into subtasks. These subtasks are distributed across many computers, which can perform the subtasks simultaneously (distribution). This is done by using the features "map" and "reduce," which are known from functional programming languages. Results are output files that are much smaller than the input files. After sending these back to the central server, the smaller output files are merged into an aggregated final file.

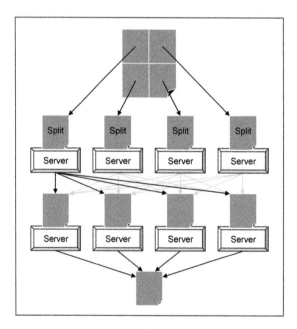

Figure 6.8 MapReduce programming model

Results

The CTR with the new method was significantly higher and almost doubled. This approach also led to cost reductions (reducing process time and having an in-house solution). Moreover, in general the method created much more interesting offers for customers. An additional result was greater cooperation between marketing and IT, which may be helpful for developing new analytical projects in the future (see also Figure 6.9).

Success factors

The keys to success for the approach can be summarized as follows:

- Marketing was responsible for the project. They did, however, work closely with IT and also adapted working methods as used by IT (e.g. agile working, scrum approaches). This stimulated a real cross-functional approach.
- By using a pilot the analyst team within the firm could show that it worked and they could also learn from their mistakes. From the pilot the project could be scaled up.
- The organization created a team dedicated to work on the project that was free to experiment with different solutions.
- The software used was free, while the hardware was rather standard and not complicated. This substantially reduced the costs, as neither advanced hardware nor software had to be purchased. In fact the hardware consisted of four standard desktops, coupled to create a more powerful engine.

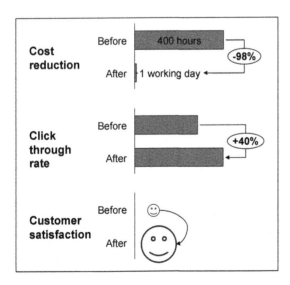

Figure 6.9 Results of new way of working

In sum, the business case was rather simple. Revenues were substantially improved by the higher CTRs and conversion rates, and there was a reduction of operational costs, all accomplished with a minimum of investment.

Case 4: Attribution modeling at an online retailer[3]

Situation

An online retailer selling multiple products was using multiple acquisition touchpoints and media to attract customers to their website. They wanted to improve their allocation of budgets over these touchpoints and media. To do so, they needed to know how many customers are attracted per touchpoint/medium and the conversion rate per touchpoint/medium. They had data on the last used touchpoint/medium when customers enter the website, whether these customers made a purchase (conversion), and how large that purchase was (order size).

Complication

The main complication here is modeling the effectiveness of each touchpoint/medium. The retailer traditionally attributed the sale to the last used touchpoint/medium. This is also known as the last-click method. That means that if a customer arrives at the website through a search engine and then subsequently buys a product, the value of this purchase is attributed to the search engine. It is unlikely that this easy method is good, as customers use multiple touchpoints and media and might be influenced by multiple touchpoints and media. In addition, touchpoints are used in multiple phases of the purchase funnel. Hence the common belief is that the last-click method leads to too high attribution values. The challenge is thus to achieve a better attribution method.

Key message

For this retailer we developed a new, more accurate attribution method which could be used to improve the allocation of marketing resources over touchpoints and media. It turned out that a more simple method than originally assumed works as effectively as the more complicated model developed originally.

Results

A more exact estimate of the true value of a touchpoint/medium can now be assessed than was possible using the traditional last-click method. This especially holds for search engine advertising, search engine organic search, and direct loads on the website. The value of email is underestimated using last-click. An Excel tool was developed to implement the new attribution method on a daily basis.

Model used

We modeled the effect of used touchpoint/medium on conversion and order size. One main issue with attribution is that the touchpoint/medium used can be endogenous (see Chapter 4.2). To correct for this we used instrumental variables and controlled for some background customer characteristics. The touchpoint medium used in a product category different from the one currently visited is used as the main instrumental variable (see Figure 6.10). By including customer background characteristics one also can already account for some endogeneity. We therefore also estimated a model without instrumental variables, as this model is less complicated and easier to use.

Insights

The last-click method usually overestimates the value of touchpoints/media. We first compared the results of last-click with a model accounting for endogeneity. In general, the new model results in lower conversion rates and average order sizes per touchpoint/media. Only for email are effects stronger in the new model (see Figure 6.11)

We next compared the complicated model with a simpler model that only included control variables. The results are rather similar, suggesting that the simpler model could be used as well and should be preferred because it is less complex (see Figure 6.12).

Additional insights

This study also achieved some collateral catches, for example:

- The sooner a customer gets back on the website the higher the conversion rate. This suggests strong opportunities for re-targeting of non-converted customers.

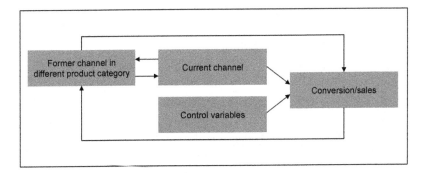

Figure 6.10 Visualization of model being used

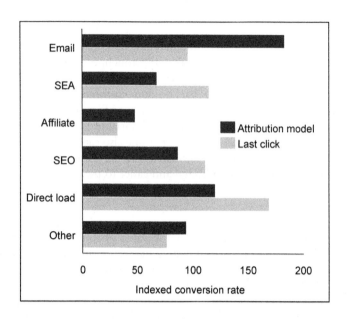

Figure 6.11 Comparison of effects for attribution model and last-click method

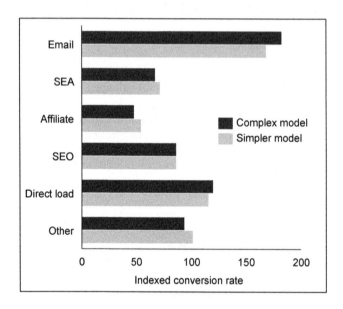

Figure 6.12 Comparison of complex model with simpler model

- Prior mobile sessions improve the conversion of consequent web sessions. (This is something we are now exploring further.)
- Conversion rates are highest for VIP customers.
- Young female customers tend to have a higher conversion rate.

Success factors

The development of the attribution model benefited from the following factors:

- The firm was able to deliver solid data.
- The models were estimated at the individual level instead of the aggregate level, which was done in a previous project. This firm is used to working at the individual level in their web-analytics and this way of modeling matches their way of working and thinking.
- There was openness to the use of complicated models, while at the same time simpler models were preferred if possible.

Case 5: Initial social network analytics at a telecom provider[4]

Situation

The telecom provider occupied a leading position in its market. They had strongly invested in a strong analytical function and were continuously looking for ways to extract more value from customers. One of the ways could be to benefit from the social networks customers are in and to use, for example, viral marketing campaigns to increase adoption of new products or reducing churn. Furthermore, the increasing relevance of social media at that point in time meant that marketing management became more interested in social networks. So far, knowledge on social networks is very limited but, given the available data in which calls between customers are being recorded, a network can be studied and relevant metrics can be calculated.

Complication

Network analysis is really a new field for this company. They have built up extensive knowledge on customer churn models, lifetime value calculations, response analysis, etc., but the analytics department have no knowledge of network analysis. They therefore defined an R&D project with the aim of gaining an understanding of customer networks and specifically to understand if social network metrics can create useful segments. They were also worried about the privacy consequences of using network data.

Key message

Social network metrics can be used to segment customers and results into very interesting social hub segments that can be used to target in viral marketing campaigns to increase, for example, cross-selling of new services or service improvements to reduce churn.

Data and model used

Data were collected on customer-to-customer interactions using call detail records (CDRs). These data showed the network of customers and with these data several social network metrics can be calculated, such as degree centrality and tie strength (see Chapter 4.2). These metrics were calculated per customer and subsequently a latent class analysis was performed (see Chapter 4.1) to come up with segments. The segments were profiled using internal and external data, such as revenue, age (internal CRM database), and innovativeness (Zip code level). This analysis resulted in five segments based on fit criteria used in these models.

Insights

Five segments are found (see Figure 6.13), of which the social hub seems to be the most relevant segment to use for social network marketing. 11.6% of the customers belong to the social hub segment. Interestingly this segment also

		Socially regular	Socially clustered	Socially involved	Social hubs	Social isolators
	Cluster size a	42.0%	26.3%	13.2%	11.6%	6.9%
Social network metrics	Degree centrality	+/-	-	+/-	++	--
	Voice symmetry ratio	+/-	+	+	+/-	++
	Text symmetry ratio	-	-	+	+/-	++
	Strength (frequency)	+/-	--	++	+/-	--
	Homophily overall gender	+/-	+	-	+/-	++
	Homophily overall age	-	+	+/-	-	++
	Homophily overall operator	-	+/-	+	+/-	++
Profiling	Age	+/-	+	+/-	-	++
	ARPU	+/-	-	+/-	++	--
	Innovativeness	+/-	-	+	++	--

Figure 6.13 Results of cluster analysis on social network variables of telecom brand

Note:
  a For confidentiality reasons we do not provide the exact figures

has a high Average Revenue (ARPU), are relatively young and innovative. This implies that by targeting young innovative customers with a high ARPU, you can target the social hub customer, that is likely to influence other customers. This also implies that in order to reach these hubs no extensive cluster analysis has to be done using the network variables, which might create problems, given privacy issues.

Success factors

After reflecting on this case, we identified two success factors:

- The project was really an R&D project that did not immediately have to result in profits, and as a consequence an extensive analysis could be done in which both theory on social networks and advanced analytics suited for these data could be used.
- Despite the fact that this project was executed in a traineeship, the report had a strong focus on managerial outcomes, which increased the impact and perceived value of the project.

Conclusions

We have discussed five actual cases on how data can be analyzed to create value. All these cases show that firms can actually benefit from analytics. Sometimes these benefits are direct, but sometimes they are indirect. For example, the online personalization case immediately resulted in higher conversion rates on personalized offers. In this case, there were also some indirect benefits, such as the increased cooperation between marketing and IT. The energy company example created nice insights for the firm into which actions it could potentially take to increase CLV. In the insurance case, there were also some direct and indirect benefits. Direct benefits included the development of marketing actions to improve the marketing performance. An important indirect benefit is that the firm now has an overview of all relevant market, brand, and customer metrics and their interrelationships. The key success factors of these cases are different, as the projects differ. However, there seems to be one common success factor, which should explicitly or implicitly be present: The firms should have a data-driven culture that is open to analytical (innovative) endeavours to create more value for the customer and the firm!

Notes

1 This case is based on L'Hoest-Snoeck, Van Nierop and Verhoef (2015); for more detail we refer to that study. We thank Sietske L'Hoest-Snoeck for sharing insights and some internally used pictures.
2 The name MapReduce originally referred to a proprietary Google technology, but this has since been genericized. A popular open-source implementation based on this technology is Apache Hadoop.

3 This case was jointly executed with Evert de Haan and Thorsten Wiesel. We kindly thank them for allowing this case to be used in this book.
4 This case is based on a master thesis project of Rico Ooievaar, which won the Dutch Marketing Master Thesis Award in 2009 and was supervised by Hans Risselada and Peter Verhoef. This study was used as a basis for later work on social influence effects as published in Risselada, Verhoef and Bijmolt (2014; 2015).

References

L'Hoest-Snoeck, S., Van Nierop, E., & Verhoef, P. C. (2015). Customer value modelling in the energy market and a practical application for marketing decision making. *International Journal of Electronic Customer Relationship Management*, 9(1), 1–32.

Risselada, H., Verhoef, P. C., & Bijmolt, T. H. A. (2014). Dynamic effects of social influence and direct marketing on the adoption of high-technology products. *Journal of Marketing*, 78(2), 52–68.

Risselada, H., Verhoef, P. C., & Bijmolt, T. H. A. (2015). Indicators of opinion leadership in customer networks: Self-reports and degree centrality. *Marketing Letters*. Forthcoming.

7 Concluding thoughts and key learning points

Concluding thoughts

Many people have claimed that the use of big data can be a new growth engine for our economies. Around the globe there are many believers in the great potential of big data and how they can transform companies, marketing strategies, and interactions with customers. For us one thing is clear: big data will change marketing analytics and how marketing will be executed in the coming decades. This will, however, not be a revolution, but more an evolution. In recent decades we have already observed many changes in how marketing departments use analytics in their marketing decisions. Marketing decisions have become more fact-based and market and customer insights have become very important in shaping marketing strategies. Whereas in the 1980s and 1990s marketing intelligence (MI) was a minor function, or absent altogether in many firms, and marketing scientists were pushing their developed models, we now observe a stronger presence of analytical functions in leading companies looking for innovative though effective ways to analyze their data and create insights. The increasing presence of large chunks of data will only fuel this development. However, it should be clear that managers should have sound expectations of these developments. The ultimate goal of marketing analytics and specifically big data analytics is to create value for customers and the firm.

In this book, we have aimed to discuss the building blocks of (big) data analytics in marketing. Following the title of this book, we believe that this should enable marketing to create smarter decisions. The basis of our discussions is the big data value creation model, in which we show that data as an asset can be transformed into powerful insights, smarter decision making, and information-based products or services, through big data capabilities. We explicitly have chosen to take a mindful step back in the big data discussion, which sometimes is too much a hype with the danger of becoming a management fad. Building on in total six decades of experience in marketing analytics, we have discussed the several elements in our big data value creation model. Importantly, it is our vision that a successful use of (big) data requires (1) good data, (2) strong embedding of the analytical function within a firm having the right set of capabilities, (3) strong and impactful analytical skills, and (4) a strong focus on value creation. Importantly, there is no need to excel at specific capabilities. For example, it is not necessary to run the most complicated model; in fact that may be more harmful as it is likely to reduce the impact of the model. Instead useful insights can be gained with relatively simple analyses.

Throughout the book we have aimed to combine both academic knowledge and practical insights. The academic marketing literature is very rich in terms of applied and developed (complicated) models for marketing insight creation and decision making. However, there is frequently a gap between academics and practice (e.g. Roberts, Kayandé, & Stremersch, 2014). Throughout our book it has been our objective to bridge this gap by focusing first on the management issues surrounding the key topics in big data analytics. Second, in the more in-depth chapters we have aimed to describe more advanced and sometimes complicated topics in a more accessible way. Third, in our approach we heavily focus on creating impact, by emphasizing the importance of storytelling and visualization. Fourth, we continuously sought good insightful examples from science and practice to visualize the discussed material, and we explicitly described insightful cases in our penultimate chapter.

Key learning points

After reading all the 13 chapters of this book, we could imagine that a kind of final summary is required on the main issues covered in each one. We aim to fulfill this need in the final section of this book. It may help the reader to further capitalize on the rich knowledge provided. The key learning points are provided in Figure 7.1.

Finally, by using text analytics, we have made a word cloud from what we have discussed in our book. This may further help in grasping the most important topics. We leave it up to the now "advanced" analyst to interpret this cloud provided in Figure 7.2.

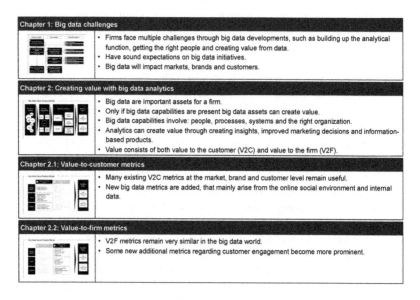

Figure 7.1 Key learning points by chapter

(Continued)

Chapter 3: Data, data, everywhere

- Two dimensions of data: data source (internal versus external) and data type (structured versus unstructured).
- A strong change is the presence of more unstructured data, that are also frequently large in size (volume).
- A distinction is made between data about either markets, brands or customers, where each can be split up in supply or demand driven data sources.

Chapter 3.1: Data integration

- The first step in data integration is the process of ETL: Extraction Transformation and Load.
- Combining declared, appended, overlaid and implied variables in the database determines the richness of the commercial data environment.
- There are three challenges organizations have to deal with in order to make maximum use of integrated data: technical, analytical an business wise.
- There are several options for data integration: individual level, intermediate level, time level or a mixture of different levels.

Chapter 3.2: Customer privacy and data security

- Privacy becomes extremely important in a big data era and firms should explicitly consider their privacy policies and even take an ethical perspective on privacy.
- However, many customers are not aware of privacy risks and there is a so-called privacy paradox.
- Data security is key in an era where criminals are looking for valuable data.

Chapter 4: How big data are changing analytics

- Analytics can create a sustainable competitive advantage for firms.
- Analytics can be performed at multiple sophistication levels.
- Big data will change analytics, but there are some important caveats.

Chapter 4.1: Classic data analytics

- Seven classic marketing analytics are at an analyst disposal to gain customer insights and improve marketing decision making:
  1. Reporting
  2. Profiling
  3. Migration analysis
  4. Segmentation analysis
  5. Trend- and market analysis and forecasting
  6. Attribute importance models
  7. Predictive customer models
- Each of the classics require specific knowledge in order to be rightfully applied.

Chapter 4.2: Big data analytics

- Big data induces the development of seven new analytical big data areas:
  1. Web analytics
  2. Customer journey analytics
  3. Attribution modelling
  4. Dynamic targeting models
  5. Social listening
  6. Social network analysis
  7. Integrated big data models
- These new methods consider new techniques and data, but frequently also build on existing techniques.

Chapter 4.3: Creating impact with story-telling and visualization

- To create impact with analytics strong storytelling and visuals are required.
- To effectively tell a good analytical story the pyramid principle can be used.
- Visualization is of essential importance to effectively communicate the results, as readers are visual instead of number oriented.

Chapter 5: Building successful big data capabilities

- Getting the right analytical people is key for a successful analytical function.
- In order to have a strong say within the firm, the analytical functions should develop sufficient knowledge on business principles, while marketing should become more open for data-based solutions.
- The right big data systems should be in place, that are typically modular without having single systems for everything.
- Organizations should make specific decision how they embed the analytical function within the firm.

Chapter 6: Every business has (big) data, let's use them

- Data analytics can indeed create value for the firm and it's customers.
- These benefits can be direct or more indirect.

Figure 7.1 (Continued)

308 Concluding thoughts and key learning points

Figure 7.2 Word cloud of our book

Reference

Roberts, J. H., Kayandé, U., & Stremersch, S. (2014). From academic research to marketing practice: Exploring the marketing science value chain. *International Journal of Research in Marketing*, 3(2), 127–40.

Index

3 "V"s of big data 15, 75, 132
5 "W"s model 85–7

Aaker, David 33
A/B testing 198–9, 294
Abela, Andrew 247
Achrol, R. S. 221
acquisition of analysts 263, 266–7
adaptive forecasting techniques 215–16
adaptive personalization system 275–6
adoption model 26
"adverse behavior" metrics 58
advertising awareness metrics 28
affective commitment 39
affective measures 28
aggregation of data 112, 114, 185, 206
Ailawadi, K. L. 44, 54–5
Allenby, Greg 211
analysis strategies (big data) 122–7
analysts, profile of 263–4, 279
analytical applications (analytical competence systems) 269, 270, 273–6
analytical challenges (of data integration) 100, 101, 103–4
analytical data platform (analytical competence systems) 269, 270, 271–3
ANCOVA (analysis of covariance) 199
anonymizing data 113, 114
ANOVA (analysis of variance) 199
Ansari, A. 208
Anscombe, Francis 238–9
APE (average prediction error) 166
appended data 96–7
APS (adaptive personalization systems) 210
ARPU (Average revenue per user) 303
Ataman, M. B. 216
ATL (above the line) campaigns 64, 71
attribute analysis (classic data analytics technique) 143, 172–80
attribution modeling 195, 203–6, 298–301

B2B (business-to-business) markets 2, 77, 88
B2C (business-to-customer) markets 2
"bagging" 135, 185
"bagging-boosting" technique 135
bar charts 243, 246
Bass, F. M. 222
BAV (Brand-Asset Valuator®) 29–30, 31, 32
Bayesian models 210–11, 216
BE (brand equity) 20–1, 32–3, 40, 53–5, 267
behavioral targeting 14, 17, 125
Berger, P. D. 65
betweenness centrality 223–5
big data analytics (big data value creation model) 9, 13–16
big data assets (big data value creation model) 9–10
big data capabilities (big data value creation model) 9, 10–13
big data dashboard 289–91
"big data hubris" 212
big data value (big data value creation model) 9, 16–21
big data value creation model 9–22, 305
big-data-based solutions 17
Blattberg, R. C. 184
Bolton, R. N. 36, 41
Boston Consulting Group 107
brand data (data source) 82–4
brand equity preference-based approach 54
brand equity price premium approach 54
brand equity share holder value approach 53
brand funnels 82
brand level changes (big data analytics) 127, 128, 130–1
brand metrics: brand awareness metrics 28, 29; brand consideration metrics 28–9; brand evaluation metrics 53–5; brand

liking metrics 28, 29; brand loyalty metrics 52–3; brand market performance metrics 51–3; brand penetration metrics 51–2; brand preference metrics 28–9, 30; brand sales metrics 51–2; V2C metrics 27–35, 36; V2F metrics 29, 32, 33, 51–5
brand repurchase rates 52–3
brand/product level analysis 4–5
Briesch, R. A. 280
BTL (below the line) campaigns 64
bubble charts 241–2, 246
Bügel, M. S. 39
building analytical competences: challenges to 253–4; organization 254, 276–82; organizational transformation 255–9; people 254, 263–8; process 254, 259–63; systems 254, 268–76
bullet charts 243, 244
business challenges (of data integration) 100, 101, 104
business questions 259–62
Buunk, A. P. 39

C2C (customer-to-customer) markets 2, 222
calculative commitment 39
case studies 285; attribution modeling 298–301; CLV calculation 286–8; holistic marketing approach 289–93; personalization through big data analytics 293–8; social network analytics 301–3
CDRs (call detail records) 223, 302
centralization/decentralization of organizations 276–7, 278
CES (customer effort score) 36, 37–8
CFMs (customer feedback metrics) 35–8, 134–5, 214–15
CHAID (Chi-square automatic interaction detection)
analysis 181–2, 183
channel switching 70
channel usage data 199–203, 205, 207
Chen, H. 217
Chi-square tests 145–6, 184
choice-based conjoint analysis 176–8
Chung, T. S. 210, 275–6
circular network charts 241–2
CIV (customer influence value) 68–9, 225
CKV (customer knowledge value) 68–9
classic data analytics: attribute analysis 143, 172–80; customer segmentation 142, 155–62; history of marketing analytics 140–1; migration analysis 142, 150–5; predictive modeling 143, 180–9;

profiling 142, 145–50; reporting 141–2, 144–5; trend analysis market and sales forecasting 142, 163–72
clickstream data 194
CLM (closed loop marketing) 206, 207
closeness centrality 223–5
cluster analysis 155–7, 159–62, 178
CLV (customer lifetime value): approach/objectives of study 5; and big data assets 10; calculating 64–6; components of 59–64; and customer equity 67, 68; and data integration 99; defining 58–9; drivers of 286–8; energy company case study 286–8; and marketing ROI 70–1; model building 66–7; and operational-analytical linkages 274–5; and predictive analyses 122; and V2F metrics 49, 58–69, 70–1
CMOs (chief marketing officers) 1
cognitive brand metrics 28
COGS (costs of goods sold) 60–1
cohort analysis 154, 155
collaborative filtering 207–8, 275
collateral catch 123, 126–7
column charts 243, 246
column histograms 245, 246
combining aggregation levels 213–14
commercial data environment 76–9, 87–8, 93, 95, 99–100, 101–2
commitment 39–40
comparison charts 242–3, 246
competitive intelligence data 77–8
completeness of data (data quality dimension) 89–90
complication (storytelling component) 235, 237, 238
composition charts 243–5, 246
computer science models 135–6, 185
conjoint analysis 54, 140, 174–80
content filtering systems 207–8
continuous data collection 134–5
contractual lifetime setting 63
conversion rate metrics 56
"coopetition" 278
Coopmans, Baptiest 257–8
corporate reputation 43
"cosmopolitans" (market data category) 80
cost allocation options 61–2
Court, D. 280
CPC (cost per click) 70
CPM (cost per mille) 70
CPO (cost per order/transaction) 70
Crawford, B. 280
credit losses (CLV driver) 286–8
creditworthiness 77

CRM (customer relationship management): and analytical competence systems 270–1; and approach/objectives of study 4–5; and classic data analytics 141; and customer lifetime value 58; development of 1, 8; dominant role of IT 3; and internal data sources of metrics 41–2; and importance of analytics 118, 131
cross-buying rates 57
Croux, C. 185
CRV (customer referral value) 68–9, 225
CSR (corporate social responsibility) 42, 43
CTR (click through rate) 294, 297, 298
culture, role of 12–13
customer crossings 145–6, 150
customer data (data source) 84–5
customer descriptors 96
customer equity 40–1, 67, 68
customer feedback loop 35–6
customer heterogeneity modeling 210–11
customer id data 84, 85, 88, 89, 101, 102, 271
"customer intimacy" 39, 40
customer journey analysis 195, 199–203
customer level analysis 4–5
customer level changes (big data analytics) 127, 128, 131–2
customer metrics: customer acquisition metrics 55, 56; customer development metrics 55, 56–8; customer engagement metrics 67–9; customer journey metrics 69–70; customer satisfaction metrics 36, 37–9; customer value metrics 55, 58; V2C metrics 35–42; V2F metrics 55–70
customer privacy: big data as threat to 3, 11, 106–7; and data security 114–16; data storage and usage 105–6, 108, 111–12; defining privacy 107; and ethics 110–11; government legislation 108–10; and internal data analytics 112–13; privacy concerns 106, 107–8, 112; privacy policies 111–12, 113
customer segmentation (classic data analytics technique) 142, 155–62
customer trust 39–40
customer-specific data 41
CVM (customer value management) 78, 88, 90, 181, 184

data being up to date (data quality dimension) 89–90
data disappointment 8
data enthusiasm 8
data fusion 87, 91, 135, 213, 271

data integration: analytical challenges 100, 101, 103–4; business challenges 100, 101, 104; in big data era 100–4; and data types 95–9; and data warehouses 100, 101; individual level integration 102; integrating data sources 93–5; intermediate level integration 102–3; technical challenges 100, 101–3; time level integration 103
data marts 271–2
data mining 123, 125–6
data modeling 123, 124–5
data protection regulations 109–10
data quality 89–90
data realism 8
data scientists 263, 268, 272–3
data security 114–16
data sources: 5 "W"s model 85–7; and analytical competence systems 269, 270–1; brand data 82–4; customer data 84–5; and data integration 93–104; and data warehouses 87–8; external 76–8; and holistic marketing approach 289, 291, 293; and integrated big data models 212–13; internal 76, 78–9; market data 80–2; multi-source data analysis 127, 130, 131, 196; structured 76, 79–80; unstructured 76, 79–80; use of 85–7
data storing (analytical competence systems) 269, 270, 271
data warehouses 87–8, 100, 101, 271
database structures 88–9
data-driven culture 280–1
Davenport, T. 119–20
De Bruin, B. 110–11
De Haan, E. 206
De Vries, L. 13, 16
decile analysis 146–7, 148
decision trees 181–2, 183
declared data 96
degree centrality 223–4
Dekimpe, M. G. 170
demand-side brand data 82–3
demand-side customer data 84
demand-side market data 80–1
dendrograms 160
departmental cooperation 277–80
descriptive analyses 144–5, 221, 261, 272
digital brand association networks 33, 34
"digital identity" 107
digital information overload 231–3
digital summary indices 33–5
digitalization of society 1, 2–3
direct marketing 141, 180, 206

discrete choice models 63
distribution charts 245–7, 246
Dixon, M. 36, 38
Donkers, A. C. 68
Donkers, B. 65, 91, 122, 136
double bar charts 245
DSI (digital sentiment index) 35, 271
duration models 63
Dutch National Bank 106
Dutch Telco (telecommunications company) 18
dynamic analyses 121–2
dynamic targeting 196, 206–11

Eberly, M. B. 267
EBITDA (earnings before interest, taxes, depreciation and amortization) 59–62
Eggers, F. 176, 177
Ehrenberg, Andrew 53
Eliashberg, J. 225
Essegaier, S. 208
ethical decision making 110–11
ETL (extraction, transformation and loading) process 93–5, 271
eWOM (electronic word-of-mouth) 34, 42
expected lifetime (CLV component) 63
Experian UK (external data provider) 97–8
explanatory analyses 121–2
explosion of data 1–3
external data sources 76–8
external profiling analyses 147
extraction stage (ETL process) 94

Facebook 35, 36
Fader, Pete 273
failure factors for creating impact 233–4
Farris, P. 20, 72, 273
feature generation 219–20
Feld, S. 56
Few, Stephen 243
flu prediction data 212
FMCGs (fast-moving consumer goods) 127, 130
Fombrun, C. J. 43
Franses, P. H. 184
Frenzen, H. 56
FTC (Federal Trade Committee) 110
F-tests 145–6
full population analysis 132–3
"fundamentalist" (privacy concern segmentation) 108
fuzzy matching 219
geographic maps 241–2

Gijsenberg, M. J. 114
Gini coefficient 186–8
GMOK (generalized mixture of Kalman filters) model 114
Goodwin, C. 107
Google (internet multinational) 27, 51
GRPs (gross rating points) 53

Hadoop (software) 11, 76, 270, 271, 294
Hagen, C. 277
Hanssens, D. M. 32, 170
Hardie, Bruce 273
Harris, J. 119–20
hierarchical cluster analysis 155, 159, 162
Hinz, O. 225
hit rate 184, 186
Hoekstra, J. C. 99
holistic marketing approach 289–93
Holtom, B. C. 267
Holtrop, N. 114
homophily 225
Hu, M. 217–18, 219
Hunneman, A. 172
hype 8

idiosyncratic models 13
implied data 96, 98–9
individual level data integration 102
infographics 232, 249
Information is Beautiful (book) 249
infrequent observations 188
ING (bank) 3, 106
insights (big data analytics) 13, 16
instrumental variables 168, 299
integrated big data models 196, 212–16
intermediate level data integration 102–3
internal data sources 41–2, 76, 78–9
invoice data 78, 79

Jacobson, R. 32
Jones, K. 106
Joshi, Y. 273
Jung, Carl 279

Kamakura, W. A. 91, 161
Keller, Kevin Lane 32
Kennedy, R. 212
key learning points 306–7
King, G. 212
K-means cluster analysis 155, 156, 159–60, 162
KNAB Bank 14
Kohli, R. 208
Konuş U. 161–2, 200, 202

Kotler, P. 140, 221
Koyck model 168
KPIs (key performance indicators): and building analytical competences 261–2, 263; and data integration 104; and holistic marketing approach 289–93; and like-4-like analysis 153; and migration matrices 152; reporting 141, 144
KPN (telecommunications company) 18, 256, 257–9
Krafft, M. 56
Kumar, V. 68

L4L (like-4-like) analysis 153–4
lagged variables 128, 169
"last-click" method 203, 205, 298–300
latent class analysis 161, 178, 200, 202, 208, 210, 302
Lattin, J. M. 155
Lazer, D. 212
Lee, T. W. 267
Leeflang, P. S. H. 1, 13, 99, 140, 165, 168, 280
Lehmann, D. R. 54–5
Lemmens, A. 136, 185
Lemon, K. N. 19, 36, 40–1
lift charts 245
Lilien, Gary 140
line charts 243, 245, 246
linear regression models 163–6
Liu, B. 217–18, 219
loading stage (ETL process) 95
logit regression models 182–5
logit-model analysis 63
log-log transformation 164

Malhotra, N. K. 146
management support 262–3, 281–2
MAPE (mean absolute percentage error) 166
MapReduce programming model 76, 296
margin (CLV component) 59–62
market data (data source) 80–2
market level analysis 4–5
market level changes (big data analytics) 127, 128–30
market metrics: market attractiveness metrics 50–1; market share metrics 51–2, 53; V2C metrics 26–7; V2F metrics 50–1
marketing accountability 280
marketing campaigns 16–17
marketing challenges 123
marketing dashboards 273–4
marketing growth objectives 123

marketing research data 77
marketing technology vendors 268–9
Markov models 154–5
McCandless, David 249
McDonalds (restaurant chain) 33, 34
McGovern, G. J. 280
McKinsey Global Institute 1
MCMC (Markov Chain Monte Carlo) method 210, 211
Meer, David 8
Mela, C. F. 216
Merkel, Angela 106
message (storytelling component) 235, 237–8
MI (marketing intelligence) 255–9, 260, 262–5, 268, 271, 280, 305
migration analysis (classic data analytics technique) 142, 150–5
migration matrices 152
Miller, George A. 235–6
Miller's law 235–6
"mind-set metrics" 32
Minto, Barbara 234
missing data values 91
Mitchell, T. R. 267
Mizik, N. 32
mobile data 79–80, 87, 226
model development (big data analytics) 13–4
moral intensity 110–11
"more advanced" analysis models 154–5
"more in-depth analysis" 154
Motivaction (research agency) 80–1
MSE (mean squared error) 166
multi-channel usage 161–2
multi-faceted customer behavior 188–9
multi-level model 214–15
multi-source data analysis 127, 130, 131, 196

Naert, P. A. 140
Nasr, N. I. 65
NBD (negative binomial distribution) models 63
Neslin, S. A. 54–5, 90, 183, 200, 202
network charts 241–2
network valuation 225
Netzer, O. 155
"neural networks" 135
new product sales metrics 51
NLP (natural language processing) 217
no mistakes in data (data quality dimension) 89–90
Nokia (telecommunications company) 19
non-contractual lifetime setting 63

non-linear additive models 164
non-stationary variables 169–70
normative commitment 39
Norton, D. 273
NPS (net promoter score) 36, 37–8, 44, 98, 124, 134, 144
NSA (National Security Agency) 3, 105
"number of levels effect" (conjoint analysis) 176

OLAP (online analytical processing) 120
OLS (ordinary least squares) regression models 164
one time investments (CLV component) 63–4
open source software 11, 272–3, 294
operational-analytical linkages 274–5
opinion analysis 217–21
opinion leadership 223
"opinion mining" 217
opinion word extraction/assessment 220
organization (analytical competence building block) 254, 276–82
organization (big data capability) 12
overhead costs 60
overlaid data 96, 97–8
oversampling 188

Paap, R. 184
"path to purchase" models 69–70, 203–4
Pauwels, K. 32, 273
"payment equity" metric 40
PCA (principal components analysis) 149, 157–9
people (analytical competence building block) 254, 263–8
people (big data capability) 10
people (data security element) 115
permission-based marketing approach 112, 113, 114
personalization systems 206, 208, 210–11
Peters, K. 56
pie charts 244, 246
Podesta, John 106
Polman, Paul 42
"polygamous loyalty" 52
POST (part-of-speech-tagging) 217, 218
"post-materialists" (market data category) 80
power of analytics 119
"pragmatist" (privacy concern segmentation) 108
pre-attentive attributes 247–8
pre-defined data 38, 123, 126
predictive analyses 121–2

predictive modeling (classic data analytics technique) 143, 180–9
predictive performance measures 185–8
price fairness metric 40
price premium metrics 54
problem solving 123, 124
process (analytical competence building block) 254, 259–63
processes (big data capability) 11–12
processes (data security element) 115, 116
product relation score 294, 295
profiling (classic data analytics technique) 142, 145–50
pruning 219–20
pseudomyzing data 113, 114
PSQ (perceived service quality) 171
purchase funnels 126, 194, 198, 203–4, 298
pyramid principle 234–5

Quelch, J. A. 280

R (open source software) 11
R&D (research and development) 13, 53, 278, 301, 303
radar charts 244
"range effect" (conjoint analysis) 176
ranking-based conjoint analysis 176
rating-based conjoint analysis 176, 178
RE (relationship equity) 41
real-time models 136–7
recommendation systems 206, 207–8, 209
"regime switching" models 216
regression-based approach attribute analysis 173–4
regression models 163–6, 167–8, 169–72, 182–5
Reibstein, D. J. 273
Reichheld, F. F. 38
relationship charts 241–2, 246
relationship costs and risk metrics 57–8
relationship expansion metrics 57
relationship length metrics 56–7
"relationship lifecycle" 55
repetition of measures/respondents 134–5
reporting (classic data analytics technique) 141–2, 144–5
reporting systems (analytical competence system) 273–4
RepTrack® measurement system 43
Reputation Institute 43
research shopping percentage 70
response rate metrics 56
retention (CLV driver) 286–8
retention of analysts 263, 267–8

revenue premium metrics 54–5
revenues (CLV driver) 286–8
"review volume" 42
"reviews valence" 42
RFM (recency, frequency and monetary value) model 180–1, 182
Risselada, H. 136
Rogers, E. M. 26
ROI (return on investment) 14, 70–1
Roose, Marteyn 258
Rosling, Hans 251
Rossi, Peter 211
Rust, R. T. 19, 40–1, 67, 210, 275–6

Sattler, H. 176, 177
SBUs (strategic business units) 127, 277, 278
scanner data 118
scanning revolution 8
SCANPRO model 140
scatter charts 241–2, 246, 247
search/purchase behavior 294, 295
seasonal effects 167, 168
security 11
selection of analysts 263–6
"self-hidden Easter eggs" 189
sentiment analysis 217–18, 220, 221
SEO (search engine optimization) 198
service costs (CLV driver) 286–8
Sethuraman, R. 280
Shah, D. 58
"share of heart" metrics 25
"share of mind" metrics 25
Sharp, Byron 53
Shepard, David 140–1
showrooming behavior 200, 201
site-centric clickstream data 194
situation (storytelling component) 235, 236–7, 238
size of effects 133–4
SKUs (stock keeping units) 294
Slice (app) 82
Sloot, L. M. 172
Snowden, Edward 3, 105
social data collection 218–19
social listening 197, 216–21
social media: and brand metrics 33, 35, 36; and customer engagement 67–9; and explosion of data 2–3; and external data sources 78, 79; and social listening 197, 216–21; and social network analysis 197, 221–5; social network analytics case study 301–3; and social targeting 225; social network data 222–3; social network metrics 223–5

social network analysis 197, 221–5
social network analytics case study 301–3
social network data 222–3
social network metrics 223–5
social targeting 225
"soft data" 80
sophistication levels of analytics 120–1
Spring, P. N. 99
SQL (structured query language) queries 271
Srinivasan, S. 32
Srinivasan, V. 155
stacked charts 244–5, 246
standardized models 13–14
star charts 243, 244
stated importance measurement 172–3
static analyses 121–2
Sternberg, R. J. 39
storytelling: and digital information overload 231–3; clear storyline checklist 236–8; core message 234, 235, 236, 237; importance of 231–2; integration with visualization 250, 251; pyramid principle 234–5
structured data sources 76, 79–80
substantive effects 133–4
summary generation 221
supply-side brand data 82–3
supply-side customer data 84–5
supply-side market data 80–1
survival analysis 154, 156
"switching matrix" 52, 67
system (data security element) 115
systems (analytical competence building block) 254, 268–76
systems (big data capability) 11

tag clouds 244
TAM (technology acceptance model) 26
team approach 265–6
technical challenges (of data integration) 100, 101–3
Tellis, G. J. 280
Tesco (retailer) 14, 123, 126
text analytics 217–21, 226, 306
Thaler, Rich 14
tie strength 225
Tillmanns, S. 68
time level data integration 103
time series data/models 42, 122, 127–9, 142–5, 163, 166, 168–72, 215
"top-2-box" customer satisfaction 37–8
top-decile lift 186, 187
touchpoint data 199–201, 203, 205–6
transaction data 96–7

transformation stage (ETL process) 95
trend analysis market/sales forecasting (classic data analytics technique) 142, 163–72
trust 39–40
Tucker, Catherine 112, 113

UGC (user generated content) 33
"unconcerned" (privacy concern segmentation) 108
"unpooled analysis" 172
unstructured data sources 76, 79–80
user-centric clickstream data 194

V2C (value to the customer) metrics 20–1, 25; balance between V2C and V2F 17–19; brand metrics 27–35, 36; and continuous data collection 134–5; customer metrics 35–42; defining 17, 22; limiting metrics collection 44; market metrics 26–7; and V2S metrics 25, 42–3, 45
V2F (value to the firm) metrics 20–1, 49; balance between V2C and V2F 17–19; brand metrics 29, 32, 33, 51–5; and customer lifetime value 49, 58–69, 70–1; customer metrics 55–70; defining 17, 22; market metrics 50–1; marketing ROI 70–1
V2S (value to society) metrics 19, 25, 42–3, 45
valence scores 34
validation process 94
value creation concepts 17
"value delivery" 17
"value extraction" 17
value of data 15, 132
Van Bruggen, G. 225
Van der Lans, R. 225
Van Heerde, H. J. 216

Van Riel, C. B. M. 43
Vanhuele, M. 32
VAR (vector-autoregressive) models 170–1, 206
variety of data 15, 75, 132
VE (value equity) 40
velocity of data 15, 132
Venkatesan, R. 68
veracity of data 15, 132
Verhoef, P. C. 1, 36, 39, 56, 91, 99, 114, 136, 172, 200, 202, 280
Vespignani, A. 212
Virgin Mobile (telecommunications company) 18
visualization: Anscombe's Quartet 238–9; choosing chart type 241–7; and digital information overload 231–3; graph design 247–9; importance of 231–2; integration with storyline 250, 251; objectives of visualizing data 240; power of 16; trends in 249, 251
volume of data 15, 132

Wald statistic 184
Ware, Colin 247–8
waterfall charts 244, 246
web analytics 194, 195, 198–9
webrooming behavior 200, 201
Wedel, M. 91, 161, 210, 275–6
WhatsApp (app) 129–30
Wierenga, B. 225
Wieringa, J. E. 114
Wiesel, T. 68
"willingness to pay" 54
win-back metrics 57
word clouds 219, 244, 249, 306, 308

Zeithaml, V. A. 19, 36, 40–1
zip code data/analysis 77, 78, 79, 97–8, 148, 149, 150, 222